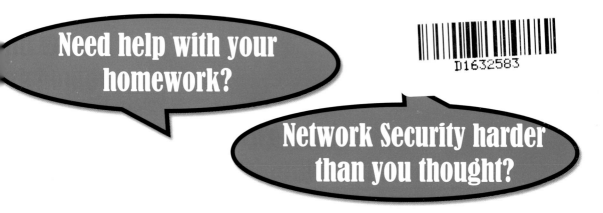

Help is here. Now.

With the purchase of a new copy of this textbook, you immediately have access to **indispensable Student Resources** and **Web Chapters.**

Use a coin to scratch off the coating and reveal your student access code. Do not use a knife or other sharp object as it may damage the code.

To redeem your access code:
1. Go to **http://www.pearsonhighered.com/stallingsinternational/**.
2. Select your textbook.
3. Click on the **Premium Content** and **Web Chapters** link.

Note to Instructors: **Instructors: Premium instructional material and Web Chapters** *for this title are available in Instructor Resource Center. Contact your Pearson representative if you do not have IRC access.*

IMPORTANT: The access code on this page can only be used once to establish a subscription to the premium content for Stallings, *Network Security Essentials: Applications and Standards, Fourth Edition.* If the access code has already been scratched off, it may no longer be valid. If this is the case, follow steps 1-3 and select **"Get Access"** to purchase a new subscription.

www.pearsonhighered.com/videonotes for information on all titles available with **VideoNotes**

Technical Support is available at **www.247pearsoned.com.**

Pearson Education | One Lake Street, Upper Saddle River, NJ 07458

NETWORK SECURITY ESSENTIALS:

APPLICATIONS AND STANDARDS

FOURTH EDITION

William Stallings

Boston   Columbus   Indianapolis   New York   San Francisco   Upper Saddle River
Amsterdam   Cape Town   Dubai   London   Madrid   Milan   Munich   Paris   Montreal   Toronto
Delhi   Mexico City   Sao Paulo   Sydney   Hong Kong   Seoul   Singapore   Taipei   Tokyo

Vice President and Editorial Director, ECS: Marcia J. Horton

Editor in Chief, Computer Science: Michael Hirsch

Executive Editor: Tracy Dunkelberger

Assistant Editor: Melinda Haggerty

Editorial Assistant: Allison Michael

Managing Editor: Scott Disanno

Production Manager: Wanda Rockwell

Art Director: Jayne Conte

Art Editor: Greg Dulles

ISBN 10:   0-13-706792-5
ISBN 13: 978-0-13-706792-3

To Antigone
never dull
never boring
always a Sage

CONTENTS

PREFACE

"The tie, if I might suggest it, sir, a shade more tightly knotted. One aims at the perfect butterfly effect. If you will permit me _"

"What does it matter, Jeeves, at a time like this? Do you realize that Mr. Little's domestic happiness is hanging in the scale?"

"There is no time, sir, at which ties do not matter."

— Very Good, Jeeves! P. G. Wodehouse

In this age of universal electronic connectivity, of viruses and hackers, of electronic eavesdropping and electronic fraud, there is indeed no time at which security does not matter. Two trends have come together to make the topic of this book of vital interest. First, the explosive growth in computer systems and their interconnections via networks has increased the dependence of both organizations and individuals on the information stored and communicated using these systems. This, in turn, has led to a heightened awareness of the need to protect data and resources from disclosure, to guarantee the authenticity of data and messages, and to protect systems from network-based attacks. Second, the disciplines of cryptography and network security have matured, leading to the development of practical, readily available applications to enforce network security.

OBJECTIVES

It is the purpose of this book to provide a practical survey of network security applications and standards. The emphasis is on applications that are widely used on the Internet and for corporate networks, and on standards (especially Internet standards) that have been widely deployed.

INTENDED AUDIENCE

This book is intended for both an academic and a professional audience. As a textbook, it is intended as a one-semester undergraduate course on network security for computer science, computer engineering, and electrical engineering majors. It covers the material in IAS2 Security Mechanisms, a core area in the Information Technology body of knowledge; and NET4 Security, another core area in the Information Technology body of knowledge. These subject areas are part of the Draft ACM/IEEE Computer Society Computing Curricula 2005.

The book also serves as a basic reference volume and is suitable for self-study.

PLAN OF THE BOOK

The book is organized in three parts:

Part One. Cryptography: A concise survey of the cryptographic algorithms and protocols underlying network security applications, including encryption, hash functions, digital signatures, and key exchange.

Part Two. Network Security Applications: Covers important network security tools and applications, including Kerberos, X.509v3 certificates, PGP, S/MIME, IP Security, SSL/TLS, SET, and SNMPv3.

Part Three. System Security: Looks at system-level security issues, including the threat of and countermeasures for intruders and viruses and the use of firewalls and trusted systems.

In addition, this book includes an extensive glossary, a list of frequently used acronyms, and a bibliography. Each chapter includes homework problems, review questions, a list of key words, suggestions for further reading, and recommended Web sites. In addition, a test bank is available to instructors.

ONLINE DOCUMENTS FOR STUDENTS

For this new edition, a tremendous amount of original supporting material has been made available online in the following categories.

- **Online chapters:** To limit the size and cost of the book, two chapters of the book are provided in PDF format. This includes a chapter on SNMP security and one on legal and ethical issues. The chapters are listed in this book's table of contents.
- **Online appendices:** There are numerous interesting topics that support material found in the text but whose inclusion is not warranted in the printed text. Seven online appendices cover these topics for the interested student. The appendices are listed in this book's table of contents.
- **Homework problems and solutions:** To aid the student in understanding the material, a separate set of homework problems with solutions are provided. These enable the students to test their understanding of the text.
- **Supporting documents:** A variety of other useful documents are referenced in the text and provided online.
- **Key papers:** Twenty-Four papers from the professional literature, many hard to find, are provided for further reading.

Purchasing this textbook new grants the reader six months of access to this online material.

INSTRUCTIONAL SUPPORT MATERIALS

To support instructors, the following materials are provided.

- **Solutions Manual:** Solutions to end-of-chapter Review Questions and Problems.
- **Projects Manual:** Suggested project assignments for all of the project categories listed subsequently in this Preface.
- **PowerPoint Slides:** A set of slides covering all chapters, suitable for use in lecturing.
- **PDF Files:** Reproductions of all figures and tables from the book.
- **Test Bank:** A chapter-by-chapter set of questions.

All of these support materials are available at the Instructor Resource Center (IRC) for this textbook, which can be reached via pearsonhighered.com/internationalstallings. To gain access to the IRC, please contact your local Prentice Hall sales representative via www.pearsonhighered.com/international or you can contact your local Pearson representative.

INTERNET SERVICES FOR INSTRUCTORS AND STUDENTS

There is a Web page for this book that provides support for students and instructors. The page includes links to other relevant sites, transparency masters of figures and tables in the book in PDF (Adobe Acrobat) format, and PowerPoint slides. The Web page is at **WilliamStallings.com/NetSec/NetSec4e.html**.

An Internet mailing list has been set up so that instructors using this book can exchange information, suggestions, and questions with each other and with the author. As soon as typos or other errors are discovered, an errata list for this book will be available at WilliamStallings.com. In addition, the Computer Science Student Resource site, at **WilliamStallings.com/StudentSupport.html**, provides documents, information, and useful links for computer science students and professionals.

PROJECTS FOR TEACHING NETWORK SECURITY

For many instructors, an important component of a network security course is a project or set of projects by which the student gets hands-on experience to reinforce concepts from the text. This book provides an unparalleled degree of support for including a projects component in the course. The IRC not only includes guidance on how to assign and structure the projects, but also includes a set of suggested projects that covers a broad range of topics from the text:

- **Research projects:** A series of research assignments that instruct the student to research a particular topic on the Internet and write a report.
- **Hacking project:** This exercise is designed to illuminate the key issues in intrusion detection and prevention.
- **Programming projects:** A series of programming projects that cover a broad range of topics and that can be implemented in any suitable language on any platform.
- **Lab exercises:** A series of projects that involve programming and experimenting with concepts from the book.
- **Practical security assessments:** A set of exercises to examine current infrastructure and practices of an existing organization.
- **Writing assignments:** A set of suggested writing assignments organized by chapter.
- **Reading/report assignments:** A list of papers in the literature, one for each chapter, that can be assigned for the student to read and then write a short report.

See Appendix B for details.

WHAT'S NEW IN THE FOURTH EDITION

The changes for this new edition of *Network Security Essentials* are more substantial and comprehensive than those for any previous revision.

In the four years since the third edition of this book was published, the field has seen continued innovations and improvements. In this fourth edition, I try to capture these changes while maintaining a broad and comprehensive coverage of the entire field. To begin this process of revision, the third edition was extensively reviewed by a number of professors who teach the subject. In addition, a number of professionals working in the field reviewed individual chapters. The result is that, in many places, the narrative has been clarified and tightened, and illustrations have been improved. Also, a large number of new "field-tested" problems have been added.

Beyond these refinements to improve pedagogy and user friendliness, there have been major substantive changes throughout the book. Highlights include:

- **Pseudorandom number generation and pseudorandom functions (revised):** The treatment of this important topic has been expanded, with the addition of new material in Chapter 2 and a new appendix on the subject.
- **Cryptographic hash functions and message authentication codes (revised):** The material on hash functions and MAC has been revised and reorganized to provide a clearer and more systematic treatment.
- **Key distribution and remote user authentication (revised):** In the third edition, these topics were scattered across three chapters. In the fourth edition, the material is revised and consolidated into a single chapter to provide a unified, systematic treatment.
- **Federated identity (new):** A new section covers this common identity management scheme across multiple enterprises and numerous applications and supporting many thousands, even millions, of users.
- **HTTPS (new):** A new section covers this protocol for providing secure communication between Web browser and Web server.
- **Secure Shell (new):** SSH, one of the most pervasive applications of encryption technology, is covered in a new section.
- **DomainKeys Identified Mail (new):** A new section covers DKIM, which has become the standard means of authenticating e-mail to counter spam.
- **Wireless network security (new):** A new chapter covers this important area of network security. The chapter deals with the IEEE 802.11 (WiFi) security standard for wireless local area networks and the Wireless Application Protocol (WAP) security standard for communication between a mobile Web browser and a Web server.
- **IPsec (revised):** The chapter on IPsec has been almost completely rewritten. It now covers IPsecv3 and IKEv2. In addition, the presentation has been revised to improve clarity and breadth.
- **Legal and ethical issues (new):** A new online chapter covers these important topics.
- **Online appendices (new):** Six online appendices provide addition breadth and depth for the interested student on a variety of topics.
- **Homework problems with solutions:** A separate set of homework problems (with solutions) is provided online for students.
- **Test bank:** A test bank of review questions is available to instructors. This can be used for quizzes or to enable the students to check their understanding of the material.
- **Firewalls (revised):** The chapter on firewalls has been significantly expanded.

With each new edition, it is a struggle to maintain a reasonable page count while adding new material. In part, this objective is realized by eliminating obsolete material and tightening the narrative. For this edition, chapters and appendices that are of less general interest have been moved online as individual PDF files. This has allowed an expansion of material without the corresponding increase in size and price.

RELATIONSHIP TO CRYPTOGRAPHY AND NETWORK SECURITY

This book is adapted from *Cryptography and Network Security, Fifth Edition* (CNS5e). CNS5e provides a substantial treatment of cryptography, including detailed analysis of algorithms and a significant mathematical component, all of which covers 400 pages. *Network Security Essentials: Applications and Standards, Fourth Edition* (NSE4e) provides instead a concise overview of these topics in Chapters 2 and 3. NSE4e includes all of the remaining material of CNS5e. NSE4e also covers SNMP security, which is not covered in CNS5e. Thus, NSE4e is intended for college courses and professional readers where the interest is primarily in the application of network security and without the need or desire to delve deeply into cryptographic theory and principles.

Pearson offers many different products around the world to facilitate learning. In countries outside the United States, some products and services related to this textbook may not be available due to copyright and/or permissions restrictions. If you have questions, you can contact your local office by visiting www.pearsonhighered.com/international or you can contact your local Pearson representative.

ACKNOWLEDGEMENTS

This new edition has benefited from review by a number of people who gave generously their time and expertise. The following people reviewed all or a large part of the manuscript: Marius Zimand (Towson State University), Shambhu Upadhyaya (University of Buffalo), Nan Zhang (George Washington University), Dongwan Shin (New Mexico Tech), Michael Kain (Drexel University), William Bard (University of Texas), David Arnold (Baylor University), Edward Allen (Wake Forest University), Michael Goodrich (UC-Irvine), Xunhua Wang (James Madison University), Xianyang Li (Illinois Institute of Technology), and Paul Jenkins (Brigham Young University).

Thanks also to the many people who provided detailed technical reviews of one or more chapters: Martin Bealby, Martin Hlavac (Department of Algebra, Charles University in Prague, Czech Republic), Martin Rublik (BSP Consulting and University of Economics in Bratislava), Rafael Lara (President of Venezuela's Association for Information Security and Cryptography Research), Amitabh Saxena, and Michael Spratte (Hewlett-Packard Company). I would especially like to thank Nikhil Bhargava (IIT Delhi) for providing detailed reviews of various chapters of the book.

Nikhil Bhargava (IIT Delhi) developed the set of online homework problems and solutions. Professor Sreekanth Malladi of Dakota State University developed the hacking exercises. Sanjay Rao and Ruben Torres of Purdue developed the laboratory exercises that appear in the IRC.

The following people contributed project assignments that appear in the instructor's supplement: Henning Schulzrinne (Columbia University), Cetin Kaya Koc (Oregon State University), and David Balenson (Trusted Information Systems and George Washington University). Kim McLaughlin developed the test bank.

Finally, I would like to thank the many people responsible for the publication of the book, all of whom did their usual excellent job. This includes my editor Tracy Dunkelberger and her assistants Melinda Hagerty and Allison Michael. Also, Jake Warde of Warde Publishers managed the reviews.

With all this assistance, little remains for which I can take full credit. However, I am proud to say that, with no help whatsoever, I selected all of the quotations.

ABOUT THE AUTHOR

William Stallings has made a unique contribution to understanding the broad sweep of technical developments in computer security, computer networking, and computer architecture. He has authored 17 titles and, counting revised editions, a total of 42 books on various aspects of these subjects. His writings have appeared in numerous ACM and IEEE publications, including the *Proceedings of the IEEE* and *ACM Computing Reviews*.

He has 11 times received the award for the best Computer Science textbook of the year from the Text and Academic Authors Association.

In over 30 years in the field, he has been a technical contributor, technical manager, and an executive with several high-technology firms. He has designed and implemented both TCP/IP-based and OSI-based protocol suites on a variety of computers and operating systems, ranging from microcomputers to mainframes. As a consultant, he has advised government agencies, computer and software vendors, and major users on the design, selection, and use of networking software and products.

He created and maintains the **Computer Science Student Resource Site** at WilliamStallings .com/StudentSupport.html. This site provides documents and links on a variety of subjects of general interest to computer science students (and professionals). He is a member of the editorial board of *Cryptologia*, a scholarly journal devoted to all aspects of cryptology.

Dr. Stallings holds a PhD from M.I.T. in Computer Science and a B.S. from Notre Dame in electrical engineering.

INTRODUCTION

The combination of space, time, and strength that must be considered as the basic elements of this theory of defense makes this a fairly complicated matter. Consequently, it is not easy to find a fixed point of departure.

—On War, Carl Von Clausewitz

The art of war teaches us to rely not on the likelihood of the enemy's not coming, but on our own readiness to receive him; not on the chance of his not attacking, but rather on the fact that we have made our position unassailable.

—The Art of War, Sun Tzu

The requirements of **information security** within an organization have undergone two major changes in the last several decades. Before the widespread use of data processing equipment, the security of information felt to be valuable to an organization was provided primarily by physical and administrative means. An example of the former is the use of rugged filing cabinets with a combination lock for storing sensitive documents. An example of the latter is personnel screening procedures used during the hiring process.

With the introduction of the computer, the need for automated tools for protecting files and other information stored on the computer became evident. This is especially the case for a shared system, such as a time-sharing system, and the need is even more acute for systems that can be accessed over a public telephone network, data network, or the Internet. The generic name for the collection of tools designed to protect data and to thwart hackers is **computer security**.

The second major change that affected security is the introduction of distributed systems and the use of networks and communications facilities for carrying data between terminal user and computer and between computer and computer. Network security measures are needed to protect data during their transmission. In fact, the term **network security** is somewhat misleading, because virtually all business, government, and academic organizations interconnect their data processing equipment with a collection of interconnected networks. Such a collection is often referred to as an internet,[1] and the term **internet security** is used.

There are no clear boundaries between these two forms of security. For example, one of the most publicized types of attack on information systems is the computer virus. A virus may be introduced into a system physically when it arrives on an optical disk and is subsequently loaded onto a computer. Viruses may also arrive over an internet. In either case, once the virus is resident on a computer system, internal computer security tools are needed to detect and recover from the virus.

This book focuses on internet security, which consists of measures to deter, prevent, detect, and correct security violations that involve the transmission of information. That is a broad statement that covers a host of possibilities. To give you a feel for the areas covered in this book, consider the following examples of security violations:

---

[1]We use the term *internet* with a lowercase "i" to refer to any interconnected collection of network. A corporate intranet is an example of an internet. The Internet with a capital "I" may be one of the facilities used by an organization to construct its internet.

1. User A transmits a file to user B. The file contains sensitive information (e.g., payroll records) that is to be protected from disclosure. User C, who is not authorized to read the file, is able to monitor the transmission and capture a copy of the file during its transmission.

2. A network manager, D, transmits a message to a computer, E, under its management. The message instructs computer E to update an authorization file to include the identities of a number of new users who are to be given access to that computer. User F intercepts the message, alters its contents to add or delete entries, and then forwards the message to E, which accepts the message as coming from manager D and updates its authorization file accordingly.

3. Rather than intercept a message, user F constructs its own message with the desired entries and transmits that message to E as if it had come from manager D. Computer E accepts the message as coming from manager D and updates its authorization file accordingly.

4. An employee is fired without warning. The personnel manager sends a message to a server system to invalidate the employee's account. When the invalidation is accomplished, the server is to post a notice to the employee's file as confirmation of the action. The employee is able to intercept the message and delay it long enough to make a final access to the server to retrieve sensitive information. The message is then forwarded, the action taken, and the confirmation posted. The employee's action may go unnoticed for some considerable time.

5. A message is sent from a customer to a stockbroker with instructions for various transactions. Subsequently, the investments lose value and the customer denies sending the message.

Although this list by no means exhausts the possible types of security violations, it illustrates the range of concerns of network security.

This chapter provides a general overview of the subject matter that structures the material in the remainder of the book. We begin with a general discussion of network security services and mechanisms and of the types of attacks they are designed for. Then we develop a general overall model within which the security services and mechanisms can be viewed.

1.1 COMPUTER SECURITY CONCEPTS

A Definition of Computer Security

The NIST *Computer Security Handbook* [NIST95] defines the term *computer security* as

---

COMPUTER SECURITY

The protection afforded to an automated information system in order to attain the applicable objectives of preserving the integrity, availability, and confidentiality of information system resources (includes hardware, software, firmware, information/data, and telecommunications).

This definition introduces three key objectives that are at the heart of computer security.

- **Confidentiality:** This term covers two related concepts:

    Data[2] confidentiality: Assures that private or confidential information is not made available or disclosed to unauthorized individuals.

    Privacy: Assures that individuals control or influence what information related to them may be collected and stored and by whom and to whom that information may be disclosed.

- **Integrity:** This term covers two related concepts:

    Data integrity: Assures that information and programs are changed only in a specified and authorized manner.

    System integrity: Assures that a system performs its intended function in an unimpaired manner, free from deliberate or inadvertent unauthorized manipulation of the system.

- **Availability:** Assures that systems work promptly and service is not denied to authorized users.

These three concepts form what is often referred to as the **CIA triad** (Figure 1.1). The three concepts embody the fundamental security objectives for both data and for information and computing services. For example, the NIST *Standards for Security Categorization of Federal Information and Information Systems* (FIPS 199) lists confidentiality, integrity, and availability as the three security objectives for information and for information systems. FIPS 199 provides a useful characterization of these three objectives in terms of requirements and the definition of a loss of security in each category.

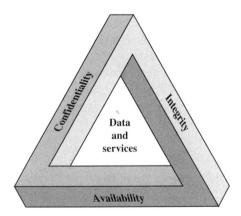

Figure 1.1 The Security Requirements Triad

---

[2]RFC 2828 defines *information* as "facts and ideas, which can be represented (encoded) as various forms of data," and *data* as "information in a specific physical representation, usually a sequence of symbols that have meaning; especially a representation of information that can be processed or produced by a computer." Security literature typically does not make much of a distinction, nor does this book.

- **Confidentiality:** Preserving authorized restrictions on information access and disclosure, including means for protecting personal privacy and proprietary information. A loss of confidentiality is the unauthorized disclosure of information.

- **Integrity:** Guarding against improper information modification or destruction, including ensuring information nonrepudiation and authenticity. A loss of integrity is the unauthorized modification or destruction of information.

- **Availability:** Ensuring timely and reliable access to and use of information. A loss of availability is the disruption of access to or use of information or an information system.

Although the use of the CIA triad to define security objectives is well established, some in the security field feel that additional concepts are needed to present a complete picture. Two of the most commonly mentioned are

- **Authenticity:** The property of being genuine and being able to be verified and trusted; confidence in the validity of a transmission, a message, or message originator. This means verifying that users are who they say they are and that each input arriving at the system came from a trusted source.

- **Accountability:** The security goal that generates the requirement for actions of an entity to be traced uniquely to that entity. This supports nonrepudiation, deterrence, fault isolation, intrusion detection and prevention, and after-action recovery and legal action. Because truly secure systems are not yet an achievable goal, we must be able to trace a security breach to a responsible party. Systems must keep records of their activities to permit later forensic analysis to trace security breaches or to aid in transaction disputes.

Examples

We now provide some examples of applications that illustrate the requirements just enumerated.[3] For these examples, we use three levels of impact on organizations or individuals should there be a breach of security (i.e., a loss of confidentiality, integrity, or availability). These levels are defined in FIPS 199:

- **Low:** The loss could be expected to have a limited adverse effect on organizational operations, organizational assets, or individuals. A limited adverse effect means that, for example, the loss of confidentiality, integrity, or availability might (i) cause a degradation in mission capability to an extent and duration that the organization is able to perform its primary functions, but the effectiveness of the functions is noticeably reduced; (ii) result in minor damage to organizational assets; (iii) result in minor financial loss; or (iv) result in minor harm to individuals.

---

[3]These examples are taken from a security policy document published by the Information Technology Security and Privacy Office at Purdue University.

- **Moderate:** The loss could be expected to have a serious adverse effect on organizational operations, organizational assets, or individuals. A serious adverse effect means that, for example, the loss might (i) cause a significant degradation in mission capability to an extent and duration that the organization is able to perform its primary functions, but the effectiveness of the functions is significantly reduced; (ii) result in significant damage to organizational assets; (iii) result in significant financial loss; or (iv) result in significant harm to individuals that does not involve loss of life or serious, life-threatening injuries.

- **High:** The loss could be expected to have a severe or catastrophic adverse effect on organizational operations, organizational assets, or individuals. A severe or catastrophic adverse effect means that, for example, the loss might (i) cause a severe degradation in or loss of mission capability to an extent and duration that the organization is not able to perform one or more of its primary functions; (ii) result in major damage to organizational assets; (iii) result in major financial loss; or (iv) result in severe or catastrophic harm to individuals involving loss of life or serious, life-threatening injuries.

CONFIDENTIALITY Student grade information is an asset whose confidentiality is considered to be highly important by students. In the United States, the release of such information is regulated by the Family Educational Rights and Privacy Act (FERPA). Grade information should only be available to students, their parents, and employees that require the information to do their job. Student enrollment information may have a moderate confidentiality rating. While still covered by FERPA, this information is seen by more people on a daily basis, is less likely to be targeted than grade information, and results in less damage if disclosed. Directory information (such as lists of students, faculty, or departmental lists) may be assigned a low confidentiality rating or indeed no rating. This information is typically freely available to the public and published on a school's Web site.

INTEGRITY Several aspects of integrity are illustrated by the example of a hospital patient's allergy information stored in a database. The doctor should be able to trust that the information is correct and current. Now suppose that an employee (e.g., a nurse) who is authorized to view and update this information deliberately falsifies the data to cause harm to the hospital. The database needs to be restored to a trusted basis quickly, and it should be possible to trace the error back to the person responsible. Patient allergy information is an example of an asset with a high requirement for integrity. Inaccurate information could result in serious harm or death to a patient and expose the hospital to massive liability.

An example of an asset that may be assigned a moderate level of integrity requirement is a Web site that offers a forum to registered users to discuss some specific topic. Either a registered user or a hacker could falsify some entries or deface the Web site. If the forum exists only for the enjoyment of the users, brings in little or no advertising revenue, and is not used for something important such as research, then potential damage is not severe. The Web master may experience some data, financial, and time loss.

An example of a low-integrity requirement is an anonymous online poll. Many Web sites, such as news organizations, offer these polls to their users with very few safeguards. However, the inaccuracy and unscientific nature of such polls is well understood.

AVAILABILITY The more critical a component or service, the higher is the level of availability required. Consider a system that provides authentication services for critical systems, applications, and devices. An interruption of service results in the inability for customers to access computing resources and for the staff to access the resources they need to perform critical tasks. The loss of the service translates into a large financial loss due to lost employee productivity and potential customer loss.

An example of an asset that typically would be rated as having a moderate availability requirement is a public Web site for a university; the Web site provides information for current and prospective students and donors. Such a site is not a critical component of the university's information system, but its unavailability will cause some embarrassment.

An online telephone directory lookup application would be classified as a low-availability requirement. Although the temporary loss of the application may be an annoyance, there are other ways to access the information, such as a hardcopy directory or the operator.

The Challenges of Computer Security

Computer and network security is both fascinating and complex. Some of the reasons include:

1. Security is not as simple as it might first appear to the novice. The requirements seem to be straightforward; indeed, most of the major requirements for security services can be given self-explanatory, one-word labels: confidentiality, authentication, nonrepudiation, integrity. But the mechanisms used to meet those requirements can be quite complex, and understanding them may involve rather subtle reasoning.

2. In developing a particular security mechanism or algorithm, one must always consider potential attacks on those security features. In many cases, successful attacks are designed by looking at the problem in a completely different way, therefore exploiting an unexpected weakness in the mechanism.

3. Because of point 2, the procedures used to provide particular services are often counterintuitive. Typically, a security mechanism is complex, and it is not obvious from the statement of a particular requirement that such elaborate measures are needed. It is only when the various aspects of the threat are considered that elaborate security mechanisms make sense.

4. Having designed various security mechanisms, it is necessary to decide where to use them. This is true both in terms of physical placement (e.g., at what points in a network are certain security mechanisms needed) and in a logical sense [e.g., at what layer or layers of an architecture such as TCP/IP (Transmission Control Protocol/Internet Protocol) should mechanisms be placed].

5. Security mechanisms typically involve more than a particular algorithm or protocol. They also require that participants be in possession of some secret information (e.g., an encryption key), which raises questions about the creation, distribution, and protection of that secret information. There also may be a reliance on communications protocols whose behavior may complicate the task of developing the security mechanism. For example, if the proper functioning of the security mechanism requires setting time limits on the transit time of a message from sender to receiver, then any protocol or network that introduces variable, unpredictable delays may render such time limits meaningless.

6. Computer and network security is essentially a battle of wits between a perpetrator who tries to find holes and the designer or administrator who tries to close them. The great advantage that the attacker has is that he or she need only find a single weakness, while the designer must find and eliminate all weaknesses to achieve perfect security.

7. There is a natural tendency on the part of users and system managers to perceive little benefit from security investment until a security failure occurs.

8. Security requires regular, even constant, monitoring, and this is difficult in today's short-term, overloaded environment.

9. Security is still too often an afterthought to be incorporated into a system after the design is complete rather than being an integral part of the design process.

10. Many users (and even security administrators) view strong security as an impediment to efficient and user-friendly operation of an information system or use of information.

The difficulties just enumerated will be encountered in numerous ways as we examine the various security threats and mechanisms throughout this book.

1.2   THE OSI SECURITY ARCHITECTURE

To assess effectively the security needs of an organization and to evaluate and choose various security products and policies, the manager responsible for computer and network security needs some systematic way of defining the requirements for security and characterizing the approaches to satisfying those requirements. This is difficult enough in a centralized data processing environment; with the use of local and wide area networks, the problems are compounded.

ITU-T[4] Recommendation X.800, *Security Architecture for OSI*, defines such a systematic approach.[5] The OSI security architecture is useful to managers as a way

---

[4]The International Telecommunication Union (ITU) Telecommunication Standardization Sector (ITU-T) is a United Nations-sponsored agency that develops standards, called Recommendations, relating to telecommunications and to open systems interconnection (OSI).

[5]The OSI security architecture was developed in the context of the OSI protocol architecture, which is described in Appendix D. However, for our purposes in this chapter, an understanding of the OSI protocol architecture is not required.

Table 1.1   Threats and Attacks (RFC 2828)

Threat A potential for violation of security, which exists when there is a circumstance, capability, action, or event that could breach security and cause harm. That is, a threat is a possible danger that might exploit a vulnerability.
Attack An assault on system security that derives from an intelligent threat. That is, an intelligent act that is a deliberate attempt (especially in the sense of a method or technique) to evade security services and violate the security policy of a system.

of organizing the task of providing security. Furthermore, because this architecture was developed as an international standard, computer and communications vendors have developed security features for their products and services that relate to this structured definition of services and mechanisms.

For our purposes, the OSI security architecture provides a useful, if abstract, overview of many of the concepts that this book deals with. The OSI security architecture focuses on security attacks, mechanisms, and services. These can be defined briefly as

- **Security attack:** Any action that compromises the security of information owned by an organization.
- **Security mechanism:** A process (or a device incorporating such a process) that is designed to detect, prevent, or recover from a security attack.
- **Security service:** A processing or communication service that enhances the security of the data processing systems and the information transfers of an organization. The services are intended to counter security attacks, and they make use of one or more security mechanisms to provide the service.

In the literature, the terms *threat* and *attack* are commonly used to mean more or less the same thing. Table 1.1 provides definitions taken from RFC 2828, *Internet Security Glossary*.

1.3 SECURITY ATTACKS

A useful means of classifying security attacks, used both in X.800 and RFC 2828, is in terms of *passive attacks* and *active attacks*. A passive attack attempts to learn or make use of information from the system but does not affect system resources. An active attack attempts to alter system resources or affect their operation.

Passive Attacks

Passive attacks are in the nature of eavesdropping on, or monitoring of, transmissions. The goal of the opponent is to obtain information that is being transmitted. Two types of passive attacks are the release of message contents and traffic analysis.

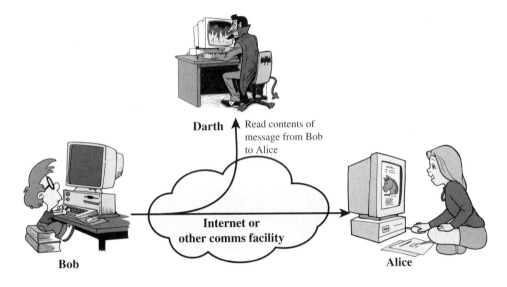

(a) Release of message contents

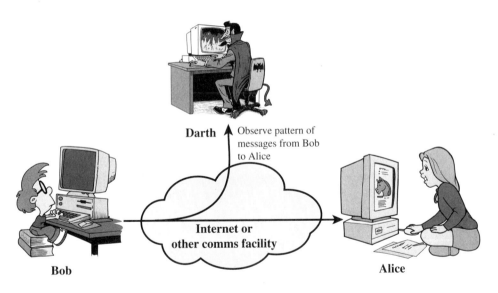

(b) Traffic analysis

Figure 1.2 Passive Network Security Attacks

The **release of message contents** is easily understood (Figure 1.2a). A telephone conversation, an electronic mail message, and a transferred file may contain sensitive or confidential information. We would like to prevent an opponent from learning the contents of these transmissions.

A second type of passive attack, **traffic analysis**, is subtler (Figure 1.2b). Suppose that we had a way of masking the contents of messages or other information traffic so that opponents, even if they captured the message, could not extract the information from the message. The common technique for masking contents is encryption. If we had encryption protection in place, an opponent still might be able to observe the pattern of these messages. The opponent could determine the location and identity of communicating hosts and could observe the frequency and length of messages being exchanged. This information might be useful in guessing the nature of the communication that was taking place.

Passive attacks are very difficult to detect, because they do not involve any alteration of the data. Typically, the message traffic is sent and received in an apparently normal fashion, and neither the sender nor the receiver is aware that a third party has read the messages or observed the traffic pattern. However, it is feasible to prevent the success of these attacks, usually by means of encryption. Thus, the emphasis in dealing with passive attacks is on prevention rather than detection.

Active Attacks

Active attacks involve some modification of the data stream or the creation of a false stream and can be subdivided into four categories: masquerade, replay, modification of messages, and denial of service.

A **masquerade** takes place when one entity pretends to be a different entity (Figure 1.3a). A masquerade attack usually includes one of the other forms of active attack. For example, authentication sequences can be captured and replayed after a valid authentication sequence has taken place, thus enabling an authorized entity with few privileges to obtain extra privileges by impersonating an entity that has those privileges.

Replay involves the passive capture of a data unit and its subsequent retransmission to produce an unauthorized effect (Figure 1.3b).

Modification of messages simply means that some portion of a legitimate message is altered, or that messages are delayed or reordered, to produce an unauthorized effect (Figure 1.3c). For example, a message meaning "Allow John Smith to read confidential file `accounts`" is modified to mean "Allow Fred Brown to read confidential file `accounts`."

The **denial of service** prevents or inhibits the normal use or management of communications facilities (Figure 1.3d). This attack may have a specific target; for example, an entity may suppress all messages directed to a particular destination (e.g., the security audit service). Another form of service denial is the disruption of an entire network—either by disabling the network or by overloading it with messages so as to degrade performance.

Active attacks present the opposite characteristics of passive attacks. Whereas passive attacks are difficult to detect, measures are available to prevent their success. On the other hand, it is quite difficult to prevent active attacks absolutely because of the wide variety of potential physical, software, and network vulnerabilities. Instead, the goal is to detect active attacks and to recover from any disruption or delays caused by them. If the detection has a deterrent effect, it also may contribute to prevention.

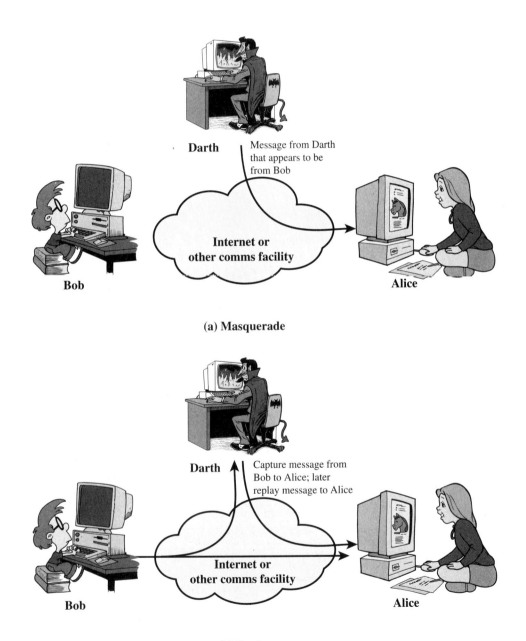

(a) Masquerade

(b) Replay

Figure 1.3 Active Attacks

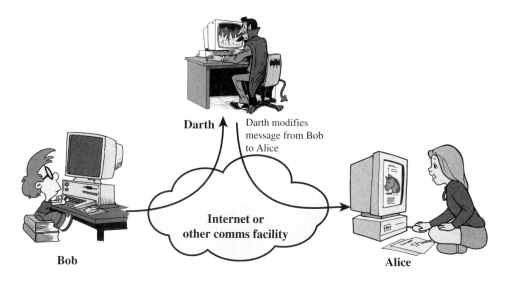

(c) Modification of messages

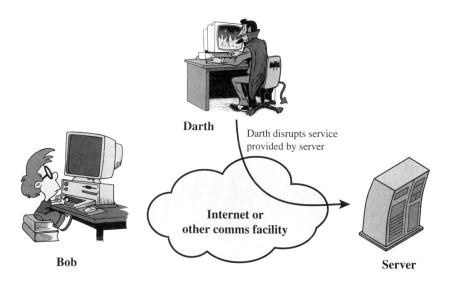

(d) Denial of service

Figure 1.3   Active Attacks (*Continued*)

1.4   SECURITY SERVICES

X.800 defines a security service as a service that is provided by a protocol layer of communicating open systems and that ensures adequate security of the systems or of data transfers. Perhaps a clearer definition is found in RFC 2828, which provides the following definition: A processing or communication service that is provided by a system to give a specific kind of protection to system resources; security services implement security policies and are implemented by security mechanisms.

X.800 divides these services into five categories and fourteen specific services (Table 1.2). We look at each category in turn.[6]

Table 1.2   Security Services (X.800)

AUTHENTICATION	DATA INTEGRITY
The assurance that the communicating entity is the one that it claims to be.	The assurance that data received are exactly as sent by an authorized entity (i.e., contain no modification, insertion, deletion, or replay).
Peer Entity Authentication Used in association with a logical connection to provide confidence in the identity of the entities connected.	**Connection Integrity with Recovery** Provides for the integrity of all user data on a connection and detects any modification, insertion, deletion, or replay of any data within an entire data sequence, with recovery attempted.
Data-Origin Authentication In a connectionless transfer, provides assurance that the source of received data is as claimed.	**Connection Integrity without Recovery** As above, but provides only detection without recovery.
ACCESS CONTROL	**Selective-Field Connection Integrity** Provides for the integrity of selected fields within the user data of a data block transferred over a connection and takes the form of determination of whether the selected fields have been modified, inserted, deleted, or replayed.
The prevention of unauthorized use of a resource (i.e., this service controls who can have access to a resource, under what conditions access can occur, and what those accessing the resource are allowed to do).	
DATA CONFIDENTIALITY	**Connectionless Integrity** Provides for the integrity of a single connectionless data block and may take the form of detection of data modification. Additionally, a limited form of replay detection may be provided.
The protection of data from unauthorized disclosure.	
Connection Confidentiality The protection of all user data on a connection.	**Selective-Field Connectionless Integrity** Provides for the integrity of selected fields within a single connectionless data block; takes the form of determination of whether the selected fields have been modified.
Connectionless Confidentiality The protection of all user data in a single data block.	**NONREPUDIATION**
Selective-Field Confidentiality The confidentiality of selected fields within the user data on a connection or in a single data block.	Provides protection against denial by one of the entities involved in a communication of having participated in all or part of the communication.
Traffic-Flow Confidentiality The protection of the information that might be derived from observation of traffic flows.	**Nonrepudiation, Origin** Proof that the message was sent by the specified party. **Nonrepudiation, Destination** Proof that the message was received by the specified party.

---

[6]There is no universal agreement about many of the terms used in the security literature. For example, the term *integrity* is sometimes used to refer to all aspects of information security. The term *authentication* is sometimes used to refer both to verification of identity and to the various functions listed under integrity in this chapter. Our usage here agrees with both X.800 and RFC 2828.

Authentication

The **authentication** service is concerned with assuring that a communication is authentic. In the case of a single message, such as a warning or alarm signal, the function of the authentication service is to assure the recipient that the message is from the source that it claims to be from. In the case of an ongoing interaction, such as the connection of a terminal to a host, two aspects are involved. First, at the time of connection initiation, the service assures that the two entities are authentic (that is, that each is the entity that it claims to be). Second, the service must assure that the connection is not interfered with in such a way that a third party can masquerade as one of the two legitimate parties for the purposes of unauthorized transmission or reception.

Two specific authentication services are defined in X.800:

- **Peer entity authentication:** Provides for the corroboration of the identity of a peer entity in an association. Two entities are considered peers if they implement the same protocol in different systems (e.g., two TCP modules in two communicating systems). Peer entity authentication is provided for use at the establishment of or during the data transfer phase of a connection. It attempts to provide confidence that an entity is not performing either a masquerade or an unauthorized replay of a previous connection.

- **Data origin authentication:** Provides for the corroboration of the source of a data unit. It does not provide protection against the duplication or modification of data units. This type of service supports applications like electronic mail, where there are no prior interactions between the communicating entities.

Access Control

In the context of network security, **access control** is the ability to limit and control the access to host systems and applications via communications links. To achieve this, each entity trying to gain access must first be identified, or authenticated, so that access rights can be tailored to the individual.

Data Confidentiality

Confidentiality is the protection of transmitted data from passive attacks. With respect to the content of a data transmission, several levels of protection can be identified. The broadest service protects all user data transmitted between two users over a period of time. For example, when a TCP connection is set up between two systems, this broad protection prevents the release of any user data transmitted over the TCP connection. Narrower forms of this service can also be defined, including the protection of a single message or even specific fields within a message. These refinements are less useful than the broad approach and may even be more complex and expensive to implement.

The other aspect of confidentiality is the protection of traffic flow from analysis. This requires that an attacker not be able to observe the source and destination, frequency, length, or other characteristics of the traffic on a communications facility.

Data Integrity

As with confidentiality, **integrity** can apply to a stream of messages, a single message, or selected fields within a message. Again, the most useful and straightforward approach is total stream protection.

A connection-oriented integrity service deals with a stream of messages and assures that messages are received as sent with no duplication, insertion, modification, reordering, or replays. The destruction of data is also covered under this service. Thus, the connection-oriented integrity service addresses both message stream modification and denial of service. On the other hand, a connectionless integrity service deals with individual messages without regard to any larger context and generally provides protection against message modification only.

We can make a distinction between service with and without recovery. Because the integrity service relates to active attacks, we are concerned with detection rather than prevention. If a violation of integrity is detected, then the service may simply report this violation, and some other portion of software or human intervention is required to recover from the violation. Alternatively, there are mechanisms available to recover from the loss of integrity of data, as we will review subsequently. The incorporation of automated recovery mechanisms is typically the more attractive alternative.

Nonrepudiation

Nonrepudiation prevents either sender or receiver from denying a transmitted message. Thus, when a message is sent, the receiver can prove that the alleged sender in fact sent the message. Similarly, when a message is received, the sender can prove that the alleged receiver in fact received the message.

Availability Service

Both X.800 and RFC 2828 define **availability** to be the property of a system or a system resource being accessible and usable upon demand by an authorized system entity, according to performance specifications for the system (i.e., a system is available if it provides services according to the system design whenever users request them). A variety of attacks can result in the loss of or reduction in availability. Some of these attacks are amenable to automated countermeasures, such as authentication and encryption, whereas others require some sort of physical action to prevent or recover from loss of availability of elements of a distributed system.

X.800 treats availability as a property to be associated with various security services. However, it makes sense to call out specifically an availability service. An availability service is one that protects a system to ensure its availability. This service addresses the security concerns raised by denial-of-service attacks. It depends on proper management and control of system resources and thus depends on access control service and other security services.

1.5 SECURITY MECHANISMS

Table 1.3 lists the security mechanisms defined in X.800. The mechanisms are divided into those that are implemented in a specific protocol layer, such as TCP or an application-layer protocol, and those that are not specific to any particular protocol layer or security

Table 1.3   Security Mechanisms (X.800)

SPECIFIC SECURITY MECHANISMS	PERVASIVE SECURITY MECHANISMS
May be incorporated into the appropriate protocol layer in order to provide some of the OSI security services.	Mechanisms that are not specific to any particular OSI security service or protocol layer.
Encipherment The use of mathematical algorithms to transform data into a form that is not readily intelligible. The transformation and subsequent recovery of the data depend on an algorithm and zero or more encryption keys.	**Trusted Functionality** That which is perceived to be correct with respect to some criteria (e.g., as established by a security policy).
Digital Signature Data appended to, or a cryptographic transformation of, a data unit that allows a recipient of the data unit to prove the source and integrity of the data unit and protect against forgery (e.g., by the recipient).	**Security Label** The marking bound to a resource (which may be a data unit) that names or designates the security attributes of that resource. **Event Detection** Detection of security-relevant events.
Access Control A variety of mechanisms that enforce access rights to resources.	**Security Audit Trail** Data collected and potentially used to facilitate a security audit, which is an independent review and examination of system records and activities.
Data Integrity A variety of mechanisms used to assure the integrity of a data unit or stream of data units.	**Security Recovery** Deals with requests from mechanisms, such as event handling and management functions, and takes recovery actions.
Authentication Exchange A mechanism intended to ensure the identity of an entity by means of information exchange.	
Traffic Padding The insertion of bits into gaps in a data stream to frustrate traffic analysis attempts.	
Routing Control Enables selection of particular physically secure routes for certain data and allows routing changes, especially when a breach of security is suspected.	
Notarization The use of a trusted third party to assure certain properties of a data exchange.	

service. These mechanisms will be covered in the appropriate places in the book, so we do not elaborate now except to comment on the definition of encipherment. X.800 distinguishes between reversible encipherment mechanisms and irreversible encipherment mechanisms. A reversible encipherment mechanism is simply an encryption algorithm that allows data to be encrypted and subsequently decrypted. Irreversible encipherment mechanisms include hash algorithms and message authentication codes, which are used in digital signature and message authentication applications.

Table 1.4, based on one in X.800, indicates the relationship between security services and security mechanisms.

Table 1.4   Relationship Between Security Services and Mechanisms

Mechanism

Service	Encipherment	Digital Signature	Access Control	Data Integrity	Authentication Exchange	Traffic Padding	Routing Control	Notarization
Peer Entity Authentication	Y	Y			Y			
Data-Origin Authentication	Y	Y						
Access Control			Y					
Confidentiality	Y						Y	
Traffic-Flow Confidentiality	Y					Y	Y	
Data Integrity	Y	Y		Y				
Nonrepudiation		Y		Y				Y
Availability				Y	Y			

1.6 A MODEL FOR NETWORK SECURITY

A model for much of what we will be discussing is captured, in very general terms, in Figure 1.4. A message is to be transferred from one party to another across some sort of Internet service. The two parties, who are the *principals* in this transaction, must cooperate for the exchange to take place. A logical information channel is established by defining a route through the Internet from source to destination and by the cooperative use of communication protocols (e.g., TCP/IP) by the two principals.

Security aspects come into play when it is necessary or desirable to protect the information transmission from an opponent who may present a threat to confidentiality, authenticity, and so on. All of the techniques for providing security have two components:

1. A security-related transformation on the information to be sent. Examples include the encryption of the message, which scrambles the message so that it is unreadable by the opponent, and the addition of a code based on the contents of the message, which can be used to verify the identity of the sender.

2. Some secret information shared by the two principals and, it is hoped, unknown to the opponent. An example is an encryption key used in conjunction with the transformation to scramble the message before transmission and unscramble it on reception.[7]

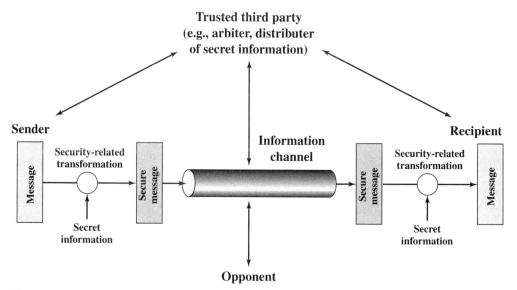

Figure 1.4 Model for Network Security

---

[7]Chapter 3 discusses a form of encryption, known as asymmetric encryption, in which only one of the two principals needs to have the secret information.

A trusted third party may be needed to achieve secure transmission. For example, a third party may be responsible for distributing the secret information to the two principals while keeping it from any opponent. Or a third party may be needed to arbitrate disputes between the two principals concerning the authenticity of a message transmission.

This general model shows that there are four basic tasks in designing a particular security service:

1. Design an algorithm for performing the security-related transformation. The algorithm should be such that an opponent cannot defeat its purpose.

2. Generate the secret information to be used with the algorithm.

3. Develop methods for the distribution and sharing of the secret information.

4. Specify a protocol to be used by the two principals that makes use of the security algorithm and the secret information to achieve a particular security service.

Parts One and Two of this book concentrate on the types of security mechanisms and services that fit into the model shown in Figure 1.4. However, there are other security-related situations of interest that do not neatly fit this model but are considered in this book. A general model of these other situations is illustrated by Figure 1.5, which reflects a concern for protecting an information system from unwanted access. Most readers are familiar with the concerns caused by the existence of hackers who attempt to penetrate systems that can be accessed over a network. The hacker can be someone who, with no malign intent, simply gets satisfaction from breaking and entering a computer system. The intruder can be a disgruntled employee who wishes to do damage or a criminal who seeks to exploit computer assets for financial gain (e.g., obtaining credit card numbers or performing illegal money transfers).

Another type of unwanted access is the placement in a computer system of logic that exploits vulnerabilities in the system and that can affect application programs as well as utility programs, such as editors and compilers. Programs can present two kinds of threats:

1. **Information access threats:** Intercept or modify data on behalf of users who should not have access to that data.

2. **Service threats:** Exploit service flaws in computers to inhibit use by legitimate users.

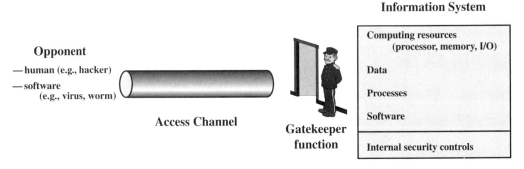

Figure 1.5   Network Access Security Model

Viruses and worms are two examples of software attacks. Such attacks can be introduced into a system by means of a disk that contains the unwanted logic concealed in otherwise useful software. They also can be inserted into a system across a network; this latter mechanism is of more concern in network security.

The **security mechanisms** needed to cope with unwanted access fall into two broad categories (see Figure 1.5). The first category might be termed a gatekeeper function. It includes password-based login procedures that are designed to deny access to all but authorized users and screening logic that is designed to detect and reject worms, viruses, and other similar attacks. Once either an unwanted user or unwanted software gains access, the second line of defense consists of a variety of internal controls that monitor activity and analyze stored information in an attempt to detect the presence of unwanted intruders. These issues are explored in Part Three.

1.7 STANDARDS

Many of the security techniques and applications described in this book have been specified as standards. Additionally, standards have been developed to cover management practices and the overall architecture of security mechanisms and services. Throughout this book, we describe the most important standards in use or being developed for various aspects of cryptography and network security. Various organizations have been involved in the development or promotion of these standards. The most important (in the current context) of these organizations are as follows.

- **National Institute of Standards and Technology:** NIST is a U.S. federal agency that deals with measurement science, standards, and technology related to U.S. government use and to the promotion of U.S. private-sector innovation. Despite its national scope, NIST **Federal Information Processing Standards (FIPS)** and **Special Publications (SP)** have a worldwide impact.

- **Internet Society:** ISOC is a professional membership society with worldwide organizational and individual membership. It provides leadership in addressing issues that confront the future of the Internet and is the organization home for the groups responsible for Internet infrastructure standards, including the Internet Engineering Task Force (IETF) and the Internet Architecture Board (IAB). These organizations develop Internet standards and related specifications, all of which are published as **Requests for Comments (RFCs)**.

A more detailed discussion of these organizations is contained in Appendix C.

1.8 OUTLINE OF THIS BOOK

This chapter serves as an introduction to the entire book. The remainder of the book is organized into three parts.

Part One: Provides a concise survey of the cryptographic algorithms and protocols underlying network security applications, including encryption, hash functions, and digital signatures.

Part Two: Examines the use of cryptographic algorithms and security protocols to provide security over networks and the Internet. Topics covered include key management, user authentication, transport-level security, wireless network security, e-mail security, and IP security.

Part Three: Deals with security facilities designed to protect a computer system from security threats, including intruders, viruses, and worms. This part also looks at firewall technology.

In addition, two online chapters cover network management security and legal and ethical issues.

1.9   RECOMMENDED READING

[STAL08] provides a broad introduction to computer security. [SCHN00] is valuable reading for any practitioner in the field of computer or network security: It discusses the limitations of technology (and cryptography in particular) in providing security and the need to consider the hardware, the software implementation, the networks, and the people involved in providing and attacking security.

It is useful to read some of the classic tutorial papers on computer security; these provide a historical perspective from which to appreciate current work and thinking. The papers to read are [WARE79], [BROW72], [SALT75], [SHAN77], and [SUMM84]. Two more recent, short treatments of computer security are [ANDR04] and [LAMP04]. [NIST95] is an exhaustive (290 pages) treatment of the subject. Another good treatment is [NRC91]. Also useful is [FRAS97].

ANDR04   Andrews, M., and Whittaker, J. "Computer Security." *IEEE Security and Privacy*, September/October 2004.

BROW72   Browne, P. "Computer Security — A Survey." *ACM SIGMIS Database*, Fall 1972.

FRAS97   Fraser, B. *Site Security Handbook.* RFC 2196, September 1997.

LAMP04   Lampson, B. "Computer Security in the Real World." *Computer*, June 2004.

NIST95   National Institute of Standards and Technology. *An Introduction to Computer Security: The NIST Handbook.* Special Publication 800–12. October 1995.

NRC91   National Research Council. *Computers at Risk: Safe Computing in the Information Age.* Washington, D.C.: National Academy Press, 1991.

SALT75   Saltzer, J., and Schroeder, M. "The Protection of Information in Computer Systems." *Proceedings of the IEEE*, September 1975.

SCHN00   Schneier, B. *Secrets and Lies: Digital Security in a Networked World.* New York: Wiley 2000.

SHAN77   Shanker, K. "The Total Computer Security Problem: An Overview." *Computer*, June 1977.

STAL08   Stallings, W., and Brown, L. *Computer Security.* Upper Saddle River, NJ: Prentice Hall, 2008.

SUMM84   Summers, R. "An Overview of Computer Security." *IBM Systems Journal*, Vol. 23, No. 4, 1984.

WARE79   Ware, W., ed. *Security Controls for Computer Systems.* RAND Report 609–1. October 1979. http://www.rand.org/pubs/reports/R609-1/R609.1.html

1.10 INTERNET AND WEB RESOURCES

There are a number of resources available on the Internet and the Web to support this book and to help one keep up with developments in this field.

Web Sites for This Book

There is a Web page for this book at **WilliamStallings.com/NetSec/NetSec4e.html**. The site includes the following:

- **Useful Web sites:** There are links to other relevant Web sites organized by chapter, including the sites listed in this section and throughout this book.

- **Online documents:** Link to the Companion Website at Pearson that includes supplemental online chapters and appendices, homework problems and solutions, important papers from the literature, and other supporting documents. See Preface for details.

- **Errata sheet:** An errata list for this book will be maintained and updated as needed. Please e-mail any errors that you spot to me. Errata sheets for my other books are at **WilliamStallings.com**.

- **Internet mailing list:** The site includes sign-up information for the book's Internet mailing list.

- **Network security courses:** There are links to home pages for courses based on this book; these pages may be useful to instructors in providing ideas about how to structure their course.

I also maintain the Computer Science Student Resource Site at **WilliamStallings.com/StudentSupport.html**. The purpose of this site is to provide documents, information, and links for computer science students and professionals. Links and documents are organized into six categories:

- **Math:** Includes a basic math refresher, a queuing analysis primer, a number system primer, and links to numerous math sites.

- **How-to:** Advice and guidance for solving homework problems, writing technical reports, and preparing technical presentations.

- **Research resources:** Links to important collections of papers, technical reports, and bibliographies.

- **Computer science careers:** Useful links and documents for those considering a career in computer science.

- **Miscellaneous:** A variety of other interesting documents and links.

- **Humor and other diversions:** You have to take your mind off your work once in a while.

Other Web Sites

There are numerous Web sites that provide information related to the topics of this book. In subsequent chapters, pointers to specific Web sites can be found in the *Recommended Reading and Web Sites* section. Because the addresses for Web sites tend to change frequently, I have not included URLs in the book. For all of the Web sites listed in the book, the appropriate link can be found at this book's Web site. Other links not mentioned in this book will be added to the Web site over time.

The following Web sites are of general interest related to cryptography and network security.

- **IETF Security Area:** Material related to Internet security standardization efforts.
- **Computer and Network Security Reference Index:** A good index to vendor and commercial products, frequently asked questions (FAQs), newsgroup archives, papers, and other Web sites.
- **The Cryptography FAQ:** Lengthy and worthwhile FAQ covering all aspects of cryptography.
- **Tom Dunigan's Security Page:** An excellent list of pointers to cryptography and network security Web sites.
- **Helger Lipmaa's Cryptology Pointers:** Another excellent list of pointers to cryptography and network security Web sites.
- **IEEE Technical Committee on Security and Privacy:** Copies of their newsletter and information on IEEE-related activities.
- **Computer Security Resource Center:** Maintained by the National Institute of Standards and Technology (NIST); contains a broad range of information on security threats, technology, and standards.
- **Security Focus:** A wide variety of security information with an emphasis on vendor products and end-user concerns.
- **SANS Institute:** Similar to Security Focus. Extensive collection of white papers.
- **Center for Internet Security:** Provides freeware benchmark and scoring tools for evaluating security of operating systems, network devices, and applications. Includes case studies and technical papers.
- **Institute for Security and Open Methodologies:** An open, collaborative security research community. Lots of interesting information.

USENET Newsgroups

A number of USENET newsgroups are devoted to some aspect of network security or cryptography. As with virtually all USENET groups, there is a high noise-to-signal ratio, but it is worth experimenting to see if any meet your needs. The most relevant are the following:

- **sci.crypt.research:** The best group to follow. This is a moderated newsgroup that deals with research topics; postings must have some relationship to the technical aspects of cryptology.

- **sci.crypt:** A general discussion of cryptology and related topics.
- **sci.crypt.random-numbers:** A discussion of cryptographic strength randomness.
- **alt.security:** A general discussion of security topics.
- **comp.security.misc:** A general discussion of computer security topics.
- **comp.security.firewalls:** A discussion of firewall products and technology.
- **comp.security.announce:** News and announcements from CERT.
- **comp.risks:** A discussion of risks to the public from computers and users.
- **comp.virus:** A moderated discussion of computer viruses.

In addition, there are a number of forums dealing with cryptography available on the Internet. Among the most worthwhile are

- **Security and Cryptography forum:** Sponsored by DevShed. Discusses issues related to coding, server applications, network protection, data protection, firewalls, ciphers, and the like.
- **Cryptography forum:** On Topix. Fairly good focus on technical issues.
- **Security forums:** On WindowsSecurity.com. Broad range of forums, including cryptographic theory, cryptographic software, firewalls, and malware.

Links to these forums are provided at this book's Web site.

1.11 KEY TERMS, REVIEW QUESTIONS, AND PROBLEMS

Key Terms

access control	denial of service	passive threat
active threat	encryption	replay
authentication	integrity	security attacks
authenticity	intruder	security mechanisms
availability	masquerade	security services
data confidentiality	nonrepudiation	traffic analysis
data integrity	OSI security architecture	

Review Questions

1.1 What is the OSI security architecture?
1.2 What is the difference between passive and active security threats?
1.3 List and briefly define categories of passive and active security attacks.
1.4 List and briefly define categories of security services.
1.5 List and briefly define categories of security mechanisms.

Problems

1.1 Consider an automated teller machine (ATM) in which users provide a personal identification number (PIN) and a card for account access. Give examples of confidentiality, integrity, and availability requirements associated with the system. In each case, indicate the degree of importance of the requirement.

1.2 Repeat Problem 1.1 for a telephone switching system that routes calls through a switching network based on the telephone number requested by the caller.

1.3 Consider a desktop publishing system used to produce documents for various organizations.
   a. Give an example of a type of publication for which confidentiality of the stored data is the most important requirement.
   b. Give an example of a type of publication in which data integrity is the most important requirement.
   c. Give an example in which system availability is the most important requirement.

1.4 For each of the following assets, assign a low, moderate, or high impact level for the loss of confidentiality, availability, and integrity, respectively. Justify your answers.
   a. An organization managing public information on its Web server.
   b. A law-enforcement organization managing extremely sensitive investigative information.
   c. A financial organization managing routine administrative information (not privacy-related information).
   d. An information system used for large acquisitions in a contracting organization that contains both sensitive, pre-solicitation phase contract information and routine administrative information. Assess the impact for the two data sets separately and the information system as a whole.
   e. A power plant contains a SCADA (supervisory control and data acquisition) system controlling the distribution of electric power for a large military installation. The SCADA system contains both real-time sensor data and routine administrative information. Assess the impact for the two data sets separately and the information system as a whole.

1.5 Draw a matrix similar to Table 1.4 that shows the relationship between security services and attacks.

1.6 Draw a matrix similar to Table 1.4 that shows the relationship between security mechanisms and attacks.

CHAPTER 2

SYMMETRIC ENCRYPTION AND MESSAGE CONFIDENTIALITY

All the afternoon Mungo had been working on Stern's code, principally with the aid of the latest messages which he had copied down at the Nevin Square drop. Stern was very confident. He must be well aware London Central knew about that drop. It was obvious that they didn't care how often Mungo read their messages, so confident were they in the impenetrability of the code.

—Talking to Strange Men, Ruth Rendell

Amongst the tribes of Central Australia every man, woman, and child has a secret or sacred name which is bestowed by the older men upon him or her soon after birth, and which is known to none but the fully initiated members of the group. This secret name is never mentioned except upon the most solemn occasions; to utter it in the hearing of men of another group would be a most serious breach of tribal custom. When mentioned at all, the name is spoken only in a whisper, and not until the most elaborate precautions have been taken that it shall be heard by no one but members of the group. The native thinks that a stranger knowing his secret name would have special power to work him ill by means of magic.

—The Golden Bough, Sir James George Frazer

Symmetric encryption, also referred to as conventional encryption, secret-key, or single-key encryption, was the only type of encryption in use prior to the development of public-key encryption in the late 1970s.[1] It remains by far the most widely used of the two types of encryption.

This chapter begins with a look at a general model for the symmetric encryption process; this will enable us to understand the context within which the algorithms are used. Then we look at three important block encryption algorithms: DES, triple DES, and AES. This is followed by a discussion of random and pseudorandom number generation. Next, the chapter introduces symmetric stream encryption and describes the widely used stream cipher RC4. Finally, we look at the important topic of block cipher modes of operation.

2.1 SYMMETRIC ENCRYPTION PRINCIPLES

A **symmetric encryption** scheme has five ingredients (Figure 2.1):

- **Plaintext:** This is the original message or data that is fed into the algorithm as input.
- **Encryption algorithm:** The encryption algorithm performs various substitutions and transformations on the plaintext.
- **Secret key:** The secret key is also input to the algorithm. The exact substitutions and transformations performed by the algorithm depend on the key.

---

[1]Public-key encryption was first described in the open literature in 1976; the National Security Agency (NSA) claims to have discovered it some years earlier.

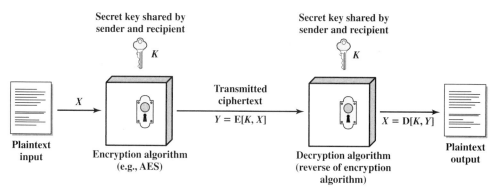

Figure 2.1   Simplified Model of Symmetric Encryption

- **Ciphertext:** This is the scrambled message produced as output. It depends on the plaintext and the secret key. For a given message, two different keys will produce two different ciphertexts.

- **Decryption algorithm:** This is essentially the encryption algorithm run in reverse. It takes the ciphertext and the same secret key and produces the original plaintext.

There are two requirements for secure use of symmetric encryption:

1. We need a strong encryption algorithm. At a minimum, we would like the algorithm to be such that an opponent who knows the algorithm and has access to one or more ciphertexts would be unable to decipher the ciphertext or figure out the key. This requirement is usually stated in a stronger form: The opponent should be unable to decrypt ciphertext or discover the key even if he or she is in possession of a number of ciphertexts together with the plaintext that produced each ciphertext.

2. Sender and receiver must have obtained copies of the secret key in a secure fashion and must keep the key secure. If someone can discover the key and knows the algorithm, all communication using this key is readable.

It is important to note that the security of symmetric encryption depends on the secrecy of the key, not the secrecy of the algorithm. That is, it is assumed that it is impractical to decrypt a message on the basis of the ciphertext *plus* knowledge of the encryption/decryption algorithm. In other words, we do not need to keep the algorithm secret; we need to keep only the key secret.

This feature of symmetric encryption is what makes it feasible for widespread use. The fact that the algorithm need not be kept secret means that manufacturers can and have developed low-cost chip implementations of data encryption algorithms. These chips are widely available and incorporated into a number of products. With the use of symmetric encryption, the principal security problem is maintaining the secrecy of the key.

Cryptography

Cryptographic systems are generically classified along three independent dimensions:

1. **The type of operations used for transforming plaintext to ciphertext.** All encryption algorithms are based on two general principles: substitution, in which each element in the plaintext (bit, letter, group of bits or letters) is mapped into another element, and transposition, in which elements in the plaintext are rearranged. The fundamental requirement is that no information be lost (that is, that all operations be reversible). Most systems, referred to as product systems, involve multiple stages of substitutions and transpositions.

2. **The number of keys used.** If both sender and receiver use the same key, the system is referred to as symmetric, single-key, secret-key, or conventional encryption. If the sender and receiver each use a different key, the system is referred to as asymmetric, two-key, or public-key encryption.

3. **The way in which the plaintext is processed.** A **block cipher** processes the input one block of elements at a time, producing an output block for each input block. A **stream cipher** processes the input elements continuously, producing output one element at a time, as it goes along.

Cryptanalysis

The process of attempting to discover the plaintext or key is known as **cryptanalysis**. The strategy used by the cryptanalyst depends on the nature of the encryption scheme and the information available to the cryptanalyst.

Table 2.1 summarizes the various types of cryptanalytic attacks based on the amount of information known to the cryptanalyst. The most difficult problem is presented when all that is available is the *ciphertext only*. In some cases, not even the encryption algorithm is known, but in general, we can assume that the opponent does know the algorithm used for encryption. One possible attack under these circumstances is the brute-force approach of trying all possible keys. If the key space is very large, this becomes impractical. Thus, the opponent must rely on an analysis of the ciphertext itself, generally applying various statistical tests to it. To use this approach, the opponent must have some general idea of the type of plaintext that is concealed, such as English or French text, an EXE file, a Java source listing, an accounting file, and so on.

The ciphertext-only attack is the easiest to defend against because the opponent has the least amount of information to work with. In many cases, however, the analyst has more information. The analyst may be able to capture one or more plaintext messages as well as their encryptions. Or the analyst may know that certain plaintext patterns will appear in a message. For example, a file that is encoded in the Postscript format always begins with the same pattern, or there may be a standardized header or banner to an electronic funds transfer message, and so on. All of these are examples of *known plaintext*. With this knowledge, the analyst may be able to deduce the key on the basis of the way in which the known plaintext is transformed.

Closely related to the known-plaintext attack is what might be referred to as a probable-word attack. If the opponent is working with the encryption of some general

Table 2.1 Types of Attacks on Encrypted Messages

Type of Attack	Known to Cryptanalyst
Ciphertext only	• Encryption algorithm • Ciphertext to be decoded
Known plaintext	• Encryption algorithm • Ciphertext to be decoded • One or more plaintext–ciphertext pairs formed with the secret key
Chosen plaintext	• Encryption algorithm • Ciphertext to be decoded • Plaintext message chosen by cryptanalyst, together with its corresponding ciphertext generated with the secret key
Chosen ciphertext	• Encryption algorithm • Ciphertext to be decoded • Purported ciphertext chosen by cryptanalyst, together with its corresponding decrypted plaintext generated with the secret key
Chosen text	• Encryption algorithm • Ciphertext to be decoded • Plaintext message chosen by cryptanalyst, together with its corresponding ciphertext generated with the secret key • Purported ciphertext chosen by cryptanalyst, together with its corresponding decrypted plaintext generated with the secret key

prose message, he or she may have little knowledge of what is in the message. However, if the opponent is after some very specific information, then parts of the message may be known. For example, if an entire accounting file is being transmitted, the opponent may know the placement of certain key words in the header of the file. As another example, the source code for a program developed by a corporation might include a copyright statement in some standardized position.

If the analyst is able somehow to get the source system to insert into the system a message chosen by the analyst, then a *chosen-plaintext* attack is possible. In general, if the analyst is able to choose the messages to encrypt, the analyst may deliberately pick patterns that can be expected to reveal the structure of the key.

Table 2.1 lists two other types of attack: chosen ciphertext and chosen text. These are less commonly employed as cryptanalytic techniques but are nevertheless possible avenues of attack.

Only relatively weak algorithms fail to withstand a ciphertext-only attack. Generally, an encryption algorithm is designed to withstand a known-plaintext attack.

An encryption scheme is **computationally secure** if the ciphertext generated by the scheme meets one or both of the following criteria:

• The cost of breaking the cipher exceeds the value of the encrypted information.

• The time required to break the cipher exceeds the useful lifetime of the information.

Unfortunately, it is very difficult to estimate the amount of effort required to cryptanalyze ciphertext successfully. However, assuming there are no inherent mathematical weaknesses in the algorithm, then a brute-force approach is indicated, and here we can make some reasonable estimates about costs and time.

A brute-force approach involves trying every possible key until an intelligible translation of the ciphertext into plaintext is obtained. On average, half of all possible keys must be tried to achieve success. Table 2.2 shows how much time is involved for various key sizes. The 56-bit key size is used with the DES (Data Encryption Standard) algorithm. For each key size, the results are shown assuming that it takes 1 μs to perform a single decryption, which is a reasonable order of magnitude for today's machines. With the use of massively parallel organizations of microprocessors, it may be possible to achieve processing rates many orders of magnitude greater. The final column of Table 2.2 considers the results for a system that can process 1 million keys per microsecond. As you can see, at this performance level, DES no longer can be considered computationally secure.

Feistel Cipher Structure

Many symmetric block encryption algorithms, including DES, have a structure first described by Horst Feistel of IBM in 1973 [FEIS73] and shown in Figure 2.2. The inputs to the encryption algorithm are a plaintext block of length $2w$ bits and a key K. The plaintext block is divided into two halves, LE_0 and RE_0. The two halves of the data pass through n rounds of processing and then combine to produce the ciphertext block. Each round i has as inputs LE_{i-1} and RE_{i-1} derived from the previous round, as well as a subkey K_i derived from the overall K. In general, the subkeys K_i are different from K and from each other and are generated from the key by a subkey generation algorithm. In Figure 2.2, 16 rounds are used, although any number of rounds could be implemented. The right-hand side of Figure 2.2 shows the decryption process.

All rounds have the same structure. A substitution is performed on the left half of the data. This is done by applying a *round function* F to the right half of the data and then taking the exclusive-OR (XOR) of the output of that function and the left half of the data. The round function has the same general structure for each round but is

Table 2.2 Average Time Required for Exhaustive Key Search

Key Size (bits)	Number of Alternative Keys	Time Required at 1 Decryption/μs	Time Required at 10^6 Decryptions/μs
32	$2^{32} = 4.3 \times 10^9$	$2^{31}\mu s = 35.8$ minutes	2.15 milliseconds
56	$2^{56} = 7.2 \times 10^{16}$	$2^{55}\mu s = 1142$ years	10.01 hours
128	$2^{128} = 3.4 \times 10^{38}$	$2^{127}\mu s = 5.4 \times 10^{24}$ years	5.4×10^{18} years
168	$2^{168} = 3.7 \times 10^{50}$	$2^{167}\mu s = 5.9 \times 10^{36}$ years	5.9×10^{30} years
26 characters (permutation)	$26! = 4 \times 10^{26}$	$2 \times 10^{26}\mu s = 6.4 \times 10^{12}$ years	6.4×10^6 years

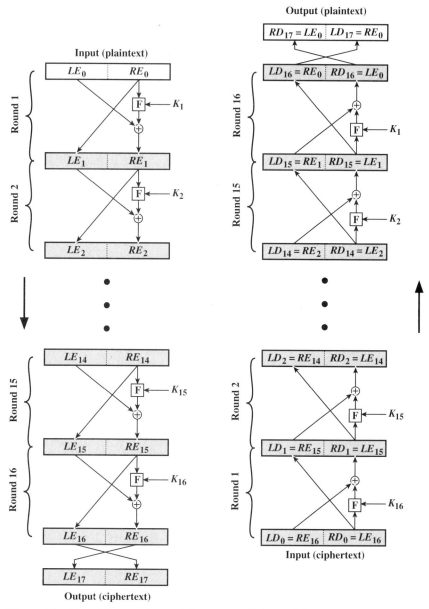

Figure 2.2   Feistel Encryption and Decryption (16 rounds)

parameterized by the round subkey K_i. Following this substitution, a permutation is performed that consists of the interchange of the two halves of the data.

The **Feistel structure** is a particular example of the more general structure used by all symmetric block ciphers. In general, a symmetric block cipher consists of a sequence of rounds, with each round performing substitutions and permutations conditioned by a secret key value. The exact realization of a symmetric block cipher depends on the choice of the following parameters and design features.

- **Block size:** Larger block sizes mean greater security (all other things being equal) but reduced encryption/decryption speed. A block size of 128 bits is a reasonable tradeoff and is nearly universal among recent block cipher designs.

- **Key size:** Larger key size means greater security but may decrease encryption/ decryption speed. The most common key length in modern algorithms is 128 bits.

- **Number of rounds:** The essence of a symmetric block cipher is that a single round offers inadequate security but that multiple rounds offer increasing security. A typical size is 16 rounds.

- **Subkey generation algorithm:** Greater complexity in this algorithm should lead to greater difficulty of cryptanalysis.

- **Round function:** Again, greater complexity generally means greater resistance to cryptanalysis.

There are two other considerations in the design of a symmetric block cipher:

- **Fast software encryption/decryption:** In many cases, encryption is embedded in applications or utility functions in such a way as to preclude a hardware implementation. Accordingly, the speed of execution of the algorithm becomes a concern.

- **Ease of analysis:** Although we would like to make our algorithm as difficult as possible to cryptanalyze, there is great benefit in making the algorithm easy to analyze. That is, if the algorithm can be concisely and clearly explained, it is easier to analyze that algorithm for cryptanalytic vulnerabilities and therefore develop a higher level of assurance as to its strength. DES, for example, does not have an easily analyzed functionality.

Decryption with a symmetric block cipher is essentially the same as the encryption process. The rule is as follows: Use the ciphertext as input to the algorithm, but use the subkeys K_i in reverse order. That is, use K_n in the first round, K_{n-1} in the second round, and so on until K_1 is used in the last round. This is a nice feature, because it means we need not implement two different algorithms—one for encryption and one for decryption.

2.2 SYMMETRIC BLOCK ENCRYPTION ALGORITHMS

The most commonly used symmetric encryption algorithms are block ciphers. A **block cipher** processes the plaintext input in fixed-sized blocks and produces a block of ciphertext of equal size for each plaintext block. This section focuses on the three most important symmetric block ciphers: the Data Encryption Standard (DES), triple DES (3DES), and the Advanced Encryption Standard (AES).

Data Encryption Standard

The most widely used encryption scheme is based on the **Data Encryption Standard (DES)** issued in 1977, as Federal Information Processing Standard 46 (FIPS 46) by the National Bureau of Standards, now known as the National Institute of Standards and Technology (NIST). The algorithm itself is referred to as the Data Encryption Algorithm (DEA).[2]

DESCRIPTION OF THE ALGORITHM The plaintext is 64 bits in length and the key is 56 bits in length; longer plaintext amounts are processed in 64-bit blocks. The DES structure is a minor variation of the Feistel network shown in Figure 2.2. There are 16 rounds of processing. From the original 56-bit key, 16 subkeys are generated, one of which is used for each round.

The process of decryption with DES is essentially the same as the encryption process. The rule is as follows: Use the ciphertext as input to the DES algorithm, but use the subkeys K_i in reverse order. That is, use K_{16} on the first iteration, K_{15} on the second iteration, and so on until K_1 is used on the 16th and last iteration.

THE STRENGTH OF DES Concerns about the strength of DES fall into two categories: concerns about the algorithm itself and concerns about the use of a 56-bit key. The first concern refers to the possibility that cryptanalysis is possible by exploiting the characteristics of the DES algorithm. Over the years, there have been numerous attempts to find and exploit weaknesses in the algorithm, making DES the most-studied encryption algorithm in existence. Despite numerous approaches, no one has so far succeeded in discovering a fatal weakness in DES.[3]

A more serious concern is key length. With a key length of 56 bits, there are 2^{56} possible keys, which is approximately 7.2×10^{16} keys. Thus, on the face of it, a brute-force attack appears impractical. Assuming that on average half the key space has to be searched, a single machine performing one DES encryption per microsecond would take more than a thousand years (see Table 2.2) to break the cipher.

However, the assumption of one encryption per microsecond is overly conservative. DES finally and definitively proved insecure in July 1998, when the Electronic Frontier Foundation (EFF) announced that it had broken a DES encryption using a special-purpose "DES cracker" machine that was built for less than $250,000. The attack took less than three days. The EFF has published a detailed description of the machine, enabling others to build their own cracker [EFF98]. And, of course, hardware prices will continue to drop as speeds increase, making DES virtually worthless.

It is important to note that there is more to a key-search attack than simply running through all possible keys. Unless known plaintext is provided, the analyst must be able to recognize plaintext as plaintext. If the message is just plain text in English, then the result pops out easily, although the task of recognizing English would have to be automated. If the text message has been compressed before encryption, then recognition is more difficult. And if the message is some more general type of data, such as a numerical file, and this has been compressed, the problem becomes even more difficult to automate. Thus, to supplement the brute-force

---

[2]The terminology is a bit confusing. Until recently, the terms *DES* and *DEA* could be used interchangeably. However, the most recent edition of the DES document includes a specification of the DEA described here plus the triple DEA (3DES) described subsequently. Both DEA and 3DES are part of the Data Encryption Standard. Furthermore, until the recent adoption of the official term *3DES*, the triple DEA algorithm was typically referred to as *triple DES* and written as 3DES. For the sake of convenience, we will use 3DES.

[3]At least, no one has publicly acknowledged such a discovery.

approach, some degree of knowledge about the expected plaintext is needed, and some means of automatically distinguishing plaintext from garble is also needed. The EFF approach addresses this issue as well and introduces some automated techniques that would be effective in many contexts.

A final point: If the only form of attack that could be made on an encryption algorithm is brute force, then the way to counter such attacks is obvious: use longer keys. To get some idea of the size of key required, let us use the EFF cracker as a basis for our estimates. The EFF cracker was a prototype, and we can assume that with today's technology a faster machine is cost effective. If we assume that a cracker can perform one million decryptions per μs, which is the rate used in Table 2.2, then a DES code would take about 10 hours to crack. This is a speed-up of approximately a factor of 7 compared to the EFF result. Using this rate, Figure 2.3 shows how long it would take to crack a DES-style algorithm as a function of key size. For example, for a 128-bit key, which is common among contemporary algorithms, it would take over 10^{18} years to break the code using the EFF cracker. Even if we managed to speed up the cracker by a factor of 1 trillion (10^{12}), it would still take over 1 million years to break the code. So a 128-bit key is guaranteed to result in an algorithm that is unbreakable by brute force.

Triple DES

Triple DES (3DES) was first standardized for use in financial applications in ANSI standard X9.17 in 1985. 3DES was incorporated as part of the Data Encryption Standard in 1999 with the publication of FIPS 46-3.

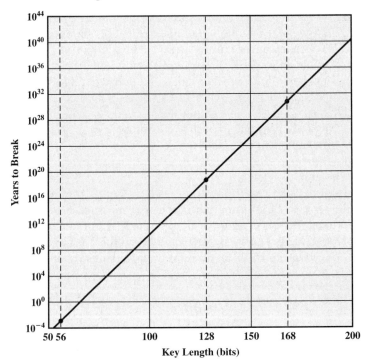

Figure 2.3   Time to Break a Code (assuming 10^6 decryptions/μs)

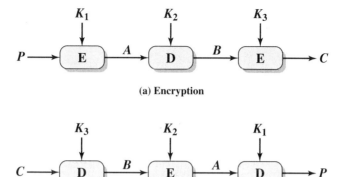

(a) Encryption

(b) Decryption

Figure 2.4   Triple DES

3DES uses three keys and three executions of the DES algorithm. The function follows an encrypt-decrypt-encrypt (EDE) sequence (Figure 2.4a):

$$C = E(K_3, D(K_2, E(K_1, P)))$$

where

$$C = \text{ciphertext}$$
$$P = \text{plaintext}$$
$$E[K, X] = \text{encryption of } X \text{ using key } K$$
$$D[K, Y] = \text{decryption of } Y \text{ using key } K$$

Decryption is simply the same operation with the keys reversed (Figure 2.4b):

$$P = D(K_1, E(K_2, D(K_3, C)))$$

There is no cryptographic significance to the use of decryption for the second stage of 3DES encryption. Its only advantage is that it allows users of 3DES to decrypt data encrypted by users of the older single DES:

$$C = E(K_1, D(K_1, E(K_1, P))) = E[K, P]$$

With three distinct keys, 3DES has an effective key length of 168 bits. FIPS 46-3 also allows for the use of two keys, with $K_1 = K_3$; this provides for a key length of 112 bits. FIPS 46-3 includes the following guidelines for 3DES.

- 3DES is the FIPS approved symmetric encryption algorithm of choice.
- The original DES, which uses a single 56-bit key, is permitted under the standard for legacy systems only. New procurements should support 3DES.
- Government organizations with legacy DES systems are encouraged to transition to 3DES.
- It is anticipated that 3DES and the Advanced Encryption Standard (AES) will coexist as FIPS-approved algorithms, allowing for a gradual transition to AES.

It is easy to see that 3DES is a formidable algorithm. Because the underlying cryptographic algorithm is DEA, 3DES can claim the same resistance to cryptanalysis based on the algorithm as is claimed for DEA. Furthermore, with a 168-bit key length, brute-force attacks are effectively impossible.

Ultimately, AES is intended to replace 3DES, but this process will take a number of years. NIST anticipates that 3DES will remain an approved algorithm (for U.S. government use) for the foreseeable future.

Advanced Encryption Standard

3DES has two attractions that assure its widespread use over the next few years. First, with its 168-bit key length, it overcomes the vulnerability to brute-force attack of DEA. Second, the underlying encryption algorithm in 3DES is the same as in DEA. This algorithm has been subjected to more scrutiny than any other encryption algorithm over a longer period of time, and no effective cryptanalytic attack based on the algorithm rather than brute force has been found. Accordingly, there is a high level of confidence that 3DES is very resistant to cryptanalysis. If security were the only consideration, then 3DES would be an appropriate choice for a standardized encryption algorithm for decades to come.

The principal drawback of 3DES is that the algorithm is relatively sluggish in software. The original DEA was designed for mid-1970s hardware implementation and does not produce efficient software code. 3DES, which has three times as many rounds as DEA, is correspondingly slower. A secondary drawback is that both DEA and 3DES use a 64-bit block size. For reasons of both efficiency and security, a larger block size is desirable.

Because of these drawbacks, 3DES is not a reasonable candidate for long-term use. As a replacement, NIST in 1997 issued a call for proposals for a new **Advanced Encryption Standard (AES)**, which should have a security strength equal to or better than 3DES and significantly improved efficiency. In addition to these general requirements, NIST specified that AES must be a symmetric block cipher with a block length of 128 bits and support for key lengths of 128, 192, and 256 bits. Evaluation criteria included security, computational efficiency, memory requirements, hardware and software suitability, and flexibility.

In a first round of evaluation, 15 proposed algorithms were accepted. A second round narrowed the field to five algorithms. NIST completed its evaluation process and published a final standard (FIPS PUB 197) in November of 2001. NIST selected Rijndael as the proposed AES algorithm. The two researchers who developed and submitted Rijndael for the AES are both cryptographers from Belgium: Dr. Joan Daemen and Dr. Vincent Rijmen.

OVERVIEW OF THE ALGORITHM AES uses a block length of 128 bits and a key length that can be 128, 192, or 256 bits. In the description of this section, we assume a key length of 128 bits, which is likely to be the one most commonly implemented.

Figure 2.5 shows the overall structure of AES. The input to the encryption and decryption algorithms is a single 128-bit block. In FIPS PUB 197, this block is depicted as a square matrix of bytes. This block is copied into the **State** array, which is modified at each stage of encryption or decryption. After the final stage, **State** is copied to an output matrix. Similarly, the 128-bit key is depicted as a square matrix of bytes. This key is then expanded into an array of key schedule words: each word is four bytes and the total key schedule is 44 words for the 128-bit key. The ordering of bytes within a

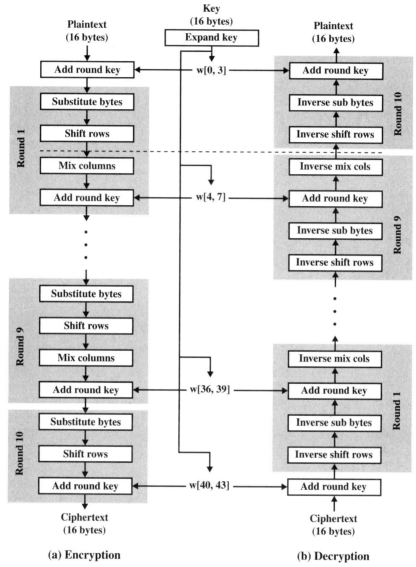

Figure 2.5 AES Encryption and Decryption

matrix is by column. So, for example, the first four bytes of a 128-bit plaintext input to the encryption cipher occupy the first column of the **in** matrix, the second four bytes occupy the second column, and so on. Similarly, the first four bytes of the expanded key, which form a word, occupy the first column of the **w** matrix.

The following comments give some insight into AES.

1. One noteworthy feature of this structure is that it is not a Feistel structure. Recall that in the classic Feistel structure, half of the data block is used to modify the other half of the data block, and then the halves are swapped. AES does not use

a Feistel structure but processes the entire data block in parallel during each round using substitutions and permutation.

2. The key that is provided as input is expanded into an array of forty-four 32-bit words, $w[i]$. Four distinct words (128 bits) serve as a round key for each round.

3. Four different stages are used, one of permutation and three of substitution:

   - **Substitute bytes:** Uses a table, referred to as an S-box,[4] to perform a byte-by-byte substitution of the block.
   - **Shift rows:** A simple permutation that is performed row by row.
   - **Mix columns:** A substitution that alters each byte in a column as a function of all of the bytes in the column.
   - **Add round key:** A simple bitwise XOR of the current block with a portion of the expanded key.

4. The structure is quite simple. For both encryption and decryption, the cipher begins with an Add Round Key stage, followed by nine rounds that each includes all four stages, followed by a tenth round of three stages. Figure 2.6 depicts the structure of a full encryption round.

5. Only the Add Round Key stage makes use of the key. For this reason, the cipher begins and ends with an Add Round Key stage. Any other stage, applied at the beginning or end, is reversible without knowledge of the key and so would add no security.

6. The Add Round Key stage by itself would not be formidable. The other three stages together scramble the bits, but by themselves, they would provide no security because they do not use the key. We can view the cipher as alternating operations of XOR encryption (Add Round Key) of a block, followed by scrambling of the block (the other three stages), followed by XOR encryption, and so on. This scheme is both efficient and highly secure.

7. Each stage is easily reversible. For the Substitute Byte, Shift Row, and Mix Columns stages, an inverse function is used in the decryption algorithm. For the Add Round Key stage, the inverse is achieved by XORing the same round key to the block, using the result that $A \oplus B \oplus B = A$.

8. As with most block ciphers, the decryption algorithm makes use of the expanded key in reverse order. However, the decryption algorithm is not identical to the encryption algorithm. This is a consequence of the particular structure of AES.

9. Once it is established that all four stages are reversible, it is easy to verify that decryption does recover the plaintext. Figure 2.5 lays out encryption and decryption going in opposite vertical directions. At each horizontal point (e.g., the dashed line in the figure), **State** is the same for both encryption and decryption.

10. The final round of both encryption and decryption consists of only three stages. Again, this is a consequence of the particular structure of AES and is required to make the cipher reversible.

---

[4]The term *S-box*, or substitution box, is commonly used in the description of symmetric ciphers to refer to a table used for a table-lookup type of substitution mechanism.

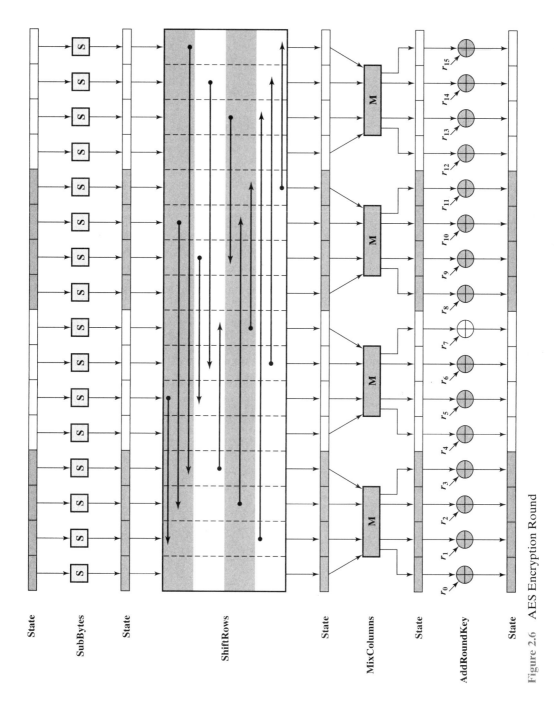

Figure 2.6 AES Encryption Round

2.3 RANDOM AND PSEUDORANDOM NUMBERS

Random numbers play an important role in the use of encryption for various network security applications. We provide an overview in this section. The topic is examined in more detail in Appendix E.

The Use of Random Numbers

A number of network security algorithms based on cryptography make use of random numbers. For example,

- Generation of keys for the RSA public-key encryption algorithm (described in Chapter 3) and other public-key algorithms.
- Generation of a stream key for symmetric stream cipher (discussed in the following section).
- Generation of a symmetric key for use as a temporary session key. This function is used in a number of networking applications, such as Transport Layer Security (Chapter 5), Wi-Fi (Chapter 6), e-mail security (Chapter 7), and IP security (Chapter 8).
- In a number of key distribution scenarios, such as Kerberos (Chapter 4), random numbers are used for handshaking to prevent replay attacks.

These applications give rise to two distinct and not necessarily compatible requirements for a sequence of random numbers: randomness and unpredictability.

RANDOMNESS Traditionally, the concern in the generation of a sequence of allegedly random numbers has been that the sequence of numbers be random in some well-defined statistical sense. The following criteria are used to validate that a sequence of numbers is random.

- **Uniform distribution:** The distribution of bits in the sequence should be uniform; that is, the frequency of occurrence of ones and zeros should be approximately the same.
- **Independence:** No one subsequence in the sequence can be inferred from the others.

Although there are well-defined tests for determining that a sequence of numbers matches a particular distribution, such as the uniform distribution, there is no such test to "prove" independence. Rather, a number of tests can be applied to demonstrate if a sequence does not exhibit independence. The general strategy is to apply a number of such tests until the confidence that independence exists is sufficiently strong.

In the context of our discussion, the use of a sequence of numbers that appear statistically random often occurs in the design of algorithms related to cryptography. For example, a fundamental requirement of the RSA public-key encryption scheme discussed in Chapter 3 is the ability to generate prime numbers. In general, it is difficult to determine if a given large number N is prime. A brute-force approach would be to divide N by every odd integer less than $\sqrt{N}$. If N is on the order, say, of 10^{150} (a not uncommon occurrence in public-key cryptography), such a brute-force approach is beyond the reach of human analysts and their computers. However, a number of effective algorithms exist that test the primality of a number by using a sequence of randomly chosen integers as input to relatively simple computations. If the sequence is sufficiently long (but far, far less than $\sqrt{10^{150}}$), the primality of a number can be determined with near certainty. This type of approach, known as randomization, crops up frequently in the design of algorithms. In essence, if a problem is too hard or time-consuming to solve exactly, a simpler, shorter approach based on randomization is used to provide an answer with any desired level of confidence.

UNPREDICTABILITY In applications such as reciprocal authentication and session key generation, the requirement is not so much that the sequence of numbers be statistically random but that the successive members of the sequence are unpredictable. With "true" random sequences, each number is statistically independent of other numbers in the sequence and therefore unpredictable. However, as is discussed shortly, true random numbers are not always used; rather, sequences of numbers that appear to be random are generated by some algorithm. In this latter case, care must be taken that an opponent not be able to predict future elements of the sequence on the basis of earlier elements.

TRNGs, PRNGs, and PRFs

Cryptographic applications typically make use of algorithmic techniques for random number generation. These algorithms are deterministic and therefore produce sequences of numbers that are not statistically random. However, if the algorithm is good, the resulting sequences will pass many reasonable tests of randomness. Such numbers are referred to as **pseudorandom numbers**.

You may be somewhat uneasy about the concept of using numbers generated by a deterministic algorithm as if they were random numbers. Despite what might be called "philosophical" objections to such a practice, it generally works. As one expert on probability theory puts it [HAMM91],

> For practical purposes we are forced to accept the awkward concept of "relatively random" meaning that with regard to the proposed use we can see no reason why they will not perform as if they were random (as the theory usually requires). This is highly subjective and is not very palatable to purists, but it is what statisticians regularly appeal to when they take "a random sample"—they hope that any results they use will have approximately the same properties as a complete counting of the whole sample space that occurs in their theory.

Figure 2.7 contrasts a **true random number generator (TRNG)** with two forms of pseudorandom number generators. A TRNG takes as input a source that is effectively random; the source is often referred to as an **entropy source**. In essence, the entropy source is drawn from the physical environment of the computer and could include things such as keystroke timing patterns, disk electrical activity, mouse movements, and instantaneous values of the system clock. The source, or combination of sources, serves as input to an algorithm that produces

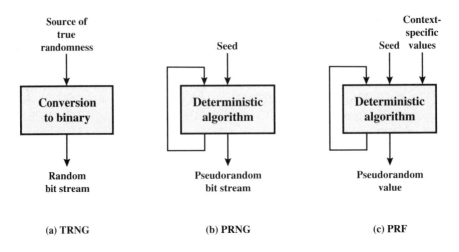

TRNG = true random number generator
PRNG = pseudorandom number generator
PRF = pseudorandom function

Figure 2.7   Random and Pseudorandom Number Generators

random binary output. The TRNG may simply involve conversion of an analog source to a binary output. The TRNG may involve additional processing to overcome any bias in the source.

In contrast, a PRNG takes as input a fixed value, called the **seed**, and produces a sequence of output bits using a deterministic algorithm. Typically, as shown in Figure 2.7, there is some feedback path by which some of the results of the algorithm are fed back as input as additional output bits are produced. The important thing to note is that the output bit stream is determined solely by the input value or values, so that an adversary who knows the algorithm and the seed can reproduce the entire bit stream.

Figure 2.7 shows two different forms of PRNGs, based on application.

- **Pseudorandom number generator:** An algorithm that is used to produce an open-ended sequence of bits is referred to as a PRNG. A common application for an open-ended sequence of bits is as input to a symmetric stream cipher, as discussed in the following section.
- **Pseudorandom function (PRF):** A PRF is used to produce a pseudorandom string of bits of some fixed length. Examples are symmetric encryption keys and nonces. Typically, the PRF takes as input a seed plus some context specific values, such as a user ID or an application ID. A number of examples of PRFs will be seen throughout this book.

Other than the number of bits produced, there is no difference between a PRNG and a PRF. The same algorithms can be used in both applications. Both require a seed and both must exhibit randomness and unpredictability. Furthermore, a PRNG application may also employ context-specific input.

Algorithm Design

Cryptographic PRNGs have been the subject of much research over the years, and a wide variety of algorithms have been developed. These fall roughly into two categories:

- **Purpose-built algorithms:** These are algorithms designed specifically and solely for the purpose of generating pseudorandom bit streams. Some of these algorithms are used for a variety of PRNG applications; several of these are described in the next section. Others are designed specifically for use in a stream cipher. The most important example of the latter is RC4, described in the next section.

- **Algorithms based on existing cryptographic algorithms:** Cryptographic algorithms have the effect of randomizing input. Indeed, this is a requirement of such algorithms. For example, if a symmetric block cipher produced ciphertext that had certain regular patterns in it, it would aid in the process of cryptanalysis. Thus, cryptographic algorithms can serve as the core of PRNGs. Three broad categories of cryptographic algorithms are commonly used to create PRNGs:

  —**Symmetric block ciphers**

  —**Asymmetric ciphers**

  —**Hash functions and message authentication codes**

  Any of these approaches can yield a cryptographically strong PRNG. A purpose-built algorithm may be provided by an operating system for general use. For applications that already use certain cryptographic algorithms for encryption or authentication, it makes sense to re-use the same code for the PRNG. Thus, all of these approaches are in common use.

2.4 STREAM CIPHERS AND RC4

A *block cipher* processes the input one block of elements at a time, producing an output block for each input block. A *stream cipher* processes the input elements continuously, producing output one element at a time as it goes along. Although block ciphers are far more common, there are certain applications in which a stream cipher is more appropriate. Examples are given subsequently in this book. In this section, we look at perhaps the most popular symmetric stream cipher, RC4. We begin with an overview of stream cipher structure, and then examine RC4.

Stream Cipher Structure

A typical stream cipher encrypts plaintext one byte at a time, although a stream cipher may be designed to operate on one bit at a time or on units larger than a byte at a time. Figure 2.8 is a representative diagram of stream cipher structure. In this structure, a key is input to a pseudorandom bit generator that produces a stream of 8-bit numbers that are apparently random. A pseudorandom stream is one that is unpredictable without knowledge of the input key and which has an apparently random character. The output of the generator, called a **keystream**, is combined one byte at a time with the plaintext stream using the bitwise exclusive-OR (XOR)

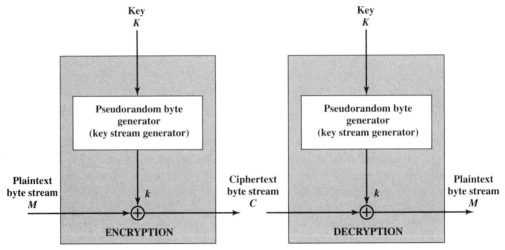

Figure 2.8 Stream Cipher Diagram

operation. For example, if the next byte generated by the generator is `01101100` and the next plaintext byte is `11001100`, then the resulting ciphertext byte is

```
  11001100  plaintext
⊕ 01101100  key stream
  10100000  ciphertext
```

Decryption requires the use of the same pseudorandom sequence:

```
  10100000  ciphertext
⊕ 01101100  key stream
  11001100  plaintext
```

[KUMA97] lists the following important design considerations for a stream cipher.

1. The encryption sequence should have a large period. A pseudorandom number generator uses a function that produces a deterministic stream of bits that eventually repeats. The longer the period of repeat, the more difficult it will be to do cryptanalysis.

2. The keystream should approximate the properties of a true random number stream as close as possible. For example, there should be an approximately equal number of 1s and 0s. If the keystream is treated as a stream of bytes, then all of the 256 possible byte values should appear approximately equally often. The more random-appearing the keystream is, the more randomized the ciphertext is, making cryptanalysis more difficult.

3. Note from Figure 2.8 that the output of the pseudorandom number generator is conditioned on the value of the input key. To guard against brute-force attacks, the key needs to be sufficiently long. The same considerations as apply for block ciphers are valid here. Thus, with current technology, a key length of at least 128 bits is desirable.

With a properly designed pseudorandom number generator, a stream cipher can be as secure as block cipher of comparable key length. The primary advantage of a stream cipher is that stream ciphers are almost always faster and use far less code than do block ciphers. The example in this section, RC4, can be implemented in just a few lines of code. Table 2.3, using data from [RESC01], compares execution times of RC4 with three well-known symmetric block ciphers. The advantage of a block cipher is that you can reuse keys. However, if two plaintexts are encrypted with the same key using a stream cipher, then cryptanalysis is often quite simple [DAWS96]. If the two ciphertext streams are XORed together, the result is the XOR of the original plaintexts. If the plaintexts are text strings, credit card numbers, or other byte streams with known properties, then cryptanalysis may be successful.

For applications that require encryption/decryption of a stream of data (such as over a data-communications channel or a browser/Web link), a stream cipher might be the better alternative. For applications that deal with blocks of data (such as file transfer, e-mail, and database), block ciphers may be more appropriate. However, either type of cipher can be used in virtually any application.

The RC4 Algorithm

RC4 is a stream cipher designed in 1987 by Ron Rivest for RSA Security. It is a variable key-size stream cipher with byte-oriented operations. The algorithm is based on the use of a random permutation. Analysis shows that the period of the cipher is overwhelmingly likely to be greater than 10^{100} [ROBS95a]. Eight to sixteen machine operations are required per output byte, and the cipher can be expected to run very quickly in software. RC4 is used in the Secure Sockets Layer/Transport Layer Security (SSL/TLS) standards that have been defined for communication between Web browsers and servers. It is also used in the Wired Equivalent Privacy (WEP) protocol and the newer WiFi Protected Access (WPA) protocol that are part of the IEEE 802.11 wireless LAN standard. RC4 was kept as a trade secret by RSA Security. In September 1994, the RC4 algorithm was anonymously posted on the Internet on the Cypherpunks anonymous remailers list.

The RC4 algorithm is remarkably simple and quite easy to explain. A variable-length key of from 1 to 256 bytes (8 to 2048 bits) is used to initialize a 256-byte state vector S, with elements S[0], S[1], ..., S[255]. At all times, S contains a permutation of all 8-bit numbers from 0 through 255. For encryption and decryption, a byte k (see Figure 2.8) is generated from S by selecting one of the 255 entries in a systematic fashion. As each value of k is generated, the entries in S are once again permuted.

Table 2.3   Speed Comparisons of Symmetric Ciphers on a Pentium II

Cipher	Key Length	Speed (Mbps)
DES	56	9
3DES	168	3
RC2	Variable	0.9
RC4	Variable	45

INITIALIZATION OF S To begin, the entries of S are set equal to the values from 0 through 255 in ascending order; that is, S[0] = 0, S[1] = 1, . . ., S[255] = 255. A temporary vector, T, is also created. If the length of the key K is 256 bytes, then K is transferred to T. Otherwise, for a key of length *keylen* bytes, the first *keylen* elements of T are copied from K, and then K is repeated as many times as necessary to fill out T. These preliminary operations can be summarized as:

```
/* Initialization */
for i = 0 to 255 do
S[i] = i;
T[i] = K[i mod keylen];
```

Next we use T to produce the initial permutation of S. This involves starting with S[0] and going through to S[255] and, for each S[i], swapping S[i] with another byte in S according to a scheme dictated by T[i]:

```
/* Initial Permutation of S */
j = 0;
for i = 0 to 255 do
    j = (j + S[i] + T[i]) mod 256;
    Swap (S[i], S[j]);
```

Because the only operation on S is a swap, the only effect is a permutation. S still contains all the numbers from 0 through 255.

STREAM GENERATION Once the S vector is initialized, the input key is no longer used. Stream generation involves cycling through all the elements of S[i] and, for each S[i], swapping S[i] with another byte in S according to a scheme dictated by the current configuration of S. After S[255] is reached, the process continues, starting over again at S[0]:

```
/* Stream Generation */
i, j = 0;
while (true)
    i = (i + 1) mod 256;
    j = (j + S[i]) mod 256;
    Swap (S[i], S[j]);
    t = (S[i] + S[j]) mod 256;
    k = S[t];
```

To encrypt, XOR the value *k* with the next byte of plaintext. To decrypt, XOR the value *k* with the next byte of ciphertext.

Figure 2.9 illustrates the RC4 logic.

STRENGTH OF RC4 A number of papers have been published analyzing methods of attacking RC4 (e.g., [KNUD98], [MIST98], [FLUH00], [MANT01], [PUDO02], [PAUL03], [PAUL04]). None of these approaches is practical against RC4 with a reasonable key length, such as 128 bits. A more serious problem is reported in

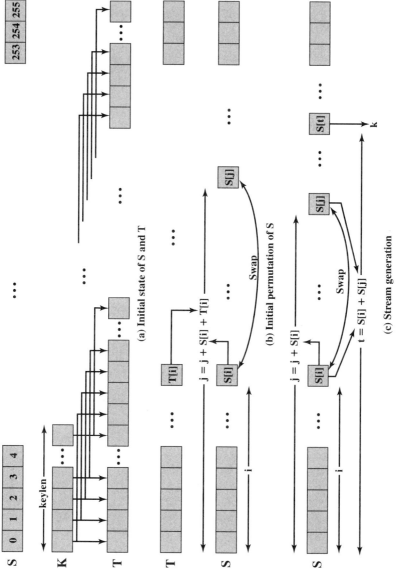

(a) Initial state of S and T

(b) Initial permutation of S

(c) Stream generation

Figure 2.9   RC4

[FLUH01]. The authors demonstrate that the WEP protocol, intended to provide confidentiality on 802.11 wireless LAN networks, is vulnerable to a particular attack approach. In essence, the problem is not with RC4 itself but the way in which keys are generated for use as input to RC4. This particular problem does not appear to be relevant to other applications using RC4 and can be remedied in WEP by changing the way in which keys are generated. This problem points out the difficulty in designing a secure system that involves both cryptographic functions and protocols that make use of them.

2.5 CIPHER BLOCK MODES OF OPERATION

A symmetric block cipher processes one block of data at a time. In the case of DES and 3DES, the block length is $b = 64$ bits; for AES, the block length is $b = 128$ bits. For longer amounts of plaintext, it is necessary to break the plaintext into b-bit blocks (padding the last block if necessary). To apply a block cipher in a variety of applications, five **modes of operation** have been defined by NIST (Special Publication 800-38A). The five modes are intended to cover virtually all of the possible applications of encryption for which a block cipher could be used. These modes are intended for use with any symmetric block cipher, including triple DES and AES. The most important modes are described briefly in the remainder of this section.

Electronic Codebook Mode

The simplest way to proceed is using what is known as **electronic codebook (ECB) mode**, in which plaintext is handled b bits at a time and each block of plaintext is encrypted using the same key. The term *codebook* is used because, for a given key, there is a unique ciphertext for every b-bit block of plaintext. Therefore, one can imagine a gigantic codebook in which there is an entry for every possible b-bit plaintext pattern showing its corresponding ciphertext.

With ECB, if the same b-bit block of plaintext appears more than once in the message, it always produces the same ciphertext. Because of this, for lengthy messages, the ECB mode may not be secure. If the message is highly structured, it may be possible for a cryptanalyst to exploit these regularities. For example, if it is known that the message always starts out with certain predefined fields, then the cryptanalyst may have a number of known plaintext–ciphertext pairs to work with. If the message has repetitive elements with a period of repetition a multiple of b bits, then these elements can be identified by the analyst. This may help in the analysis or may provide an opportunity for substituting or rearranging blocks.

To overcome the security deficiencies of ECB, we would like a technique in which the same plaintext block, if repeated, produces different ciphertext blocks.

Cipher Block Chaining Mode

In the **cipher block chaining (CBC) mode** (Figure 2.10), the input to the encryption algorithm is the XOR of the current plaintext block and the preceding ciphertext block; the same key is used for each block. In effect, we have chained together the processing of the sequence of plaintext blocks. The input to the encryption function

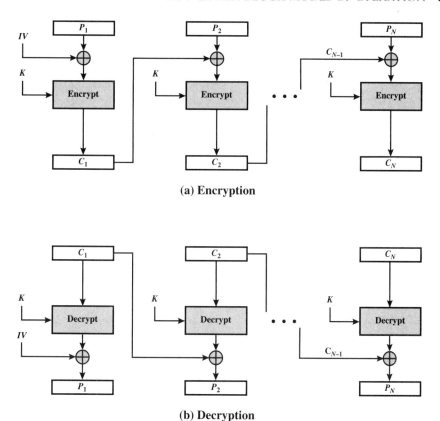

(a) Encryption

(b) Decryption

Figure 2.10 Cipher Block Chaining (CBC) Mode

for each plaintext block bears no fixed relationship to the plaintext block. Therefore, repeating patterns of b bits are not exposed.

For decryption, each cipher block is passed through the decryption algorithm. The result is XORed with the preceding ciphertext block to produce the plaintext block. To see that this works, we can write

$$C_j = E(K, [C_{j-1} \oplus P_j])$$

where $E[K, X]$ is the encryption of plaintext X using key K, and $\oplus$ is the exclusive-OR operation. Then

$$D(K, C_j) = D(K, E(K, [C_{j-1} \oplus P_j]))$$
$$D(K, C_j) = C_{j-1} \oplus P_j$$
$$C_{j-1} \oplus D(K, C_j) = C_{j-1} \oplus C_{j-1} \oplus P_j = P_j$$

which verifies Figure 2.10b.

To produce the first block of ciphertext, an initialization vector (IV) is XORed with the first block of plaintext. On decryption, the IV is XORed with the output of the decryption algorithm to recover the first block of plaintext.

The IV must be known to both the sender and receiver. For maximum security, the IV should be protected as well as the key. This could be done by sending the IV using ECB encryption. One reason for protecting the IV is as follows: If an opponent is able to fool the receiver into using a different value for IV, then the opponent is able to invert selected bits in the first block of plaintext. To see this, consider the following:

$$C_1 = E(K, [IV \oplus P_1])$$
$$P_1 = IV \oplus D(K, C_1)$$

Now use the notation that $X[j]$ denotes the jth bit of the b-bit quantity X. Then

$$P_1[i] = IV[i] \oplus D(K, C_1)[i]$$

Then, using the properties of XOR, we can state

$$P_1[i]' = IV[i]' \oplus D(K, C_1)[i]$$

where the prime notation denotes bit complementation. This means that if an opponent can predictably change bits in IV, the corresponding bits of the received value of P_1 can be changed.

Cipher Feedback Mode

It is possible to convert any block cipher into a stream cipher by using the **cipher feedback (CFB) mode**. A stream cipher eliminates the need to pad a message to be an integral number of blocks. It also can operate in real time. Thus, if a character stream is being transmitted, each character can be encrypted and transmitted immediately using a character-oriented stream cipher.

One desirable property of a stream cipher is that the ciphertext be of the same length as the plaintext. Thus, if 8-bit characters are being transmitted, each character should be encrypted using 8 bits. If more than 8 bits are used, transmission capacity is wasted.

Figure 2.11 depicts the CFB scheme. In the figure, it is assumed that the unit of transmission is s bits; a common value is $s = 8$. As with CBC, the units of plaintext are chained together, so that the ciphertext of any plaintext unit is a function of all the preceding plaintext.

First, consider encryption. The input to the encryption function is a b-bit shift register that is initially set to some initialization vector (IV). The leftmost (most significant) s bits of the output of the encryption function are XORed with the first unit of plaintext P_1 to produce the first unit of ciphertext C_1, which is then transmitted. In addition, the contents of the shift register are shifted left by s bits, and C_1 is placed in the rightmost (least significant) s bits of the shift register. This process continues until all plaintext units have been encrypted.

For decryption, the same scheme is used, except that the received ciphertext unit is XORed with the output of the encryption function to produce the plaintext unit. Note that it is the *encryption* function that is used, not the decryption function. This is easily explained. Let $S_s(X)$ be defined as the most significant s bits of X. Then

$$C_1 = P_1 \oplus S_s[E(K, IV)]$$

Therefore,

$$P_1 = C_1 \oplus S_s[E(K, IV)]$$

The same reasoning holds for subsequent steps in the process.

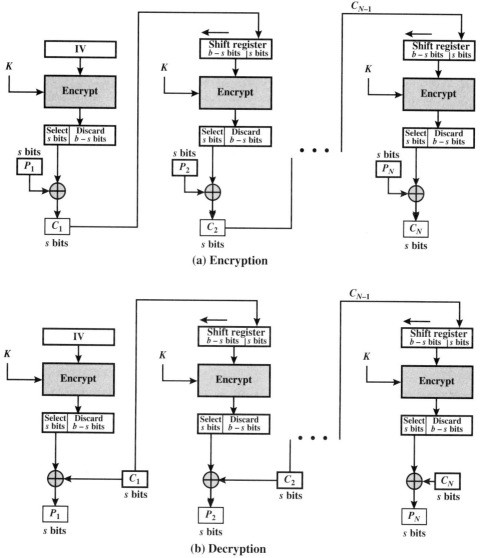

Figure 2.11   *s*-bit Cipher Feedback (CFB) Mode

Counter Mode

Although interest in the **counter mode (CTR)** has increased recently, with applications to ATM (asynchronous transfer mode) network security and IPSec (IP security), this mode was proposed early on (e.g., [DIFF79]).

Figure 2.12 depicts the CTR mode. A counter equal to the plaintext block size is used. The only requirement stated in SP 800-38A is that the counter value must be different for each plaintext block that is encrypted. Typically, the counter is initialized to some value and then incremented by 1 for each subsequent block (modulo

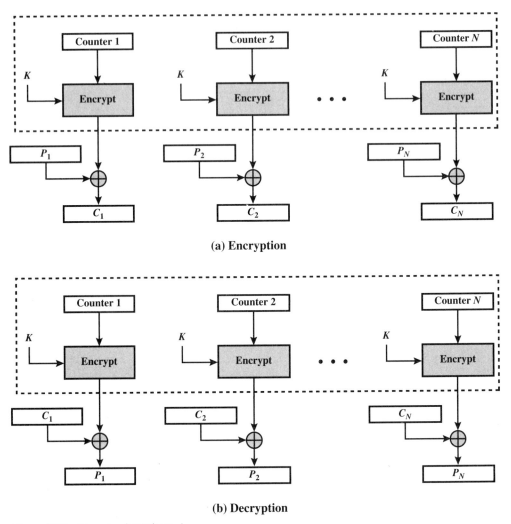

(a) Encryption

(b) Decryption

Figure 2.12 Counter (CTR) Mode

2^b, where b is the block size). For encryption, the counter is encrypted and then XORed with the plaintext block to produce the ciphertext block; there is no chaining. For decryption, the same sequence of counter values is used, with each encrypted counter XORed with a ciphertext block to recover the corresponding plaintext block.

[LIPM00] lists the following advantages of CTR mode.

- **Hardware efficiency:** Unlike the chaining modes, encryption (or decryption) in CTR mode can be done in parallel on multiple blocks of plaintext or ciphertext. For the chaining modes, the algorithm must complete the computation on one block before beginning on the next block. This limits the maximum throughput of the algorithm to the reciprocal of the time for one execution of block encryption or decryption. In CTR mode, the throughput is only limited by the amount of parallelism that is achieved.

- **Software efficiency:** Similarly, because of the opportunities for parallel execution in CTR mode, processors that support parallel features (such as aggressive pipelining, multiple instruction dispatch per clock cycle, a large number of registers, and SIMD instructions) can be effectively utilized.

- **Preprocessing:** The execution of the underlying encryption algorithm does not depend on input of the plaintext or ciphertext. Therefore, if sufficient memory is available and security is maintained, preprocessing can be used to prepare the output of the encryption boxes that feed into the XOR functions in Figure 2.12. When the plaintext or ciphertext input is presented, then the only computation is a series of XORs. Such a strategy greatly enhances throughput.

- **Random access:** The ith block of plaintext or ciphertext can be processed in random-access fashion. With the chaining modes, block C_i cannot be computed until the $i - 1$ prior block are computed. There may be applications in which a ciphertext is stored, and it is desired to decrypt just one block; for such applications, the random access feature is attractive.

- **Provable security:** It can be shown that CTR is at least as secure as the other modes discussed in this section.

- **Simplicity:** Unlike ECB and CBC modes, CTR mode requires only the implementation of the encryption algorithm and not the decryption algorithm. This matters most when the decryption algorithm differs substantially from the encryption algorithm, as it does for AES. In addition, the decryption key scheduling need not be implemented.

2.6 RECOMMENDED READING AND WEB SITES

The topics in this chapter are covered in greater detail in [STAL11]. For coverage of cryptographic algorithms, [SCHN96] is an essential reference work; it contains descriptions of virtually every cryptographic algorithm and protocol published up to the time of the writing of the book. Another worthwhile and detailed survey is [MENE97]. A more in-depth treatment, with rigorous mathematical discussion, is [STIN06].

MENE97   Menezes, A.; van Oorschot, P.; and Vanstone, S. *Handbook of Applied Cryptography.* Boca Raton, FL: CRC Press, 1997.

SCHN96   Schneier, B. *Applied Cryptography.* New York: Wiley, 1996.

STAL11   Stallings, W. *Cryptography and Network Security: Principles and Practice, Fifth Edition.* Upper Saddle River, NJ: Prentice Hall, 2011.

STIN06   Stinson, D. *Cryptography: Theory and Practice.* Boca Raton, FL: Chapman&Hall/ CRC Press, 2006.

Recommended Web Sites:

- **AES home page:** NIST's page on AES. Contains the standard plus a number of other relevant documents.
- **AES Lounge:** Contains a comprehensive bibliography of documents and papers on AES with access to electronic copies.
- **Block Cipher Modes of Operation:** NIST page with full information on NIST-approved modes of operation.

2.7 KEY TERMS, REVIEW QUESTIONS, AND PROBLEMS

Key Terms

Advanced Encryption Standard (AES)	Cryptography	keystream
block cipher	Data Encryption Standard (DES)	link encryption
brute-force attack	decryption	plaintext
cipher block chaining (CBC) mode	electronic codebook (ECB) mode	session key
cipher feedback (CFB) mode	encryption	stream cipher
ciphertext	end-to-end encryption	subkey
counter mode (CTR)	Feistel cipher	symmetric encryption
cryptanalysis	key distribution	triple DES (3DES)

Review Questions

2.1 What are the essential ingredients of a symmetric cipher?

2.2 What are the two basic functions used in encryption algorithms?

2.3 How many keys are required for two people to communicate via a symmetric cipher?

2.4 What is the difference between a block cipher and a stream cipher?

2.5 What are the two general approaches to attacking a cipher?

2.6 Why do some block cipher modes of operation only use encryption while others use both encryption and decryption?

2.7 What is triple encryption?

2.8 Why is the middle portion of 3DES a decryption rather than an encryption?

Problems

2.1 This problem uses a real-world example of a symmetric cipher, from an old U.S. Special Forces manual (public domain). The document, filename *SpecialForces.pdf*, is available at this book's Web site.

a. Using the two keys (memory words) *cryptographic* and *network security*, encrypt the following message:

> Be at the third pillar from the left outside the lyceum theatre tonight at seven. If you are distrustful bring two friends.

> Make reasonable assumptions about how to treat redundant letters and excess letters in the memory words and how to treat spaces and punctuation. Indicate what your assumptions are. *Note:* The message is from the Sherlock Holmes novel, *The Sign of Four.*

b. Decrypt the ciphertext. Show your work.

c. Comment on when it would be appropriate to use this technique and what its advantages are.

2.2 Consider a very simple symmetric block encryption algorithm in which 32-bits blocks of plaintext are encrypted using a 64-bit key. Encryption is defined as

$$C = (P \oplus K_0) \boxplus K_1$$

where C = ciphertext, K = secret key, K_0 = leftmost 64 bits of K, K_1 = rightmost 64 bits of K, $\oplus$ = bitwise exclusive OR, and $\boxplus$ is addition mod 2^{64}.

a. Show the decryption equation. That is, show the equation for P as a function of C, K_0, and K_1.

b. Suppose and adversary has access to two sets of plaintexts and their corresponding ciphertexts and wishes to determine K. We have the two equations:

$$C = (P \oplus K_0) \boxplus K_1; C' = (P' \oplus K_0) \boxplus K_1$$

First, derive an equation in one unknown (e.g., K_0). Is it possible to proceed further to solve for K_0?

2.3 Perhaps the simplest "serious" symmetric block encryption algorithm is the Tiny Encryption Algorithm (TEA). TEA operates on 64-bit blocks of plaintext using a 128-bit key. The plaintext is divided into two 32-bit blocks (L_0, R_0), and the key is divided into four 32-bit blocks (K_0, K_1, K_2, K_3). Encryption involves repeated application of a pair of rounds, defined as follows for rounds i and $i+1$:

$$L_i = R_{i-1}$$
$$R_i = L_{i-1} \boxplus F(R_{i-1}, K_0, K_1, \delta_i)$$
$$L_{i+1} = R_i$$
$$R_{i+1} = L_i \boxplus F(R_i, K_2, K_3, \delta_{i+1})$$

where F is defined as

$$F(M, K_j, K_k, \delta_i) = ((M << 4) \boxplus K_j) \oplus ((M >> 5) \boxplus K_k) \oplus (M \boxplus \delta_i)$$

and where the logical shift of x by y bits is denoted by $x << y$, the logical right shift of x by y bits is denoted by $x >> y$, and δ_i is a sequence of predetermined constants.

a. Comment on the significance and benefit of using the sequence of constants.

b. Illustrate the operation of TEA using a block diagram or flow chart type of depiction.

c. If only one pair of rounds is used, then the ciphertext consists of the 64-bit block (L_2, R_2). For this case, express the decryption algorithm in terms of equations.

d. Repeat part (c) using an illustration similar to that used for part (b).

2.4 Show that Feistel decryption is the inverse of Feistel encryption.

2.5 Consider a Feistel cipher composed of 16 rounds with block length 128 bits and key length 128 bits. Suppose that, for a given k, the key scheduling algorithm determines values for the first eight round keys, $k_1, k_2, \ldots, k_8$, and then sets

$$k_9 = k_8, k_{10} = k_7, k_{11} = k_6, \ldots, k_{16} = k_1$$

Suppose you have a ciphertext c. Explain how, with access to an encryption oracle, you can decrypt c and determine m using just a single oracle query. This shows that such a cipher is vulnerable to a chosen plaintext attack. (An encryption oracle can be thought of as a device that, when given a plaintext, returns the corresponding ciphertext. The internal details of the device are not known to you, and you cannot break open the device. You can only gain information from the oracle by making queries to it and observing its responses.)

2.6 For any block cipher, the fact that it is a nonlinear function is crucial to its security. To see this, suppose that we have a linear block cipher EL that encrypts 128-bit blocks of plaintext into 128-bit blocks of ciphertext. Let $EL(k, m)$ denote the encryption of a 128-bit message m under a key k (the actual bit length of k is irrelevant). Thus,

$$EL(k, [m_1 \oplus m_2]) = EL(k, m_1) \oplus EL(k, m_2) \text{ for all 128-bit patterns } m_1, m_2$$

Describe how, with 128 chosen ciphertexts, an adversary can decrypt any ciphertext without knowledge of the secret key k. (A "chosen ciphertext" means that an adversary has the ability to choose a ciphertext and then obtain its decryption. Here, you have 128 plaintext–ciphertext pairs to work with, and you have the ability to chose the value of the ciphertexts.)

2.7 Suppose you have a true random bit generator where each bit in the generated stream has the same probability of being a 0 or 1 as any other bit in the stream and that the bits are not correlated; that is, the bits are generated from identical independent distribution. However, the bit stream is biased. The probability of a 1 is $0.5 + \delta$ and the probability of a 0 is $0.5 - \delta$, where $0 < \delta < 0.5$. A simple deskewing algorithm is as follows: Examine the bit stream as a sequence of non-overlapping pairs. Discard all 00 and 11 pairs. Replace each 01 pair with 0 and each 10 pair with 1.

   a. What is the probability of occurrence of each pair in the original sequence?
   b. What is the probability of occurrence of 0 and 1 in the modified sequence?
   c. What is the expected number of input bits to produce x output bits?
   d. Suppose that the algorithm uses overlapping successive bit pairs instead of nonoverlapping successive bit pairs. That is, the first output bit is based on input bits 1 and 2, the second output bit is based on input bits 2 and 3, and so on. What can you say about the output bit stream?

2.8 Another approach to deskewing is to consider the bit stream as a sequence of non-overlapping groups of n bits each and output the parity of each group. That is, if a group contains an odd number of ones, the output is 1; otherwise the output is 0.

   a. Express this operation in terms of a basic Boolean function.
   b. Assume, as in the Problem 2.7, that the probability of a 1 is $0.5 + \delta$. If each group consists of 2 bits, what is the probability of an output of 1?
   c. If each group consists of 4 bits, what is the probability of an output of 1?
   d. Generalize the result to find the probability of an output of 1 for input groups of n bits.

2.9 What RC4 key value will leave S unchanged during initialization? That is, after the initial permutation of S, the entries of S will be equal to the values from 0 through 255 in ascending order.

2.10 RC4 has a secret internal state which is a permutation of all the possible values of the vector **S** and the two indices i and j.

   a. Using a straightforward scheme to store the internal state, how many bits are used?
   b. Suppose we think of it from the point of view of how much information is represented by the state. In that case, we need to determine how may different states

there are, then take the log to the base 2 to find out how many bits of information this represents. Using this approach, how many bits would be needed to represent the state?

2.11 Alice and Bob agree to communicate privately via e-mail using a scheme based on RC4, but they want to avoid using a new secret key for each transmission. Alice and Bob privately agree on a 128-bit key k. To encrypt a message m consisting of a string of bits, the following procedure is used.

1. Choose a random 80-bit value v
2. Generate the ciphertext $c = RC4(v \| k) \oplus m$
3. Send the bit string $(v \| c)$

a. Suppose Alice uses this procedure to send a message m to Bob. Describe how Bob can recover the message m from $(v \| c)$ using k.

b. If an adversary observes several values $(v_1 \| c_1), (v_2 \| c_2), \ldots$ transmitted between Alice and Bob, how can he/she determine when the same key stream has been used to encrypt two messages?

2.12 With the ECB mode, if there is an error in a block of the transmitted ciphertext, only the corresponding plaintext block is affected. However, in the CBC mode, this error propagates. For example, an error in the transmitted C_1 (Figure 2.10) obviously corrupts P_1 and P_2.

a. Are any blocks beyond P_2 affected?

b. Suppose that there is a bit error in the source version of P_1. Through how many ciphertext blocks is this error propagated? What is the effect at the receiver?

2.13 Is it possible to perform encryption operations in parallel on multiple blocks of plaintext in CBC mode? How about decryption?

2.14 Suppose an error occurs in a block of ciphertext on transmission using CBC. What effect is produced on the recovered plaintext blocks?

2.15 CBC-Pad is a block cipher mode of operation used in the RC5 block cipher, but it could be used in any block cipher. CBC-Pad handles plaintext of any length. The ciphertext is longer than the plaintext by at most the size of a single block. Padding is used to assure that the plaintext input is a multiple of the block length. It is assumed that the original plaintext is an integer number of bytes. This plaintext is padded at the end by from 1 to bb bytes, where bb equals the block size in bytes. The pad bytes are all the same and set to a byte that represents the number of bytes of padding. For example, if there are 8 bytes of padding, each byte has the bit pattern **00001000**. Why not allow zero bytes of padding? That is, if the original plaintext is an integer multiple of the block size, why not refrain from padding?

2.16 Padding may not always be appropriate. For example, one might wish to store the encrypted data in the same memory buffer that originally contained the plaintext. In that case, the ciphertext must be the same length as the original plaintext. A mode for that purpose is the ciphertext stealing (CTS) mode. Figure 2.13a shows an implementation of this mode.

a. Explain how it works.

b. Describe how to decrypt C_{n-1} and C_n.

2.17 Figure 2.13b shows an alternative to CTS for producing ciphertext of equal length to the plaintext when the plaintext is not an integer multiple of the block size.

a. Explain the algorithm.

b. Explain why CTS is preferable to this approach illustrated in Figure 2.13b.

2.18 If a bit error occurs in the transmission of a ciphertext character in 8-bit CFB mode, how far does the error propagate?

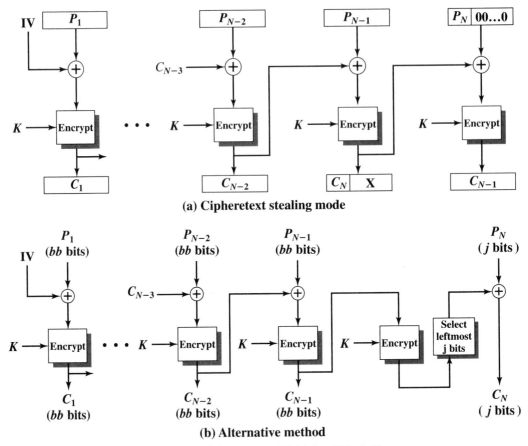

(a) Cipheretext stealing mode

(b) Alternative method

Figure 2.13   Block Cipher Modes for Plaintext not a Multiple of Block Size

CHAPTER 3

PUBLIC-KEY CRYPTOGRAPHY AND MESSAGE AUTHENTICATION

Every Egyptian received two names, which were known respectively as the true name and the good name, or the great name and the little name; and while the good or little name was made public, the true or great name appears to have been carefully concealed.

— *The Golden Bough*, Sir James George Frazer

To guard against the baneful influence exerted by strangers is therefore an elementary dictate of savage prudence. Hence before strangers are allowed to enter a district, or at least before they are permitted to mingle freely with the inhabitants, certain ceremonies are often performed by the natives of the country for the purpose of disarming the strangers of their magical powers, or of disinfecting, so to speak, the tainted atmosphere by which they are supposed to be surrounded.

— *The Golden Bough*, Sir James George Frazer

In addition to message confidentiality, message authentication is an important network security function. This chapter examines three aspects of message authentication. First, we look at the use of message authentication codes and hash functions to provide message authentication. Then we look at public-key encryption principles and two specific public-key algorithms. These algorithms are useful in the exchange of conventional encryption keys. Then we look at the use of public-key encryption to produce digital signatures, which provides an enhanced form of message authentication.

3.1 APPROACHES TO MESSAGE AUTHENTICATION

Encryption protects against passive attack (eavesdropping). A different requirement is to protect against active attack (falsification of data and transactions). Protection against such attacks is known as message authentication.

A message, file, document, or other collection of data is said to be authentic when it is genuine and comes from its alleged source. Message authentication is a procedure that allows communicating parties to verify that received messages are authentic.[1] The two important aspects are to verify that the contents of the message have not been altered and that the source is authentic. We may also wish to verify a message's timeliness (it has not been artificially delayed and replayed) and sequence relative to other messages flowing between two parties. All of these concerns come under the category of data integrity as described in Chapter 1.

Authentication Using Conventional Encryption

It would seem possible to perform authentication simply by the use of symmetric encryption. If we assume that only the sender and receiver share a key (which is as it should be), then only the genuine sender would be able to encrypt a message

---

[1]For simplicity, for the remainder of this chapter, we refer to *message authentication*. By this we mean both authentication of transmitted messages and of stored data (*data authentication*).

successfully for the other participant, provided the receiver can recognize a valid message. Furthermore, if the message includes an error-detection code and a sequence number, the receiver is assured that no alterations have been made and that sequencing is proper. If the message also includes a timestamp, the receiver is assured that the message has not been delayed beyond that normally expected for network transit.

In fact, symmetric encryption alone is not a suitable tool for data authentication. To give one simple example, in the ECB mode of encryption, if an attacker reorders the blocks of ciphertext, then each block will still decrypt successfully. However, the reordering may alter the meaning of the overall data sequence. Although sequence numbers may be used at some level (e.g., each IP packet), it is typically not the case that a separate sequence number will be associated with each b-bit block of plaintext. Thus, block reordering is a threat.

Message Authentication without Message Encryption

In this section, we examine several approaches to message authentication that do not rely on encryption. In all of these approaches, an authentication tag is generated and appended to each message for transmission. The message itself is not encrypted and can be read at the destination independent of the authentication function at the destination.

Because the approaches discussed in this section do not encrypt the message, message confidentiality is not provided. As was mentioned, message encryption by itself does not provide a secure form of authentication. However, it is possible to combine authentication and confidentiality in a single algorithm by encrypting a message plus its authentication tag. Typically, however, message authentication is provided as a separate function from message encryption. [DAVI89] suggests three situations in which message authentication without confidentiality is preferable:

1. There are a number of applications in which the same message is broadcast to a number of destinations. Two examples are notification to users that the network is now unavailable and an alarm signal in a control center. It is cheaper and more reliable to have only one destination responsible for monitoring authenticity. Thus, the message must be broadcast in plaintext with an associated message authentication tag. The responsible system performs authentication. If a violation occurs, the other destination systems are alerted by a general alarm.

2. Another possible scenario is an exchange in which one side has a heavy load and cannot afford the time to decrypt all incoming messages. Authentication is carried out on a selective basis with messages being chosen at random for checking.

3. Authentication of a computer program in plaintext is an attractive service. The computer program can be executed without having to decrypt it every time, which would be wasteful of processor resources. However, if a message authentication tag were attached to the program, it could be checked whenever assurance is required of the integrity of the program.

Thus, there is a place for both authentication and encryption in meeting security requirements.

MESSAGE AUTHENTICATION CODE One authentication technique involves the use of a secret key to generate a small block of data, known as a **message authentication code (MAC)**, that is appended to the message. This technique assumes that two communicating parties, say A and B, share a common secret key K_{AB}. When A has a message to send to B, it calculates the message authentication code as a function of the message and the key: $MAC_M = F(K_{AB}, M)$. The message plus code are transmitted to the intended recipient. The recipient performs the same calculation on the received message, using the same secret key, to generate a new message authentication code. The received code is compared to the calculated code (Figure 3.1). If we assume that only the receiver and the sender know the identity of the secret key, and if the received code matches the calculated code, then the following statements apply:

1. The receiver is assured that the message has not been altered. If an attacker alters the message but does not alter the code, then the receiver's calculation of the code will differ from the received code. Because the attacker is assumed not to know the secret key, the attacker cannot alter the code to correspond to the alterations in the message.

2. The receiver is assured that the message is from the alleged sender. Because no one else knows the secret key, no one else could prepare a message with a proper code.

3. If the message includes a sequence number (such as is used with HDLC and TCP), then the receiver can be assured of the proper sequence, because an attacker cannot successfully alter the sequence number.

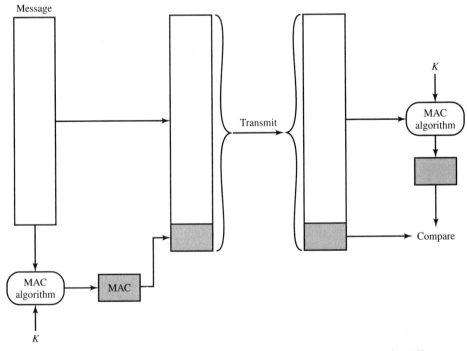

Figure 3.1   Message Authentication Using a Message Authentication Code (MAC)

A number of algorithms could be used to generate the code. The NIST specification, FIPS PUB 113, recommends the use of DES. DES is used to generate an encrypted version of the message, and the last number of bits of ciphertext are used as the code. A 16- or 32-bit code is typical.

The process just described is similar to encryption. One difference is that the authentication algorithm need not be reversible, as it must for decryption. Because of the mathematical properties of the authentication function, it is less vulnerable to being broken than encryption.

ONE-WAY HASH FUNCTION An alternative to the message authentication code is the **one-way hash function**. As with the message authentication code, a hash function accepts a variable-size message M as input and produces a fixed-size message digest $H(M)$ as output. Unlike the MAC, a hash function does not take a secret key as input. To authenticate a message, the message digest is sent with the message in such a way that the message digest is authentic.

Figure 3.2 illustrates three ways in which the message can be authenticated. The message digest can be encrypted using conventional encryption (part a); if it is assumed that only the sender and receiver share the encryption key, then authenticity is assured. The message digest can be encrypted using public-key encryption (part b); this is explained in Section 3.5. The public-key approach has two advantages: (1) It provides a digital signature as well as message authentication. (2) It does not require the distribution of keys to communicating parties.

These two approaches also have an advantage over approaches that encrypt the entire message in that less computation is required. Nevertheless, there has been interest in developing a technique that avoids encryption altogether. Several reasons for this interest are pointed out in [TSUD92]:

- Encryption software is quite slow. Even though the amount of data to be encrypted per message is small, there may be a steady stream of messages into and out of a system.

- Encryption hardware costs are nonnegligible. Low-cost chip implementations of DES are available, but the cost adds up if all nodes in a network must have this capability.

- Encryption hardware is optimized toward large data sizes. For small blocks of data, a high proportion of the time is spent in initialization/invocation overhead.

- An encryption algorithm may be protected by a patent.

Figure 3.2c shows a technique that uses a hash function but no encryption for message authentication. This technique assumes that two communicating parties, say A and B, share a common secret value S_{AB}. When A has a message to send to B, it calculates the hash function over the concatenation of the secret value and the message: $MD_M = H(S_{AB}\|M)$.[2] It then sends $[M\|MD_M]$ to B. Because B possesses S_{AB}, it can recompute $H(S_{AB}\|M)$ and verify MD_M. Because the secret value itself is

---

[2] $\|$ denotes concatenation.

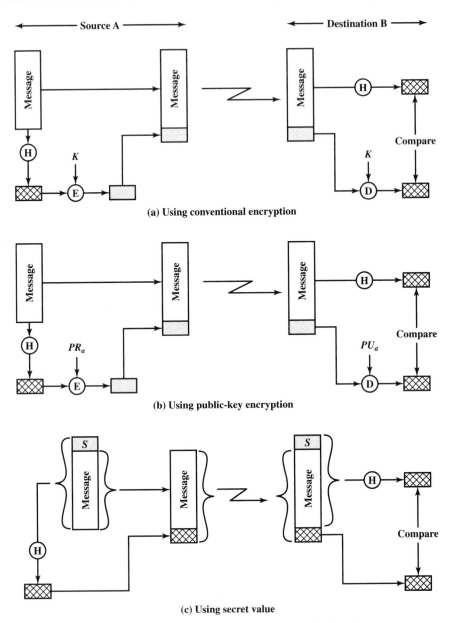

Figure 3.2 Message Authentication Using a One-Way Hash Function

not sent, it is not possible for an attacker to modify an intercepted message. As long as the secret value remains secret, it is also not possible for an attacker to generate a false message.

A variation on the third technique, called HMAC, is the one adopted for IP security (described in Chapter 8); it also has been specified for SNMPv3 (Chapter 12).

3.2 SECURE HASH FUNCTIONS

The one-way hash function, or **secure hash function**, is important not only in message authentication but in digital signatures. In this section, we begin with a discussion of requirements for a secure hash function. Then we look at the most important hash function, SHA.

Hash Function Requirements

The purpose of a hash function is to produce a "fingerprint" of a file, message, or other block of data. To be useful for message authentication, a hash function H must have the following properties:

1. H can be applied to a block of data of any size.
2. H produces a fixed-length output.
3. $H(x)$ is relatively easy to compute for any given x, making both hardware and software implementations practical.
4. For any given code h, it is computationally infeasible to find x such that $H(x) = h$. A hash function with this property is referred to as **one-way** or **preimage resistant**.[3]
5. For any given block x, it is computationally infeasible to find $y \neq x$ with $H(y) = H(x)$. A hash function with this property is referred to as **second preimage resistant**. This is sometimes referred to as **weak collision resistant**.
6. It is computationally infeasible to find any pair (x, y) such that $H(x) = H(y)$. A hash function with this property is referred to as **collision resistant**. This is sometimes referred to as **strong collision resistant**.

The first three properties are requirements for the practical application of a hash function to message authentication. The fourth property, preimage resistant, is the "one-way" property: It is easy to generate a code given a message, but virtually impossible to generate a message given a code. This property is important if the authentication technique involves the use of a secret value (Figure 3.2c). The secret value itself is not sent; however, if the hash function is not one way, an attacker can easily discover the secret value: If the attacker can observe or intercept a transmission, the attacker obtains the message M and the hash code $C = H(S_{AB}\|M)$. The attacker then inverts the hash function to obtain $S_{AB}\|M = H^{-1}(C)$. Because the attacker now has both M and $S_{AB}\|M$, it is a trivial matter to recover S_{AB}.

The second preimage resistant property guarantees that it is impossible to find an alternative message with the same hash value as a given message. This prevents forgery when an encrypted hash code is used (Figures 3.2a and b). If this property were not true, an attacker would be capable of the following sequence: First, observe or intercept a message plus its encrypted hash code; second, generate an unencrypted hash code from the message; third, generate an alternate message with the same hash code.

---

[3]For $f(x) = y$, x is said to be a preimage of y. Unless f is one-to-one, there may be multiple preimage values for a given y.

A hash function that satisfies the first five properties in the preceding list is referred to as a weak hash function. If the sixth property is also satisfied, then it is referred to as a strong hash function. The sixth property, collision resistant, protects against a sophisticated class of attack known as the birthday attack. Details of this attack are beyond the scope of this book. The attack reduces the strength of an m-bit hash function from 2^m to $2^{m/2}$. See [STAL11] for details.

In addition to providing authentication, a message digest also provides data integrity. It performs the same function as a frame check sequence: If any bits in the message are accidentally altered in transit, the message digest will be in error.

Security of Hash Functions

As with symmetric encryption, there are two approaches to attacking a secure hash function: cryptanalysis and brute-force attack. As with symmetric encryption algorithms, cryptanalysis of a hash function involves exploiting logical weaknesses in the algorithm.

The strength of a hash function against brute-force attacks depends solely on the length of the hash code produced by the algorithm. For a hash code of length n, the level of effort required is proportional to the following:

Preimage resistant	2^n
Second preimage resistant	2^n
Collision resistant	$2^{n/2}$

If collision resistance is required (and this is desirable for a general-purpose secure hash code), then the value $2^{n/2}$ determines the strength of the hash code against brute-force attacks. Van Oorschot and Wiener [VANO94] presented a design for a $10 million collision search machine for MD5, which has a 128-bit hash length, that could find a collision in 24 days. Thus, a 128-bit code may be viewed as inadequate. The next step up, if a hash code is treated as a sequence of 32 bits, is a 160-bit hash length. With a hash length of 160 bits, the same search machine would require over four thousand years to find a collision. With today's technology, the time would be much shorter, so that 160 bits now appears suspect.

Simple Hash Functions

All hash functions operate using the following general principles. The input (message, file, etc.) is viewed as a sequence of n-bit blocks. The input is processed one block at a time in an iterative fashion to produce an n-bit hash function.

One of the simplest hash functions is the bit-by-bit exclusive-OR (XOR) of every block. This can be expressed as

$$C_i = b_{i1} \oplus b_{i2} \oplus \ldots \oplus b_{im}$$

where

$C_i = $ ith bit of the hash code, $1 \leq i \leq n$

$m = $ number of n-bit blocks in the input

$b_{ij} = $ ith bit in jth block

$\oplus = $ XOR operation

	bit 1	bit 2	• • •	bit n
Block 1	b_{11}	b_{21}		b_{n1}
Block 2	b_{12}	b_{22}		b_{n2}
	• • •	• • •	• • •	• • •
Block m	b_{1m}	b_{2m}		b_{nm}
Hash code	C_1	C_2		C_n

Figure 3.3   Simple Hash Function Using Bitwise XOR

Figure 3.3 illustrates this operation; it produces a simple parity for each bit position and is known as a longitudinal redundancy check. It is reasonably effective for random data as a data integrity check. Each n-bit hash value is equally likely. Thus, the probability that a data error will result in an unchanged hash value is 2^{-n}. With more predictably formatted data, the function is less effective. For example, in most normal text files, the high-order bit of each octet is always zero. So if a 128-bit hash value is used, instead of an effectiveness of 2^{-128}, the hash function on this type of data has an effectiveness of 2^{-112}.

A simple way to improve matters is to perform a 1-bit circular shift, or rotation, on the hash value after each block is processed. The procedure can be summarized as

1. Initially set the n-bit hash value to zero.
2. Process each successive n-bit block of data:
   a. Rotate the current hash value to the left by one bit.
   b. XOR the block into the hash value.

This has the effect of "randomizing" the input more completely and overcoming any regularities that appear in the input.

Although the second procedure provides a good measure of data integrity, it is virtually useless for data security when an encrypted hash code is used with a plaintext message, as in Figures 3.2a and b. Given a message, it is an easy matter to produce a new message that yields that hash code: Simply prepare the desired alternate message and then append an n-bit block that forces the combined new message plus block to yield the desired hash code.

Although a simple XOR or rotated XOR (RXOR) is insufficient if only the hash code is encrypted, you may still feel that such a simple function could be useful when the message as well as the hash code are encrypted. But one must be careful. A technique originally proposed by the National Bureau of Standards used the simple XOR applied to 64-bit blocks of the message and then an encryption of the entire message using the cipher block chaining (CBC) mode. We can define the scheme as follows: Given a message consisting of a sequence of 64-bit blocks $X_1, X_2, \ldots, X_N$, define the hash code C as the block-by-block XOR or all blocks and append the hash code as the final block:

$$C = X_{N+1} = X_1 \oplus X_2 \oplus \ldots \oplus X_N$$

Next, encrypt the entire message plus hash code using CBC mode to produce the encrypted message $Y_1, Y_2, \ldots, Y_{N+1}$. [JUEN85] points out several ways in which the ciphertext of this message can be manipulated in such a way that it is not detectable by the hash code. For example, by the definition of CBC (Figure 2.10), we have

$$X_1 = IV \oplus D(K, Y_1)$$
$$X_i = Y_{i-1} \oplus D(K, Y_i)$$
$$X_{N+1} = Y_N \oplus D(K, Y_{N+1})$$

But X_{N+1} is the hash code:

$$X_{N+1} = X_1 \oplus X_2 \oplus \ldots \oplus X_N$$
$$= [IV \oplus D(K, Y_1)] \oplus [Y_1 \oplus D(K, Y_2)] \oplus \ldots \oplus [Y_{N-1} \oplus D(K, Y_N)]$$

Because the terms in the preceding equation can be XORed in any order, it follows that the hash code would not change if the ciphertext blocks were permuted.

The SHA Secure Hash Function

In recent years, the most widely used hash function has been the Secure Hash Algorithm (SHA). Indeed, because virtually every other widely used hash function had been found to have substantial cryptanalytic weaknesses, SHA was more or less the last remaining standardized hash algorithm by 2005. SHA was developed by the National Institute of Standards and Technology (NIST) and published as a federal information processing standard (FIPS 180) in 1993. When weaknesses were discovered in SHA (now known as SHA-0), a revised version was issued as FIPS 180-1 in 1995 and is referred to as **SHA-1**. The actual standards document is entitled "Secure Hash Standard." SHA is based on the hash function MD4, and its design closely models MD4. SHA-1 is also specified in RFC 3174, which essentially duplicates the material in FIPS 180-1 but adds a C code implementation.

SHA-1 produces a hash value of 160 bits. In 2002, NIST produced a revised version of the standard, FIPS 180-2, that defined three new versions of SHA with hash value lengths of 256, 384, and 512 bits known as SHA-256, SHA-384, and SHA-512, respectively. Collectively, these hash algorithms are known as **SHA-2**. These new versions have the same underlying structure and use the same types of modular arithmetic and logical binary operations as SHA-1. A revised document was issued as FIP PUB 180-3 in 2008, which added a 224-bit version (Table 3.1). SHA-2 is also specified in RFC 4634, which essentially duplicates the material in FIPS 180-3 but adds a C code implementation.

In 2005, NIST announced the intention to phase out approval of SHA-1 and move to a reliance on SHA-2 by 2010. Shortly thereafter, a research team described an attack in which two separate messages could be found that deliver the same SHA-1 hash using 2^{69} operations, far fewer than the 2^{80} operations previously thought needed to find a collision with an SHA-1 hash [WANG05]. This result should hasten the transition to SHA-2.

In this section, we provide a description of SHA-512. The other versions are quite similar.

Table 3.1   Comparison of SHA Parameters

	SHA-1	SHA-224	SHA-256	SHA-384	SHA-512
Message Digest Size	160	224	256	384	512
Message Size	$< 2^{64}$	$< 2^{64}$	$< 2^{64}$	$< 2^{128}$	$< 2^{128}$
Block Size	512	512	512	1024	1024
Word Size	32	32	32	64	64
Number of Steps	80	64	64	80	80
Security	80	112	128	192	256

Notes: 1. All sizes are measured in bits.
2. Security refers to the fact that a birthday attack on a message digest of size n produces a collision with a workfactor of approximately $2^{n/2}$.

The algorithm takes as input a message with a maximum length of less than 2^{128} bits and produces as output a 512-bit message digest. The input is processed in 1024-bit blocks. Figure 3.4 depicts the overall processing of a message to produce a digest. The processing consists of the following steps.

Step 1 Append padding bits: The message is padded so that its length is congruent to 896 modulo 1024 [length $\equiv$ 896 (mod 1024)]. Padding is always added, even if the message is already of the desired length. Thus, the number of padding bits is in the range of 1 to 1024. The padding consists of a single 1 bit followed by the necessary number of 0 bits.

Step 2 Append length: A block of 128 bits is appended to the message. This block is treated as an unsigned 128-bit integer (most significant byte first) and contains the length of the original message (before the padding).

The outcome of the first two steps yields a message that is an integer multiple of 1024 bits in length. In Figure 3.4, the expanded message is represented as the sequence of 1024-bit blocks $M_1, M_2, \ldots, M_N$, so that the total length of the expanded message is $N \times 1024$ bits.

Step 3 Initialize hash buffer: A 512-bit buffer is used to hold intermediate and final results of the hash function. The buffer can be represented as eight 64-bit registers (a, b, c, d, e, f, g, h). These registers are initialized to the following 64-bit integers (hexadecimal values):

$$a = \text{6A09E667F3BCC908} \qquad e = \text{510E527FADE682D1}$$
$$b = \text{BB67AE8584CAA73B} \qquad f = \text{9B05688C2B3E6C1F}$$
$$c = \text{3C6EF372FE94F82B} \qquad g = \text{1F83D9ABFB41BD6B}$$
$$d = \text{A54FF53A5F1D36F1} \qquad h = \text{5BE0CD19137E2179}$$

These values are stored in big-endian format, which is the most significant byte of a word in the low-address (leftmost) byte position. These words were obtained by taking the first sixty-four bits of the fractional parts of the square roots of the first eight prime numbers.

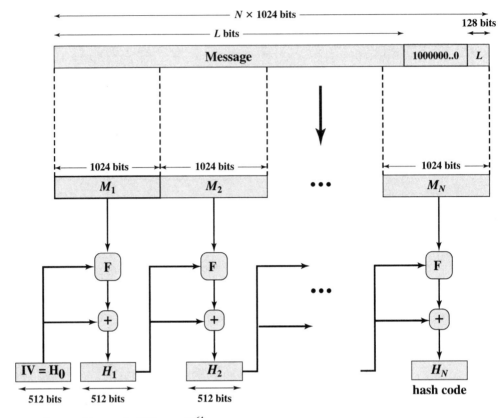

Figure 3.4   Message Digest Generation Using SHA-512

Step 4 **Process message in 1024-bit (128-word) blocks:** The heart of the algorithm is a module that consists of 80 rounds; this module is labeled F in Figure 3.4. The logic is illustrated in Figure 3.5.

Each round takes as input the 512-bit buffer value **abcdefgh** and updates the contents of the buffer. At input to the first round, the buffer has the value of the intermediate hash value, H_{i-1}. Each round t makes use of a 64-bit value W_t derived from the current 1024-bit block being processed (M_i). Each round also makes use of an additive constant K_t, where $0 \le t \le 79$ indicates one of the 80 rounds. These words represent the first 64 bits of the fractional parts of the cube roots of the first 80 prime numbers. The constants provide a "randomized" set of 64-bit patterns, which should eliminate any regularities in the input data.

The output of the 80th round is added to the input to the first round (H_{i-1}) to produce H_i. The addition is done independently for each of the eight words in the buffer with each of the corresponding words in H_{i-1}, using addition modulo 2^{64}.

Step 5 **Output:** After all N 1024-bit blocks have been processed, the output from the Nth stage is the 512-bit message digest.

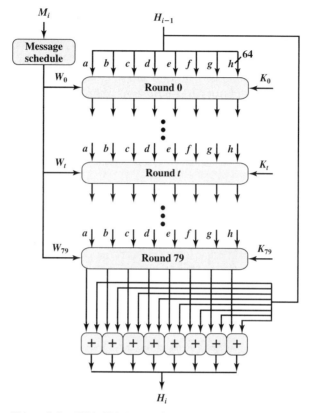

Figure 3.5   SHA-512 Processing of a Single 1024-Bit Block

The SHA-512 algorithm has the property that every bit of the hash code is a function of every bit of the input. The complex repetition of the basic function F produces results that are well mixed; that is, it is unlikely that two messages chosen at random, even if they exhibit similar regularities, will have the same hash code. Unless there is some hidden weakness in SHA-512, which has not so far been published, the difficulty of coming up with two messages having the same message digest is on the order of 2^{256} operations, while the difficulty of finding a message with a given digest is on the order of 2^{512} operations.

3.3 MESSAGE AUTHENTICATION CODES

HMAC

In recent years, there has been increased interest in developing a MAC derived from a cryptographic hash code, such as SHA-1. The motivations for this interest are

- Cryptographic hash functions generally execute faster in software than conventional encryption algorithms such as DES.
- Library code for cryptographic hash functions is widely available.

A hash function such as SHA-1 was not designed for use as a MAC and cannot be used directly for that purpose because it does not rely on a secret key. There have been a number of proposals for the incorporation of a secret key into an existing hash algorithm. The approach that has received the most support is HMAC [BELL96a, BELL96b]. HMAC has been issued as RFC 2104, has been chosen as the mandatory-to-implement MAC for IP Security, and is used in other Internet protocols, such as Transport Layer Security (TLS) and Secure Electronic Transaction (SET).

HMAC DESIGN OBJECTIVES RFC 2104 lists the following design objectives for HMAC.

- To use, without modifications, available hash functions. In particular, hash functions that perform well in software, and for which code is freely and widely available
- To allow for easy replaceability of the embedded hash function in case faster or more secure hash functions are found or required
- To preserve the original performance of the hash function without incurring a significant degradation
- To use and handle keys in a simple way
- To have a well-understood cryptographic analysis of the strength of the authentication mechanism based on reasonable assumptions on the embedded hash function

The first two objectives are important to the acceptability of HMAC. HMAC treats the hash function as a "black box." This has two benefits. First, an existing implementation of a hash function can be used as a module in implementing HMAC. In this way, the bulk of the HMAC code is prepackaged and ready to use without modification. Second, if it is ever desired to replace a given hash function in an HMAC implementation, all that is required is to remove the existing hash function module and drop in the new module. This could be done if a faster hash function were desired. More important, if the security of the embedded hash function were compromised, the security of HMAC could be retained simply by replacing the embedded hash function with a more secure one.

The last design objective in the preceding list is, in fact, the main advantage of HMAC over other proposed hash-based schemes. HMAC can be proven secure provided that the embedded hash function has some reasonable cryptographic strengths. We return to this point later in this section, but first we examine the structure of HMAC.

HMAC ALGORITHM Figure 3.6 illustrates the overall operation of HMAC. The following terms are defined:

H = embedded hash function (e.g., SHA-1)

M = message input to HMAC (including the padding specified in the embedded hash function)

Y_i = ith block of M, $0 \le i \le (L - 1)$

L = number of blocks in M

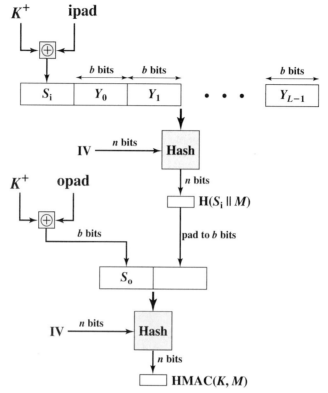

Figure 3.6 HMAC Structure

b = number of bits in a block

n = length of hash code produced by embedded hash function

K = secret key; if key length is greater than b, the key is input to the hash function to produce an n-bit key; recommended length is $> n$

K^+ = K padded with zeros on the left so that the result is b bits in length

ipad = 00110110 (36 in hexadecimal) repeated $b/8$ times

opad = 01011100 (5C in hexadecimal) repeated $b/8$ times

Then HMAC can be expressed as

$$\text{HMAC}(K, M) = \text{H}[(K^+ \oplus \text{opad}) \| \text{H}[(K^+ \oplus \text{ipad}) \| M]]$$

In words, HMAC is defined as follows:

1. Append zeros to the left end of K to create a b-bit string K^+ (e.g., if K is of length 160 bits and $b = 512$, then K will be appended with 44 zero bytes).
2. XOR (bitwise exclusive-OR) K^+ with ipad to produce the b-bit block S_i.

3. Append M to S_i.
4. Apply H to the stream generated in step 3.
5. XOR K^+ with opad to produce the b-bit block S_0.
6. Append the hash result from step 4 to S_0.
7. Apply H to the stream generated in step 6 and output the result.

Note that the XOR with ipad results in flipping one-half of the bits of K. Similarly, the XOR with opad results in flipping one-half of the bits of K, but a different set of bits. In effect, by passing S_i and S_0 through the hash algorithm, we have pseudorandomly generated two keys from K.

HMAC should execute in approximately the same time as the embedded hash function for long messages. HMAC adds three executions of the basic hash function (for S_i, S_0, and the block produced from the inner hash).

MACs Based on Block Ciphers

In this section, we look at several MACs based on the use of a block cipher.

CIPHER-BASED MESSAGE AUTHENTICATION CODE (CMAC) The Cipher-based Message Authentication Code (CMAC) mode of operation is for use with AES and triple DES. It is specified in NIST Special Publication 800-38B.

First, let us consider the operation of CMAC when the message is an integer multiple n of the cipher block length b. For AES, $b = 128$, and for triple DES, $b = 64$. The message is divided into n blocks ($M_1, M_2, \ldots, M_n$). The algorithm makes use of a k-bit encryption key K and an n-bit key, K_1. For AES, the key size k is 128, 192, or 256 bits; for triple DES, the key size is 112 or 168 bits. CMAC is calculated as follows (Figure 3.7).

$$C_1 = E(K, M_1)$$
$$C_2 = E(K, [M_2 \oplus C_1])$$
$$C_3 = E(K, [M_3 \oplus C_2])$$
$$\bullet$$
$$\bullet$$
$$\bullet$$
$$C_n = E(K, [M_N \oplus C_{n-1} \oplus K_1])$$
$$T = \text{MSB}_{Tlen}(C_n)$$

where

T = message authentication code, also referred to as the tag

$Tlen$ = bit length of T

$\text{MSB}_s(X)$ = the s leftmost bits of the bit string X

If the message is not an integer multiple of the cipher block length, then the final block is padded to the right (least significant bits) with a 1 and as many 0s as necessary so that the final block is also of length b. The CMAC operation then proceeds as before, except that a different n-bit key K_2 is used instead of K_1.

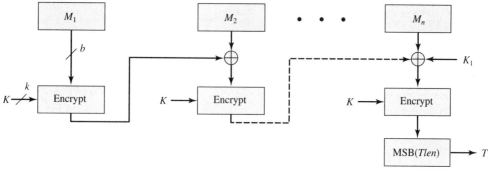

(a) Message length is integer multiple of block size

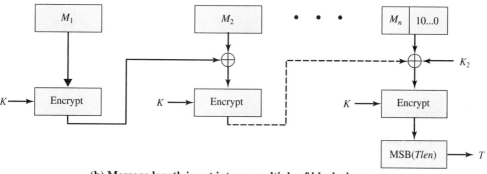

(b) Message length is not integer multiple of block size

Figure 3.7 Cipher-Based Message Authentication Code (CMAC)

To generate the two n-bit keys, the block cipher is applied to the block that consists entirely of 0 bits. The first subkey is derived from the resulting ciphertext by a left shift of one bit and, conditionally, by XORing a constant that depends on the block size. The second subkey is derived in the same manner from the first subkey.

COUNTER WITH CIPHER BLOCK CHAINING-MESSAGE AUTHENTICATION CODE The CCM mode of operation, defined in NIST SP 800-38C, is referred to as an **authenticated encryption** mode. Authenticated encryption is a term used to describe encryption systems that simultaneously protect confidentiality and authenticity (integrity) of communications. Many applications and protocols require both forms of security, but until recently the two services have been designed separately.

The key algorithmic ingredients of CCM are the AES encryption algorithm (Section 2.2), the CTR mode of operation (Section 2.5), and the CMAC authentication algorithm. A single key K is used for both encryption and MAC algorithms. The input to the CCM encryption process consists of three elements.

1. Data that will be both authenticated and encrypted. This is the plaintext message P of data block.

2. Associated data A that will be authenticated but not encrypted. An example is a protocol header that must be transmitted in the clear for proper protocol operation but which needs to be authenticated.

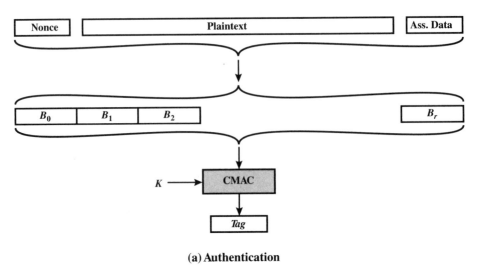

(a) Authentication

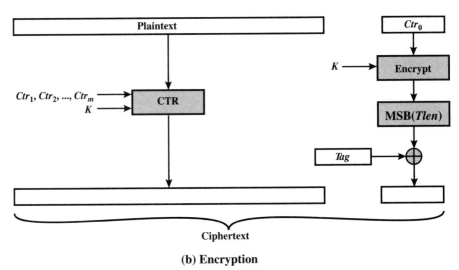

(b) Encryption

Figure 3.8   Counter with Cipher Block Chaining-Message Authentication Code (CCM)

3. A nonce N that is assigned to the payload and the associated data. This is a unique value that is different for every instance during the lifetime of a protocol association and is intended to prevent replay attacks and certain other types of attacks.

Figure 3.8 illustrates the operation of CCM. For authentication, the input includes the nonce, the associated data, and the plaintext. This input is formatted as a sequence of blocks B_0 through B_r. The first block contains the nonce plus some formatting bits that indicate the lengths of the N, A, and P elements. This is followed by zero or more blocks that contain A, followed by zero of more blocks that contain P. The resulting sequence of blocks serves as input to the CMAC algorithm, which produces a MAC value with length $Tlen$, which is less than or equal to the block length (Figure 3.8a).

For encryption, a sequence of counters is generated that must be independent of the nonce. The authentication tag is encrypted in CTR mode using the single counter Ctr_0. The $Tlen$ most significant bits of the output are XORed with the tag to produce an encrypted tag. The remaining counters are used for the CTR mode encryption of the plaintext (Figure 2.12). The encrypted plaintext is concatenated with the encrypted tag to form the ciphertext output (Figure 3.8b).

3.4 PUBLIC-KEY CRYPTOGRAPHY PRINCIPLES

Of equal importance to conventional encryption is **public-key encryption**, which finds use in message authentication and key distribution. This section looks first at the basic concept of public-key encryption and takes a preliminary look at key distribution issues. Section 3.5 examines the two most important public-key algorithms: RSA and Diffie-Hellman. Section 3.6 introduces digital signatures.

Public-Key Encryption Structure

Public-key encryption, first publicly proposed by Diffie and Hellman in 1976 [DIFF76], is the first truly revolutionary advance in encryption in literally thousands of years. Public-key algorithms are based on mathematical functions rather than on simple operations on bit patterns, such as are used in symmetric encryption algorithms. More important, public-key cryptography is asymmetric, involving the use of two separate keys—in contrast to the symmetric conventional encryption, which uses only one key. The use of two keys has profound consequences in the areas of confidentiality, key distribution, and authentication.

Before proceeding, we should first mention several common misconceptions concerning public-key encryption. One is that public-key encryption is more secure from cryptanalysis than conventional encryption. In fact, the security of any encryption scheme depends on (1) the length of the key and (2) the computational work involved in breaking a cipher. There is nothing in principle about either conventional or public-key encryption that makes one superior to another from the point of view of resisting cryptanalysis. A second misconception is that public-key encryption is a general-purpose technique that has made conventional encryption obsolete. On the contrary, because of the computational overhead of current public-key encryption schemes, there seems no foreseeable likelihood that conventional encryption will be abandoned. Finally, there is a feeling that key distribution is trivial when using public-key encryption, compared to the rather cumbersome handshaking involved with key distribution centers for conventional encryption. In fact, some form of protocol is needed, often involving a central agent, and the procedures involved are no simpler or any more efficient than those required for conventional encryption.

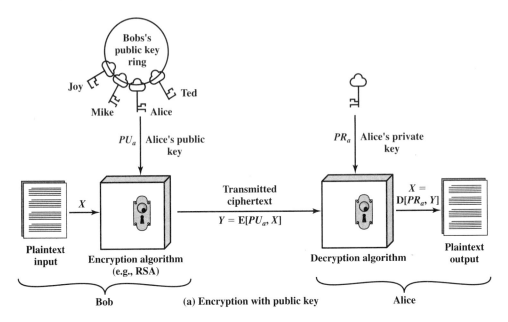

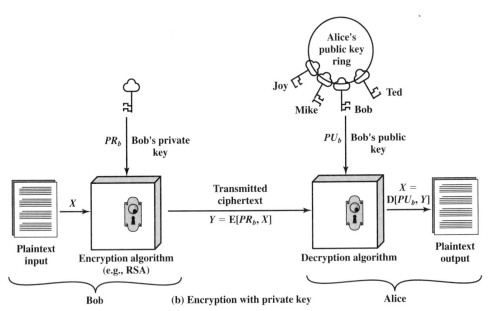

Figure 3.9 Public-Key Cryptography

A public-key encryption scheme has six ingredients (Figure 3.9a).

- **Plaintext:** This is the readable message or data that is fed into the algorithm as input.
- **Encryption algorithm:** The encryption algorithm performs various transformations on the plaintext.

- **Public and private key:** This is a pair of keys that have been selected so that if one is used for encryption, the other is used for decryption. The exact transformations performed by the encryption algorithm depend on the public or private key that is provided as input.
- **Ciphertext:** This is the scrambled message produced as output. It depends on the plaintext and the key. For a given message, two different keys will produce two different ciphertexts.
- **Decryption algorithm:** This algorithm accepts the ciphertext and the matching key and produces the original plaintext.

As the names suggest, the public key of the pair is made public for others to use, while the private key is known only to its owner. A general-purpose public-key cryptographic algorithm relies on one key for encryption and a different but related key for decryption.

The essential steps are the following:

1. Each user generates a pair of keys to be used for the encryption and decryption of messages.
2. Each user places one of the two keys in a public register or other accessible file. This is the public key. The companion key is kept private. As Figure 3.9a suggests, each user maintains a collection of public keys obtained from others.
3. If Bob wishes to send a private message to Alice, Bob encrypts the message using Alice's public key.
4. When Alice receives the message, she decrypts it using her private key. No other recipient can decrypt the message because only Alice knows Alice's private key.

With this approach, all participants have access to public keys, and private keys are generated locally by each participant and therefore need never be distributed. As long as a user protects his or her private key, incoming communication is secure. At any time, a user can change the private key and publish the companion public key to replace the old public key.

The key used in conventional encryption is typically referred to as a **secret key**. The two keys used for public-key encryption are referred to as the **public key** and the **private key**. Invariably, the private key is kept secret, but it is referred to as a private key rather than a secret key to avoid confusion with conventional encryption.

Applications for Public-Key Cryptosystems

Before proceeding, we need to clarify one aspect of public-key cryptosystems that is otherwise likely to lead to confusion. Public-key systems are characterized by the use of a cryptographic type of algorithm with two keys, one held private and one available publicly. Depending on the application, the sender uses either the sender's private key, the receiver's public key, or both to perform some type of cryptographic function. In broad terms, we can classify the use of public-key cryptosystems into three categories:

- **Encryption/decryption:** The sender encrypts a message with the recipient's public key.

Table 3.2 Applications for Public-Key Cryptosystems

Algorithm	Encryption/Decryption	Digital Signature	Key Exchange
RSA	Yes	Yes	Yes
Diffie-Hellman	No	No	Yes
DSS	No	Yes	No
Elliptic curve	Yes	Yes	Yes

- **Digital signature:** The sender "signs" a message with its private key. Signing is achieved by a cryptographic algorithm applied to the message or to a small block of data that is a function of the message.

- **Key exchange:** Two sides cooperate to exchange a session key. Several different approaches are possible, involving the private key(s) of one or both parties.

Some algorithms are suitable for all three applications, whereas others can be used only for one or two of these applications. Table 3.2 indicates the applications supported by the algorithms discussed in this chapter: RSA and Diffie Hellman. This table also includes the Digital Signature Standard (DSS) and elliptic-curve cryptography, also mentioned later in this chapter.

Requirements for Public-Key Cryptography

The cryptosystem illustrated in Figure 3.9 depends on a cryptographic algorithm based on two related keys. Diffie and Hellman postulated this system without demonstrating that such algorithms exist. However, they did lay out the conditions that such algorithms must fulfill [DIFF76]:

1. It is computationally easy for a party B to generate a pair (public key PU_b, private key PR_b).

2. It is computationally easy for a sender A, knowing the public key and the message to be encrypted, M, to generate the corresponding ciphertext:

$$C = E(PU_b, M)$$

3. It is computationally easy for the receiver B to decrypt the resulting ciphertext using the private key to recover the original message:

$$M = D(PR_b, C) = D[PR_b, E(PU_b, M)]$$

4. It is computationally infeasible for an opponent, knowing the public key, PU_b, to determine the private key, PR_b.

5. It is computationally infeasible for an opponent, knowing the public key, PU_b, and a ciphertext, C, to recover the original message, M.

We can add a sixth requirement that, although useful, is not necessary for all public-key applications.

6. Either of the two related keys can be used for encryption, with the other used for decryption.

$$M = D[PU_b, E(PR_b, M)] = D[PR_b, E(PU_b, M)]$$

The two most widely used public-key algorithms are RSA and Diffie-Hellman. We look at both of these in this section and then briefly introduce two other algorithms.[4]

The RSA Public-Key Encryption Algorithm

One of the first public-key schemes was developed in 1977 by Ron Rivest, Adi Shamir, and Len Adleman at MIT and first published in 1978 [RIVE78]. The RSA scheme has since that time reigned supreme as the most widely accepted and implemented approach to public-key encryption. **RSA** is a block cipher in which the plaintext and ciphertext are integers between 0 and $n-1$ for some n.

Encryption and decryption are of the following form period for some plaintext block M and ciphertext block C:

$$C = M^e \bmod n$$

$$M = C^d \bmod n = (M^e)^d \bmod n = M^{ed} \bmod n$$

Both sender and receiver must know the values of n and e, and only the receiver knows the value of d. This is a public-key encryption algorithm with a public key of $KU = \{e, n\}$ and a private key of $KR = \{d, n\}$. For this algorithm to be satisfactory for public-key encryption, the following requirements must be met.

1. It is possible to find values of e, d, n such that $M^{ed} \bmod n = M$ for all $M < n$.
2. It is relatively easy to calculate M^e and C^d for all values of $M < n$.
3. It is infeasible to determine d given e and n.

The first two requirements are easily met. The third requirement can be met for large values of e and n.

Figure 3.10 summarizes the RSA algorithm. Begin by selecting two prime numbers p and q and calculating their product n, which is the modulus for encryption and decryption. Next, we need the quantity $\phi(n)$, referred to as the Euler totient of n, which is the number of positive integers less than n and relatively prime to n. Then select an integer e that is relatively prime to $\phi(n)$ [i.e., the greatest common divisor of e and $\phi(n)$ is 1]. Finally, calculate d as the multiplicative inverse of e, modulo $\phi(n)$. It can be shown that d and e have the desired properties.

Suppose that user A has published its public key and that user B wishes to send the message M to A. Then B calculates $C = M^e \ (\bmod \ n)$ and transmits C. On receipt of this ciphertext, user A decrypts by calculating $M = C^d \ (\bmod \ n)$.

An example, from [SING99], is shown in Figure 3.11. For this example, the keys were generated as follows:

1. Select two prime numbers, $p = 17$ and $q = 11$.
2. Calculate $n = pq = 17 \times 11 = 187$.

---

[4]This section uses some elementary concepts from number theory. For a review, see Appendix A.

Key Generation	
Select p, q	p and q both prime, $p \neq q$
Calculate $n = p \times q$	
Calculate $\phi(n) = (p - 1)(q - 1)$	
Select integer e	$\gcd(\phi(n), e) = 1; 1 < e < \phi(n)$
Calculate d	$de \bmod \phi(n) = 1$
Public key	$KU = \{e, n\}$
Private key	$KR = \{d, n\}$

Encryption	
Plaintext:	$M < n$
Ciphertext:	$C = M^e \pmod{n}$

Decryption	
Ciphertext:	C
Plaintext:	$M = C^d \pmod{n}$

Figure 3.10   The RSA Algorithm

3. Calculate $\phi(n) = (p - 1)(q - 1) = 16 \times 10 = 160$.

4. Select e such that e is relatively prime to $\phi(n) = 160$ and less than $\phi(n)$; we choose $e = 7$.

5. Determine d such that $de \bmod 160 = 1$ and $d < 160$. The correct value is $d = 23$, because $23 \times 7 = 161 = (1 \times 160) + 1$.

The resulting keys are public key $PU = \{7, 187\}$ and private key $PR = \{23, 187\}$. The example shows the use of these keys for a plaintext input of $M = 88$. For

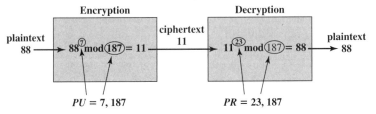

Figure 3.11   Example of RSA Algorithm

encryption, we need to calculate $C = 88^7$ mod 187. Exploiting the properties of modular arithmetic, we can do this as follows:

88^7 mod 187 = $[(88^4$ mod 187$) \times (88^2$ mod 187$) \times (88^1$ mod 187$)]$ mod 187

88^1 mod 187 = 88

88^2 mod 187 = 7744 mod 187 = 77

88^4 mod 187 = 59,969,536 mod 187 = 132

88^7 mod 187 = $(88 \times 77 \times 132)$ mod 187 = 894,432 mod 187 = 11

For decryption, we calculate $M = 11^{23}$ mod 187:

11^{23} mod 187 = $[(11^1$ mod 187$) \times (11^2$ mod 187$) \times (11^4$ mod 187$) \times$
$\qquad (11^8$ mod 187$) \times (11^8$ mod 187$)]$ mod 187

11^1 mod 187 = 11

11^2 mod 187 = 121

11^4 mod 187 = 14,641 mod 187 = 55

11^8 mod 187 = 214,358,881 mod 187 = 33

11^{23} mod 187 = $(11 \times 121 \times 55 \times 33 \times 33)$ mod 187
$\qquad\qquad\qquad = 79,720,245$ mod 187 = 88

There are two possible approaches to defeating the RSA algorithm. The first is the brute-force approach: Try all possible private keys. Thus, the larger the number of bits in e and d, the more secure the algorithm. However, because the calculations involved (both in key generation and in encryption/decryption) are complex, the larger the size of the key, the slower the system will run.

Most discussions of the cryptanalysis of RSA have focused on the task of factoring n into its two prime factors. For a large n with large prime factors, factoring is a hard problem, but not as hard as it used to be. A striking illustration of this occurred in 1977; the three inventors of RSA challenged *Scientific American* readers to decode a cipher they printed in Martin Gardner's "Mathematical Games" column [GARD77]. They offered a $100 reward for the return of a plaintext sentence, an event they predicted might not occur for some 40 quadrillion years. In April of 1994, a group working over the Internet and using over 1600 computers claimed the prize after only eight months of work [LEUT94]. This challenge used a public-key size (length of n) of 129 decimal digits (approximately 428 bits). This result does not invalidate the use of RSA; it simply means that larger key sizes must be used. Currently, a 1024-bit key size (about 300 decimal digits) is considered strong enough for virtually all applications.

Diffie–Hellman Key Exchange

The first published public-key algorithm appeared in the seminal paper by Diffie and Hellman that defined public-key cryptography [DIFF76] and is generally referred to as the **Diffie-Hellman key exchange**. A number of commercial products employ this key exchange technique.

The purpose of the algorithm is to enable two users to exchange a secret key securely that then can be used for subsequent encryption of messages. The algorithm itself is limited to the exchange of the keys.

The Diffie-Hellman algorithm depends for its effectiveness on the difficulty of computing discrete logarithms. Briefly, we can define the discrete logarithm in the following way. First, we define a primitive root of a prime number p as one whose powers generate all the integers from 1 to $p - 1$. That is, if a is a primitive root of the prime number p, then the numbers

$$a \bmod p, a^2 \bmod p, \ldots, ap^{-1} \bmod p$$

are distinct and consist of the integers from 1 through $p - 1$ in some permutation. For any integer b less than p and a primitive root a of prime number p, one can find a unique exponent i such that

$$b = a^i \bmod p \quad 0 \leq i \leq (p - 1)$$

The exponent i is referred to as the discrete logarithm, or index, of b for the base a, mod p. We denote this value as $\mathrm{dlog}_{a,p}(b)$.[5]

THE ALGORITHM With this background, we can define the Diffie-Hellman key exchange, which is summarized in Figure 3.12. For this scheme, there are two publicly known numbers: a prime number q and an integer α that is a primitive root of q. Suppose the users A and B wish to exchange a key. User A selects a random integer $X_A < q$ and computes $Y_A = \alpha^{X_A} \bmod q$. Similarly, user B independently selects a random integer $X_B < q$ and computes $Y_B = \alpha^{X_B} \bmod q$. Each side keeps the X value private and makes the Y value available publicly to the other side. User A computes the key as $K = (Y_B)^{X_A} \bmod q$ and user B computes the key as $K = (Y_A)^{X_B} \bmod q$. These two calculations produce identical results:

$$
\begin{aligned}
K &= (Y_B)^{X_A} \bmod q \\
&= (\alpha^{X_B} \bmod q)^{X_A} \bmod q \\
&= (\alpha^{X_B})^{X_A} \bmod q \\
&= \alpha^{X_B X_A} \bmod q \\
&= (\alpha^{X_A})^{X_B} \bmod q \\
&= (\alpha^{X_A} \bmod q)^{X_B} \bmod q \\
&= (Y_A)^{X_B} \bmod q
\end{aligned}
$$

The result is that the two sides have exchanged a secret value. Furthermore, because X_A and X_B are private, an adversary only has the following ingredients to work with: q, α, Y_A, and Y_B. Thus, the adversary is forced to take a discrete logarithm to determine the key. For example, to determine the private key of user B, an adversary must compute

$$X_B = \mathrm{dlog}_{\alpha,q}(Y_B)$$

---

[5]Many texts refer to the discrete logarithm as the *index*. There is no generally agreed notation for this concept, much less an agreed name.

<table>
<tr><td colspan="2" align="center">Global Public Elements</td></tr>
<tr><td>q</td><td>prime number</td></tr>
<tr><td>α</td><td>$\alpha < q$ and α a primitive root of q</td></tr>
</table>

<table>
<tr><td colspan="2" align="center">User A Key Generation</td></tr>
<tr><td>Select private X_A</td><td>$X_A < q$</td></tr>
<tr><td>Calculate public Y_A</td><td>$Y_A = \alpha^{X_A} \bmod q$</td></tr>
</table>

<table>
<tr><td colspan="2" align="center">User B Key Generation</td></tr>
<tr><td>Select private X_B</td><td>$X_B < q$</td></tr>
<tr><td>Calculate public Y_B</td><td>$Y_B = \alpha^{X_B} \bmod q$</td></tr>
</table>

<table>
<tr><td align="center">Generation of Secret Key by User A</td></tr>
<tr><td>$K = (Y_B)^{X_A} \bmod q$</td></tr>
</table>

<table>
<tr><td align="center">Generation of Secret Key by User B</td></tr>
<tr><td>$K = (Y_A)^{X_B} \bmod q$</td></tr>
</table>

Figure 3.12   The Diffie-Hellman Key Exchange Algorithm

The adversary can then calculate the key K in the same manner as user B does.

The security of the Diffie-Hellman key exchange lies in the fact that, while it is relatively easy to calculate exponentials modulo a prime, it is very difficult to calculate discrete logarithms. For large primes, the latter task is considered infeasible.

Here is an example. Key exchange is based on the use of the prime number $q = 353$ and a primitive root of 353, in this case $\alpha = 3$. A and B select secret keys $X_A = 97$ and $X_B = 233$, respectively. Each computes its public key:

$$\text{A computes } Y_A = 3^{97} \bmod 353 = 40.$$
$$\text{B computes } Y_B = 3^{233} \bmod 353 = 248.$$

After they exchange public keys, each can compute the common secret key:

$$\text{A computes } K = (Y_B)^{X_A} \bmod 353 = 248^{97} \bmod 353 = 160.$$
$$\text{B computes } K = (Y_A)^{X_B} \bmod 353 = 40^{233} \bmod 353 = 160.$$

We assume an attacker would have available the following information:

$$q = 353; \quad \alpha = 3; \quad Y_A = 40; \quad Y_B = 248$$

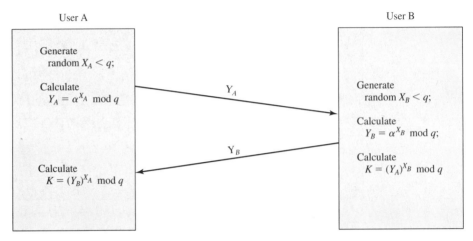

Figure 3.13 Diffie-Hellman Key Exchange

In this simple example, it would be possible to determine the secret key 160 by brute force. In particular, an attacker E can determine the common key by discovering a solution to the equation $3^a \bmod 353 = 40$ or the equation $3^b \bmod 353 = 248$. The brute-force approach is to calculate powers of 3 modulo 353, stopping when the result equals either 40 or 248. The desired answer is reached with the exponent value of 97, which provides $3^{97} \bmod 353 = 40$.

With larger numbers, the problem becomes impractical.

KEY EXCHANGE PROTOCOLS Figure 3.13 shows a simple protocol that makes use of the Diffie-Hellman calculation. Suppose that user A wishes to set up a connection with user B and use a secret key to encrypt messages on that connection. User A can generate a one-time private key X_A, calculate Y_A, and send that to user B. User B responds by generating a private value X_B, calculating Y_B, and sending Y_B to user A. Both users can now calculate the key. The necessary public values q and α would need to be known ahead of time. Alternatively, user A could pick values for q and α and include those in the first message.

As an example of another use of the Diffie-Hellman algorithm, suppose that a group of users (e.g., all users on a LAN) each generate a long-lasting private value X_A and calculate a public value Y_A. These public values, together with global public values for q and α, are stored in some central directory. At any time, user B can access user A's public value, calculate a secret key, and use that to send an encrypted message to user A. If the central directory is trusted, then this form of communication provides both confidentiality and a degree of authentication. Because only A and B can determine the key, no other user can read the message (confidentiality). Recipient A knows that only user B could have created a message using this key (authentication). However, the technique does not protect against replay attacks.

MAN-IN-THE-MIDDLE ATTACK The protocol depicted in Figure 3.13 is insecure against a man-in-the-middle attack. Suppose Alice and Bob wish to exchange keys, and Darth is the adversary. The attack proceeds as follows:

1. Darth prepares for the attack by generating two random private keys X_{D1} and X_{D2}, and then computing the corresponding public keys Y_{D1} and Y_{D2}.

2. Alice transmits Y_A to Bob.

3. Darth intercepts Y_A and transmits Y_{D1} to Bob. Darth also calculates $K2 = (Y_A)^{X_{D2}} \bmod q$.

4. Bob receives Y_{D1} and calculates $K1 = (Y_{D1})^{X_B} \bmod q$.

5. Bob transmits Y_B to Alice.

6. Darth intercepts Y_B and transmits Y_{D2} to Alice. Darth calculates $K1 = (Y_B)^{X_{D1}} \bmod q$.

7. Alice receives Y_{D2} and calculates $K2 = (Y_{D2})^{X_A} \bmod q$.

At this point, Bob and Alice think that they share a secret key. Instead Bob and Darth share secret key $K1$, and Alice and Darth share secret key $K2$. All future communication between Bob and Alice is compromised in the following way:

1. Alice sends an encrypted message M: $E(K2, M)$.

2. Darth intercepts the encrypted message and decrypts it to recover M.

3. Darth sends Bob $E(K1, M)$ or $E(K1, M')$, where M' is any message. In the first case, Darth simply wants to eavesdrop on the communication without altering it. In the second case, Darth wants to modify the message going to Bob.

The key exchange protocol is vulnerable to such an attack because it does not authenticate the participants. This vulnerability can be overcome with the use of digital signatures and public-key certificates; these topics are explored later in this chapter and in Chapter 4.

Other Public-Key Cryptography Algorithms

Two other public-key algorithms have found commercial acceptance: DSS and elliptic-curve cryptography.

DIGITAL SIGNATURE STANDARD The National Institute of Standards and Technology (NIST) has published Federal Information Processing Standard FIPS PUB 186, known as the **Digital Signature Standard (DSS)**. The DSS makes use of the SHA-1 and presents a new digital signature technique, the Digital Signature Algorithm (DSA). The DSS was originally proposed in 1991 and revised in 1993 in response to public feedback concerning the security of the scheme. There was a further minor revision in 1996. The DSS uses an algorithm that is designed to provide only the digital signature function. Unlike RSA, it cannot be used for encryption or key exchange.

ELLIPTIC-CURVE CRYPTOGRAPHY The vast majority of the products and standards that use public-key cryptography for encryption and digital signatures use RSA. The bit length for secure RSA use has increased over recent years, and this has put a heavier processing load on applications using RSA. This burden has ramifications, especially for electronic commerce sites that conduct large numbers of secure transactions. Recently, a competing system has begun to challenge RSA: **elliptic curve cryptography (ECC)**. Already, ECC is showing up in standardization efforts, including the IEEE P1363 Standard for Public-Key Cryptography.

The principal attraction of ECC compared to RSA is that it appears to offer equal security for a far smaller bit size, thereby reducing processing overhead. On the other hand, although the theory of ECC has been around for some time, it is only recently that products have begun to appear and that there has been sustained cryptanalytic interest in probing for weaknesses. Thus, the confidence level in ECC is not yet as high as that in RSA.

ECC is fundamentally more difficult to explain than either RSA or Diffie-Hellman, and a full mathematical description is beyond the scope of this book. The technique is based on the use of a mathematical construct known as the elliptic curve.

3.6 DIGITAL SIGNATURES

Public-key encryption can be used in another way, as illustrated in Figure 3.9b. Suppose that Bob wants to send a message to Alice, and although it is not important that the message be kept secret, he wants Alice to be certain that the message is indeed from him. In this case, Bob uses his own private key to encrypt the message. When Alice receives the ciphertext, she finds that she can decrypt it with Bob's public key, thus proving that the message must have been encrypted by Bob. No one else has Bob's private key, and therefore no one else could have created a ciphertext that could be decrypted with Bob's public key. Therefore, the entire encrypted message serves as a **digital signature**. In addition, it is impossible to alter the message without access to Bob's private key, so the message is authenticated both in terms of source and in terms of data integrity.

In the preceding scheme, the entire message is encrypted. Although validating both author and contents, this requires a great deal of storage. Each document must be kept in plaintext to be used for practical purposes. A copy also must be stored in ciphertext so that the origin and contents can be verified in case of a dispute. A more efficient way of achieving the same results is to encrypt a small block of bits that is a function of the document. Such a block, called an authenticator, must have the property that it is infeasible to change the document without changing the authenticator. If the authenticator is encrypted with the sender's private key, it serves as a signature that verifies origin, content, and sequencing. A secure hash code such as SHA-1 can serve this function. Figure 3.2b illustrates this scenario.

It is important to emphasize that the encryption process just described does not provide confidentiality. That is, the message being sent is safe from alteration but not safe from eavesdropping. This is obvious in the case of a signature based on a portion of the message, because the rest of the message is transmitted in the clear. Even in the case of complete encryption, there is no protection of confidentiality because any observer can decrypt the message by using the sender's public key.

3.7 RECOMMENDED READING AND WEB SITES

Solid treatments of hash functions and message authentication codes are found in [STIN06] and {MENE97].

The recommended treatments of encryption provided in Chapter 2 cover public-key as well as conventional encryption. [DIFF88] describes in detail the several attempts to devise secure two-key cryptoalgorithms and the gradual evolution of a variety of protocols based on them.

DIFF88 Diffie, W. "The First Ten Years of Public-Key Cryptography." *Procedings of the IEEE,* May 1988.

MENE97 Menezes, A.; Oorschot, P.; and Vanstone, S. *Handbook of Applied Cryptography.* Boca Raton, FL: CRC Press, 1997.

STIN06 Stinson, D. *Cryptography: Theory and Practice.* Boca Raton, FL: Chapman&Hall/ CRC Press, 2006.

Recommended Web Sites:

- **NIST Secure Hashing Page:** SHA FIPS and related documents.
- **RSA Laboratories:** Extensive collection of technical material on RSA and other topics in cryptography.
- **Digital Signatures:** NIST page with information on NIST-approved digital signature options.

3.8 KEY TERMS, REVIEW QUESTIONS, AND PROBLEMS

Key Terms

authenticated encryption	MD5	public-key encryption
Diffie-Hellman key exchange	message authentication	RIPEMD-160
digital signature	message authentication code	RSA
Digital Signature Standard	(MAC)	secret key
(DSS)	message digest	secure hash function
elliptic-curve cryptography	one-way hash function	SHA-1
(ECC)	private key	strong collision resistance
HMAC	public key	weak collision resistance
key exchange	public-key certificate	

Review Questions

3.1 List three approaches to message authentication.

3.2 What is a message authentication code?

3.3 Briefly describe the three schemes illustrated in Figure 3.2.

3.4 What properties must a hash function have to be useful for message authentication?

3.5 In the context of a hash function, what is a compression function?

3.6 What are the principal ingredients of a public-key cryptosystem?

3.7 List and briefly define three uses of a public-key cryptosystem.

3.8   What is the difference between a private key and a secret key?

3.9   What is a digital signature?

Problems

3.1   Consider a 32-bit hash function defined as the concatenation of two 16-bit functions: XOR and RXOR, which are defined in Section 3.2 as "two simple hash functions."

   a.   Will this checksum detect all errors caused by an odd number of error bits? Explain.
   b.   Will this checksum detect all errors caused by an even number of error bits? If not, characterize the error patterns that will cause the checksum to fail.
   c.   Comment on the effectiveness of this function for use as a hash function for authentication.

3.2   Suppose $H(m)$ is a collision-resistant hash function that maps a message of arbitrary bit length into an n-bit hash value. Is it true that, for all messages x, x' with $x \neq x'$, we have $H(x) \neq H(x')$? Explain your answer.

3.3   State the value of the padding field in SHA-512 if the length of the message is

   a.   1919 bits
   b.   1920 bits
   c.   1921 bits

3.4   State the value of the length field in SHA-512 if the length of the message is

   a.   1919 bits
   b.   1920 bits
   c.   1921 bits

3.5   a.   Consider the following hash function. Messages are in the form of a sequence of decimal numbers, $M = (a_1, a_2, \ldots, a_t)$. The hash value h is calculated as $\left(\sum_{i=1}^{t} a_i \right) \bmod n$, for some predefined value n. Does this hash function satisfy any of the requirements for a hash function listed in Section 3.2? Explain your answer.

   b.   Repeat part (a) for the hash function $h = \left(\sum_{i=1}^{t} (a_i)^2 \right) \bmod n$.

   c.   Calculate the hash function of part (b) for $M = (189, 632, 900, 722, 349)$ and $n = 989$.

3.6   This problem introduces a hash function similar in spirit to SHA that operates on letters instead of binary data. It is called the *toy tetragraph hash* (tth).[6] Given a message consisting of a sequence of letters, tth produces a hash value consisting of four letters. First, tth divides the message into blocks of 16 letters, ignoring spaces, punctuation, and capitalization. If the message length is not divisible by 16, it is padded out with nulls. A four-number running total is maintained that starts out with the value $(0,0,0,0)$; this is input to the compression function for processing the first block. The compression function consists of two rounds. **Round 1:** Get the next block of text and arrange it as a row-wise 4×4 block of text and covert it to numbers ($A = 0, B = 1$, etc.). For example, for the block ABCDEFGHIJKLMNOP, we have

A	B	C	D
E	F	G	H
I	J	K	L
M	N	O	P

0	1	2	3
4	5	6	7
8	9	10	11
12	13	14	15

---

[6]I thank William K. Mason of the magazine staff of *The Cryptogram* for providing this example.

Then, add each column mod 26 and add the result to the running total, mod 26. In this example, the running total is (24, 2, 6, 10). **Round 2:** Using the matrix from round 1, rotate the first row left by 1, second row left by 2, third row left by 3, and reverse the order of the fourth row. In our example:

B	C	D	A
G	H	E	F
L	I	J	K
P	O	N	M

1	2	3	0
6	7	4	5
11	8	9	10
15	14	13	12

Now, add each column mod 26 and add the result to the running total. The new running total is (5, 7, 9, 11). This running total is now the input into the first round of the compression function for the next block of text. After the final block is processed, convert the final running total to letters. For example, if the message is ABCDE FGHIJKLMNOP, then the hash is FHJL.

a. Draw figures comparable to Figures 3.4 and 3.5 to depict the overall tth logic and the compression function logic.
b. Calculate the hash function for the 48-letter message "I leave twenty million dollars to my friendly cousin Bill."
c. To demonstrate the weakness of tth, find a 48-letter block that produces the same hash as that just derived. *Hint:* Use lots of A's.

3.7 It is possible to use a hash function to construct a block cipher with a structure similar to DES. Because a hash function is one way and a block cipher must be reversible (to decrypt), how is it possible?

3.8 Now consider the opposite problem: Use an encryption algorithm to construct a one-way hash function. Consider using RSA with a known key. Then process a message consisting of a sequence of blocks as follows: Encrypt the first block, XOR the result with the second block and encrypt again, and so on. Show that this scheme is not secure by solving the following problem. Given a two-block message B1, B2, and its hash, we have

$$\text{RSAH}(B1, B2) = \text{RSA}(\text{RSA}(B1) \oplus B2)$$

Given an arbitrary block C1, choose C2 so that $\text{RSAH}(C1, C2) = \text{RSAH}(B1, B2)$. Thus, the hash function does not satisfy weak collision resistance.

3.9 One of the most widely used MACs, referred to as the Data Authentication Algorithm, is based on DES. The algorithm is both a FIPS publication (FIPS PUB 113) and an ANSI standard (X9.17). The algorithm can be defined as using the cipher block chaining (CBC) mode of operation of DES with an initialization vector of zero (Figure 2.10). The data (e.g., message, record, file, or program) to be authenticated is grouped into contiguous 64-bit blocks: $P_1, P_2, \ldots, P_N$. If necessary, the final block is padded on the right with 0s to form a full 64-bit block. The MAC consists of either the entire ciphertext block C_N or the leftmost M bits of the block with $16 \leq M \leq 64$. Show that the same result can be produced using the cipher feedback mode.

3.10 In this problem, we will compare the security services that are provided by digital signatures (DS) and message authentication codes (MAC). We assume that Oscar is able to observe all messages send from Alice to Bob and vice versa. Oscar has no knowledge of any keys but the public one in case of DS. State whether and how (i) DS and (ii) MAC protect against each attack. The value `auth(x)` is computed with a DS or a MAC algorithm, respectively.

a. (Message integrity) Alice sends a message x = `"Transfer $1000 to Mark"` in the clear and also sends `auth(x)` to Bob. Oscar intercepts the message and replaces "Mark" with "Oscar". Will Bob detect this?

    b. (Replay) Alice sends a message x = "Transfer $1000 to Oscar" in the clear and also sends auth(x) to Bob. Oscar observes the message and signature and sends them 100 times to Bob. Will Bob detect this?

    c. (Sender Authentication with cheating third party) Oscar claims that he sent some message x with a valid auth(x) to Bob, but Alice claims the same. Can Bob clear the question in either case?

    d. (Authentication with Bob cheating) Bob claims that he received a message x with a valid signature auth(x) from Alice (e.g., "Transfer $1000 from Alice to Bob") but Alice claims she has never sent it. Can Alice clear this question in either case?

3.11 Figure 3.14 shows an alternative means of implementing HMAC.

    a. Describe the operation of this implementation.

    b. What potential benefit does this implementation have over that shown in Figure 3.6?

3.12 In this problem, we demonstrate that for CMAC, a variant that XORs the second key after applying the final encryption doesn't work. Let us consider this for the case of the message being an integer multiple of the block size. Then the variant can be expressed as $VMAC(K, M) = CBC(K, M) \oplus K_1$. Now suppose an adversary is able to ask for the MACs of three messages: the message $\mathbf{0} = 0^n$, where n is the cipher block size; the message $\mathbf{1} = 1^n$; and the message $\mathbf{1} \parallel \mathbf{0}$. As a result of these three queries, the

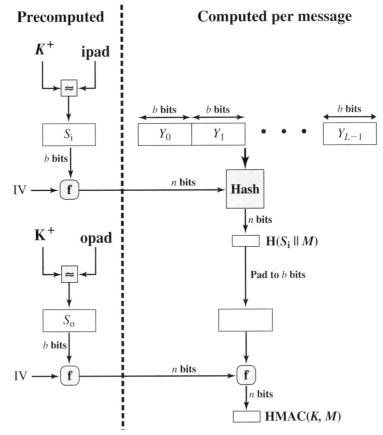

Figure 3.14 Efficient Implementation of HMAC

adversary gets $T_0 = CBC(K, \mathbf{0}) \oplus K_1$; $T_1 = CBC(K, \mathbf{1}) \oplus K_1$ and $T_2 = CBC(K, [CBC(K, \mathbf{1})]) \oplus K_1$. Show that the adversary can compute the correct MAC for the (unqueried) message $\mathbf{0} \| (T_0 \oplus T_1)$.

3.13   Prior to the discovery of any specific public-key schemes, such as RSA, an existence proof was developed whose purpose was to demonstrate that public-key encryption is possible in theory. Consider the functions $f_1(x_1) = z_1$; $f_2(x_2, y_2) = z_2$; $f_3(x_3, y_3) = z_3$, where all values are integers with $1 \leq x_i, y_i, z_i \leq N$. Function f_1 can be represented by a vector M1 of length N in which the kth entry is the value of $f_1(k)$. Similarly, f_2 and f_3 can be represented by $N \times N$ matrices M2 and M3. The intent is to represent the encryption/decryption process by table lookups for tables with very large values of N. Such tables would be impractically huge but in principle could be constructed. The scheme works as follows: construct M1 with a random permutation of all integers between 1 and N; that is, each integer appears exactly once in M1. Construct M2 so that each row contains a random permutation of the first N integers. Finally, fill in M3 to satisfy the condition:

$$f_3(f_2(f_1(k), p), k) = p \quad \text{for all } k, p \text{ with } 1 \leq k, p \leq N$$

In words,

1. M1 takes an input k and produces an output x.
2. M2 takes inputs x and p giving output z.
3. M3 takes inputs z and k and produces p.

The three tables, once constructed, are made public.

a.   It should be clear that it is possible to construct M3 to satisfy the preceding condition. As an example, fill in M3 for the following simple case:

$$M1 = \begin{bmatrix} 5 \\ 4 \\ 2 \\ 3 \\ 1 \end{bmatrix} \quad M2 = \begin{bmatrix} 5 & 2 & 3 & 4 & 1 \\ 4 & 2 & 5 & 1 & 3 \\ 1 & 3 & 2 & 4 & 5 \\ 3 & 1 & 4 & 2 & 5 \\ 2 & 5 & 3 & 4 & 1 \end{bmatrix} \quad M3 = \begin{bmatrix} & & & & \\ & & & & \\ & & & & \\ & & & & \\ & & & & \end{bmatrix}$$

Convention: The ith element of M1 corresponds to $k = i$. The ith row of M2 corresponds to $x = i$; the jth column of M2 corresponds to $p = j$. The ith row of M3 corresponds to $z = i$; the jth column of M3 corresponds to $k = j$.

b.   Describe the use of this set of tables to perform encryption and decryption between two users.

c.   Argue that this is a secure scheme.

3.14   Perform encryption and decryption using the RSA algorithm (Figure 3.10) for the following:

a. $p = 3; q = 11, e = 7; M = 5$
b. $p = 5; q = 11, e = 3; M = 9$
c. $p = 7; q = 11, e = 17; M = 8$
d. $p = 11; q = 13, e = 11; M = 7$
e. $p = 17; q = 31, e = 7; M = 2$

Hint: Decryption is not as hard as you think; use some finesse.

3.15   In a public-key system using RSA, you intercept the ciphertext $C = 10$ sent to a user whose public key is $e = 5, n = 35$. What is the plaintext M?

3.16   In an RSA system, the public key of a given user is $e = 31, n = 3599$. What is the private key of this user?

3.17   Suppose we have a set of blocks encoded with the RSA algorithm and we don't have the private key. Assume $n = pq$, e is the public key. Suppose also someone tells us they know one of the plaintext blocks has a common factor with n. Does this help us in any way?

3.18 Show how RSA can be represented by matrices M1, M2, and M3 of Problem 3.4.

3.19 Consider the following scheme.

1. Pick an odd number, E.
2. Pick two prime numbers, P and Q, where $(P - 1)(Q - 1) - 1$ is evenly divisible by E.
3. Multiply P and Q to get N.
4. Calculate $D = \dfrac{(P - 1)(Q - 1)(E - 1) + 1}{E}$.

Is this scheme equivalent to RSA? Show why or why not.

3.20 Suppose Bob uses the RSA cryptosystem with a very large modulus n for which the factorization cannot be found in a reasonable amount of time. Suppose Alice sends a message to Bob by representing each alphabetic character as an integer between 0 and 25 (A $\rightarrow$ 0, . . ., Z $\rightarrow$ 25), and then encrypting each number separately using RSA with large e and large n. Is this method secure? If not, describe the most efficient attack against this encryption method.

3.21 Consider a Diffie-Hellman scheme with a common prime $q = 11$ and a primitive root $\alpha = 2$.

a. If user A has public key $Y_A = 9$, what is A's private key X_A?
b. If user B has public key $Y_B = 3$, what is the shared secret key K?

CHAPTER 4

KEY DISTRIBUTION AND USER AUTHENTICATION

No Singhalese, whether man or woman, would venture out of the house without a bunch of keys in his hand, for without such a talisman he would fear that some devil might take advantage of his weak state to slip into his body.

— *The Golden Bough*, Sir James George Frazer

This chapter covers two important, related concepts. First is the complex topic of cryptographic key distribution, involving cryptographic, protocol, and management considerations. This chapter gives the reader a feel for the issues involved and provides a broad survey of the various aspects of key management and distribution.

This chapter also examines some of the authentication functions that have been developed to support network-based user authentication. The chapter includes a detail discussion of one of the earliest and also one of the most widely used key distribution and user authentication services: Kerberos. Next, the chapter looks at key distribution schemes that rely on asymmetric encryption. This is followed by a discussion of X.509 certificates and public-key infrastructure. Finally, the concept of federated identity management is introduced.

4.1 SYMMETRIC KEY DISTRIBUTION USING SYMMETRIC ENCRYPTION

For symmetric encryption to work, the two parties to an exchange must share the same key, and that key must be protected from access by others. Furthermore, frequent key changes are usually desirable to limit the amount of data compromised if an attacker learns the key. Therefore, the strength of any cryptographic system rests with the key distribution technique, a term that refers to the means of delivering a key to two parties that wish to exchange data, without allowing others to see the key. Key distribution can be achieved in a number of ways. For two parties A and B, there are the following options:

1. A key could be selected by A and physically delivered to B.
2. A third party could select the key and physically deliver it to A and B.
3. If A and B have previously and recently used a key, one party could transmit the new key to the other, using the old key to encrypt the new key.
4. If A and B each have an encrypted connection to a third party C, C could deliver a key on the encrypted links to A and B.

Options 1 and 2 call for manual delivery of a key. For link encryption, this is a reasonable requirement, because each link encryption device is only going to be exchanging data with its partner on the other end of the link. However, for end-to-end encryption over a network, manual delivery is awkward. In a distributed system, any given host or terminal may need to engage in exchanges with many other hosts and terminals over time. Thus, each device needs a number of keys supplied dynamically. The problem is especially difficult in a wide-area distributed system.

Option 3 is a possibility for either link encryption or end-to-end encryption, but if an attacker ever succeeds in gaining access to one key, then all subsequent keys are revealed. Even if frequent changes are made to the link encryption keys, these should be done manually. To provide keys for end-to-end encryption, option 4 is preferable.

For **option 4**, two kinds of keys are used:

- **Session key:** When two end systems (hosts, terminals, etc.) wish to communicate, they establish a logical connection (e.g., virtual circuit). For the duration of that logical connection, called a session, all user data are encrypted with a one-time session key. At the conclusion of the session the session key is destroyed.

- **Permanent key:** A permanent key is a key used between entities for the purpose of distributing session keys.

A necessary element of option 4 is a **key distribution center (KDC)**. The KDC determines which systems are allowed to communicate with each other. When permission is granted for two systems to establish a connection, the key distribution center provides a one-time session key for that connection.

In general terms, the operation of a KDC proceeds as follows:

1. When host A wishes to set up a connection to host B, it transmits a connection-request packet to the KDC. The communication between A and the KDC is encrypted using a master key shared only by A and the KDC.

2. If the KDC approves the connection request, it generates a unique one-time session key. It encrypts the session key using the permanent key it shares with A and delivers the encrypted session key to A. Similarly, it encrypts the session key using the permanent key it shares with B and delivers the encrypted session key to B.

3. A and B can now set up a logical connection and exchange messages and data, all encrypted using the temporary session key.

The automated key distribution approach provides the flexibility and dynamic characteristics needed to allow a number of users to access a number of servers and for the servers to exchange data with each other. The most widely used application that implements this approach is Kerberos, described in the next section.

4.2 KERBEROS

Kerberos is a key distribution and user authentication service developed at MIT. The problem that Kerberos addresses is this: Assume an open distributed environment in which users at workstations wish to access services on servers distributed throughout the network. We would like for servers to be able to restrict access to authorized users and to be able to authenticate requests for service. In this environment, a workstation cannot be trusted to identify its users correctly to network services. In particular, the following three threats exist:

1. A user may gain access to a particular workstation and pretend to be another user operating from that workstation.

2. A user may alter the network address of a workstation so that the requests sent from the altered workstation appear to come from the impersonated workstation.

3. A user may eavesdrop on exchanges and use a replay attack to gain entrance to a server or to disrupt operations.

In any of these cases, an unauthorized user may be able to gain access to services and data that he or she is not authorized to access. Rather than building elaborate authentication protocols at each server, Kerberos provides a centralized authentication server whose function is to authenticate users to servers and servers to users. Kerberos relies exclusively on symmetric encryption, making no use of public-key encryption.

Two versions of Kerberos are in use. Version 4 [MILL88, STEI88] implementations still exist, although this version is being phased out. Version 5 [KOHL94] corrects some of the security deficiencies of version 4 and has been issued as a proposed Internet Standard (RFC 4120).

Because of the complexity of Kerberos, it is best to start with a description of version 4. This enables us to see the essence of the Kerberos strategy without considering some of the details required to handle subtle security threats. Then, we examine version 5.

Kerberos Version 4

Version 4 of Kerberos makes use of DES, in a rather elaborate protocol, to provide the authentication service. Viewing the protocol as a whole, it is difficult to see the need for the many elements contained therein. Therefore, we adopt a strategy used by Bill Bryant [BRYA88] and build up to the full protocol by looking first at several hypothetical dialogues. Each successive dialogue adds additional complexity to counter security vulnerabilities revealed in the preceding dialogue.

After examining the protocol, we look at some other aspects of version 4.

A SIMPLE AUTHENTICATION DIALOGUE In an unprotected network environment, any client can apply to any server for service. The obvious security risk is that of impersonation. An opponent can pretend to be another client and obtain unauthorized privileges on server machines. To counter this threat, servers must be able to confirm the identities of clients who request service. Each server can be required to undertake this task for each client/server interaction, but in an open environment, this places a substantial burden on each server.

An alternative is to use an **authentication server (AS)** that knows the passwords of all users and stores these in a centralized database. In addition, the AS shares a unique secret key with each server. These keys have been distributed physically or in some other secure manner. Consider the following hypothetical dialogue:[1]

$$\textbf{(1) } C \rightarrow AS: \quad ID_C \| P_C \| ID_V$$

$$\textbf{(2) } AS \rightarrow C: \quad Ticket$$

$$\textbf{(3) } C \rightarrow V: \quad ID_C \| Ticket$$

$$Ticket = E(K_v, [ID_C \| AD_C \| ID_V])$$

---

[1]The portion to the left of the colon indicates the sender and receiver, the portion to the right indicates the contents of the message, and the symbol $\|$ indicates concatenation.

where

C   = client
AS = authentication server
V   = server
ID_C = identifier of user on C
ID_V = identifier of V
P_C = password of user on C
AD_C = network address of C
K_v = secret encryption key shared by AS and V

In this scenario, the user logs on to a workstation and requests access to server V. The client module C in the user's workstation requests the user's password and then sends a message to the AS that includes the user's ID, the server's ID, and the user's password. The AS checks its database to see if the user has supplied the proper password for this user ID and whether this user is permitted access to server V. If both tests are passed, the AS accepts the user as authentic and must now convince the server that this user is authentic. To do so, the AS creates a **ticket** that contains the user's ID and network address and the server's ID. This ticket is encrypted using the secret key shared by the AS and this server. This ticket is then sent back to C. Because the ticket is encrypted, it cannot be altered by C or by an opponent.

With this ticket, C can now apply to V for service. C sends a message to V containing C's ID and the ticket. V decrypts the ticket and verifies that the user ID in the ticket is the same as the unencrypted user ID in the message. If these two match, the server considers the user authenticated and grants the requested service.

Each of the ingredients of message (3) is significant. The ticket is encrypted to prevent alteration or forgery. The server's ID (ID_V) is included in the ticket so that the server can verify that it has decrypted the ticket properly. ID_C is included in the ticket to indicate that this ticket has been issued on behalf of C. Finally, AD_C serves to counter the following threat. An opponent could capture the ticket transmitted in message (2), then use the name ID_C, and transmit a message of form (3) from another workstation. The server would receive a valid ticket that matches the user ID and grant access to the user on that other workstation. To prevent this attack, the AS includes in the ticket the network address from which the original request came. Now the ticket is valid only if it is transmitted from the same workstation that initially requested the ticket.

A MORE SECURE AUTHENTICATION DIALOGUE Although the foregoing scenario solves some of the problems of authentication in an open network environment, problems remain. Two in particular stand out. First, we would like to minimize the number of times that a user has to enter a password. Suppose each ticket can be used only once. If user C logs on to a workstation in the morning and wishes to check his or her mail at a mail server, C must supply a password to get a ticket for the mail server. If C wishes to check the mail several times during the day, each attempt requires reentering the password. We can improve matters by saying that tickets are reusable. For a single logon session, the workstation can store the mail-server ticket after it is received and use it on behalf of the user for multiple accesses to the mail server.

However, under this scheme, it remains the case that a user would need a new ticket for every different service. If a user wished to access a print server, a mail server, a file server, and so on, the first instance of each access would require a new ticket and hence require the user to enter the password.

The second problem is that the earlier scenario involved a plaintext transmission of the password [message (1)]. An eavesdropper could capture the password and use any service accessible to the victim.

To solve these additional problems, we introduce a scheme for avoiding plaintext passwords and a new server, known as the **ticket-granting server (TGS)**. The new (but still hypothetical) scenario is as follows.

Once per user logon session:

    (1) $C \rightarrow AS$: $ID_C \| ID_{tgs}$

    (2) $AS \rightarrow C$: $E(K_c, Ticket_{tgs})$

Once per type of service:

    (3) $C \rightarrow TGS$: $ID_C \| ID_V \| Ticket_{tgs}$

    (4) $TGS \rightarrow C$: $Ticket_v$

Once per service session:

    (5) $C \rightarrow V$: $ID_C \| Ticket_v$

$$Ticket_{tgs} = E(K_{tgs}, [ID_C \| AD_C \| ID_{tgs} \| TS_1 \| Lifetime_1])$$

$$Ticket_v = E(K_v, [ID_C \| AD_C \| ID_v \| TS_2 \| Lifetime_2])$$

The new service, TGS, issues **tickets** to users who have been authenticated to AS. Thus, the user first requests a ticket-granting ticket ($Ticket_{tgs}$) from the AS. The client module in the user workstation saves this ticket. Each time the user requires access to a new service, the client applies to the TGS, using the ticket to authenticate itself. The TGS then grants a ticket for the particular service. The client saves each service-granting ticket and uses it to authenticate its user to a server each time a particular service is requested. Let us look at the details of this scheme:

1. The client requests a ticket-granting ticket on behalf of the user by sending its user's ID to the AS, together with the TGS ID, indicating a request to use the TGS service.

2. The AS responds with a ticket that is encrypted with a key that is derived from the user's password (K_C), which is already stored at the AS. When this response arrives at the client, the client prompts the user for his or her password, generates the key, and attempts to decrypt the incoming message. If the correct password is supplied, the ticket is successfully recovered.

Because only the correct user should know the password, only the correct user can recover the ticket. Thus, we have used the password to obtain credentials from Kerberos without having to transmit the password in plaintext. The ticket itself consists of the ID and network address of the user and the ID of the TGS.

This corresponds to the first scenario. The idea is that the client can use this ticket to request multiple service-granting tickets. So the ticket-granting ticket is to be reusable. However, we do not wish an opponent to be able to capture the ticket and use it. Consider the following scenario: An opponent captures the login ticket and waits until the user has logged off his or her workstation. Then the opponent either gains access to that workstation or configures his workstation with the same network address as that of the victim. The opponent would be able to reuse the ticket to spoof the TGS. To counter this, the ticket includes a **timestamp**, indicating the date and time at which the ticket was issued, and a **lifetime**, indicating the length of time for which the ticket is valid (e.g., eight hours). Thus, the client now has a reusable ticket and need not bother the user for a password for each new service request. Finally, note that the ticket-granting ticket is encrypted with a secret key known only to the AS and the TGS. This prevents alteration of the ticket. The ticket is reencrypted with a key based on the user's password. This assures that the ticket can be recovered only by the correct user, providing the authentication.

Now that the client has a ticket-granting ticket, access to any server can be obtained with steps 3 and 4.

3. The client requests a service-granting ticket on behalf of the user. For this purpose, the client transmits a message to the TGS containing the user's ID, the ID of the desired service, and the ticket-granting ticket.

4. The TGS decrypts the incoming ticket using a key shared only by the AS and the TGS (K_{tgs}) and verifies the success of the decryption by the presence of its ID. It checks to make sure that the lifetime has not expired. Then it compares the user ID and network address with the incoming information to authenticate the user. If the user is permitted access to the server V, the TGS issues a ticket to grant access to the requested service.

The service-granting ticket has the same structure as the ticket-granting ticket. Indeed, because the TGS is a server, we would expect that the same elements are needed to authenticate a client to the TGS and to authenticate a client to an application server. Again, the ticket contains a timestamp and lifetime. If the user wants access to the same service at a later time, the client can simply use the previously acquired service-granting ticket and need not bother the user for a password. Note that the ticket is encrypted with a secret key (K_v) known only to the TGS and the server, preventing alteration.

Finally, with a particular service-granting ticket, the client can gain access to the corresponding service with step 5.

5. The client requests access to a service on behalf of the user. For this purpose, the client transmits a message to the server containing the user's ID and the service-granting ticket. The server authenticates by using the contents of the ticket.

This new scenario satisfies the two requirements of only one password query per user session and protection of the user password.

THE VERSION 4 AUTHENTICATION DIALOGUE Although the foregoing scenario enhances security compared to the first attempt, two additional problems remain. The heart of the first problem is the lifetime associated with the ticket-granting ticket. If this lifetime is very short (e.g., minutes), then the user will be repeatedly asked for a password. If the lifetime is long (e.g., hours), then an opponent has a greater opportunity for replay. An opponent could eavesdrop on the network and capture a copy of the ticket-granting ticket and then wait for the legitimate user to log out. Then the opponent could forge the legitimate user's network address and send the message of step (3) to the TGS. This would give the opponent unlimited access to the resources and files available to the legitimate user.

Similarly, if an opponent captures a service-granting ticket and uses it before it expires, the opponent has access to the corresponding service.

Thus, we arrive at an additional requirement. A network service (the TGS or an application service) must be able to prove that the person using a ticket is the same person to whom that ticket was issued.

The second problem is that there may be a requirement for servers to authenticate themselves to users. Without such authentication, an opponent could sabotage the configuration so that messages to a server were directed to another location. The false server then would be in a position to act as a real server, capture any information from the user, and deny the true service to the user.

We examine these problems in turn and refer to Table 4.1, which shows the actual Kerberos protocol.

First, consider the problem of captured ticket-granting tickets and the need to determine that the ticket presenter is the same as the client for whom the ticket was issued. The threat is that an opponent will steal the ticket and use it before it expires.

Table 4.1 Summary of Kerberos Version 4 Message Exchanges

---

(1) $C \rightarrow AS \quad ID_c \| ID_{tgs} \| TS_1$

(2) $AS \rightarrow C \quad E(K_c, [K_{c,tgs} \| ID_{tgs} \| TS_2 \| Lifetime_2 \| Ticket_{tgs}])$

$\qquad Ticket_{tgs} = E(K_{tgs}, [K_{c,tgs} \| ID_C \| AD_C \| ID_{tgs} \| TS_2 \| Lifetime_2])$

(a) Authentication Service Exchange to obtain ticket-granting ticket

---

(3) $C \rightarrow TGS \quad ID_v \| Ticket_{tgs} \| Authenticator_c$

(4) $TGS \rightarrow C \quad E(K_{c,tgs}, [K_{c,v} \| ID_v \| TS_4 \| Ticket_v])$

$\qquad Ticket_{tgs} = E(K_{tgs}, [K_{c,tgs} \| ID_C \| AD_C \| ID_{tgs} \| TS_2 \| Lifetime_2])$

$\qquad Ticket_v = E(K_v, [K_{c,v} \| ID_C \| AD_C \| ID_v \| TS_4 \| Lifetime_4])$

$\qquad Authenticator_c = E(K_{c,tgs}, [ID_C \| AD_C \| TS_3])$

(b) Ticket-Granting Service Exchange to obtain service-granting ticket

---

(5) $C \rightarrow V \quad Ticket_v \| Authenticator_c$

(6) $V \rightarrow C \quad E(K_{c,v}, [TS_5 + 1])$ (for mutual authentication)

$\qquad Ticket_v = E(K_v, [K_{c,v} \| ID_C \| AD_C \| ID_v \| TS_4 \| Lifetime_4])$

$\qquad Authenticator_c = E(K_{c,v}, [ID_C \| AD_C \| TS_5])$

(c) Client/Server Authentication Exchange to obtain service

To get around this problem, let us have the AS provide both the client and the TGS with a secret piece of information in a secure manner. Then the client can prove its identity to the TGS by revealing the secret information, again in a secure manner. An efficient way of accomplishing this is to use an encryption key as the secure information; this is referred to as a session key in Kerberos.

Table 4.1a shows the technique for distributing the session key. As before, the client sends a message to the AS requesting access to the TGS. The AS responds with a message, encrypted with a key derived from the user's password (K_C), that contains the ticket. The encrypted message also contains a copy of the session key, $K_{C,tgs}$, where the subscripts indicate that this is a session key for C and TGS. Because this session key is inside the message encrypted with K_C, only the user's client can read it. The same session key is included in the ticket, which can be read only by the TGS. Thus, the session key has been securely delivered to both C and the TGS.

Note that several additional pieces of information have been added to this first phase of the dialogue. Message (1) includes a timestamp, so that the AS knows that the message is timely. Message (2) includes several elements of the ticket in a form accessible to C. This enables C to confirm that this ticket is for the TGS and to learn its expiration time.

Armed with the ticket and the session key, C is ready to approach the TGS. As before, C sends the TGS a message that includes the ticket plus the ID of the requested service (message (3) in Table 4.1b). In addition, C transmits an authenticator, which includes the ID and address of C's user and a timestamp. Unlike the ticket, which is reusable, the authenticator is intended for use only once and has a very short lifetime. The TGS can decrypt the ticket with the key that it shares with the AS. This ticket indicates that user C has been provided with the session key $K_{C,tgs}$. In effect, the ticket says, "Anyone who uses $K_{C,tgs}$ must be C." The TGS uses the session key to decrypt the authenticator. The TGS can then check the name and address from the authenticator with that of the ticket and with the network address of the incoming message. If all match, then the TGS is assured that the sender of the ticket is indeed the ticket's real owner. In effect, the authenticator says, "At time TS_3, I hereby use $K_{C,tgs}$." Note that the ticket does not prove anyone's identity but is a way to distribute keys securely. It is the authenticator that proves the client's identity. Because the authenticator can be used only once and has a short lifetime, the threat of an opponent stealing both the ticket and the authenticator for presentation later is countered.

The reply from the TGS in message (4) follows the form of message (2). The message is encrypted with the session key shared by the TGS and C and includes a session key to be shared between C and the server V, the ID of V, and the timestamp of the ticket. The ticket itself includes the same session key.

C now has a reusable service-granting ticket for V. When C presents this ticket, as shown in message (5), it also sends an authenticator. The server can decrypt the ticket, recover the session key, and decrypt the authenticator.

If mutual authentication is required, the server can reply as shown in message (6) of Table 4.1. The server returns the value of the timestamp from the authenticator, incremented by 1, and encrypted in the session key. C can decrypt this message to recover the incremented timestamp. Because the message was encrypted by the session key, C is assured that it could have been created only by V. The contents of the message assure C that this is not a replay of an old reply.

Finally, at the conclusion of this process, the client and server share a secret key. This key can be used to encrypt future messages between the two or to exchange a new random session key for that purpose.

Table 4.2 summarizes the justification for each of the elements in the Kerberos protocol, and Figure 4.1 provides a simplified overview of the action.

Table 4.2   Rationale for the Elements of the Kerberos Version 4 Protocol

Message (1)	Client requests ticket-granting ticket.
ID_C	Tells AS identity of user from this client.
ID_{tgs}	Tells AS that user requests access to TGS.
TS_1	Allows AS to verify that client's clock is synchronized with that of AS.
Message (2)	AS returns ticket-granting ticket.
K_c	Encryption is based on user's password, enabling AS and client to verify password, and protecting contents of message (2).
$K_{c,tgs}$	Copy of session key accessible to client created by AS to permit secure exchange between client and TGS without requiring them to share a permanent key.
ID_{tgs}	Confirms that this ticket is for the TGS.
TS_2	Informs client of time this ticket was issued.
$Lifetime_2$	Informs client of the lifetime of this ticket.
$Ticket_{tgs}$	Ticket to be used by client to access TGS.

(a) Authentication Service Exchange

Message (3)	Client requests service-granting ticket.
ID_V	Tells TGS that user requests access to server V.
$Ticket_{tgs}$	Assures TGS that this user has been authenticated by AS.
$Authenticator_c$	Generated by client to validate ticket.
Message (4)	TGS returns service-granting ticket.
$K_{c,tgs}$	Key shared only by C and TGS protects contents of message (4).
$K_{c,v}$	Copy of session key accessible to client created by TGS to permit secure exchange between client and server without requiring them to share a permanent key.
ID_V	Confirms that this ticket is for server V.
TS_4	Informs client of time this ticket was issued.
$Ticket_V$	Ticket to be used by client to access server V.
$Ticket_{tgs}$	Reusable so that user does not have to reenter password.
K_{tgs}	Ticket is encrypted with key known only to AS and TGS, to prevent tampering.
$K_{c,tgs}$	Copy of session key accessible to TGS used to decrypt authenticator, thereby authenticating ticket.

ID_C	Indicates the rightful owner of this ticket.
AD_C	Prevents use of ticket from workstation other than one that initially requested the ticket.
ID_{tgs}	Assures server that it has decrypted ticket properly.
TS_2	Informs TGS of time this ticket was issued.
$Lifetime_2$	Prevents replay after ticket has expired.
$Authenticator_c$	Assures TGS that the ticket presenter is the same as the client for whom the ticket was issued has very short lifetime to prevent replay.
$K_{c,tgs}$	Authenticator is encrypted with key known only to client and TGS, to prevent tampering.
ID_C	Must match ID in ticket to authenticate ticket.
AD_C	Must match address in ticket to authenticate ticket.
TS_3	Informs TGS of time this authenticator was generated.

(b) Ticket-Granting Service Exchange

Message (5)	Client requests service.
$Ticket_V$	Assures server that this user has been authenticated by AS.
$Authenticator_c$	Generated by client to validate ticket.
Message (6)	Optional authentication of server to client.
$K_{c,v}$	Assures C that this message is from V.
$TS_5 + 1$	Assures C that this is not a replay of an old reply.
$Ticket_v$	Reusable so that client does not need to request a new ticket from TGS for each access to the same server.
K_v	Ticket is encrypted with key known only to TGS and server, to prevent tampering.
$K_{c,v}$	Copy of session key accessible to client; used to decrypt authenticator, thereby authenticating ticket.
ID_C	Indicates the rightful owner of this ticket.
AD_C	Prevents use of ticket from workstation other than one that initially requested the ticket.
ID_V	Assures server that it has decrypted ticket properly.
TS_4	Informs server of time this ticket was issued.
$Lifetime_4$	Prevents replay after ticket has expired.
$Authenticator_c$	Assures server that the ticket presenter is the same as the client for whom the ticket was issued; has very short lifetime to prevent replay.
$K_{c,v}$	Authenticator is encrypted with key known only to client and server, to prevent tampering.
ID_C	Must match ID in ticket to authenticate ticket.
AD_c	Must match address in ticket to authenticate ticket.
TS_5	Informs server of time this authenticator was generated.

(c) Client/Server Authentication Exchange

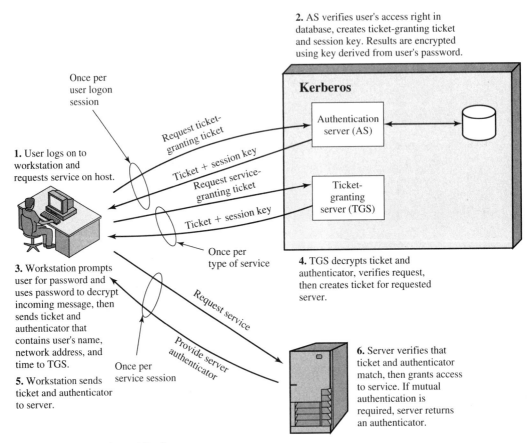

Figure 4.1 Overview of Kerberos

KERBEROS REALMS AND MULTIPLE KERBERI A full-service Kerberos environment consisting of a Kerberos server, a number of clients, and a number of application servers requires the following:

1. The Kerberos server must have the user ID and hashed passwords of all participating users in its database. All users are registered with the Kerberos server.

2. The Kerberos server must share a secret key with each server. All servers are registered with the Kerberos server.

Such an environment is referred to as a **Kerberos realm**. The concept of **realm** can be explained as follows. A Kerberos realm is a set of managed nodes that share the same Kerberos database. The Kerberos database resides on the Kerberos master computer system, which should be kept in a physically secure room. A read-only copy of the Kerberos database might also reside on other Kerberos computer systems. However, all changes to the database must be made on the master computer system. Changing or accessing the contents of a Kerberos database requires the Kerberos master password. A related concept is that of a **Kerberos principal**, which is a service or user that is known to the Kerberos system. Each Kerberos principal is identified by its principal name. Principal names consist of three parts: a service or user name, an instance name, and a realm name

Networks of clients and servers under different administrative organizations typically constitute different realms. That is, it generally is not practical or does not conform to administrative policy to have users and servers in one administrative domain registered with a Kerberos server elsewhere. However, users in one realm may need access to servers in other realms, and some servers may be willing to provide service to users from other realms, provided that those users are authenticated.

Kerberos provides a mechanism for supporting such interrealm authentication. For two realms to support interrealm authentication, a third requirement is added:

3. The Kerberos server in each interoperating realm shares a secret key with the server in the other realm. The two Kerberos servers are registered with each other.

The scheme requires that the Kerberos server in one realm trust the Kerberos server in the other realm to authenticate its users. Furthermore, the participating servers in the second realm also must be willing to trust the Kerberos server in the first realm.

With these ground rules in place, we can describe the mechanism as follows (Figure 4.2): A user wishing service on a server in another realm needs a ticket for that server. The user's client follows the usual procedures to gain access to the local TGS and then requests a ticket-granting ticket for a remote TGS (TGS in another realm). The client can then apply to the remote TGS for a service-granting ticket for the desired server in the realm of the remote TGS.

The details of the exchanges illustrated in Figure 4.2 are as follows (compare Table 4.1).

(1) $C \rightarrow AS$: $ID_C \| ID_{tgs} \| TS_1$

(2) $AS \rightarrow C$: $E(K_C, [K_{C,tgs} \| ID_{tgs} \| TS_2 \| Lifetime_2 \| Ticket_{tgs}])$

(3) $C \rightarrow TGS$: $ID_{tgsrem} \| Ticket_{tgs} \| Authenticator_C$

(4) $TGS \rightarrow C$: $E(K_{C,tgs}, [K_{C,tgsrem} \| ID_{tgsrem} \| TS_4 \| Ticket_{tgsrem}])$

(5) $C \rightarrow TGS_{rem}$: $ID_{Vrem} \| Ticket_{tgsrem} \| Authenticator_C$

(6) $TGS_{rem} \rightarrow C$: $E(K_{C,tgsrem}, [K_{C,Vrem} \| ID_{Vrem} \| TS_6 \| Ticket_{Vrem}])$

(7) $C \rightarrow V_{rem}$: $Ticket_{Vrem} \| Authenticator_C$

The ticket presented to the remote server (V_{rem}) indicates the realm in which the user was originally authenticated. The server chooses whether to honor the remote request.

One problem presented by the foregoing approach is that it does not scale well to many realms. If there are N realms, then there must be $N(N-1)/2$ secure key exchanges so that each Kerberos realm can interoperate with all other Kerberos realms.

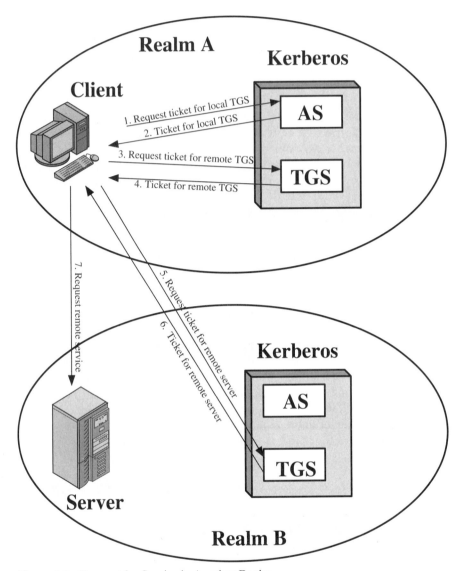

Figure 4.2 Request for Service in Another Realm

Kerberos Version 5

Kerberos version 5 is specified in RFC 4120 and provides a number of improvements over version 4 [KOHL94]. To begin, we provide an overview of the changes from version 4 to version 5 and then look at the version 5 protocol.

DIFFERENCES BETWEEN VERSIONS 4 AND 5 Version 5 is intended to address the limitations of version 4 in two areas: environmental shortcomings and technical deficiencies. We briefly summarize the improvements in each area. Kerberos version

4 did not fully address the need to be of general purpose. This led to the following **environmental shortcomings**.

1. **Encryption system dependence:** Version 4 requires the use of DES. Export restriction on DES as well as doubts about the strength of DES were thus of concern. In version 5, ciphertext is tagged with an encryption-type identifier so that any encryption technique may be used. Encryption keys are tagged with a type and a length, allowing the same key to be used in different algorithms and allowing the specification of different variations on a given algorithm.

2. **Internet protocol dependence:** Version 4 requires the use of Internet Protocol (IP) addresses. Other address types, such as the ISO network address, are not accommodated. Version 5 network addresses are tagged with type and length, allowing any network address type to be used.

3. **Message byte ordering:** In version 4, the sender of a message employs a byte ordering of its own choosing and tags the message to indicate least significant byte in lowest address or most significant byte in lowest address. This techniques works but does not follow established conventions. In version 5, all message structures are defined using Abstract Syntax Notation One (ASN.1) and Basic Encoding Rules (BER), which provide an unambiguous byte ordering.

4. **Ticket lifetime:** Lifetime values in version 4 are encoded in an 8-bit quantity in units of five minutes. Thus, the maximum lifetime that can be expressed is $2^8 \times 5 = 1280$ minutes (a little over 21 hours). This may be inadequate for some applications (e.g., a long-running simulation that requires valid Kerberos credentials throughout execution). In version 5, tickets include an explicit start time and end time, allowing tickets with arbitrary lifetimes.

5. **Authentication forwarding:** Version 4 does not allow credentials issued to one client to be forwarded to some other host and used by some other client. This capability would enable a client to access a server and have that server access another server on behalf of the client. For example, a client issues a request to a print server that then accesses the client's file from a file server, using the client's credentials for access. Version 5 provides this capability.

6. **Interrealm authentication:** In version 4, interoperability among N realms requires on the order of N^2 Kerberos-to-Kerberos relationships, as described earlier. Version 5 supports a method that requires fewer relationships, as described shortly.

Apart from these environmental limitations, there are **technical deficiencies** in the version 4 protocol itself. Most of these deficiencies were documented in [BELL90], and version 5 attempts to address these. The deficiencies are the following.

1. **Double encryption:** Note in Table 4.1 [messages (2) and (4)] that tickets provided to clients are encrypted twice—once with the secret key of the target server and then again with a secret key known to the client. The second encryption is not necessary and is computationally wasteful.

2. **PCBC encryption:** Encryption in version 4 makes use of a nonstandard mode of DES known as **propagating cipher block chaining (PCBC)**.[2] It has been demonstrated that this mode is vulnerable to an attack involving the interchange of ciphertext blocks [KOHL89]. PCBC was intended to provide an integrity check as part of the encryption operation. Version 5 provides explicit integrity mechanisms, allowing the standard CBC mode to be used for encryption. In particular, a checksum or hash code is attached to the message prior to encryption using CBC.

3. **Session keys:** Each ticket includes a session key that is used by the client to encrypt the authenticator sent to the service associated with that ticket. In addition, the session key subsequently may be used by the client and the server to protect messages passed during that session. However, because the same ticket may be used repeatedly to gain service from a particular server, there is the risk that an opponent will replay messages from an old session to the client or the server. In version 5, it is possible for a client and server to negotiate a subsession key, which is to be used only for that one connection. A new access by the client would result in the use of a new subsession key.

4. **Password attacks:** Both versions are vulnerable to a password attack. The message from the AS to the client includes material encrypted with a key based on the client's password.[3] An opponent can capture this message and attempt to decrypt it by trying various passwords. If the result of a test decryption is of the proper form, then the opponent has discovered the client's password and may subsequently use it to gain authentication credentials from Kerberos. This is the same type of password attack described in Chapter 9, with the same kinds of countermeasures being applicable. Version 5 does provide a mechanism known as preauthentication, which should make password attacks more difficult, but it does not prevent them.

THE VERSION 5 AUTHENTICATION DIALOGUE Table 4.3 summarizes the basic version 5 dialogue. This is best explained by comparison with version 4 (Table 4.1).

First, consider the **authentication service exchange**. Message (1) is a client request for a ticket-granting ticket. As before, it includes the ID of the user and the TGS. The following new elements are added:

- **Realm:** Indicates realm of user.
- **Options:** Used to request that certain flags be set in the returned ticket.
- **Times:** Used by the client to request the following time settings in the ticket:

    from: the desired start time for the requested ticket

    till: the requested expiration time for the requested ticket

    rtime: requested renew-till time

- **Nonce:** A random value to be repeated in message (2) to assure that the response is fresh and has not been replayed by an opponent.

---

[2]This is described in Appendix F.

[3]Appendix F describes the mapping of passwords to encryption keys.

Table 4.3 Summary of Kerberos Version 5 Message Exchanges

(1) C → AS $Options \parallel ID_c \parallel Realm_c \parallel ID_{tgs} \parallel Times \parallel Nonce_1$
(2) AS → C $Realm_c \parallel ID_C \parallel Ticket_{tgs} \parallel E(K_c, [K_{c,tgs} \parallel Times \parallel Nonce_1 \parallel Realm_{tgs} \parallel ID_{tgs}])$
$\qquad Ticket_{tgs} = E(K_{tgs}, [Flags \parallel K_{c,tgs} \parallel Realm_c \parallel ID_C \parallel AD_C \parallel Times])$

(a) Authentication Service Exchange to obtain ticket-granting ticket

(3) C → TGS $Options \parallel ID_v \parallel Times \parallel Nonce_2 \parallel Ticket_{tgs} \parallel Authenticator_c$
(4) TGS → C $Realm_c \parallel ID_C \parallel Ticket_v \parallel E(K_{c,tgs}, [K_{c,v} \parallel Times \parallel Nonce_2 \parallel Realm_v \parallel ID_v])$
$\qquad Ticket_{tgs} = E(K_{tgs}, [Flags \parallel K_{c,tgs} \parallel Realm_c \parallel ID_C \parallel AD_C \parallel Times])$
$\qquad Ticket_v = E(K_v, [Flags \parallel K_{c,v} \parallel Realm_c \parallel ID_C \parallel AD_C \parallel Times])$
$\qquad Authenticator_c = E(K_{c,tgs}, [ID_C \parallel Realm_c \parallel TS_1])$

(b) Ticket-Granting Service Exchange to obtain service-granting ticket

(5) C → V $Options \parallel Ticket_v \parallel Authenticator_c$
(6) V → C $E_{KC,v} [TS_2 \parallel Subkey \parallel Seq\#]$
$\qquad Ticket_v = E(K_v, [Flags \parallel K_{c,v} \parallel Realm_c \parallel ID_C \parallel AD_C \parallel Times])$
$\qquad Authenticator_c = E(K_{c,v}, [ID_C \parallel Realm_c \parallel TS_2 \parallel Subkey \parallel Seq\#])$

(c) Client/Server Authentication Exchange to obtain service

Message (2) returns a ticket-granting ticket, identifying information for the client, and a block encrypted using the encryption key based on the user's password. This block includes the session key to be used between the client and the TGS, times specified in message (1), the nonce from message (1), and TGS identifying information. The ticket itself includes the session key, identifying information for the client, the requested time values, and flags that reflect the status of this ticket and the requested options. These flags introduce significant new functionality to version 5. For now, we defer a discussion of these flags and concentrate on the overall structure of the version 5 protocol.

Let us now compare the **ticket-granting service exchange** for versions 4 and 5. We see that message (3) for both versions includes an authenticator, a ticket, and the name of the requested service. In addition, version 5 includes requested times and options for the ticket and a nonce—all with functions similar to those of message (1). The authenticator itself is essentially the same as the one used in version 4.

Message (4) has the same structure as message (2). It returns a ticket plus information needed by the client, with the information encrypted using the session key now shared by the client and the TGS.

Finally, for the **client/server authentication exchange**, several new features appear in version 5. In message (5), the client may request as an option that mutual authentication is required. The authenticator includes several new fields:

- **Subkey:** The client's choice for an encryption key to be used to protect this specific application session. If this field is omitted, the session key from the ticket ($K_{C,V}$) is used.

- **Sequence number:** An optional field that specifies the starting sequence number to be used by the server for messages sent to the client during this session. Messages may be sequence numbered to detect replays.

If mutual authentication is required, the server responds with message (6). This message includes the timestamp from the authenticator. Note that in version 4, the timestamp was incremented by one. This is not necessary in version 5, because the nature of the format of messages is such that it is not possible for an opponent to create message (6) without knowledge of the appropriate encryption keys. The subkey field, if present, overrides the subkey field, if present, in message (5). The optional sequence number field specifies the starting sequence number to be used by the client.

4.3   KEY DISTRIBUTION USING ASYMMETRIC ENCRYPTION

One of the major roles of public-key encryption is to address the problem of key distribution. There are actually two distinct aspects to the use of public-key encryption in this regard.

- The distribution of public keys.
- The use of public-key encryption to distribute secret keys.

We examine each of these areas in turn.

Public-Key Certificates

On the face of it, the point of public-key encryption is that the public key is public. Thus, if there is some broadly accepted public-key algorithm, such as RSA, any participant can send his or her public key to any other participant or broadcast the key to the community at large. Although this approach is convenient, it has a major weakness. Anyone can forge such a public announcement. That is, some user could pretend to be user A and send a public key to another participant or broadcast such a public key. Until such time as user A discovers the forgery and alerts other participants, the forger is able to read all encrypted messages intended for A and can use the forged keys for authentication.

The solution to this problem is the **public-key certificate**. In essence, a certificate consists of a public key plus a user ID of the key owner, with the whole block signed by a trusted third party. Typically, the third party is a certificate authority (CA) that is trusted by the user community, such as a government agency or a financial institution. A user can present his or her public key to the authority in a secure manner and obtain a certificate. The user can then publish the certificate. Anyone needing this user's public key can obtain the certificate and verify that it is valid by way of the attached trusted signature. Figure 4.3 illustrates the process.

One scheme has become universally accepted for formatting public-key certificates: the X.509 standard. X.509 certificates are used in most network security applications, including IP security, secure sockets layer (SSL), secure electronic

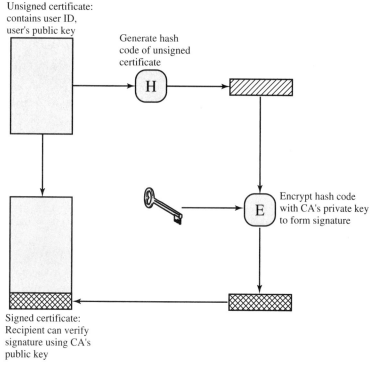

Unsigned certificate:
contains user ID,
user's public key

Generate hash
code of unsigned
certificate

H

Encrypt hash code
with CA's private key
to form signature

E

Signed certificate:
Recipient can verify
signature using CA's
public key

Figure 4.3   Public-Key Certificate Use

transactions (SET), and S/MIME — all of which are discussed in Part Two. X.509 is examined in detail in the next section.

Public-Key Distribution of Secret Keys

With conventional encryption, a fundamental requirement for two parties to communicate securely is that they share a secret key. Suppose Bob wants to create a messaging application that will enable him to exchange e-mail securely with anyone who has access to the Internet or to some other network that the two of them share. Suppose Bob wants to do this using conventional encryption. With conventional encryption, Bob and his correspondent, say, Alice, must come up with a way to share a unique secret key that no one else knows. How are they going to do that? If Alice is in the next room from Bob, Bob could generate a key and write it down on a piece of paper or store it on a diskette and hand it to Alice. But if Alice is on the other side of the continent or the world, what can Bob do? He could encrypt this key using conventional encryption and e-mail it to Alice, but this means that Bob and Alice must share a secret key to encrypt this new secret key. Furthermore, Bob and everyone else who uses this new e-mail package faces the same problem with every potential correspondent: Each pair of correspondents must share a unique secret key.

One approach is the use of Diffie-Hellman key exchange. This approach is indeed widely used. However, it suffers the drawback that, in its simplest form, Diffie-Hellman provides no authentication of the two communicating partners.

A powerful alternative is the use of public-key certificates. When Bob wishes to communicate with Alice, Bob can do the following:

1. Prepare a message.
2. Encrypt that message using conventional encryption with a one-time conventional session key.
3. Encrypt the session key using public-key encryption with Alice's public key.
4. Attach the encrypted session key to the message and send it to Alice.

Only Alice is capable of decrypting the session key and therefore of recovering the original message. If Bob obtained Alice's public key by means of Alice's public-key certificate, then Bob is assured that it is a valid key.

4.4   X.509 CERTIFICATES

ITU-T recommendation X.509 is part of the X.500 series of recommendations that define a directory service. The directory is, in effect, a server or distributed set of servers that maintains a database of information about users. The information includes a mapping from user name to network address, as well as other attributes and information about the users.

X.509 defines a framework for the provision of authentication services by the X.500 directory to its users. The directory may serve as a repository of public-key certificates. Each certificate contains the public key of a user and is signed with the private key of a trusted certification authority. In addition, X.509 defines alternative authentication protocols based on the use of public-key certificates.

X.509 is an important standard because the certificate structure and authentication protocols defined in X.509 are used in a variety of contexts. For example, the X.509 certificate format is used in S/MIME (Chapter 7), IP Security (Chapter 8), and SSL/TLS (Chapter 5).

X.509 was initially issued in 1988. The standard was subsequently revised to address some of the security concerns documented in [IANS90] and [MITC90]; a revised recommendation was issued in 1993. A third version was issued in 1995 and revised in 2000.

X.509 is based on the use of public-key cryptography and digital signatures. The standard does not dictate the use of a specific algorithm but recommends RSA. The digital signature scheme is assumed to require the use of a hash function. Again, the standard does not dictate a specific hash algorithm. The 1988 recommendation included the description of a recommended hash algorithm; this algorithm has since been shown to be insecure and was dropped from the 1993 recommendation. Figure 4.3 illustrates the generation of a public-key certificate.

Certificates

The heart of the X.509 scheme is the public-key certificate associated with each user. These user certificates are assumed to be created by some trusted certification authority (CA) and placed in the directory by the CA or by the user. The directory server itself is not responsible for the creation of public keys or for the

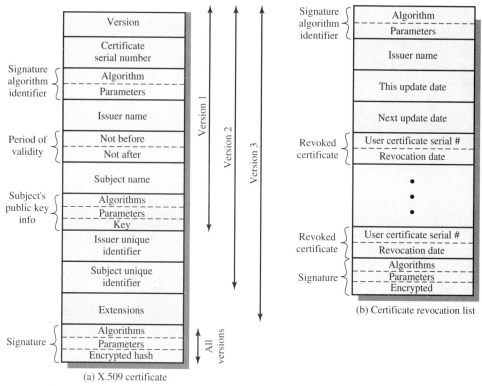

Figure 4.4   X.509 Formats

certification function; it merely provides an easily accessible location for users to obtain certificates.

Figure 4.4a shows the general format of a certificate, which includes the following elements.

- **Version:** Differentiates among successive versions of the certificate format; the default is version 1. If the Issuer Unique Identifier or Subject Unique Identifier are present, the value must be version 2. If one or more extensions are present, the version must be version 3.
- **Serial number:** An integer value, unique within the issuing CA, that is unambiguously associated with this certificate.
- **Signature algorithm identifier:** The algorithm used to sign the certificate, together with any associated parameters. Because this information is repeated in the Signature field at the end of the certificate, this field has little, if any, utility.
- **Issuer name:** X.500 name of the CA that created and signed this certificate.
- **Period of validity:** Consists of two dates: the first and last on which the certificate is valid.
- **Subject name:** The name of the user to whom this certificate refers. That is, this certificate certifies the public key of the subject who holds the corresponding private key.

- **Subject's public-key information:** The public key of the subject, plus an identifier of the algorithm for which this key is to be used, together with any associated parameters.
- **Issuer unique identifier:** An optional bit string field used to identify uniquely the issuing CA in the event the X.500 name has been reused for different entities.
- **Subject unique identifier:** An optional bit string field used to identify uniquely the subject in the event the X.500 name has been reused for different entities.
- **Extensions:** A set of one or more extension fields. Extensions were added in version 3 and are discussed later in this section.
- **Signature:** Covers all of the other fields of the certificate; it contains the hash code of the other fields encrypted with the CA's private key. This field includes the signature algorithm identifier.

The unique identifier fields were added in version 2 to handle the possible reuse of subject and/or issuer names over time. These fields are rarely used.

The standard uses the following notation to define a certificate:

$$CA<<A>> = CA \{V, SN, AI, CA, UCA, A, UA, Ap, T^A\}$$

where

$Y<<X>>$ = the certificate of user X issued by certification authority Y

$Y \{I\}$ = the signing of I by Y; consists of I with an encrypted hash code appended

V = version of the certificate

SN = serial number of the certificate

AI = identifier of the algorithm used to sign the certificate

CA = name of certificate authority

UCA = optional unique identifier of the CA

A = name of user A

UA = optional unique identifier of the user A

Ap = public key of user A

T^A = period of validity of the certificate

The CA signs the certificate with its private key. If the corresponding public key is known to a user, then that user can verify that a certificate signed by the CA is valid. This is the typical digital signature approach, as illustrated in Figure 4.5.

OBTAINING A USER'S CERTIFICATE User certificates generated by a CA have the following characteristics:

- Any user with access to the public key of the CA can verify the user public key that was certified.
- No party other than the certification authority can modify the certificate without this being detected.

Bob   ## Alice

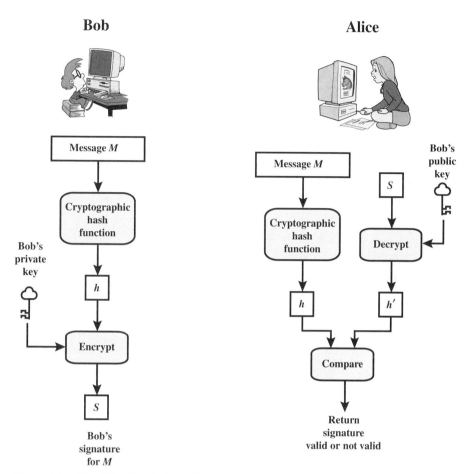

Figure 4.5   Simplified Depiction of Essential Elements of Digital Signature Process

Because certificates are unforgeable, they can be placed in a directory without the need for the directory to make special efforts to protect them.

If all users subscribe to the same CA, then there is a common trust of that CA. All user certificates can be placed in the directory for access by all users. In addition, a user can transmit his or her certificate directly to other users. In either case, once B is in possession of A's certificate, B has confidence that messages it encrypts with A's public key will be secure from eavesdropping and that messages signed with A's private key are unforgeable.

If there is a large community of users, it may not be practical for all users to subscribe to the same CA. Because it is the CA that signs certificates, each partic-ipating user must have a copy of the CA's own public key to verify signatures. This public key must be provided to each user in an absolutely secure way (with respect to integrity and authenticity) so that the user has confidence in the associated certificates. Thus, with many users, it may be more practical for there to be a number of CAs, each of which securely provides its public key to some fraction of the users.

Now suppose that A has obtained a certificate from certification authority X_1 and B has obtained a certificate from CA X_2. If A does not securely know the public key of X_2, then B's certificate, issued by X_2, is useless to A. A can read B's certificate, but A cannot verify the signature. However, if the two CAs have securely exchanged their own public keys, the following procedure will enable A to obtain B's public key.

1. A obtains (from the directory) the certificate of X_2 signed by X_1. Because A securely knows X_1's public key, A can obtain X_2's public key from its certificate and verify it by means of X_1's signature on the certificate.

2. A then goes back to the directory and obtains the certificate of B signed by X_2. Because A now has a trusted copy of X_2's public key, A can verify the signature and securely obtain B's public key.

A has used a chain of certificates to obtain B's public key. In the notation of X.509, this chain is expressed as

$$X_1 <<X_2>>\ X_2<<B>>$$

In the same fashion, B can obtain A's public key with the reverse chain:

$$X_2 <<X_1>>\ X_1<<A>>$$

This scheme need not be limited to a chain of two certificates. An arbitrarily long path of CAs can be followed to produce a chain. A chain with N elements would be expressed as

$$X_1 <<X_2>>\ X_2<<X_3>>.\ .\ .\ X_N<<B>>$$

In this case, each pair of CAs in the chain (X_i, X_{i+1}) must have created certificates for each other.

All of these certificates of CAs by CAs need to appear in the directory, and the user needs to know how they are linked to follow a path to another user's public-key certificate. X.509 suggests that CAs be arranged in a hierarchy so that navigation is straightforward.

Figure 4.6, taken from X.509, is an example of such a hierarchy. The connected circles indicate the hierarchical relationship among the CAs; the associated boxes indicate certificates maintained in the directory for each CA entry. The directory entry for each CA includes two types of certificates:

- **Forward certificates:** Certificates of X generated by other CAs
- **Reverse certificates:** Certificates generated by X that are the certificates of other CAs

In this example, user A can acquire the following certificates from the directory to establish a certification path to B:

$$X <<W>>\ W<<V>>\ V<<Y>>\ Y<<Z>>\ Z<<B>>$$

When A has obtained these certificates, it can unwrap the certification path in sequence to recover a trusted copy of B's public key. Using this public key, A can send encrypted messages to B. If A wishes to receive encrypted messages back from

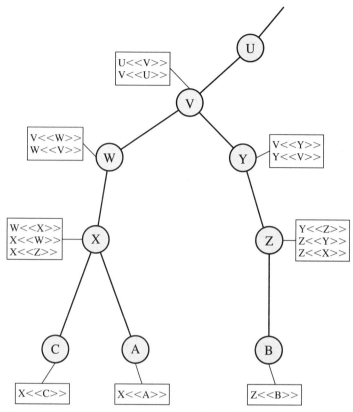

Figure 4.6 X.509 Hierarchy: A Hypothetical Example

B, or to sign messages sent to B, then B will require A's public key, which can be obtained from the certification path:

$$Z<<Y>> \; Y<<V>> \; V<<W>> \; W<<X>> \; X<<A>>$$

B can obtain this set of certificates from the directory, or A can provide them as part of its initial message to B.

REVOCATION OF CERTIFICATES Recall from Figure 4.4 that each certificate includes a period of validity, much like a credit card. Typically, a new certificate is issued just before the expiration of the old one. In addition, it may be desirable on occasion to revoke a certificate before it expires for one of the following reasons.

1. The user's private key is assumed to be compromised.
2. The user is no longer certified by this CA. Reasons for this include subject's name has changed, the certificate is superseded, or the certificate was not issued in conformance with the CA's policies.
3. The CA's certificate is assumed to be compromised.

Each CA must maintain a list consisting of all revoked but not expired certificates issued by that CA, including both those issued to users and to other CAs. These lists also should be posted on the directory.

Each certificate revocation list (CRL) posted to the directory is signed by the issuer and includes (Figure 4.4b) the issuer's name, the date the list was created, the date the next CRL is scheduled to be issued, and an entry for each revoked certificate. Each entry consists of the serial number of a certificate and revocation date for that certificate. Because serial numbers are unique within a CA, the serial number is sufficient to identify the certificate.

When a user receives a certificate in a message, the user must determine whether the certificate has been revoked. The user could check the directory each time a certificate is received. To avoid the delays (and possible costs) associated with directory searches, it is likely that the user would maintain a local cache of certificates and lists of revoked certificates.

X.509 Version 3

The X.509 version 2 format does not convey all of the information that recent design and implementation experience has shown to be needed. [FORD95] lists the following requirements not satisfied by version 2:

1. The Subject field is inadequate to convey the identity of a key owner to a public-key user. X.509 names may be relatively short and lacking in obvious identification details that may be needed by the user.

2. The Subject field is also inadequate for many applications, which typically recognize entities by an Internet e-mail address, a URL, or some other Internet-related identification.

3. There is a need to indicate security policy information. This enables a security application or function, such as IPSec, to relate an X.509 certificate to a given policy.

4. There is a need to limit the damage that can result from a faulty or malicious CA by setting constraints on the applicability of a particular certificate.

5. It is important to be able to identify different keys used by the same owner at different times. This feature supports key life cycle management, in particular the ability to update key pairs for users and CAs on a regular basis or under exceptional circumstances.

Rather than continue to add fields to a fixed format, standards developers felt that a more flexible approach was needed. Thus, version 3 includes a number of optional extensions that may be added to the version 2 format. Each extension consists of an extension identifier, a criticality indicator, and an extension value. The criticality indicator indicates whether an extension can be safely ignored. If the indicator has a value of TRUE and an implementation does not recognize the extension, it must treat the certificate as invalid.

The certificate extensions fall into three main categories: key and policy information, subject and issuer attributes, and certification path constraints.

KEY AND POLICY INFORMATION These extensions convey additional information about the subject and issuer keys, plus indicators of certificate policy. A certificate policy is a named set of rules that indicates the applicability of a certificate to a particular community and/or class of application with common security requirements. For example, a policy might be applicable to the authentication of electronic data interchange (EDI) transactions for the trading of goods within a given price range.

This area includes:

- **Authority key identifier:** Identifies the public key to be used to verify the signature on this certificate or CRL. Enables distinct keys of the same CA to be differentiated. One use of this field is to handle CA key pair updating.

- **Subject key identifier:** Identifies the public key being certified. Useful for subject key pair updating. Also, a subject may have multiple key pairs and, correspondingly, different certificates for different purposes (e.g., digital signature and encryption key agreement).

- **Key usage:** Indicates a restriction imposed as to the purposes for which, and the policies under which, the certified public key may be used. May indicate one or more of the following: digital signature, nonrepudiation, key encryption, data encryption, key agreement, CA signature verification on certificates, and CA signature verification on CRLs.

- **Private-key usage period:** Indicates the period of use of the private key corresponding to the public key. Typically, the private key is used over a different period from the validity of the public key. For example, with digital signature keys, the usage period for the signing private key is typically shorter than that for the verifying public key.

- **Certificate policies:** Certificates may be used in environments where multiple policies apply. This extension lists policies that the certificate is recognized as supporting, together with optional qualifier information.

- **Policy mappings:** Used only in certificates for CAs issued by other CAs. Policy mappings allow an issuing CA to indicate that one or more of that issuer's policies can be considered equivalent to another policy used in the subject CA's domain.

CERTIFICATE SUBJECT AND ISSUER ATTRIBUTES These extensions support alternative names, in alternative formats, for a certificate subject or certificate issuer and can convey additional information about the certificate subject to increase a certificate user's confidence that the certificate subject is a particular person or entity. For example, information such as postal address, position within a corporation, or picture image may be required.

The extension fields in this area include:

- **Subject alternative name:** Contains one or more alternative names, using any of a variety of forms. This field is important for supporting certain applications, such as electronic mail, EDI, and IPSec, which may employ their own name forms.

- **Issuer alternative name:** Contains one or more alternative names, using any of a variety of forms.

- **Subject directory attributes:** Conveys any desired X.500 directory attribute values for the subject of this certificate.

CERTIFICATION PATH CONSTRAINTS These extensions allow constraint specifications to be included in certificates issued for CAs by other CAs. The constraints may restrict the types of certificates that can be issued by the subject CA or that may occur subsequently in a certification chain.

The extension fields in this area include:

- **Basic constraints:** Indicates if the subject may act as a CA. If so, a certification path length constraint may be specified.
- **Name constraints:** Indicates a name space within which all subject names in subsequent certificates in a certification path must be located.
- **Policy constraints:** Specifies constraints that may require explicit certificate policy identification or inhibit policy mapping for the remainder of the certification path.

4.5 PUBLIC-KEY INFRASTRUCTURE

RFC 2822 (*Internet Security Glossary*) defines public-key infrastructure (PKI) as the set of hardware, software, people, policies, and procedures needed to create, manage, store, distribute, and revoke digital certificates based on asymmetric cryptography. The principal objective for developing a PKI is to enable secure, convenient, and efficient acquisition of public keys. The Internet Engineering Task Force (IETF) Public Key Infrastructure X.509 (PKIX) working group has been the driving force behind setting up a formal (and generic) model based on X.509 that is suitable for deploying a certificate-based architecture on the Internet. This section describes the PKIX model.

Figure 4.7 shows the interrelationship among the key elements of the PKIX model. These elements are

- **End entity:** A generic term used to denote end users, devices (e.g., servers, routers), or any other entity that can be identified in the subject field of a public key certificate. End entities typically consume and/or support PKI-related services.
- **Certification authority (CA):** The issuer of certificates and (usually) certificate revocation lists (CRLs). It may also support a variety of administrative functions, although these are often delegated to one or more registration authorities.
- **Registration authority (RA):** An optional component that can assume a number of administrative functions from the CA. The RA is often associated with the end entity registration process, but can assist in a number of other areas as well.
- **CRL issuer:** An optional component that a CA can delegate to publish CRLs.
- **Repository:** A generic term used to denote any method for storing certificates and CRLs so that they can be retrieved by end entities.

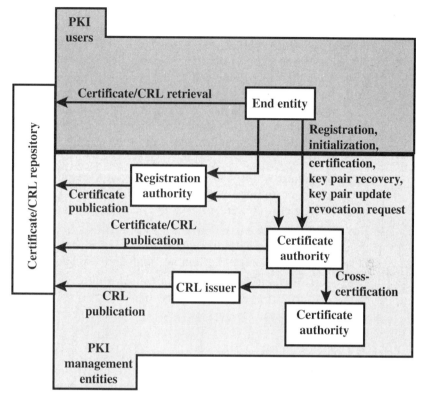

Figure 4.7   PKIX Architectural Model

PKIX Management Functions

PKIX identifies a number of management functions that potentially need to be supported by management protocols. These are indicated in Figure 4.7 and include the following:

- **Registration:** This is the process whereby a user first makes itself known to a CA (directly, or through an RA), prior to that CA issuing a certificate or certificates for that user. Registration begins the process of enrolling in a PKI. Registration usually involves some off-line or online procedure for mutual authentication. Typically, the end entity is issued one or more shared secret keys used for subsequent authentication.

- **Initialization:** Before a client system can operate securely, it is necessary to install key materials that have the appropriate relationship with keys stored elsewhere in the infrastructure. For example, the client needs to be securely initialized with the public key and other assured information of the trusted CA(s) to be used in validating certificate paths.

- **Certification:** This is the process in which a CA issues a certificate for a user's public key and returns that certificate to the user's client system and/or posts that certificate in a repository.

- **Key pair recovery:** Key pairs can be used to support digital signature creation and verification, encryption and decryption, or both. When a key pair is used for encryption/decryption, it is important to provide a mechanism to recover the necessary decryption keys when normal access to the keying material is no longer possible, otherwise it will not be possible to recover the encrypted data. Loss of access to the decryption key can result from forgotten passwords/PINs, corrupted disk drives, damage to hardware tokens, and so on. Key pair recovery allows end entities to restore their encryption/decryption key pair from an authorized key backup facility (typically, the CA that issued the end entity's certificate).

- **Key pair update:** All key pairs need to be updated regularly (i.e., replaced with a new key pair) and new certificates issued. Update is required when the certificate lifetime expires and as a result of certificate revocation.

- **Revocation request:** An authorized person advises a CA of an abnormal situation requiring certificate revocation. Reasons for revocation include private key compromise, change in affiliation, and name change.

- **Cross certification:** Two CAs exchange information used in establishing a cross-certificate. A cross-certificate is a certificate issued by one CA to another CA that contains a CA signature key used for issuing certificates.

PKIX Management Protocols

The PKIX working group has defines two alternative management protocols between PKIX entities that support the management functions listed in the preceding subsection. RFC 2510 defines the certificate management protocols (CMP). Within CMP, each of the management functions is explicitly identified by specific protocol exchanges. CMP is designed to be a flexible protocol able to accommodate a variety of technical, operational, and business models.

RFC 2797 defines certificate management messages over CMS (CMC), where CMS refers to RFC 2630, cryptographic message syntax. CMC is built on earlier work and is intended to leverage existing implementations. Although all of the PKIX functions are supported, the functions do not all map into specific protocol exchanges.

4.6   FEDERATED IDENTITY MANAGEMENT

Federated identity management is a relatively new concept dealing with the use of a common identity management scheme across multiple enterprises and numerous applications and supporting many thousands, even millions, of users. We begin our overview with a discussion of the concept of identity management and then examine federated identity management.

Identity Management

Identity management is a centralized, automated approach to provide enterprise-wide access to resources by employees and other authorized individuals. The focus of identity management is defining an identity for each user (human or process), associating attributes with the identity, and enforcing a means by which a user can verify identity. The central concept of an identity management system is the use of single sign-on (SSO). SSO enables a user to access all network resources after a single authentication.

[PELT07] lists the following as the principal elements of an identity management system.

- **Authentication:** Confirmation that a user corresponds to the user name provided.

- **Authorization:** Granting access to specific services and/or resources based on the authentication.

- **Accounting:** A process for logging access and authorization.

- **Provisioning:** The enrollment of users in the system.

- **Workflow automation:** Movement of data in a business process.

- **Delegated administration:** The use of role-based access control to grant permissions.

- **Password synchronization:** Creating a process for single sign-on (SSO) or reduced sign-on (RSO). Single sign-on enables a user to access all network resources after a single authentication. RSO may involve multiple sign-ons but requires less user effort than if each resource and service maintained its own authentication facility.

- **Self-service password reset:** Enables the user to modify his or her password.

- **Federation:** A process where authentication and permission will be passed on from one system to another—usually across multiple enterprises, thereby reducing the number of authentications needed by the user.

Note that Kerberos contains a number of the elements of an identity management system.

Figure 4.8 [LINN06] illustrates entities and data flows in a generic identity management architecture. A **principal** is an identity holder. Typically, this is a human user that seeks access to resources and services on the network. User devices, agent processes, and server systems may also function as principals. Principals authenticate themselves to an **identity provider**. The identity provider associates authentication information with a principal, as well as attributes and one or more identifiers.

Increasingly, digital identities incorporate attributes other than simply an identifier and authentication information (such as passwords and biometric information). An **attribute service** manages the creation and maintenance of such attributes. For example, a user needs to provide a shipping address each time an order is placed at a new Web merchant, and this information needs to be revised when the user moves. Identity management enables the user to provide this information once, so that it is maintained in a single place and released to data consumers in accordance with authorization and privacy policies. Users may create some of the attributes to be associated with their digital identity, such as address. **Administrators** may also assign attributes to users, such as roles, access permissions, and employee information.

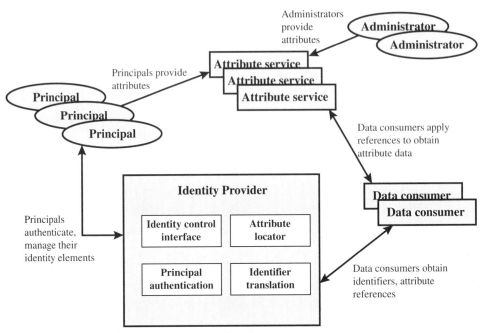

Figure 4.8   Generic Identity Management Architecture

Data consumers are entities that obtain and employ data maintained and provided by identity and attribute providers, which are often used to support authorization decisions and to collect audit information. For example, a database server or file server is a data consumer that needs a client's credentials so as to know what access to provide to that client.

Identity Federation

Identity federation is, in essence, an extension of identity management to multiple security domains. Such domains include autonomous internal business units, external business partners, and other third-party applications and services. The goal is to provide the sharing of digital identities so that a user can be authenticated a single time and then access applications and resources across multiple domains. Because these domains are relatively autonomous or independent, no centralized control is possible. Rather, the cooperating organizations must form a federation based on agreed standards and mutual levels of trust to securely share digital identities.

Federated identity management refers to the agreements, standards, and technologies that enable the portability of identities, identity attributes, and entitlements across multiple enterprises and numerous applications and supporting many thousands, even millions, of users. When multiple organizations implement interoperable federated identity schemes, an employee in one organization can use a single sign-on to access services across the federation with trust relationships associated with the identity. For example, an employee may log onto her corporate intranet and be authenticated to perform authorized functions and access authorized services on that intranet. The employee could then access their health benefits from an outside health-care provider without having to reauthenticate.

Beyond SSO, federated identity management provides other capabilities. One is a standardized means of representing attributes. Increasingly, digital identities incorporate attributes other than simply an identifier and authentication information (such as passwords and biometric information). Examples of attributes include account numbers, organizational roles, physical location, and file ownership. A user may have multiple identifiers; for example, each identifier may be associated with a unique role with its own access permissions.

Another key function of federated identity management is identity mapping. Different security domains may represent identities and attributes differently. Furthermore, the amount of information associated with an individual in one domain may be more than is necessary in another domain. The federated identity management protocols map identities and attributes of a user in one domain to the requirements of another domain.

Figure 4.9 illustrates entities and data flows in a generic federated identity management architecture.

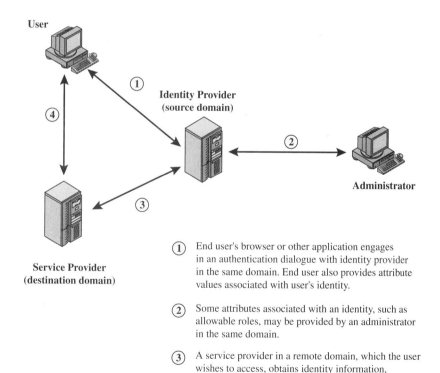

User

Identity Provider (source domain)

Administrator

Service Provider (destination domain)

(1) End user's browser or other application engages in an authentication dialogue with identity provider in the same domain. End user also provides attribute values associated with user's identity.

(2) Some attributes associated with an identity, such as allowable roles, may be provided by an administrator in the same domain.

(3) A service provider in a remote domain, which the user wishes to access, obtains identity information, authentication information, and associated attributes from the identity provider in the source domain.

(4) Service provider opens session with remote user and enforces access control restrictions based on user's identity and attributes.

Figure 4.9   Federated Identity Operation

The identity provider acquires attribute information through dialogue and protocol exchanges with users and administrators. For example, a user needs to provide a shipping address each time an order is placed at a new Web merchant, and this information needs to be revised when the user moves. Identity management enables the user to provide this information once, so that it is maintained in a single place and released to data consumers in accordance with authorization and privacy policies.

Service providers are entities that obtain and employ data maintained and provided by identity providers, often to support authorization decisions and to collect audit information. For example, a database server or file server is a data consumer that needs a client's credentials so as to know what access to provide to that client. A service provider can be in the same domain as the user and the identity provider. The power of this approach is for federated identity management, in which the service provider is in a different domain (e.g., a vendor or supplier network).

STANDARDS Federated identity management uses a number of standards as the building blocks for secure identity exchange across different domains or heterogeneous systems. In essence, organizations issue some form of security tickets for their users that can be processed by cooperating partners. Identity federation standards are thus concerned with defining these tickets in terms of content and format, providing protocols for exchanging tickets, and performing a number of management tasks. These tasks include configuring systems to perform attribute transfers and identity mapping and performing logging and auditing functions.

The principal underlying standard for federated identity is the Security Assertion Markup Language (SAML), which defines the exchange of security information between online business partners. SAML conveys authentication information in the form of assertions about subjects. Assertions are statements about the subject issued by an authoritative entity.

SAML is part of a broader collection of standards being issued by the Organization for the Advancement of Structured Information Standards (OASIS) for federated identity management. For example, WS-Federation enables browser-based federation; it relies on a security token service to broker trust of identities, attributes, and authentication between participating Web services.

The challenge with federated identity management is to integrate multiple technologies, standards, and services to provide a secure, user-friendly utility. The key, as in most areas of security and networking, is the reliance on a few mature standards widely accepted by industry. Federated identity management seems to have reached this level of maturity.

EXAMPLES To get some feel for the functionality of identity federation, we look at three scenarios, taken from [COMP06]. In the first scenario (Figure 4.10a), Workplace.com contracts with Health.com to provide employee health benefits. An employee uses a Web interface to sign on to Workplace.com and goes through an authentication procedure there. This enables the employee to access authorized services and resources at Workplace.com. When the employee clicks

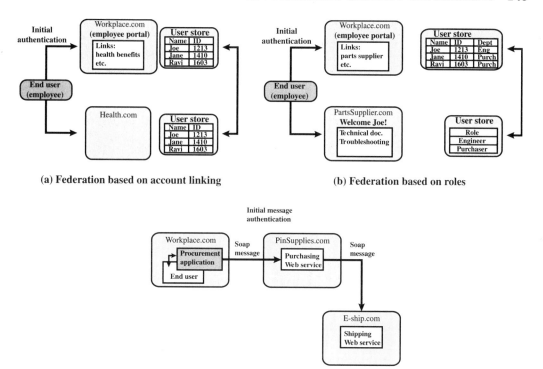

(a) Federation based on account linking

(b) Federation based on roles

(b) Chained Web services

Figure 4.10   Federated Identity Scenarios

on a link to access health benefits, her browser is redirected to Health.com. At the same time, the Workplace.com software passes the user's identifier to Health.com in a secure manner. The two organizations are part of a federation that cooperatively exchanges user identifiers. Health.com maintains user identities for every employee at Workplace.com and associates with each identity health-benefits information and access rights. In this example, the linkage between the two companies is based on account information and user participation is browser based.

Figure 4.10b shows a second type of browser-based scheme. PartsSupplier.com is a regular supplier of parts to Workplace.com. In this case, a role-based access-control (RBAC) scheme is used for access to information. An engineer of Workplace.com authenticates at the employee portal at Workplace.com and clicks on a link to access information at PartsSupplier.com. Because the user is authenticated in the role of an engineer, he is taken to the technical documentation and troubleshooting portion of PartSupplier.com's Web site without having to sign on. Similarly, an employee in a purchasing role signs on at Workplace.com and is authorized, in that role, to place purchases at PartSupplier.com without having to authenticate to PartSupplier.com. For this scenario, PartSupplier.com does not have identity information for individual employees at Workplace.com. Rather, the linkage between the two federated partners is in terms of roles.

The scenario illustrated in Figure 4.10c can be referred to as document based rather than browser based. In this third example, Workplace.com has a purchasing agreement with PinSupplies.com, and PinSupplies.com has a business relationship with E-Ship.com. An employee of Workplace.com signs on and is authenticated to make purchases. The employee goes to a procurement application that provides a list of Workplace.com's suppliers and the parts that can be ordered. The user clicks on the PinSupplies button and is presented with a purchase order Web page (HTML page). The employee fills out the form and clicks the submit button. The procurement application generates an XML/SOAP document that it inserts into the envelope body of an XML-based message. The procurement application then inserts the user's credentials in the envelope header of the message, together with Workplace.com's organizational identity. The procurement application posts the message to the PinSupplies.com's purchasing Web service. This service authenticates the incoming message and processes the request. The purchasing Web service then sends a SOAP message its shipping partner to fulfill the order. The message includes a PinSupplies.com security token in the envelope header and the list of items to be shipped as well as the end user's shipping information in the envelope body. The shipping Web service authenticates the request and processes the shipment order.

4.7   RECOMMENDED READING AND WEB SITES

An exhaustive and essential resource on the topics of this chapter is the three-volume NIST SP800-57 [BARK07b. BARK07c, BARK08]. [FUMY93] is a good survey of key management principles. Another interesting survey, which looks at many key management techniques, is [HEGL06].

A painless way to get a grasp of Kerberos concepts is found in [BRYA88]. One of the best treatments of Kerberos is [KOHL94].

[PERL99] reviews various trust models that can be used in a PKI. [GUTM02] highlights difficulties in PKI use and recommends approaches for an effective PKI.

[SHIM05] provides a brief overview of federated identity management and examines one approach to standardization. [BHAT07] describes an integrated approach to federated identity management couple with management of access control privileges.

BARK07b   Barker, E., et al. *Recommendation for Key Management—Part 1: General.* NIST SP800-57, March 2007.

BARK07c   Barker, E., et al. *Recommendation for Key Management—Part 2: Best Practices for Key Management Organization.* NIST SP800-57, March 2007.

BARK08   Barker, E., et al. *Recommendation for Key Management—Part 3: Specific Key Management Guidance.* NIST SP800-57, August 2008.

BHAT07   Bhatti, R.; Bertino, E.; and Ghafoor, A. "An Integrated Approach to Federated Identity and Privilege Management in Open Systems." *Communications of the ACM,* February 2007.

BRYA88 Bryant, W. *Designing an Authentication System: A Dialogue in Four Scenes.* Project Athena document, February 1988. Available at http://web.mit.edu/kerberos/www/dialogue.html.

FUMY93 Fumy, S., and Landrock, P. "Principles of Key Management." *IEEE Journal on Selected Areas in Communications*, June 1993.

GUTM02 Gutmann, P. "PKI: It's Not Dead, Just Resting." *Computer*, August 2002.

HEGL06 Hegland, A., et al. "A Survey of Key Management in Ad Hoc Networks." *IEEE Communications Surveys & Tutorials.* 3rd Quarter, 2006.

KOHL94 Kohl, J.; Neuman, B.; and Ts'o, T. "The Evolution of the Kerberos Authentication Service." in Brazier, F., and Johansen, D. *Distributed Open Systems.* Los Alamitos, CA: IEEE Computer Society Press, 1994. Available at http://web.mit.edu/kerberos/www/papers.html.

PERL99 Perlman, R. "An Overview of PKI Trust Models." *IEEE Network*, November/December 1999.

SHIM05 Shim, S.; Bhalla, G.; and Pendyala, V. "Federated Identity Management." *Computer*, December 2005.

Recommended Web Sites:

- **MIT Kerberos Site:** Information about Kerberos, including the FAQ, papers and documents, and pointers to commercial product sites.
- **MIT Kerberos Consortium:** Created to establish Kerberos as the universal authentication platform for the world's computer networks.
- **USC/ISI Kerberos Page:** Another good source of Kerberos material.
- **Kerberos Working Group:** IETF group developing standards based on Kerberos.
- **Public-Key Infrastructure Working Group:** IETF group developing standards based on X.509v3.
- **Verisign:** A leading commercial vendor of X.509-related products; white papers and other worthwhile material at this site.
- **NIST PKI Program:** Good source of information.

4.8 KEY TERMS, REVIEW QUESTIONS, AND PROBLEMS

Key Terms

authentication	Kerberos	key management
authentication server (AS)	Kerberos realm	master key
federated identity management	key distribution	mutual authentication
identity management	key distribution center (KDC)	nonce
		one-way authentication

| propagating cipher block chaining (PCBC) mode public-key certificate public-key directory | realm replay attack ticket | ticket-granting server (TGS) timestamp X.509 certificate |

Review Questions

4.1 List ways in which secret keys can be distributed to two communicating parties.

4.2 What is the difference between a session key and a master key?

4.3 What is a key distribution center?

4.4 What entities constitute a full-service Kerberos environment?

4.5 In the context of Kerberos, what is a realm?

4.6 What are the principal differences between version 4 and version 5 of Kerberos?

4.7 What is a nonce?

4.8 What are two different uses of public-key cryptography related to key distribution?

4.9 What are the essential ingredients of a public-key directory?

4.10 What is a public-key certificate?

4.11 What are the requirements for the use of a public-key certificate scheme?

4.12 What is the purpose of the X.509 standard?

4.13 What is a chain of certificates?

4.14 How is an X.509 certificate revoked?

Problems

4.1 "We are under great pressure, Holmes." Detective Lestrade looked nervous. "We have learned that copies of sensitive government documents are stored in computers of one foreign embassy here in London. Normally these documents exist in electronic form only on a selected few government computers that satisfy the most stringent security requirements. However, sometimes they must be sent through the network connecting all government computers. But all messages in this network are encrypted using a top secret encryption algorithm certified by our best crypto experts. Even the NSA and the KGB are unable to break it. And now these documents have appeared in hands of diplomats of a small, otherwise insignificant, country. And we have no idea how it could happen."

"But you do have some suspicion who did it, do you?" asked Holmes.

"Yes, we did some routine investigation. There is a man who has legal access to one of the government computers and has frequent contacts with diplomats from the embassy. But the computer he has access to is not one of the trusted ones where these documents are normally stored. He is the suspect, but we have no idea how he could obtain copies of the documents. Even if he could obtain a copy of an encrypted document, he couldn't decrypt it."

"Hmm, please describe the communication protocol used on the network." Holmes opened his eyes, thus proving that he had followed Lestrade's talk with an attention that contrasted with his sleepy look.

"Well, the protocol is as follows. Each node N of the network has been assigned a unique secret key K_n. This key is used to secure communication between the node and a trusted server. That is, all the keys are stored also on the server. User A, wishing to send a secret message M to user B, initiates the following protocol:

1. A generates a random number R and sends to the server his name A, destination B, and $E(K_a, R)$.

2. Server responds by sending $E(K_b, R)$ to A.
3. A sends $E(R, M)$ together with $E(K_b, R)$ to B.
4. B knows K_b, thus decrypts $E(K_b, R)$ to get R and will subsequently use R to decrypt $E(R, M)$ to get M.

You see that a random key is generated every time a message has to be sent. I admit the man could intercept messages sent between the top secret trusted nodes, but I see no way he could decrypt them."

"Well, I think you have your man, Lestrade. The protocol isn't secure because the server doesn't authenticate users who send him a request. Apparently designers of the protocol have believed that sending $E(K_x, R)$ implicitly authenticates user X as the sender, as only X (and the server) knows K_x. But you know that $E(K_x, R)$ can be intercepted and later replayed. Once you understand where the hole is, you will be able to obtain enough evidence by monitoring the man's use of the computer he has access to. Most likely he works as follows: After intercepting $E(K_a, R)$ and $E(R, M)$ (see steps 1 and 3 of the protocol), the man, let's denote him as Z, will continue by pretending to be A and...

Finish the sentence for Holmes.

4.2 There are three typical ways to use nonces as challenges. Suppose N_a is a nonce generated by A, A and B share key K, and f() is a function (such as increment). The three usages are

Usage 1	Usage 2	Usage 3
(1) A $\rightarrow$ B: N_a	(1) A $\rightarrow$ B: $E(K, N_a)$	(1) A $\rightarrow$ B: $E(K, N_a)$
(2) B $\rightarrow$ A: $E(K, N_a)$	(2) B $\rightarrow$ A: N_a	(2) B $\rightarrow$ A: $E(K, f(N_a))$

Describe situations for which each usage is appropriate.

4.3 Show that a random error in one block of ciphertext is propagated to all subsequent blocks of plaintext in PCBC mode (see Figure F.2 in Appendix F).

4.4 Suppose that, in PCBC mode, blocks C_i and C_{i+1} are interchanged during transmission. Show that this affects only the decrypted blocks P_i and P_{i+1} but not subsequent blocks.

4.5 In addition to providing a standard for public-key certificate formats, X.509 specifies an authentication protocol. The original version of X.509 contains a security flaw. The essence of the protocol is

$$A \rightarrow B: \quad A \{t_A, r_A, ID_B\}$$

$$B \rightarrow A: \quad B \{t_B, r_B, ID_A, r_A\}$$

$$A \rightarrow B: \quad A \{r_B\}$$

where t_A and t_B are timestamps, r_A and r_B are nonces, and the notation X{Y} indicates that the message Y is transmitted, encrypted, and signed by X.

The text of X.509 states that checking timestamps t_A and t_B is optional for three-way authentication. But consider the following example: Suppose A and B have used the preceding protocol on some previous occasion, and that opponent C has intercepted the preceding three messages. In addition, suppose that timestamps are not used and are all set to 0. Finally, suppose C wishes to impersonate A to B. C initially sends the first captured message to B:

$$C \rightarrow B: \quad A \{0, r_A, ID_B\}$$

B responds, thinking it is talking to A but is actually talking to C:

$$B \rightarrow C: \quad B\{0, r'_B, ID_A, r_A\}$$

C meanwhile causes A to initiate authentication with C by some means. As a result, A sends C the following:

$$A \rightarrow C: \quad A \{0, r'_A, ID_C\}$$

C responds to A using the same nonce provided to C by B.

$$C \rightarrow A: \quad C \{0, r'_B, ID_A, r'_A\}$$

A responds with

$$A \rightarrow C: \quad A \{r'_B\}$$

This is exactly what C needs to convince B that it is talking to A, so C now repeats the incoming message back out to B.

$$C \rightarrow B: \quad A \{r'_B\}$$

So B will believe it is talking to A, whereas it is actually talking to C. Suggest a simple solution to this problem that does not involve the use of timestamps.

4.6 Consider a one-way authentication technique based on asymmetric encryption:

$$A \rightarrow B: \quad ID_A$$
$$B \rightarrow A: \quad R_1$$
$$A \rightarrow B: \quad E(PR_a, R_1)$$

a. Explain the protocol.
b. What type of attack is this protocol susceptible to?

4.7 Consider a one-way authentication technique based on asymmetric encryption:

$$A \rightarrow B: \quad ID_A$$
$$B \rightarrow A: \quad E(PU_a, R_2)$$
$$A \rightarrow B: \quad R_2$$

a. Explain the protocol.
b. What type of attack is this protocol susceptible to?

4.8 In Kerberos, when Bob receives a ticket from Alice, how does he know it is genuine?

4.9 In Kerberos, when Bob receives a ticket from Alice, how does he know it came from Alice?

4.10 In Kerberos, Alice receives a reply, how does she know it came from Bob (that it's not a replay of an earlier message from Bob)?

4.11 In Kerberos, what does the ticket contain that allows Alice and Bob to talk securely?

4.12 The 1988 version of X.509 lists properties that RSA keys must satisfy to be secure, given current knowledge about the difficulty of factoring large numbers. The discussion concludes with a constraint on the public exponent and the modulus n:

It must be ensured that $e > \log_2(n)$ to prevent attack by taking the eth root mod n to disclose the plaintext.

Although the constraint is correct, the reason given for requiring it is incorrect. What is wrong with the reason given and what is the correct reason?

4.13 Find at least one intermediate certification authority's certificate and one trusted root certification authority's certificate on your computer (e.g. in the browser). Print screenshots of both the general and details tab for each certificate.

4.14 NIST defines the term cryptoperiod as the time span during which a specific key is authorized for use or in which the keys for a given system or application may remain in effect. One document on key management uses the following time diagram for a shared secret key.

Originator Usage Period

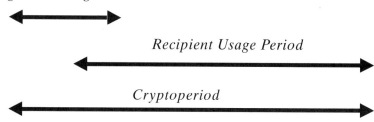

Recipient Usage Period

Cryptoperiod

Explain the overlap by giving an example application in which the originator's usage period for the shared secret key begins before the recipient's usage period and also ends before the recipient's usage period.

4.15 Consider the following protocol, designed to let A and B decide on a fresh, shared session key K'_{AB}. We assume that they already share a long-term key K_{AB}.
1. $A \rightarrow B: A, N_A$
2. $B \rightarrow A: E(K_{AB}, [N_A, K'_{AB}])$
3. $A \rightarrow B: E(K'_{AB}, N_A)$

a. We first try to understand the protocol designer's reasoning:
   - Why would A and B believe after the protocol ran that they share K'_{AB} with the other party?
   - Why would they believe that this shared key is fresh?

In both cases, you should explain both the reasons of both A and B, so your answer should complete the following sentences.

   A believes that she shares K'_{AB} with B since . . .
   B believes that he shares K'_{AB} with A since . . .
   A believes that K'_{AB} is fresh since . . .
   B believes that K'_{AB} is fresh since . . .

b. Assume now that A starts a run of this protocol with B. However, the connection is intercepted by the adversary C. Show how C can start a new run of the protocol using reflection, causing A to believe that she has agreed on a fresh key with B (in spite of the fact that she has only been communicating with C). Thus, in particular, the belief in (a) is false.

c. Propose a modification of the protocol that prevents this attack.

4.16 What are the core components of a PKI? Briefly describe each component.

4.17 Explain the problems with key management and how it affects symmetric cryptography.

4.18 Consider the following protocol:

$$A \rightarrow KDC: \quad ID_A \| ID_B \| N_1$$

$$KDC \rightarrow A: \quad E(K_a, [K_S \| ID_B \| N_1 \| E(K_b, [K_S \| ID_A])])$$

$$A \rightarrow B: \quad E(K_b, [K_S \| ID_A])$$

$$B \rightarrow A: \quad E(K_S, N_2)$$

$$A \rightarrow B: \quad E(K_S, f(N_2))$$

a. Explain the protocol.

b. Can you think of a possible attack on this protocol? Explain how it can be done.

c. Mention a possible technique to get around the attack—not a detailed mechanism, just the basics of the idea.

Note: The remaining problems deal with a cryptographic product developed by IBM, which is briefly described in a document at this book's Web site in `IBMCrypto.pdf`. *Try these problems after reviewing the document.*

4.19   What is the effect of adding the instruction EMK_i?

$$EMK_i: X \rightarrow E(KMH_i, X) \quad i = 0, 1$$

4.20   Suppose N different systems use the IBM Cryptographic Subsystem with host master keys KMH[i] ($i = 1, 2, \ldots, N$). Devise a method for communicating between systems without requiring the system to either share a common host master key or to divulge their individual host master keys. *Hint:* Each system needs three variants of its host master key.

4.21   The principal objective of the IBM Cryptographic Subsystem is to protect transmissions between a terminal and the processing system. Devise a procedure, perhaps adding instructions, which will allow the processor to generate a session key KS and distribute it to Terminal i and Terminal j without having to store a key-equivalent variable in the host.

CHAPTER 5

TRANSPORT-LEVEL SECURITY

Use your mentality
Wake up to reality

— *From the song*, "I've Got You Under My Skin" by Cole Porter

KEY POINTS

◆ Secure Socket Layer (SSL) provides security services between TCP and applications that use TCP. The Internet standard version is called Transport Layer Service (TLS).

◆ SSL/TLS provides confidentiality using symmetric encryption and message integrity using a message authentication code.

◆ SSL/TLS includes protocol mechanisms to enable two TCP users to determine the security mechanisms and services they will use.

◆ HTTPS (HTTP over SSL) refers to the combination of HTTP and SSL to implement secure communication between a Web browser and a Web server.

◆ Secure Shell (SSH) provides secure remote logon and other secure client/server facilities.

Virtually all businesses, most government agencies, and many individuals now have Web sites. The number of individuals and companies with Internet access is expanding rapidly and all of these have graphical Web browsers. As a result, businesses are enthusiastic about setting up facilities on the Web for electronic commerce. But the reality is that the Internet and the Web are extremely vulnerable to compromises of various sorts. As businesses wake up to this reality, the demand for secure Web services grows.

The topic of Web security is a broad one and can easily fill a book. In this chapter, we begin with a discussion of the general requirements for Web security and then focus on three standardized schemes that are becoming increasingly important as part of Web commerce and that focus on security at the transport layer: SSL/TLS, HTTPS, and SSH.

5.1 WEB SECURITY CONSIDERATIONS

The World Wide Web is fundamentally a client/server application running over the Internet and TCP/IP intranets. As such, the security tools and approaches discussed so far in this book are relevant to the issue of Web security. But, as pointed out in [GARF02], the Web presents new challenges not generally appreciated in the context of computer and network security.

• The Internet is two-way. Unlike traditional publishing environments—even electronic publishing systems involving teletext, voice response, or fax-back— the Web is vulnerable to attacks on the Web servers over the Internet.

- The Web is increasingly serving as a highly visible outlet for corporate and product information and as the platform for business transactions. Reputations can be damaged and money can be lost if the Web servers are subverted.

- Although Web browsers are very easy to use, Web servers are relatively easy to configure and manage, and Web content is increasingly easy to develop, the underlying software is extraordinarily complex. This complex software may hide many potential security flaws. The short history of the Web is filled with examples of new and upgraded systems, properly installed, that are vulnerable to a variety of security attacks.

- A Web server can be exploited as a launching pad into the corporation's or agency's entire computer complex. Once the Web server is subverted, an attacker may be able to gain access to data and systems not part of the Web itself but connected to the server at the local site.

- Casual and untrained (in security matters) users are common clients for Web-based services. Such users are not necessarily aware of the security risks that exist and do not have the tools or knowledge to take effective countermeasures.

Web Security Threats

Table 5.1 provides a summary of the types of security threats faced when using the Web. One way to group these threats is in terms of passive and active attacks. Passive attacks include eavesdropping on network traffic between browser and server and gaining access to information on a Web site that is supposed to be restricted. Active attacks include impersonating another user, altering messages in transit between client and server, and altering information on a Web site.

Another way to classify Web security threats is in terms of the location of the threat: Web server, Web browser, and network traffic between browser and server. Issues of server and browser security fall into the category of computer system security; Part Four of this book addresses the issue of system security in general but is also applicable to Web system security. Issues of traffic security fall into the category of network security and are addressed in this chapter.

Web Traffic Security Approaches

A number of approaches to providing Web security are possible. The various approaches that have been considered are similar in the services they provide and, to some extent, in the mechanisms that they use, but they differ with respect to their scope of applicability and their relative location within the TCP/IP protocol stack.

Figure 5.1 illustrates this difference. One way to provide Web security is to use IP security (IPsec) (Figure 5.1a). The advantage of using IPsec is that it is transparent to end users and applications and provides a general-purpose solution. Furthermore, IPsec includes a filtering capability so that only selected traffic need incur the overhead of IPsec processing.

Another relatively general-purpose solution is to implement security just above TCP (Figure 5.1b). The foremost example of this approach is the Secure

Table 5.1 A Comparison of Threats on the Web

	Threats	Consequences	Countermeasures
Integrity	• Modification of user data • Trojan horse browser • Modification of memory • Modification of message traffic in transit	• Loss of information • Compromise of machine • Vulnerabilty to all other threats	Cryptographic checksums
Confidentiality	• Eavesdropping on the net • Theft of info from server • Theft of data from client • Info about network configuration • Info about which client talks to server	• Loss of information • Loss of privacy	Encryption, Web proxies
Denial of Service	• Killing of user threads • Flooding machine with bogus requests • Filling up disk or memory • Isolating machine by DNS attacks	• Disruptive • Annoying • Prevent user from getting work done	Difficult to prevent
Authentication	• Impersonation of legitimate users • Data forgery	• Misrepresentation of user • Belief that false information is valid	Cryptographic techniques

Sockets Layer (SSL) and the follow-on Internet standard known as Transport Layer Security (TLS). At this level, there are two implementation choices. For full generality, SSL (or TLS) could be provided as part of the underlying protocol suite and therefore be transparent to applications. Alternatively, SSL can be embedded in specific packages. For example, Netscape and Microsoft Explorer browsers come equipped with SSL, and most Web servers have implemented the protocol.

Application-specific security services are embedded within the particular application. Figure 5.1c shows examples of this architecture. The advantage of this approach is that the service can be tailored to the specific needs of a given application.

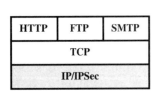

HTTP	FTP	SMTP
TCP		
IP/IPSec		

(a) Network level

HTTP	FTP	SMTP
SSL or TLS		
TCP		
IP		

(b) Transport level

	S/MIME	
Kerberos	SMTP	HTTP
UDP		TCP
IP		

(c) Application level

Figure 5.1 Relative Location of Security Facilities in the TCP/IP Protocol Stack

5.2 SECURE SOCKET LAYER AND TRANSPORT LAYER SECURITY

Netscape originated SSL. Version 3 of the protocol was designed with public review and input from industry and was published as an Internet draft document. Subsequently, when a consensus was reached to submit the protocol for Internet standardization, the TLS working group was formed within IETF to develop a common standard. This first published version of TLS can be viewed as essentially an SSLv3.1 and is very close to and backward compatible with SSLv3.

This section is devoted to a discussion of SSLv3. In the next section, the principal differences between SSLv3 and TLS are described.

SSL Architecture

SSL is designed to make use of TCP to provide a reliable end-to-end secure service. SSL is not a single protocol but rather two layers of protocols, as illustrated in Figure 5.2.

The SSL Record Protocol provides basic security services to various higher-layer protocols. In particular, the Hypertext Transfer Protocol (HTTP), which provides the transfer service for Web client/server interaction, can operate on top of SSL. Three higher-layer protocols are defined as part of SSL: the Handshake Protocol, The Change Cipher Spec Protocol, and the Alert Protocol. These SSL-specific protocols are used in the management of SSL exchanges and are examined later in this section.

Two important SSL concepts are the SSL session and the SSL connection, which are defined in the specification as follows.

- **Connection:** A connection is a transport (in the OSI layering model definition) that provides a suitable type of service. For SSL, such connections are peer-to-peer relationships. The connections are transient. Every connection is associated with one session.
- **Session:** An SSL session is an association between a client and a server. Sessions are created by the Handshake Protocol. Sessions define a set of cryptographic

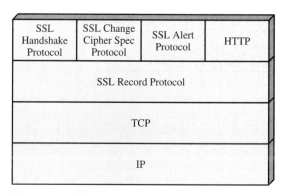

Figure 5.2   SSL Protocol Stack

security parameters which can be shared among multiple connections. Sessions are used to avoid the expensive negotiation of new security parameters for each connection.

Between any pair of parties (applications such as HTTP on client and server), there may be multiple secure connections. In theory, there may also be multiple simultaneous sessions between parties, but this feature is not used in practice.

There are a number of states associated with each session. Once a session is established, there is a current operating state for both read and write (i.e., receive and send). In addition, during the Handshake Protocol, pending read and write states are created. Upon successful conclusion of the Handshake Protocol, the pending states become the current states.

A session state is defined by the following parameters.

- **Session identifier:** An arbitrary byte sequence chosen by the server to identify an active or resumable session-state.
- **Peer certificate:** An X509.v3 certificate of the peer. This element of the state may be null.
- **Compression method:** The algorithm used to compress data prior to encryption.
- **Cipher spec:** Specifies the bulk data encryption algorithm (such as null, AES, etc.) and a hash algorithm (such as MD5 or SHA-1) used for MAC calculation. It also defines cryptographic attributes such as the hash_size.
- **Master secret:** 48-byte secret shared between the client and server.
- **Is resumable:** A flag indicating whether the session can be used to initiate new connections.

A connection state is defined by the following parameters.

- **Server and client random:** Byte sequences that are chosen by the server and client for each connection.
- **Server write MAC secret:** The secret key used in MAC operations on data sent by the server.
- **Client write MAC secret:** The secret key used in MAC operations on data sent by the client.
- **Server write key:** The secret encryption key for data encrypted by the server and decrypted by the client.
- **Client write key:** The symmetric encryption key for data encrypted by the client and decrypted by the server.
- **Initialization vectors:** When a block cipher in CBC mode is used, an initialization vector (IV) is maintained for each key. This field is first initialized by the SSL Handshake Protocol. Thereafter, the final ciphertext block from each record is preserved for use as the IV with the following record.
- **Sequence numbers:** Each party maintains separate sequence numbers for transmitted and received messages for each connection. When a party sends or receives a change cipher spec message, the appropriate sequence number is set to zero. Sequence numbers may not exceed $2^{64} - 1$.

SSL Record Protocol

The SSL Record Protocol provides two services for SSL connections:

- **Confidentiality:** The Handshake Protocol defines a shared secret key that is used for conventional encryption of SSL payloads.
- **Message Integrity:** The Handshake Protocol also defines a shared secret key that is used to form a message authentication code (MAC).

Figure 5.3 indicates the overall operation of the SSL Record Protocol. The Record Protocol takes an application message to be transmitted, fragments the data into manageable blocks, optionally compresses the data, applies a MAC, encrypts, adds a header, and transmits the resulting unit in a TCP segment. Received data are decrypted, verified, decompressed, and reassembled before being delivered to higher-level users.

The first step is **fragmentation**. Each upper-layer message is fragmented into blocks of 2^{14} bytes (16384 bytes) or less. Next, **compression** is optionally applied. Compression must be lossless and may not increase the content length by more than 1024 bytes.[1] In SSLv3 (as well as the current version of TLS), no compression algorithm is specified, so the default compression algorithm is null.

The next step in processing is to compute a **message authentication code** over the compressed data. For this purpose, a shared secret key is used. The calculation is defined as

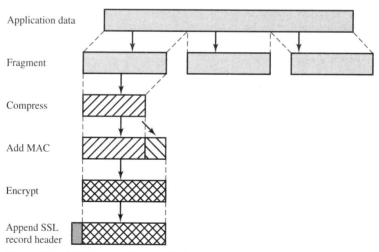

Application data

Fragment

Compress

Add MAC

Encrypt

Append SSL
record header

Figure 5.3 SSL Record Protocol Operation

---

[1]Of course, one hopes that compression shrinks rather than expands the data. However, for very short blocks, it is possible, because of formatting conventions, that the compression algorithm will actually provide output that is longer than the input.

```
hash(MAC_write_secret || pad_2 ||
     hash(MAC_write_secret || pad_1 || seq_num ||
     SSLCompressed.type || SSLCompressed.length ||
     SSLCompressed.fragment))
```

where

$\|$	= concatenation
MAC_write_secret	= shared secret key
hash	= cryptographic hash algorithm; either MD5 or SHA-1
pad_1	= the byte 0x36 (0011 0110) repeated 48 times (384 bits) for MD5 and 40 times (320 bits) for SHA-1
pad_2	= the byte 0x5C (0101 1100) repeated 48 times for MD5 and 40 times for SHA-1
seq_num	= the sequence number for this message
SSLCompressed.type	= the higher-level protocol used to process this fragment
SSLCompressed.length	= the length of the compressed fragment
SSLCompressed.fragment	= the compressed fragment (if compression is not used, this is the plaintext fragment)

Note that this is very similar to the HMAC algorithm defined in Chapter 3. The difference is that the two pads are concatenated in SSLv3 and are XORed in HMAC. The SSLv3 MAC algorithm is based on the original Internet draft for HMAC, which used concatenation. The final version of HMAC (defined in RFC 2104) uses the XOR.

Next, the compressed message plus the MAC are **encrypted** using symmetric encryption. Encryption may not increase the content length by more than 1024 bytes, so that the total length may not exceed $2^{14} + 2048$. The following encryption algorithms are permitted:

Block Cipher		Stream Cipher	
Algorithm	**Key Size**	**Algorithm**	**Key Size**
AES	128, 256	RC4-40	40
IDEA	128	RC4-128	128
RC2-40	40		
DES-40	40		
DES	56		
3DES	168		
Fortezza	80		

Fortezza can be used in a smart card encryption scheme.

For stream encryption, the compressed message plus the MAC are encrypted. Note that the MAC is computed before encryption takes place and that the MAC is then encrypted along with the plaintext or compressed plaintext.

For block encryption, padding may be added after the MAC prior to encryption. The padding is in the form of a number of padding bytes followed by a one-byte indication of the length of the padding. The total amount of padding is the smallest amount such that the total size of the data to be encrypted (plaintext plus MAC plus padding) is a multiple of the cipher's block length. An example is a plaintext (or compressed text if compression is used) of 58 bytes, with a MAC of 20 bytes (using SHA-1), that is encrypted using a block length of 8 bytes (e.g., DES). With the padding-length byte, this yields a total of 79 bytes. To make the total an integer multiple of 8, one byte of padding is added.

The final step of SSL Record Protocol processing is to prepare a header consisting of the following fields:

- **Content Type (8 bits):** The higher-layer protocol used to process the enclosed fragment.

- **Major Version (8 bits):** Indicates major version of SSL in use. For SSLv3, the value is 3.

- **Minor Version (8 bits):** Indicates minor version in use. For SSLv3, the value is 0.

- **Compressed Length (16 bits):** The length in bytes of the plaintext fragment (or compressed fragment if compression is used). The maximum value is $2^{14}+2048$.

The content types that have been defined are change_cipher_spec, alert, handshake, and application_data. The first three are the SSL-specific protocols, discussed next. Note that no distinction is made among the various applications (e.g., HTTP) that might use SSL; the content of the data created by such applications is opaque to SSL.

Figure 5.4 illustrates the SSL record format.

Change Cipher Spec Protocol

The Change Cipher Spec Protocol is one of the three SSL-specific protocols that use the SSL Record Protocol, and it is the simplest. This protocol consists of a single message (Figure 5.5a), which consists of a single byte with the value 1. The sole purpose of this message is to cause the pending state to be copied into the current state, which updates the cipher suite to be used on this connection.

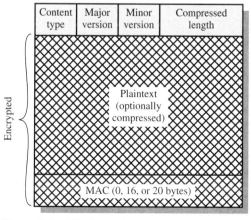

Figure 5.4   SSL Record Format

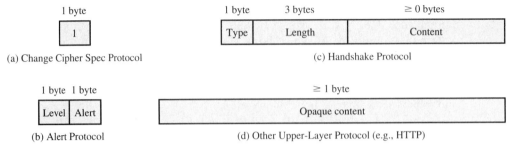

Figure 5.5   SSL Record Protocl Payload

Alert Protocol

The Alert Protocol is used to convey SSL-related alerts to the peer entity. As with other applications that use SSL, alert messages are compressed and encrypted, as specified by the current state.

Each message in this protocol consists of two bytes (Figure 5.5b). The first byte takes the value warning (1) or fatal (2) to convey the severity of the message. If the level is fatal, SSL immediately terminates the connection. Other connections on the same session may continue, but no new connections on this session may be established. The second byte contains a code that indicates the specific alert. First, we list those alerts that are always fatal (definitions from the SSL specification):

- **unexpected_message:** An inappropriate message was received.
- **bad_record_mac:** An incorrect MAC was received.
- **decompression_failure:** The decompression function received improper input (e.g., unable to decompress or decompress to greater than maximum allowable length).
- **handshake_failure:** Sender was unable to negotiate an acceptable set of security parameters given the options available.
- **illegal_parameter:** A field in a handshake message was out of range or inconsistent with other fields.

The remaining alerts are the following.

- **close_notify:** Notifies the recipient that the sender will not send any more messages on this connection. Each party is required to send a **close_notify** alert before closing the write side of a connection.
- **no_certificate:** May be sent in response to a certificate request if no appropriate certificate is available.
- **bad_certificate:** A received certificate was corrupt (e.g., contained a signature that did not verify).
- **unsupported_certificate:** The type of the received certificate is not supported.
- **certificate_revoked:** A certificate has been revoked by its signer.
- **certificate_expired:** A certificate has expired.

- **certificate_unknown:** Some other unspecified issue arose in processing the certificate, rendering it unacceptable.

Handshake Protocol

The most complex part of SSL is the Handshake Protocol. This protocol allows the server and client to authenticate each other and to negotiate an encryption and MAC algorithm and cryptographic keys to be used to protect data sent in an SSL record. The Handshake Protocol is used before any application data is transmitted.

The Handshake Protocol consists of a series of messages exchanged by client and server. All of these have the format shown in Figure 5.5c. Each message has three fields:

- **Type (1 byte):** Indicates one of 10 messages. Table 5.2 lists the defined message types.
- **Length (3 bytes):** The length of the message in bytes.
- **Content ($\geq$ 0 bytes):** The parameters associated with this message; these are listed in Table 5.2.

Figure 5.6 shows the initial exchange needed to establish a logical connection between client and server. The exchange can be viewed as having four phases.

PHASE 1. ESTABLISH SECURITY CAPABILITIES This phase is used to initiate a logical connection and to establish the security capabilities that will be associated with it. The exchange is initiated by the client, which sends a **client_hello message** with the following parameters:

- **Version:** The highest SSL version understood by the client.
- **Random:** A client-generated random structure consisting of a 32-bit timestamp and 28 bytes generated by a secure random number generator. These values serve as nonces and are used during key exchange to prevent replay attacks.

Table 5.2   SSL Handshake Protocol Message Types

Message Type	Parameters
hello_request	null
client_hello	version, random, session id, cipher suite, compression method
server_hello	version, random, session id, cipher suite, compression method
certificate	chain of X.509v3 certificates
server_key_exchange	parameters, signature
certificate_request	type, authorities
server_done	null
certificate_verify	signature
client_key_exchange	parameters, signature
finished	hash value

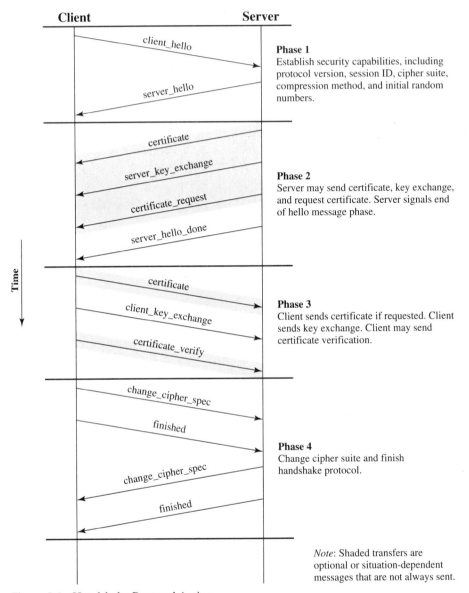

Figure 5.6 Handshake Protocol Action

- **Session ID:** A variable-length session identifier. A nonzero value indicates that the client wishes to update the parameters of an existing connection or to create a new connection on this session. A zero value indicates that the client wishes to establish a new connection on a new session.
- **CipherSuite:** This is a list that contains the combinations of cryptographic algorithms supported by the client, in decreasing order of preference. Each element of the list (each cipher suite) defines both a key exchange algorithm and a CipherSpec; these are discussed subsequently.

- **Compression Method:** This is a list of the compression methods the client supports.

After sending the client_hello message, the client waits for the server_hello message, which contains the same parameters as the client_hello message. For the server_hello message, the following conventions apply. The Version field contains the lower of the versions suggested by the client and the highest supported by the server. The Random field is generated by the server and is independent of the client's Random field. If the SessionID field of the client was nonzero, the same value is used by the server; otherwise the server's SessionID field contains the value for a new session. The CipherSuite field contains the single cipher suite selected by the server from those proposed by the client. The Compression field contains the compression method selected by the server from those proposed by the client.

The first element of the CipherSuite parameter is the key exchange method (i.e., the means by which the cryptographic keys for conventional encryption and MAC are exchanged). The following key exchange methods are supported.

- **RSA:** The secret key is encrypted with the receiver's RSA public key. A public-key certificate for the receiver's key must be made available.
- **Fixed Diffie-Hellman:** This is a Diffie-Hellman key exchange in which the server's certificate contains the Diffie-Hellman public parameters signed by the certificate authority (CA). That is, the public-key certificate contains the Diffie-Hellman public-key parameters. The client provides its Diffie-Hellman public-key parameters either in a certificate, if client authentication is required, or in a key exchange message. This method results in a fixed secret key between two peers based on the Diffie-Hellman calculation using the fixed public keys.
- **Ephemeral Diffie-Hellman:** This technique is used to create ephemeral (temporary, one-time) secret keys. In this case, the Diffie-Hellman public keys are exchanged, signed using the sender's private RSA or DSS key. The receiver can use the corresponding public key to verify the signature. Certificates are used to authenticate the public keys. This would appear to be the most secure of the three Diffie-Hellman options, because it results in a temporary, authenticated key.
- **Anonymous Diffie-Hellman:** The base Diffie-Hellman algorithm is used with no authentication. That is, each side sends its public Diffie-Hellman parameters to the other with no authentication. This approach is vulnerable to man-in-the-middle attacks, in which the attacker conducts anonymous Diffie-Hellman with both parties.
- **Fortezza:** The technique defined for the Fortezza scheme.

Following the definition of a key exchange method is the CipherSpec, which includes the following fields.

- **CipherAlgorithm:** Any of the algorithms mentioned earlier: RC4, RC2, DES, 3DES, DES40, IDEA, or Fortezza

- **MACAlgorithm:** MD5 or SHA-1
- **CipherType:** Stream or Block
- **IsExportable:** True or False
- **HashSize:** 0, 16 (for MD5), or 20 (for SHA-1) bytes
- **Key Material:** A sequence of bytes that contain data used in generating the write keys
- **IV Size:** The size of the Initialization Value for Cipher Block Chaining (CBC) encryption

PHASE 2. SERVER AUTHENTICATION AND KEY EXCHANGE The server begins this phase by sending its certificate if it needs to be authenticated; the message contains one or a chain of X.509 certificates. The **certificate message** is required for any agreed-on key exchange method except anonymous Diffie-Hellman. Note that if fixed Diffie-Hellman is used, this certificate message functions as the server's key exchange message because it contains the server's public Diffie-Hellman parameters.

Next, a `server_key_exchange message` may be sent if it is required. It is not required in two instances: (1) The server has sent a certificate with fixed Diffie-Hellman parameters or (2) a RSA key exchange is to be used. The `server_key_exchange` message is needed for the following:

- **Anonymous Diffie-Hellman:** The message content consists of the two global Diffie-Hellman values (a prime number and a primitive root of that number) plus the server's public Diffie-Hellman key (see Figure 3.12).
- **Ephemeral Diffie-Hellman:** The message content includes the three Diffie-Hellman parameters provided for anonymous Diffie-Hellman plus a signature of those parameters.
- **RSA key exchange (in which the server is using RSA but has a signature-only RSA key):** Accordingly, the client cannot simply send a secret key encrypted with the server's public key. Instead, the server must create a temporary RSA public/private key pair and use the `server_key_exchange` message to send the public key. The message content includes the two parameters of the temporary RSA public key (exponent and modulus; see Figure 3.10) plus a signature of those parameters.
- **Fortezza**

Some further details about the signatures are warranted. As usual, a signature is created by taking the hash of a message and encrypting it with the sender's private key. In this case, the hash is defined as

```
hash(ClientHello.random  ||  ServerHello.random  ||
ServerParams)
```

So the hash covers not only the Diffie-Hellman or RSA parameters but also the two nonces from the initial hello messages. This ensures against replay attacks and misrepresentation. In the case of a DSS signature, the hash is performed using the

SHA-1 algorithm. In the case of an RSA signature, both an MD5 and an SHA-1 hash are calculated, and the concatenation of the two hashes (36 bytes) is encrypted with the server's private key.

Next, a nonanonymous server (server not using anonymous Diffie-Hellman) can request a certificate from the client. The **certificate_request message** includes two parameters: certificate_type and certificate_authorities. The certificate type indicates the public-key algorithm and its use:

- RSA, signature only
- DSS, signature only
- RSA for fixed Diffie-Hellman; in this case the signature is used only for authentication, by sending a certificate signed with RSA
- DSS for fixed Diffie-Hellman; again, used only for authentication
- RSA for ephemeral Diffie-Hellman
- DSS for ephemeral Diffie-Hellman
- Fortezza

The second parameter in the certificate_request message is a list of the distinguished names of acceptable certificate authorities.

The final message in phase 2, and one that is always required, is the server_done message, which is sent by the server to indicate the end of the server hello and associated messages. After sending this message, the server will wait for a client response. This message has no parameters.

PHASE 3. CLIENT AUTHENTICATION AND KEY EXCHANGE Upon receipt of the server_done message, the client should verify that the server provided a valid certificate (if required) and check that the server_hello parameters are acceptable. If all is satisfactory, the client sends one or more messages back to the server.

If the server has requested a certificate, the client begins this phase by sending a **certificate message**. If no suitable certificate is available, the client sends a no_certificate alert instead.

Next is the **client_key_exchange message**, which must be sent in this phase. The content of the message depends on the type of key exchange, as follows.

- **RSA:** The client generates a 48-byte *pre-master secret* and encrypts with the public key from the server's certificate or temporary RSA key from a server_key_exchange message. Its use to compute a *master secret* is explained later.
- **Ephemeral or Anonymous Diffie-Hellman:** The client's public Diffie-Hellman parameters are sent.
- **Fixed Diffie-Hellman:** The client's public Diffie-Hellman parameters were sent in a certificate message, so the content of this message is null.
- **Fortezza:** The client's Fortezza parameters are sent.

Finally, in this phase, the client may send a **certificate_verify message** to provide explicit verification of a client certificate. This message is only sent following any client certificate that has signing capability (i.e., all certificates except those containing fixed Diffie-Hellman parameters). This message signs a hash code based on the preceding messages, defined as

```
CertificateVerify.signature.md5_hash=
    MD5(master_secret || pad_2 || MD5(handshake_messages ||
        master_secret || pad_1));
CertificateVerify.signature.sha_hash=
    SHA(master_secret || pad_2 || SHA(handshake_messages ||
        master_secret || pad_1));
```

where `pad_1` and `pad_2` are the values defined earlier for the MAC, **handshake_messages** refers to all Handshake Protocol messages sent or received starting at `client_hello` but not including this message, and `master_secret` is the calculated secret whose construction is explained later in this section. If the user's private key is DSS, then it is used to encrypt the SHA-1 hash. If the user's private key is RSA, it is used to encrypt the concatenation of the MD5 and SHA-1 hashes. In either case, the purpose is to verify the client's ownership of the private key for the client certificate. Even if someone is misusing the client's certificate, he or she would be unable to send this message.

PHASE 4. FINISH This phase completes the setting up of a secure connection. The client sends a `change_cipher_spec` message and copies the pending CipherSpec into the current CipherSpec. Note that this message is not considered part of the Handshake Protocol but is sent using the Change Cipher Spec Protocol. The client then immediately sends the **finished message** under the new algorithms, keys, and secrets. The finished message verifies that the key exchange and authentication processes were successful. The content of the finished message is the concatenation of two hash values:

```
MD5(master_secret || pad2 || MD5(handshake_messages ||
    Sender || master_secret || pad1))
SHA(master_secret || pad2 || SHA(handshake_messages ||
    Sender || master_secret || pad1))
```

where `Sender` is a code that identifies that the sender is the client and `handshake_messages` is all of the data from all handshake messages up to but not including this message.

In response to these two messages, the server sends its own `change_cipher_spec` message, transfers the pending to the current CipherSpec, and sends its finished message. At this point, the handshake is complete and the client and server may begin to exchange application-layer data.

Cryptographic Computations

Two further items are of interest: (1) the creation of a shared master secret by means of the key exchange and (2) the generation of cryptographic parameters from the master secret.

MASTER SECRET CREATION The shared master secret is a one-time 48-byte value (384 bits) generated for this session by means of secure key exchange. The creation is in two stages. First, a `pre_master_secret` is exchanged. Second, the `master_secret` is calculated by both parties. For `pre_master_secret` exchange, there are two possibilities.

- **RSA:** A 48-byte `pre_master_secret` is generated by the client, encrypted with the server's public RSA key, and sent to the server. The server decrypts the ciphertext using its private key to recover the pre_master_secret.
- **Diffie-Hellman:** Both client and server generate a Diffie-Hellman public key. After these are exchanged, each side performs the Diffie-Hellman calculation to create the shared `pre_master_secret`.

Both sides now compute the `master_secret` as

```
master_secret = MD5(pre_master_secret || SHA('A' ||
                    pre_master_secret || ClientHello.random ||
                    ServerHello.random)) ||
                MD5(pre_master_secret || SHA('BB' ||
                    pre_master_secret || ClientHello.random ||
                    ServerHello.random)) ||
                MD5(pre_master_secret || SHA('CCC' ||
                    pre_master_secret || ClientHello.random ||
                    ServerHello.random))
```

where `ClientHello.random` and `ServerHello.random` are the two nonce values exchanged in the initial hello messages.

GENERATION OF CRYPTOGRAPHIC PARAMETERS CipherSpecs require a client write MAC secret, a server write MAC secret, a client write key, a server write key, a client write IV, and a server write IV, which are generated from the master secret in that order. These parameters are generated from the master secret by hashing the master secret into a sequence of secure bytes of sufficient length for all needed parameters.

The generation of the key material from the master secret uses the same format for generation of the master secret from the pre-master secret as

```
key_block = MD5(master_secret || SHA('A' || master_secret ||
                ServerHello.random || ClientHello.random)) ||
            MD5(master_secret || SHA('BB' || master_secret ||
                ServerHello.random || ClientHello.random)) ||
            MD5(master_secret || SHA('CCC' || master_secret ||
                ServerHello.random || ClientHello.random)) || . . .
```

until enough output has been generated. The result of this algorithmic structure is a pseudorandom function. We can view the `master_secret` as the pseudorandom seed value to the function. The client and server random numbers can be viewed as salt values to complicate cryptanalysis (see Chapter 9 for a discussion of the use of salt values).

5.3 TRANSPORT LAYER SECURITY

TLS is an IETF standardization initiative whose goal is to produce an Internet standard version of SSL. TLS is defined as a Proposed Internet Standard in RFC 5246. RFC 5246 is very similar to SSLv3. In this section, we highlight the differences.

Version Number

The TLS Record Format is the same as that of the SSL Record Format (Figure 5.4), and the fields in the header have the same meanings. The one difference is in version values. For the current version of TLS, the major version is 3 and the minor version is 3.

Message Authentication Code

There are two differences between the SSLv3 and TLS MAC schemes: the actual algorithm and the scope of the MAC calculation. TLS makes use of the HMAC algorithm defined in RFC 2104. Recall from Chapter 3 that HMAC is defined as

$$\text{HMAC}_K(M) = \text{H}[(K^+ \oplus \text{opad}) \| \text{H}[(K^+ \oplus \text{ipad}) \| M]]$$

where

H = embedded hash function (for TLS, either MD5 or SHA-1)

M = message input to HMAC

K^+ = secret key padded with zeros on the left so that the result is equal to the block length of the hash code (for MD5 and SHA-1, block length = 512 bits)

ipad = 00110110 (36 in hexadecimal) repeated 64 times (512 bits)

opad = 01011100 (5C in hexadecimal) repeated 64 times (512 bits)

SSLv3 uses the same algorithm, except that the padding bytes are concatenated with the secret key rather than being XORed with the secret key padded to the block length. The level of security should be about the same in both cases.

For TLS, the MAC calculation encompasses the fields indicated in the following expression:

```
MAC(MAC_write_secret,seq_num || TLSCompressed.type ||
    TLSCompressed.version || TLSCompressed.length ||
    TLSCompressed.fragment)
```

The MAC calculation covers all of the fields covered by the SSLv3 calculation, plus the field TLSCompressed.version, which is the version of the protocol being employed.

Pseudorandom Function

TLS makes use of a pseudorandom function referred to as PRF to expand secrets into blocks of data for purposes of key generation or validation. The objective is to make use of a relatively small shared secret value but to generate longer blocks of data in a way that is secure from the kinds of attacks made on hash functions and MACs. The PRF is based on the data expansion function (Figure 5.7) given as

```
P_hash(secret, seed) = HMAC_hash(secret,A(1) || seed) ||
                       HMAC_hash(secret, A(2) || seed) ||
                       HMAC_hash(secret, A(3) || seed) || . . .
```

where `A()` is defined as

$$A(0) = \text{seed}$$
$$A(i) = \text{HMAC\_hash}(\text{secret}, A(i-1))$$

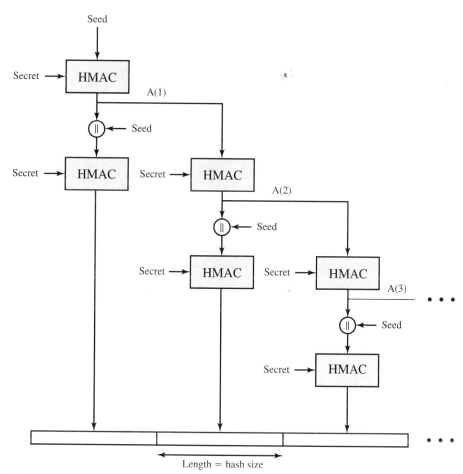

Figure 5.7   TLS Function `P_hash(secret, seed)`

The data expansion function makes use of the HMAC algorithm with either MD5 or SHA-1 as the underlying hash function. As can be seen, P_hash can be iterated as many times as necessary to produce the required quantity of data. For example, if P_SHA-1 was used to generate 64 bytes of data, it would have to be iterated four times, producing 80 bytes of data of which the last 16 would be discarded. In this case, P_MD5 would also have to be iterated four times, producing exactly 64 bytes of data. Note that each iteration involves two executions of HMAC—each of which in turn involves two executions of the underlying hash algorithm.

To make PRF as secure as possible, it uses two hash algorithms in a way that should guarantee its security if either algorithm remains secure. PRF is defined as

$$PRF(secret, label, seed) = P\_hash(S1, label \parallel seed)$$

PRF takes as input a secret value, an identifying label, and a seed value and produces an output of arbitrary length.

Alert Codes

TLS supports all of the alert codes defined in SSLv3 with the exception of no_certificate. A number of additional codes are defined in TLS; of these, the following are always fatal.

- **record_overflow:** A TLS record was received with a payload (ciphertext) whose length exceeds $2^{14}+2048$ bytes, or the ciphertext decrypted to a length of greater than $2^{14}+1024$ bytes.
- **unknown_ca:** A valid certificate chain or partial chain was received, but the certificate was not accepted because the CA certificate could not be located or could not be matched with a known, trusted CA.
- **access_denied:** A valid certificate was received, but when access control was applied, the sender decided not to proceed with the negotiation.
- **decode_error:** A message could not be decoded, because either a field was out of its specified range or the length of the message was incorrect.
- **protocol_version:** The protocol version the client attempted to negotiate is recognized but not supported.
- **insufficient_security:** Returned instead of handshake_failure when a negotiation has failed specifically because the server requires ciphers more secure than those supported by the client.
- **unsupported_extension:** Sent by clients that receive an extended server hello containing an extension not in the corresponding client hello.
- **internal_error:** An internal error unrelated to the peer or the correctness of the protocol makes it impossible to continue.
- **decrypt_error:** A handshake cryptographic operation failed, including being unable to verify a signature, decrypt a key exchange, or validate a finished message.

The remaining alerts include the following.

- **user_canceled:** This handshake is being canceled for some reason unrelated to a protocol failure.
- **no_renegotiation:** Sent by a client in response to a hello request or by the server in response to a client hello after initial handshaking. Either of these messages would normally result in renegotiation, but this alert indicates that the sender is not able to renegotiate. This message is always a warning.

Cipher Suites

There are several small differences between the cipher suites available under SSLv3 and under TLS:

- **Key Exchange:** TLS supports all of the key exchange techniques of SSLv3 with the exception of Fortezza.
- **Symmetric Encryption Algorithms:** TLS includes all of the symmetric encryption algorithms found in SSLv3, with the exception of Fortezza.

Client Certificate Types

TLS defines the following certificate types to be requested in a certificate_request message: rsa_sign, dss_sign, rsa_fixed_dh, and dss_fixed_dh. These are all defined in SSLv3. In addition, SSLv3 includes rsa_ephemeral_dh, dss_ephemeral_dh, and fortezza_kea. Ephemeral Diffie-Hellman involves signing the Diffie-Hellman parameters with either RSA or DSS. For TLS, the rsa_sign and dss_sign types are used for that function; a separate signing type is not needed to sign Diffie-Hellman parameters. TLS does not include the Fortezza scheme.

Certificate_Verify and Finished Messages

In the TLS certificate_verify message, the MD5 and SHA-1 hashes are calculated only over handshake_messages. Recall that for SSLv3, the hash calculation also included the master secret and pads. These extra fields were felt to add no additional security.

As with the finished message in SSLv3, the finished message in TLS is a hash based on the shared master_secret, the previous handshake messages, and a label that identifies client or server. The calculation is somewhat different. For TLS, we have

```
PRF(master_secret,finished_label,MD5(handshake_messages)‖
    SHA-1(handshake_messages))
```

where finished_label is the string "client finished" for the client and "server finished" for the server.

Cryptographic Computations

The `pre_master_secret` for TLS is calculated in the same way as in SSLv3. As in SSLv3, the `master_secret` in TLS is calculated as a hash function of the `pre_master_secret` and the two hello random numbers. The form of the TLS calculation is different from that of SSLv3 and is defined as

```
master_secret= PRF(pre_master_secret,"master secret",
                ClientHello.random‖ServerHello.random)
```

The algorithm is performed until 48 bytes of pseudorandom output are produced. The calculation of the key block material (MAC secret keys, session encryption keys, and IVs) is defined as

```
key_block = PRF(master_secret, "key expansion",
                SecurityParameters.server_random‖
                SecurityParameters.client_random)
```

until enough output has been generated. As with SSLv3, the `key_block` is a function of the `master_secret` and the client and server random numbers, but for TLS, the actual algorithm is different.

Padding

In SSL, the padding added prior to encryption of user data is the minimum amount required so that the total size of the data to be encrypted is a multiple of the cipher's block length. In TLS, the padding can be any amount that results in a total that is a multiple of the cipher's block length, up to a maximum of 255 bytes. For example, if the plaintext (or compressed text if compression is used) plus MAC plus padding.length byte is 79 bytes long, then the padding length (in bytes) can be 1, 9, 17, and so on, up to 249. A variable padding length may be used to frustrate attacks based on an analysis of the lengths of exchanged messages.

5.4 HTTPS

HTTPS (HTTP over SSL) refers to the combination of HTTP and SSL to implement secure communication between a Web browser and a Web server. The HTTPS capability is built into all modern Web browsers. Its use depends on the Web server supporting HTTPS communication. For example, search engines do not support HTTPS.

The principal difference seen by a user of a Web browser is that URL (uniform resource locator) addresses begin with https:// rather than http://. A normal HTTP connection uses port 80. If HTTPS is specified, port 443 is used, which invokes SSL.

When HTTPS is used, the following elements of the communication are encrypted:

- URL of the requested document
- Contents of the document
- Contents of browser forms (filled in by browser user)
- Cookies sent from browser to server and from server to browser
- Contents of HTTP header

HTTPS is documented in RFC 2818, *HTTP Over TLS*. There is no fundamental change in using HTTP over either SSL or TLS, and both implementations are referred to as HTTPS.

Connection Initiation

For HTTPS, the agent acting as the HTTP client also acts as the TLS client. The client initiates a connection to the server on the appropriate port and then sends the TLS ClientHello to begin the TLS handshake. When the TLS handshake has finished, the client may then initiate the first HTTP request. All HTTP data is to be sent as TLS application data. Normal HTTP behavior, including retained connections, should be followed.

We need to be clear that there are three levels of awareness of a connection in HTTPS. At the HTTP level, an HTTP client requests a connection to an HTTP server by sending a connection request to the next lowest layer. Typically, the next lowest layer is TCP, but it also may be TLS/SSL. At the level of TLS, a session is established between a TLS client and a TLS server. This session can support one or more connections at any time. As we have seen, a TLS request to establish a connection begins with the establishment of a TCP connection between the TCP entity on the client side and the TCP entity on the server side.

Connection Closure

An HTTP client or server can indicate the closing of a connection by including the following line in an HTTP record: `Connection: close`. This indicates that the connection will be closed after this record is delivered.

The closure of an HTTPS connection requires that TLS close the connection with the peer TLS entity on the remote side, which will involve closing the underlying TCP connection. At the TLS level, the proper way to close a connection is for each side to use the TLS alert protocol to send a `close_notify` alert. TLS implementations must initiate an exchange of closure alerts before closing a connection. A TLS implementation may, after sending a closure alert, close the connection without waiting for the peer to send its closure alert, generating an "incomplete close". Note that an implementation that does this may choose to reuse the session. This should only be done when the application knows (typically through detecting HTTP message boundaries) that it has received all the message data that it cares about.

HTTP clients also must be able to cope with a situation in which the underlying TCP connection is terminated without a prior `close_notify` alert and without a `Connection: close` indicator. Such a situation could be due to a programming error on the server or a communication error that causes the TCP connection to drop. However, the unannounced TCP closure could be evidence of some sort of attack. So the HTTPS client should issue some sort of security warning when this occurs.

5.5 SECURE SHELL (SSH)

Secure Shell (SSH) is a protocol for secure network communications designed to be relatively simple and inexpensive to implement. The initial version, SSH1 was focused on providing a secure remote logon facility to replace TELNET and other remote logon schemes that provided no security. SSH also provides a more general client/server capability and can be used for such network functions as file transfer and e-mail. A new version, SSH2, fixes a number of security flaws in the original scheme. SSH2 is documented as a proposed standard in IETF RFCs 4250 through 4256.

SSH client and server applications are widely available for most operating systems. It has become the method of choice for remote login and X tunneling and is rapidly becoming one of the most pervasive applications for encryption technology outside of embedded systems.

SSH is organized as three protocols that typically run on top of TCP (Figure 5.8):

- **Transport Layer Protocol:** Provides server authentication, data confidentiality, and data integrity with forward secrecy (i.e., if a key is compromised during one session, the knowledge does not affect the security of earlier sessions). The transport layer may optionally provide compression.

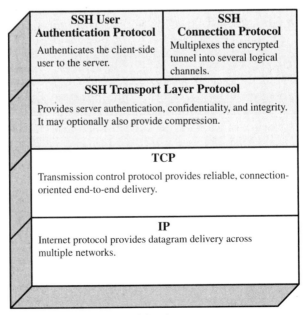

Figure 5.8   SSH Protocol Stack

- **User Authentication Protocol:** Authenticates the user to the server.
- **Connection Protocol:** Multiplexes multiple logical communications channels over a single, underlying SSH connection.

Transport Layer Protocol

HOST KEYS Server authentication occurs at the transport layer, based on the server possessing a public/private key pair. A server may have multiple host keys using multiple different asymmetric encryption algorithms. Multiple hosts may share the same host key. In any case, the server host key is used during key exchange to authenticate the identity of the host. For this to be possible, the client must have a priori knowledge of the server's public host key. RFC 4251 dictates two alternative trust models that can be used:

1. The client has a local database that associates each host name (as typed by the user) with the corresponding public host key. This method requires no centrally administered infrastructure and no third-party coordination. The downside is that the database of name-to-key associations may become burdensome to maintain.

2. The host name-to-key association is certified by a trusted certification authority (CA). The client only knows the CA root key and can verify the validity of all host keys certified by accepted CAs. This alternative eases the maintenance problem, since ideally, only a single CA key needs to be securely stored on the client. On the other hand, each host key must be appropriately certified by a central authority before authorization is possible.

PACKET EXCHANGE Figure 5.9 illustrates the sequence of events in the SSH Transport Layer Protocol. First, the client establishes a TCP connection to the server. This is done via the TCP protocol and is not part of the Transport Layer Protocol. Once the connection is established, the client and server exchange data, referred to as packets, in the data field of a TCP segment. Each packet is in the following format (Figure 5.10).

- **Packet length:** Length of the packet in bytes, not including the packet length and MAC fields.
- **Padding length:** Length of the random padding field.
- **Payload:** Useful contents of the packet. Prior to algorithm negotiation, this field is uncompressed. If compression is negotiated, then in subsequent packets, this field is compressed.
- **Random padding:** Once an encryption algorithm has been negotiated, this field is added. It contains random bytes of padding so that that total length of the packet (excluding the MAC field) is a multiple of the cipher block size, or 8 bytes for a stream cipher.
- **Message authentication code (MAC):** If message authentication has been negotiated, this field contains the MAC value. The MAC value is computed over the entire packet plus a sequence number, excluding the MAC field. The sequence number is an implicit 32-bit packet sequence that is initialized to

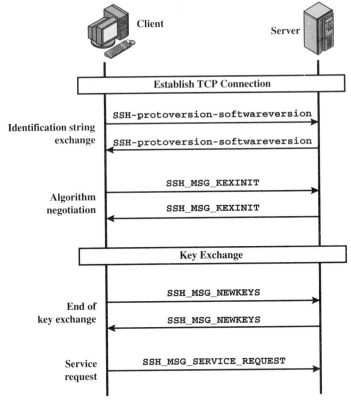

Figure 5.9 SSH Transport Layer Protocol Packet Exchanges

zero for the first packet and incremented for every packet. The sequence number is not included in the packet sent over the TCP connection.

Once an encryption algorithm has been negotiated, the entire packet (excluding the MAC field) is encrypted after the MAC value is calculated.

The SSH Transport Layer packet exchange consists of a sequence of steps (Figure 5.9). The first step, the **identification string exchange**, begins with the client sending a packet with an identification string of the form:

```
SSH-protoversion-softwareversion SP comments CR LF
```

where SP, CR, and LF are space character, carriage return, and line feed, respectively. An example of a valid string is SSH-2.0-billsSSH_3.6.3q3<CR><LF>. The server responds with its own identification string. These strings are used in the Diffie-Hellman key exchange.

Next comes **algorithm negotiation**. Each side sends an SSH_MSG_KEXINIT containing lists of supported algorithms in the order of preference to the sender. There is one list for each type of cryptographic algorithm. The algorithms include key exchange, encryption, MAC algorithm, and compression algorithm. Table 5.3 shows the allowable options for encryption, MAC, and compression. For each category, the algorithm chosen is the first algorithm on the client's list that is also supported by the server.

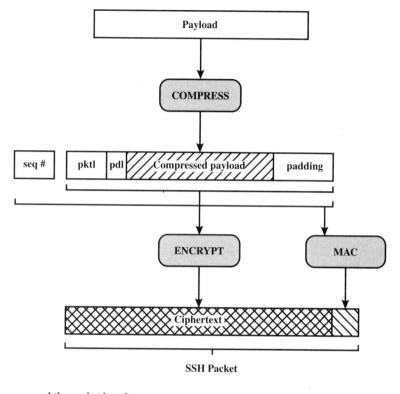

pktl = packet length
pdl = padding length

Figure 5.10   SSH Transport Layer Protocol Packet Formation

The next step is **key exchange**. The specification allows for alternative methods of key exchange, but at present, only two versions of Diffie-Hellman key exchange are specified. Both versions are defined in RFC 2409 and require only one packet in each direction. The following steps are involved in the exchange. In this, C is the client; S is the server; p is a large safe prime; g is a generator for a subgroup of GF(p); q is the order of the subgroup; V_S is S's identification string; V_C is C's identification string; K_S is S's public host key; I_C is C's SSH_MSG_KEXINIT message and I_S is S's SSH_MSG_KEXINIT message that have been exchanged before this part begins. The values of p, g, and q are known to both client and server as a result of the algorithm selection negotiation. The hash function hash() is also decided during algorithm negotiation.

1. C generates a random number $x(1 < x < q)$ and computes $e = g^x \bmod p$. C sends e to S.

2. S generates a random number $y(0 < y < q)$ and computes $f = g^y \bmod p$. S receives e. It computes $K = e^y \bmod p$, $H = \text{hash}(V\_C \,\|\, V\_S \,\|\, I\_C \,\|\, I\_S \,\|\, K\_S \,\|\, e \,\|\, f \,\|\, K)$, and signature s on H with its private host key. S sends $(K\_S \,\|\, f \,\|\, s)$ to C. The signing operation may involve a second hashing operation.

Table 5.3   SSH Transport Layer Cryptographic Algorithms

Cipher	
`3des-cbc`*	Three-key 3DES in CBC mode
`blowfish-cbc`	Blowfish in CBC mode
`twofish256-cbc`	Twofish in CBC mode with a 256-bit key
`twofish192-cbc`	Twofish with a 192-bit key
`twofish128-cbc`	Twofish with a 128-bit key
`aes256-cbc`	AES in CBC mode with a 256-bit key
`aes192-cbc`	AES with a 192-bit key
`aes128-cbc`**	AES with a 128-bit key
`Serpent256-cbc`	Serpent in CBC mode with a 256-bit key
`Serpent192-cbc`	Serpent with a 192-bit key
`Serpent128-cbc`	Serpent with a 128-bit key
`arcfour`	RC4 with a 128-bit key
`cast128-cbc`	CAST-128 in CBC mode

MAC algorithm	
`hmac-sha1`*	HMAC-SHA1; digest length = key length = 20
`hmac-sha1-96`**	First 96 bits of HMAC-SHA1; digest length = 12; key length = 20
`hmac-md5`	HMAC-SHA1; digest length = key length = 16
`hmac-md5-96`	First 96 bits of HMAC-SHA1; digest length = 12; key length = 16

Compression algorithm	
`none`*	No compression
`zlib`	Defined in RFC 1950 and RFC 1951

* = Required

** = Recommended

3. C verifies that K_S really is the host key for S (e.g., using certificates or a local database). C is also allowed to accept the key without verification; however, doing so will render the protocol insecure against active attacks (but may be desirable for practical reasons in the short term in many environments). C then computes $K = f^x \bmod p$, $H = \text{hash}(V\_C \parallel V\_S \parallel I\_C \parallel I\_S \parallel K\_S \parallel e \parallel f \parallel K)$, and verifies the signature s on H.

As a result of these steps, the two sides now share a master key K. In addition, the server has been authenticated to the client, because the server has used its private key to sign its half of the Diffie-Hellman exchange. Finally, the hash value H serves as a session identifier for this connection. Once computed, the session identifier is not changed, even if the key exchange is performed again for this connection to obtain fresh keys.

The **end of key exchange** is signaled by the exchange of SSH_MSG_NEWKEYS packets. At this point, both sides may start using the keys generated from K, as discussed subsequently.

The final step is **service request**. The client sends an SSH_MSG_SERVICE_REQUEST packet to request either the User Authentication or the Connection Protocol. Subsequent to this, all data is exchanged as the payload of an SSH Transport Layer packet, protected by encryption and MAC.

KEY GENERATION The keys used for encryption and MAC (and any needed IVs) are generated from the shared secret key K, the hash value from the key exchange H, and the session identifier, which is equal to H unless there has been a subsequent key exchange after the initial key exchange. The values are computed as follows.

- Initial IV client to server: HASH($K \parallel H \parallel$ "A" $\parallel$ session_id)
- Initial IV server to client: HASH($K \parallel H \parallel$ "B" $\parallel$ session_id)
- Encryption key client to server: HASH($K \parallel H \parallel$ "C" $\parallel$ session_id)
- Encryption key server to client: HASH($K \parallel H \parallel$ "D" $\parallel$ session_id)
- Integrity key client to server: HASH($K \parallel H \parallel$ "E" $\parallel$ session_id)
- Integrity key server to client: HASH($K \parallel H \parallel$ "F" $\parallel$ session_id)

where HASH() is the hash function determined during algorithm negotiation.

User Authentication Protocol

The User Authentication Protocol provides the means by which the client is authenticated to the server.

MESSAGE TYPES AND FORMATS Three types of messages are always used in the User Authentication Protocol. Authentication requests from the client have the format:

byte	SSH_MSG_USERAUTH_REQUEST (50)
string	user name
string	service name
string	method name
...	method specific fields

where user name is the authorization identity the client is claiming, service name is the facility to which the client is requesting access (typically the SSH Connection Protocol), and method name is the authentication method being used in this request. The first byte has decimal value 50, which is interpreted as SSH_MSG_USERAUTH_REQUEST.

If the server either (1) rejects the authentication request or (2) accepts the request but requires one or more additional authentication methods, the server sends a message with the format:

byte	SSH_MSG_USERAUTH_FAILURE (51)
name-list	authentications that can continue
boolean	partial success

where the name-list is a list of methods that may productively continue the dialog. If the server accepts authentication, it sends a single byte message: SSH_MSG_USERAUTH_SUCCESS (52).

MESSAGE EXCHANGE The message exchange involves the following steps.

1. The client sends a SSH_MSG_USERAUTH_REQUEST with a requested method of none.

2. The server checks to determine if the user name is valid. If not, the server returns SSH_MSG_USERAUTH_FAILURE with the partial success value of false. If the user name is valid, the server proceeds to step 3.

3. The server returns SSH_MSG_USERAUTH_FAILURE with a list of one or more authentication methods to be used.

4. The client selects one of the acceptable authentication methods and sends a SSH_MSG_USERAUTH_REQUEST with that method name and the required method-specific fields. At this point, there may be a sequence of exchanges to perform the method.

5. If the authentication succeeds and more authentication methods are required, the server proceeds to step 3, using a partial success value of true. If the authentication fails, the server proceeds to step 3, using a partial success value of false.

6. When all required authentication methods succeed, the server sends a SSH_MSG_USERAUTH_SUCCESS message, and the Authentication Protocol is over.

AUTHENTICATION METHODS The server may require one or more of the following authentication methods.

- **publickey:** The details of this method depend on the public-key algorithm chosen. In essence, the client sends a message to the server that contains the client's public key, with the message signed by the client's private key. When the server receives this message, it checks whether the supplied key is acceptable for authentication and, if so, it checks whether the signature is correct.

- **password:** The client sends a message containing a plaintext password, which is protected by encryption by the Transport Layer Protocol.

- **hostbased:** Authentication is performed on the client's host rather than the client itself. Thus, a host that supports multiple clients would provide authentication for all its clients. This method works by having the client send a signature created with the private key of the client host. Thus, rather than directly verifying the user's identity, the SSH server verifies the identity of the client host—and then believes the host when it says the user has already authenticated on the client side.

Connection Protocol

The SSH Connection Protocol runs on top of the SSH Transport Layer Protocol and assumes that a secure authentication connection is in use.[2] That secure authentication

---

[2]RFC 4254, *The Secure Shell (SSH) Connection Protocol*, states that the Connection Protocol runs on top of the Transport Layer Protocol and the User Authentication Protocol. RFC 4251, *SSH Protocol Architecture*, states that the Connection Protocol runs over the User Authentication Protocol. In fact, the Connection Protocol runs over the Transport Layer Protocol, but assumes that the User Authentication Protocol has been previously invoked.

connection, referred to as a **tunnel**, is used by the Connection Protocol to multiplex a number of logical channels.

CHANNEL MECHANISM All types of communication using SSH, such as a terminal session, are supported using separate channels. Either side may open a channel. For each channel, each side associates a unique channel number, which need not be the same on both ends. Channels are flow controlled using a window mechanism. No data may be sent to a channel until a message is received to indicate that window space is available.

The life of a channel progresses through three stages: opening a channel, data transfer, and closing a channel.

When either side wishes to **open a new channel**, it allocates a local number for the channel and then sends a message of the form:

byte	SSH_MSG_CHANNEL_OPEN
string	channel type
uint32	sender channel
uint32	initial window size
uint32	maximum packet size
....	channel type specific data follows

where uint32 means unsigned 32-bit integer. The channel type identifies the application for this channel, as described subsequently. The sender channel is the local channel number. The initial window size specifies how many bytes of channel data can be sent to the sender of this message without adjusting the window. The maximum packet size specifies the maximum size of an individual data packet that can be sent to the sender. For example, one might want to use smaller packets for interactive connections to get better interactive response on slow links.

If the remote side is able to open the channel, it returns a SSH_MSG_CHANNEL_OPEN_CONFIRMATION message, which includes the sender channel number, the recipient channel number, and window and packet size values for incoming traffic. Otherwise, the remote side returns a SSH_MSG_CHANNEL_OPEN_FAILURE message with a reason code indicating the reason for failure.

Once a channel is open, **data transfer** is performed using a SSH_MSG_CHANNEL_DATA message, which includes the recipient channel number and a block of data. These messages, in both directions, may continue as long as the channel is open.

When either side wishes to **close a channel**, it sends a SSH_MSG_CHANNEL_CLOSE message, which includes the recipient channel number.

Figure 5.11 provides an example of Connection Protocol Message Exchange.

CHANNEL TYPES Four channel types are recognized in the SSH Connection Protocol specification.

- **session:** The remote execution of a program. The program may be a shell, an application such as file transfer or e-mail, a system command, or some built-in subsystem. Once a session channel is opened, subsequent requests are used to start the remote program.

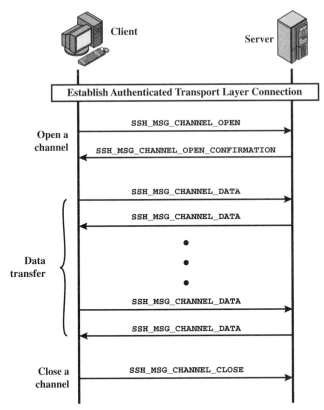

Figure 5.11 Example SSH Connection Protocol Message Exchange

- **x11:** This refers to the X Window System, a computer software system and network protocol that provides a graphical user interface (GUI) for networked computers. X allows applications to run on a network server but to be displayed on a desktop machine.
- **forwarded-tcpip:** This is remote port forwarding, as explained in the next subsection.
- **direct-tcpip:** This is local port forwarding, as explained in the next subsection.

PORT FORWARDING One of the most useful features of SSH is port forwarding. In essence, port forwarding provides the ability to convert any insecure TCP connection into a secure SSH connection. This is also referred to as SSH tunneling. We need to know what a port is in this context. A **port** is an identifier of a user of TCP. So, any application that runs on top of TCP has a port number. Incoming TCP traffic is delivered to the appropriate application on the basis of the port number. An application may employ multiple port numbers. For example, for the Simple Mail Transfer Protocol (SMTP), the server side generally listens on port 25, so an incoming SMTP request uses TCP and addresses the data to destination port 25. TCP recognizes that this is the SMTP server address and routes the data to the SMTP server application.

Figure 5.12 illustrates the basic concept behind port forwarding. We have a client application that is identified by port number x and a server application identified by port number y. At some point, the client application invokes the local TCP entity and requests a connection to the remote server on port y. The local TCP entity negotiates a TCP connection with the remote TCP entity, such that the connection links local port x to remote port y.

To secure this connection, SSH is configured so that the SSH Transport Layer Protocol establishes a TCP connection between the SSH client and server entities with TCP port numbers a and b, respectively. A secure SSH tunnel is established over this TCP connection. Traffic from the client at port x is redirected to the local

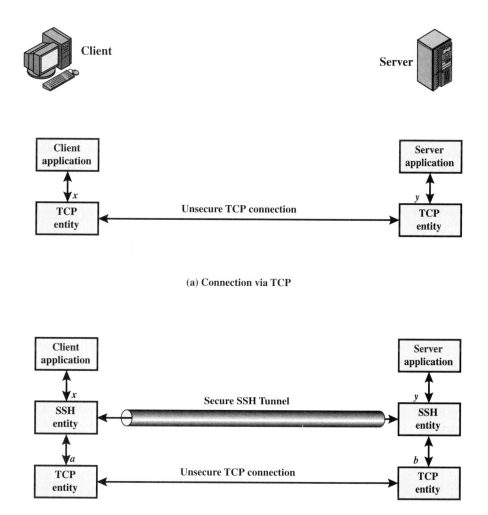

(a) Connection via TCP

(b) Connection via SSH tunnel

Figure 5.12   SSH Transport Layer Packet Exchanges

SSH entity and travels through the tunnel where the remote SSH entity delivers the data to the server application on port y. Traffic in the other direction is similarly redirected.

SSH supports two types of port forwarding: local forwarding and remote forwarding. **Local forwarding** allows the client to set up a "hijacker" process. This will intercept selected application-level traffic and redirect it from an unsecured TCP connection to a secure SSH tunnel. SSH is configured to listen on selected ports. SSH grabs all traffic using a selected port and sends it through an SSH tunnel. On the other end, the SSH server sends the incoming traffic to the destination port dictated by the client application.

The following example should help clarify local forwarding. Suppose you have an e-mail client on your desktop and use it to get e-mail from your mail server via the Post Office Protocol (POP). The assigned port number for POP3 is port 110. We can secure this traffic in the following way:

1. The SSH client sets up a connection to the remote server.
2. Select an unused local port number, say 9999, and configure SSH to accept traffic from this port destined for port 110 on the server.
3. The SSH client informs the SSH server to create a connection to the destination, in this case mailserver port 110.
4. The client takes any bits sent to local port 9999 and sends them to the server inside the encrypted SSH session. The SSH server decrypts the incoming bits and sends the plaintext to port 110.
5. In the other direction, the SSH server takes any bits received on port 110 and sends them inside the SSH session back to the client, who decrypts and sends them to the process connected to port 9999.

With **remote forwarding**, the user's SSH client acts on the server's behalf. The client receives traffic with a given destination port number, places the traffic on the correct port and sends it to the destination the user chooses. A typical example of remote forwarding is the following. You wish to access a server at work from your home computer. Because the work server is behind a firewall, it will not accept an SSH request from your home computer. However, from work you can set up an SSH tunnel using remote forwarding. This involves the following steps.

1. From the work computer, set up an SSH connection to your home computer. The firewall will allow this, because it is a protected outgoing connection.
2. Configure the SSH server to listen on a local port, say 22, and to deliver data across the SSH connection addressed to remote port, say 2222.
3. You can now go to your home computer, and configure SSH to accept traffic on port 2222.
4. You now have an SSH tunnel that can be used for remote logon to the work server.

5.6 RECOMMENDED READING AND WEB SITES

[RESC01] is a good detailed treatment of SSL and TLS. [BARR05] provides a thorough treatment of SSH. The original version (SSH-1) of SSH was introduced in [YLON96].

BARR05 Barrett, D.; Silverman, R.; and Byrnes, R. *SSH The Secure Shell: The Definitive Guide.* Sebastopol, CA: O'Reilly, 2005.

RESC01 Rescorla, E. *SSL and TLS: Designing and Building Secure Systems.* Reading, MA: Addison-Wesley, 2001.

YLON96 Ylonen, T. "SSH - Secure Login Connections over the Internet." *Proceedings, Sixth USENIX Security Symposium,* July 1996.

Recommended Web Sites:

- **Transport Layer Security Charter:** Latest RFCs and Internet drafts for TLS.
- **OpenSSL Project:** Project to develop open-source SSL and TLS software. Site includes documents and links.

5.7 KEY TERMS, REVIEW QUESTIONS, AND PROBLEMS

Key Terms

Alert protocol	HTTPS (HTTP over SSL)	Secure Socket Layer (SSL)
Change Cipher Spec protocol	Master Secret	Transport Layer Security
Handshake protocol	Secure Shell (SSH)	(TLS)

Review Questions

5.1   What are the advantages of each of the three approaches shown in Figure 5.1?

5.2   What protocols comprise SSL?

5.3   What is the difference between an SSL connection and an SSL session?

5.4   List and briefly define the parameters that define an SSL session state.

5.5   List and briefly define the parameters that define an SSL session connection.

5.6   What services are provided by the SSL Record Protocol?

5.7   What steps are involved in the SSL Record Protocol transmission?

5.8   What is the purpose of HTTPS?

5.9   For what applications is SSH useful?

5.10   List and briefly define the SSH protocols.

Problems

5.1 In SSL and TLS, why is there a separate Change Cipher Spec Protocol rather than including a `change_cipher_spec` message in the Handshake Protocol?

5.2 What purpose does the MAC serve during the change cipher spec SSL exchange?

5.3 Consider the following threats to Web security and describe how each is countered by a particular feature of SSL.

a. Brute-Force Cryptanalytic Attack: An exhaustive search of the key space for a conventional encryption algorithm.

b. Known Plaintext Dictionary Attack: Many messages will contain predictable plaintext, such as the HTTP GET command. An attacker constructs a dictionary containing every possible encryption of the known-plaintext message. When an encrypted message is intercepted, the attacker takes the portion containing the encrypted known plaintext and looks up the ciphertext in the dictionary. The ciphertext should match against an entry that was encrypted with the same secret key. If there are several matches, each of these can be tried against the full cipher-text to determine the right one. This attack is especially effective against small key sizes (e.g., 40-bit keys).

c. Replay Attack: Earlier SSL handshake messages are replayed.

d. Man-in-the-Middle Attack: An attacker interposes during key exchange, acting as the client to the server and as the server to the client.

e. Password Sniffing: Passwords in HTTP or other application traffic are eaves-dropped.

f. IP Spoofing: Uses forged IP addresses to fool a host into accepting bogus data.

g. IP Hijacking: An active, authenticated connection between two hosts is disrupted and the attacker takes the place of one of the hosts.

h. SYN Flooding: An attacker sends TCP SYN messages to request a connection but does not respond to the final message to establish the connection fully. The attacked TCP module typically leaves the "half-open connection" around for a few minutes. Repeated SYN messages can clog the TCP module.

5.4 Based on what you have learned in this chapter, is it possible in SSL for the receiver to reorder SSL record blocks that arrive out of order? If so, explain how it can be done. If not, why not?

5.5 For SSH packets, what is the advantage, if any, of not including the MAC in the scope of the packet encryption?

CHAPTER 6

WIRELESS NETWORK SECURITY

Investigators have published numerous reports of birds taking turns vocalizing; the bird spoken to gave its full attention to the speaker and never vocalized at the same time, as if the two were holding a conversation.

Researchers and scholars who have studied the data on avian communication carefully write (a) the communication code of birds, such as crows, has not been broken by any means; (b) probably all birds have wider vocabularies than anyone realizes; and (c) greater complexity and depth are recognized in avian communication as research progresses.

— The Human Nature of Birds, Theodore Barber

KEY POINTS

◆ IEEE 802.11 is a standard for wireless LANs. Interoperable standards-compliant implementations are referred to as Wi-Fi.

◆ IEEE 802.11i specifies security standards for IEEE 802.11 LANs, including authentication, data integrity, data confidentiality, and key management. Interoperable implementations are also referred to as Wi-Fi Protected Access (WPA).

◆ The Wireless Application Protocol (WAP) is a standard to provide mobile users of wireless phones and other wireless terminals access to telephony and information services, including the Internet and the Web.

◆ WAP security is primarily provided by the Wireless Transport Layer Security (WTLS), which provides security services between the mobile device and the WAP gateway to the Internet.

◆ There are several approaches to WAP end-to-end security. One notable approach assumes that the mobile device implements TLS over TCP/IP and the wireless network supports transfer of IP packets.

This chapter looks at two important wireless network security schemes. First, we look at the IEEE 802.11i standard for wireless LAN security. This standard is part of IEEE 802.11, also referred to as Wi-Fi. We begin the discussion with an overview of IEEE 802.11, and we then look in some detail at IEEE 802.11i.

The remainder of the chapter is devoted to security standards for Web access from mobile wireless devices, such as cell phones. We begin this part of the chapter with an overview of the Wireless Application Protocol (WAP), which is a set of standards for communication between mobile devices attached to a cellular network and a Web server. Then we examine the Wireless Transport Layer Security (WTLS) protocol, which provides security between the mobile device and a gateway that operates between the cellular network and the Internet. Finally, we cover end-to-end security services between WAP devices and Web servers.

6.1 IEEE 802.11 WIRELESS LAN OVERVIEW

IEEE 802 is a committee that has developed standards for a wide range of local area networks (LANs). In 1990, the IEEE 802 Committee formed a new working group, IEEE 802.11, with a charter to develop a protocol and transmission specifications for wireless LANs (WLANs). Since that time, the demand for WLANs at different frequencies and data rates has exploded. Keeping pace with this demand, the IEEE 802.11 working group has issued an ever-expanding list of standards. Table 6.1 briefly defines key terms used in the IEEE 802.11 standard.

The Wi-Fi Alliance

The first 802.11 standard to gain broad industry acceptance was 802.11b. Although 802.11b products are all based on the same standard, there is always a concern whether products from different vendors will successfully interoperate. To meet this concern, the Wireless Ethernet Compatibility Alliance (WECA), an industry consortium, was formed in 1999. This organization, subsequently renamed the Wi-Fi (Wireless Fidelity) Alliance, created a test suite to certify interoperability for 802.11b products. The term used for certified 802.11b products is *Wi-Fi*. Wi-Fi certification has been extended to 802.11g products. The Wi-Fi Alliance has also developed a certification process for 802.11a products, called *Wi-Fi5*. The Wi-Fi Alliance is concerned with a range of market areas for WLANs, including enterprise, home, and hot spots.

More recently, the Wi-Fi Alliance has developed certification procedures for IEEE 802.11 security standards, referred to as Wi-Fi Protected Access (WPA). The most recent version of WPA, known as WPA2, incorporates all of the features of the IEEE 802.11i WLAN security specification.

Table 6.1   IEEE 802.11 Terminology

Access point (AP)	Any entity that has station functionality and provides access to the distribution system via the wireless medium for associated stations.
Basic service set (BSS)	A set of stations controlled by a single coordination function.
Coordination function	The logical function that determines when a station operating within a BSS is permitted to transmit and may be able to receive PDUs.
Distribution system (DS)	A system used to interconnect a set of BSSs and integrated LANs to create an ESS.
Extended service set (ESS)	A set of one or more interconnected BSSs and integrated LANs that appear as a single BSS to the LLC layer at any station associated with one of these BSSs.
MAC protocol data unit (MPDU)	The unit of data exchanged between two peer MAC entities using the services of the physical layer.
MAC service data unit (MSDU)	Information that is delivered as a unit between MAC users.
Station	Any device that contains an IEEE 802.11 conformant MAC and physical layer.

IEEE 802 Protocol Architecture

Before proceeding, we need to briefly preview the IEEE 802 protocol architecture. IEEE 802.11 standards are defined within the structure of a layered set of protocols. This structure, used for all IEEE 802 standards, is illustrated in Figure 6.1.

PHYSICAL LAYER The lowest layer of the IEEE 802 reference model is the **physical layer**, which includes such functions as encoding/decoding of signals and bit transmission/reception. In addition, the physical layer includes a specification of the transmission medium. In the case of IEEE 802.11, the physical layer also defines frequency bands and antenna characteristics.

MEDIA ACCESS CONTROL All LANs consist of collections of devices that share the network's transmission capacity. Some means of controlling access to the transmission medium is needed to provide an orderly and efficient use of that capacity. This is the function of a **media access control (MAC)** layer. The MAC layer receives data from a higher-layer protocol, typically the Logical Link Control (LLC) layer, in the form of a block of data known as the **MAC service data unit (MSDU)**. In general, the MAC layer performs the following functions:

- On transmission, assemble data into a frame, known as a **MAC protocol data unit (MPDU)** with address and error-detection fields.
- On reception, disassemble frame, and perform address recognition and error detection.
- Govern access to the LAN transmission medium.

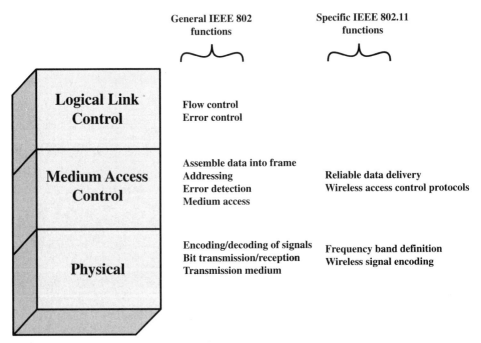

Figure 6.1 IEEE 802.11 Protocol Stack

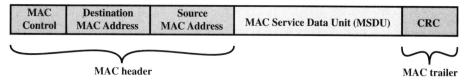

Figure 6.2 General IEEE 802 MPDU Format

The exact format of the MPDU differs somewhat for the various MAC protocols in use. In general, all of the MPDUs have a format similar to that of Figure 6.2. The fields of this frame are as follows.

- **MAC Control:** This field contains any protocol control information needed for the functioning of the MAC protocol. For example, a priority level could be indicated here.
- **Destination MAC Address:** The destination physical address on the LAN for this MPDU.
- **Source MAC Address:** The source physical address on the LAN for this MPDU.
- **MAC Service Data Unit:** The data from the next higher layer.
- **CRC:** The cyclic redundancy check field; also known as the Frame Check Sequence (FCS) field. This is an error-detecting code, such as that which is used in other data-link control protocols. The CRC is calculated based on the bits in the entire MPDU. The sender calculates the CRC and adds it to the frame. The receiver performs the same calculation on the incoming MPDU and compares that calculation to the CRC field in that incoming MPDU. If the two values don't match, then one or more bits have been altered in transit.

The fields preceding the MSDU field are referred to as the **MAC header**, and the field following the MSDU field is referred to as the **MAC trailer**. The header and trailer contain control information that accompany the data field and that are used by the MAC protocol.

LOGICAL LINK CONTROL In most data-link control protocols, the data-link protocol entity is responsible not only for detecting errors using the CRC, but for recovering from those errors by retransmitting damaged frames. In the LAN protocol architecture, these two functions are split between the MAC and LLC layers. The MAC layer is responsible for detecting errors and discarding any frames that contain errors. The LLC layer optionally keeps track of which frames have been successfully received and retransmits unsuccessful frames.

IEEE 802.11 Network Components and Architectural Model

Figure 6.3 illustrates the model developed by the 802.11 working group. The smallest building block of a wireless LAN is a **basic service set (BSS)**, which consists of wireless stations executing the same MAC protocol and competing for access to the same shared wireless medium. A BSS may be isolated, or it may connect to a backbone

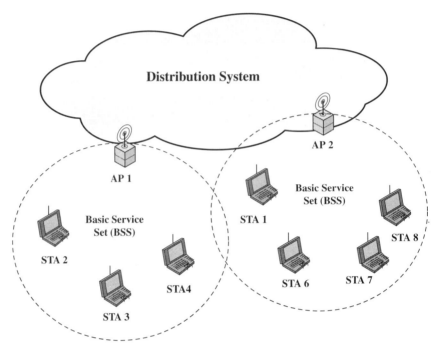

Figure 6.3   IEEE 802.11 Extended Service Set

distribution system (DS) through an **access point (AP)**. The AP functions as a bridge and a relay point. In a BSS, client stations do not communicate directly with one another. Rather, if one station in the BSS wants to communicate with another station in the same BSS, the MAC frame is first sent from the originating station to the AP and then from the AP to the destination station. Similarly, a MAC frame from a station in the BSS to a remote station is sent from the local station to the AP and then relayed by the AP over the DS on its way to the destination station. The BSS generally corresponds to what is referred to as a cell in the literature. The DS can be a switch, a wired network, or a wireless network.

When all the stations in the BSS are mobile stations that communicate directly with one another (not using an AP), the BSS is called an **independent BSS (IBSS)**. An IBSS is typically an ad hoc network. In an IBSS, the stations all communicate directly, and no AP is involved.

A simple configuration is shown in Figure 6.3, in which each station belongs to a single BSS; that is, each station is within wireless range only of other stations within the same BSS. It is also possible for two BSSs to overlap geographically, so that a single station could participate in more than one BSS. Furthermore, the association between a station and a BSS is dynamic. Stations may turn off, come within range, and go out of range.

An **extended service set (ESS)** consists of two or more basic service sets interconnected by a distribution system. The extended service set appears as a single logical LAN to the logical link control (LLC) level.

IEEE 802.11 Services

IEEE 802.11 defines nine services that need to be provided by the wireless LAN to achieve functionality equivalent to that which is inherent to wired LANs. Table 6.2 lists the services and indicates two ways of categorizing them.

1. The service provider can be either the station or the DS. Station services are implemented in every 802.11 station, including AP stations. Distribution services are provided between BSSs; these services may be implemented in an AP or in another special-purpose device attached to the distribution system.

2. Three of the services are used to control IEEE 802.11 LAN access and confidentiality. Six of the services are used to support delivery of MSDUs between stations. If the MSDU is too large to be transmitted in a single MPDU, it may be fragmented and transmitted in a series of MPDUs.

Following the IEEE 802.11 document, we next discuss the services in an order designed to clarify the operation of an IEEE 802.11 ESS network. **MSDU delivery**, which is the basic service, already has been mentioned. Services related to security are introduced in Section 6.2.

DISTRIBUTION OF MESSAGES WITHIN A DS The two services involved with the distribution of messages within a DS are distribution and integration. **Distribution** is the primary service used by stations to exchange MPDUs when the MPDUs must traverse the DS to get from a station in one BSS to a station in another BSS. For example, suppose a frame is to be sent from station 2 (STA 2) to station 7 (STA 7) in Figure 6.3. The frame is sent from STA 2 to AP 1, which is the AP for this BSS. The AP gives the frame to the DS, which has the job of directing the frame to the AP associated with STA 7 in the target BSS. AP 2 receives the frame and forwards it to STA 7. How the message is transported through the DS is beyond the scope of the IEEE 802.11 standard.

If the two stations that are communicating are within the same BSS, then the distribution service logically goes through the single AP of that BSS.

Table 6.2   IEEE 802.11 Services

Service	Provider	Used to support
Association	Distribution system	MSDU delivery
Authentication	Station	LAN access and security
Deauthentication	Station	LAN access and security
Disassociation	Distribution system	MSDU delivery
Distribution	Distribution system	MSDU delivery
Integration	Distribution system	MSDU delivery
MSDU delivery	Station	MSDU delivery
Privacy	Station	LAN access and security
Reassociation	Distribution system	MSDU delivery

The **integration** service enables transfer of data between a station on an IEEE 802.11 LAN and a station on an integrated IEEE 802.x LAN. The term *integrated* refers to a wired LAN that is physically connected to the DS and whose stations may be logically connected to an IEEE 802.11 LAN via the integration service. The integration service takes care of any address translation and media conversion logic required for the exchange of data.

ASSOCIATION-RELATED SERVICES The primary purpose of the MAC layer is to transfer MSDUs between MAC entities; this purpose is fulfilled by the distribution service. For that service to function, it requires information about stations within the ESS that is provided by the association-related services. Before the distribution service can deliver data to or accept data from a station, that station must be *associated*. Before looking at the concept of association, we need to describe the concept of mobility. The standard defines three transition types, based on mobility:

- **No transition:** A station of this type is either stationary or moves only within the direct communication range of the communicating stations of a single BSS.
- **BSS transition:** This is defined as a station movement from one BSS to another BSS within the same ESS. In this case, delivery of data to the station requires that the addressing capability be able to recognize the new location of the station.
- **ESS transition:** This is defined as a station movement from a BSS in one ESS to a BSS within another ESS. This case is supported only in the sense that the station can move. Maintenance of upper-layer connections supported by 802.11 cannot be guaranteed. In fact, disruption of service is likely to occur.

To deliver a message within a DS, the distribution service needs to know where the destination station is located. Specifically, the DS needs to know the identity of the AP to which the message should be delivered in order for that message to reach the destination station. To meet this requirement, a station must maintain an association with the AP within its current BSS. Three services relate to this requirement:

- **Association:** Establishes an initial association between a station and an AP. Before a station can transmit or receive frames on a wireless LAN, its identity and address must be known. For this purpose, a station must establish an association with an AP within a particular BSS. The AP can then communicate this information to other APs within the ESS to facilitate routing and delivery of addressed frames.
- **Reassociation:** Enables an established association to be transferred from one AP to another, allowing a mobile station to move from one BSS to another.
- **Disassociation:** A notification from either a station or an AP that an existing association is terminated. A station should give this notification before leaving an ESS or shutting down. However, the MAC management facility protects itself against stations that disappear without notification.

6.2 IEEE 802.11i WIRELESS LAN SECURITY

There are two characteristics of a wired LAN that are not inherent in a wireless LAN.

1. In order to transmit over a wired LAN, a station must be physically connected to the LAN. On the other hand, with a wireless LAN, any station within radio range of the other devices on the LAN can transmit. In a sense, there is a form of authentication with a wired LAN in that it requires some positive and presumably observable action to connect a station to a wired LAN.

2. Similarly, in order to receive a transmission from a station that is part of a wired LAN, the receiving station also must be attached to the wired LAN. On the other hand, with a wireless LAN, any station within radio range can receive. Thus, a wired LAN provides a degree of privacy, limiting reception of data to stations connected to the LAN.

These differences between wired and wireless LANs suggest the increased need for robust security services and mechanisms for wireless LANs. The original 802.11 specification included a set of security features for privacy and authentication that were quite weak. For privacy, 802.11 defined the **Wired Equivalent Privacy (WEP)** algorithm. The privacy portion of the 802.11 standard contained major weaknesses. Subsequent to the development of WEP, the 802.11i task group has developed a set of capabilities to address the WLAN security issues. In order to accelerate the introduction of strong security into WLANs, the Wi-Fi Alliance promulgated **Wi-Fi Protected Access (WPA)** as a Wi-Fi standard. WPA is a set of security mechanisms that eliminates most 802.11 security issues and was based on the current state of the 802.11i standard. The final form of the 802.11i standard is referred to as **Robust Security Network (RSN)**. The Wi-Fi Alliance certifies vendors in compliance with the full 802.11i specification under the WPA2 program.

IEEE 802.11i Services

The 802.11i RSN security specification defines the following services.

- **Authentication:** A protocol is used to define an exchange between a user and an AS that provides mutual authentication and generates temporary keys to be used between the client and the AP over the wireless link.

- **Access control:**[1] This function enforces the use of the authentication function, routes the messages properly, and facilitates key exchange. It can work with a variety of authentication protocols.

- **Privacy with message integrity:** MAC-level data (e.g., an LLC PDU) are encrypted along with a message integrity code that ensures that the data have not been altered.

Figure 6.4a indicates the security protocols used to support these services, while Figure 6.4b lists the cryptographic algorithms used for these services.

---

[1]In this context, we are discussing access control as a security function. This is a different function than media access control (MAC) as described in Section 6.1. Unfortunately, the literature and the standards use the term *access control* in both contexts.

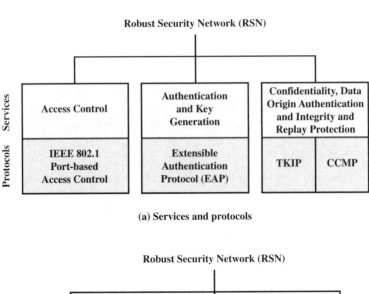

(a) Services and protocols

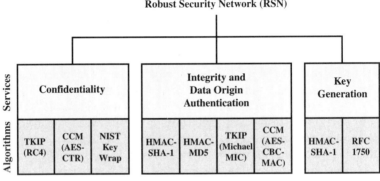

(b) Cryptographic algorithms

CBC-MAC	= Cipher Block Block Chaining Message Authentication Code (MAC)
CCM	= Counter Mode with Cipher Block Chaining Message Authentication Code
CCMP	= Counter Mode with Cipher Block Chaining MAC Protocol
TKIP	= Temporal Key Integrity Protocol

Figure 6.4   Elements of IEEE 802.11i

IEEE 802.11i Phases of Operation

The operation of an IEEE 802.11i RSN can be broken down into five distinct phases of operation. The exact nature of the phases will depend on the configuration and the end points of the communication. Possibilities include (see Figure 6.3):

1. Two wireless stations in the same BSS communicating via the access point (AP) for that BSS.
2. Two wireless stations (STAs) in the same ad hoc IBSS communicating directly with each other.
3. Two wireless stations in different BSSs communicating via their respective APs across a distribution system.
4. A wireless station communicating with an end station on a wired network via its AP and the distribution system.

IEEE 802.11i security is concerned only with secure communication between the STA and its AP. In case 1 in the preceding list, secure communication is assured if each STA establishes secure communications with the AP. Case 2 is similar, with the AP functionality residing in the STA. For case 3, security is not provided across the distribution system at the level of IEEE 802.11, but only within each BSS. End-to-end security (if required) must be provided at a higher layer. Similarly, in case 4, security is only provided between the STA and its AP.

With these considerations in mind, Figure 6.5 depicts the five phases of operation for an RSN and maps them to the network components involved. One new component is the authentication server (AS). The rectangles indicate the exchange of sequences of MPDUs. The five phases are defined as follows.

- **Discovery:** An AP uses messages called Beacons and Probe Responses to advertise its IEEE 802.11i security policy. The STA uses these to identify an AP for a WLAN with which it wishes to communicate. The STA associates with the AP, which it uses to select the cipher suite and authentication mechanism when the Beacons and Probe Responses present a choice.

- **Authentication:** During this phase, the STA and AS prove their identities to each other. The AP blocks non-authentication traffic between the STA and AS until the authentication transaction is successful. The AP does not participate in the authentication transaction other than forwarding traffic between the STA and AS.

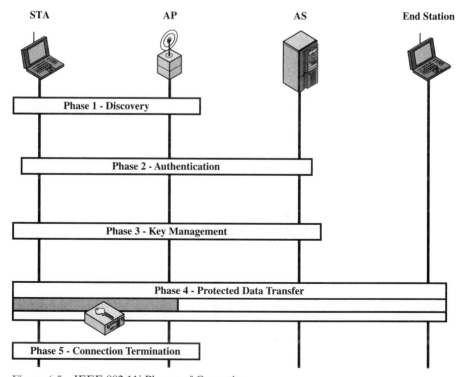

Figure 6.5 IEEE 802.11i Phases of Operation

- **Key generation and distribution:** The AP and the STA perform several operations that cause cryptographic keys to be generated and placed on the AP and the STA. Frames are exchanged between the AP and STA only.

- **Protected data transfer:** Frames are exchanged between the STA and the end station through the AP. As denoted by the shading and the encryption module icon, secure data transfer occurs between the STA and the AP only; security is not provided end-to-end.

- **Connection termination:** The AP and STA exchange frames. During this phase, the secure connection is torn down and the connection is restored to the original state.

Discovery Phase

We now look in more detail at the RSN phases of operation, beginning with the discovery phase, which is illustrated in the upper portion of Figure 6.6. The purpose of this phase is for an STA and an AP to recognize each other, agree on a set of security capabilities, and establish an association for future communication using those security capabilities.

SECURITY CAPABILITIES During this phase, the STA and AP decide on specific techniques in the following areas:

- Confidentiality and MPDU integrity protocols for protecting unicast traffic (traffic only between this STA and AP)
- Authentication method
- Cryptography key management approach

Confidentiality and integrity protocols for protecting multicast/broadcast traffic are dictated by the AP, since all STAs in a multicast group must use the same protocols and ciphers. The specification of a protocol, along with the chosen key length (if variable) is known as a *cipher suite*. The options for the confidentiality and integrity cipher suite are

- WEP, with either a 40-bit or 104-bit key, which allows backward compatibility with older IEEE 802.11 implementations
- TKIP
- CCMP
- Vendor-specific methods

The other negotiable suite is the authentication and key management (AKM) suite, which defines (1) the means by which the AP and STA perform mutual authentication and (2) the means for deriving a root key from which other keys may be generated. The possible AKM suites are

- IEEE 802.1X
- Pre-shared key (no explicit authentication takes place and mutual authentication is implied if the STA and AP share a unique secret key)
- Vendor-specific methods

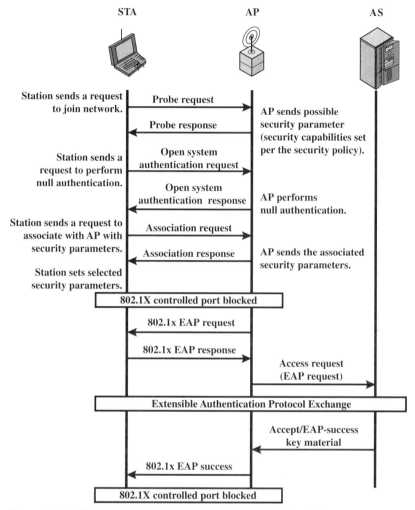

Figure 6.6   IEEE 802.11i Phases of Operation: Capability Discovery, Authentication, and Association

MPDU Exchange The discovery phase consists of three exchanges.

- **Network and security capability discovery:** During this exchange, STAs discover the existence of a network with which to communicate. The AP either periodically broadcasts its security capabilities (not shown in figure), indicated by RSN IE (Robust Security Network Information Element), in a specific channel through the Beacon frame; or responds to a station's Probe Request through a Probe Response frame. A wireless station may discover available access points and corresponding security capabilities by either passively monitoring the Beacon frames or actively probing every channel.

- **Open system authentication:** The purpose of this frame sequence, which provides no security, is simply to maintain backward compatibility with the

IEEE 802.11 state machine, as implemented in existing IEEE 802.11 hardware. In essence, the two devices (STA and AP) simply exchange identifiers.

- **Association:** The purpose of this stage is to agree on a set of security capabilities to be used. The STA then sends an Association Request frame to the AP. In this frame, the STA specifies one set of matching capabilities (one authentication and key management suite, one pairwise cipher suite, and one group-key cipher suite) from among those advertised by the AP. If there is no match in capabilities between the AP and the STA, the AP refuses the Association Request. The STA blocks it too, in case it has associated with a rogue AP or someone is inserting frames illicitly on its channel. As shown in Figure 6.6, the IEEE 802.1X controlled ports are blocked, and no user traffic goes beyond the AP. The concept of blocked ports is explained subsequently.

Authentication Phase

As was mentioned, the authentication phase enables mutual authentication between an STA and an authentication server (AS) located in the DS. Authentication is designed to allow only authorized stations to use the network and to provide the STA with assurance that it is communicating with a legitimate network.

IEEE 802.1X ACCESS CONTROL APPROACH IEEE 802.11i makes use of another standard that was designed to provide access control functions for LANs. The standard is IEEE 802.1X, Port-Based Network Access Control. The authentication protocol that is used, the Extensible Authentication Protocol (EAP), is defined in the IEEE 802.1X standard. IEEE 802.1X uses the terms *supplicant*, *authenticator*, and *authentication server* (AS). In the context of an 802.11 WLAN, the first two terms correspond to the wireless station and the AP. The AS is typically a separate device on the wired side of the network (i.e., accessible over the DS) but could also reside directly on the authenticator.

Before a supplicant is authenticated by the AS using an authentication protocol, the authenticator only passes control or authentication messages between the supplicant and the AS; the 802.1X control channel is unblocked, but the 802.11 data channel is blocked. Once a supplicant is authenticated and keys are provided, the authenticator can forward data from the supplicant, subject to predefined access control limitations for the supplicant to the network. Under these circumstances, the data channel is unblocked.

As indicated in Figure 6.7, 802.1X uses the concepts of controlled and uncontrolled ports. Ports are logical entities defined within the authenticator and refer to physical network connections. For a WLAN, the authenticator (the AP) may have only two physical ports: one connecting to the DS and one for wireless communication within its BSS. Each logical port is mapped to one of these two physical ports. An uncontrolled port allows the exchange of PDUs between the supplicant and the other AS, regardless of the authentication state of the supplicant. A controlled port allows the exchange of PDUs between a supplicant and other systems on the LAN only if the current state of the supplicant authorizes such an exchange.

The 802.1X framework, with an upper-layer authentication protocol, fits nicely with a BSS architecture that includes a number of wireless stations and an AP.

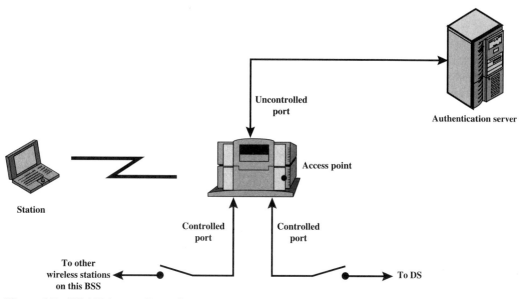

Authentication server

Access point

Station

Controlled
port

Controlled
port

To other
wireless stations
on this BSS

To DS

Figure 6.7   802.1X Access Control

However, for an IBSS, there is no AP. For an IBSS, 802.11i provides a more complex solution that, in essence, involves pairwise authentication between stations on the IBSS.

MPDU EXCHANGE The lower part of Figure 6.6 shows the MPDU exchange dictated by IEEE 802.11 for the authentication phase. We can think of authentication phase as consisting of the following three phases.

- **Connect to AS:** The STA sends a request to its AP (the one with which it has an association) for connection to the AS. The AP acknowledges this request and sends an access request to the AS.
- **EAP exchange:** This exchange authenticates the STA and AS to each other. A number of alternative exchanges are possible, as explained subsequently.
- **Secure key delivery:** Once authentication is established, the AS generates a master session key (MSK), also known as the Authentication, Authorization, and Accounting (AAA) key and sends it to the STA. As explained subsequently, all the cryptographic keys needed by the STA for secure communication with its AP are generated from this MSK. IEEE 802.11i does not prescribe a method for secure delivery of the MSK but relies on EAP for this. Whatever method is used, it involves the transmission of an MPDU containing an encrypted MSK from the AS, via the AP, to the AS.

EAP EXCHANGE As mentioned, there are a number of possible EAP exchanges that can be used during the authentication phase. Typically, the message flow between STA and AP employs the EAP over LAN (EAPOL) protocol, and the message flow between the AP and AS uses the Remote Authentication Dial In User Service (RADIUS) protocol, although other options are available for both STA-to-AP and AP-to-AS exchanges. [FRAN07] provides the following summary of the authentication exchange using EAPOL and RADIUS.

1. The EAP exchange begins with the AP issuing an EAP-Request/Identity frame to the STA.

2. The STA replies with an EAP-Response/Identity frame, which the AP receives over the uncontrolled port. The packet is then encapsulated in RADIUS over EAP and passed on to the RADIUS server as a RADIUS-Access-Request packet.

3. The AAA server replies with a RADIUS-Access-Challenge packet, which is passed on to the STA as an EAP-Request. This request is of the appropriate authentication type and contains relevant challenge information.

4. The STA formulates an EAP-Response message and sends it to the AS. The response is translated by the AP into a Radius-Access-Request with the response to the challenge as a data field. Steps 3 and 4 may be repeated multiple times, depending on the EAP method in use. For TLS tunneling methods, it is common for authentication to require 10 to 20 round trips.

5. The AAA server grants access with a Radius-Access-Accept packet. The AP issues an EAP-Success frame. (Some protocols require confirmation of the EAP success inside the TLS tunnel for authenticity validation.) The controlled port is authorized, and the user may begin to access the network.

Note from Figure 6.6 that the AP controlled port is still blocked to general user traffic. Although the authentication is successful, the ports remain blocked until the temporal keys are installed in the STA and AP, which occurs during the 4-Way Handshake.

Key Management Phase

During the key management phase, a variety of cryptographic keys are generated and distributed to STAs. There are two types of keys: pairwise keys used for communication between an STA and an AP and group keys used for multicast communication. Figure 6.8, based on [FRAN07], shows the two key hierarchies, and Table 6.3 defines the individual keys.

PAIRWISE KEYS Pairwise keys are used for communication between a pair of devices, typically between an STA and an AP. These keys form a hierarchy beginning with a master key from which other keys are derived dynamically and used for a limited period of time.

At the top level of the hierarchy are two possibilities. A **pre-shared key (PSK)** is a secret key shared by the AP and a STA and installed in some fashion outside the scope of IEEE 802.11i. The other alternative is the **master session key (MSK)**, also known as the AAAK, which is generated using the IEEE 802.1X protocol

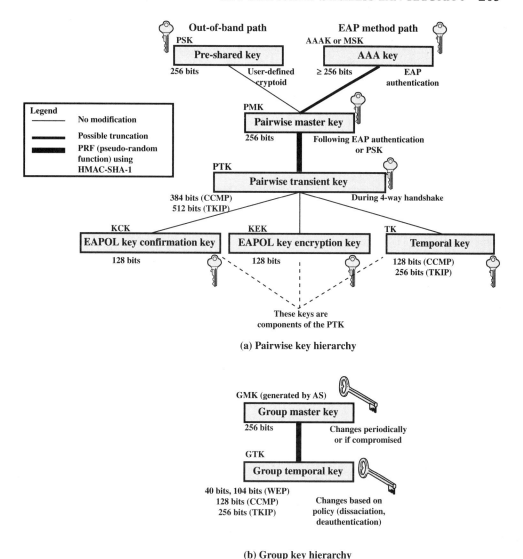

Figure 6.8   IEEE 802.11i Key Hierarchies

during the authentication phase, as described previously. The actual method of key generation depends on the details of the authentication protocol used. In either case (PSK or MSK), there is a unique key shared by the AP with each STA with which it communicates. All the other keys derived from this master key are also unique between an AP and an STA. Thus, each STA, at any time, has one set of keys, as depicted in the hierarchy of Figure 6.8a, while the AP has one set of such keys for each of its STAs.

The **pairwise master key (PMK)** is derived from the master key. If a PSK is used, then the PSK is used as the PMK; if a MSK is used, then the PMK is derived from the MSK by truncation (if necessary). By the end of the authentication phase,

Table 6.3   IEEE 802.11i Keys for Data Confidentiality and Integrity Protocols

Abbrev-iation	Name	Description / Purpose	Size (bits)	Type
AAA Key	Authentication, Accounting, and Authorization Key	Used to derive the PMK. Used with the IEEE 802.1X authentication and key management approach. Same as MMSK.	≥ 256	Key generation key, root key
PSK	Pre-shared Key	Becomes the PMK in pre-shared key environments.	256	Key generation key, root key
PMK	Pairwise Master Key	Used with other inputs to derive the PTK.	256	Key generation key
GMK	Group Master Key	Used with other inputs to derive the GTK.	128	Key generation key
PTK	Pair-wise Transient Key	Derived from the PMK. Comprises the EAPOL-KCK, EAPOL-KEK, and TK and (for TKIP) the MIC key.	512 (TKIP) 384 (CCMP)	Composite key
TK	Temporal Key	Used with TKIP or CCMP to provide confidentiality and integrity protection for unicast user traffic.	256 (TKIP) 128 (CCMP)	Traffic key
GTK	Group Temporal Key	Derived from the GMK. Used to provide confidentiality and integrity protection for multicast/broadcast user traffic.	256 (TKIP) 128 (CCMP) 40, 104 (WEP)	Traffic key
MIC Key	Message Integrity Code Key	Used by TKIP's Michael MIC to provide integrity protection of messages.	64	Message integrity key
EAPOL-KCK	EAPOL-Key Confirmation Key	Used to provide integrity protection for key material distributed during the 4-Way Handshake.	128	Message integrity key
EAPOL-KEK	EAPOL-Key Encryption Key	Used to ensure the confidentiality of the GTK and other key material in the 4-Way Handshake.	128	Traffic key / key encryption key
WEP Key	Wired Equivalent Privacy Key	Used with WEP.	40, 104	Traffic key

marked by the 802.1x EAP Success message (Figure 6.6), both the AP and the STA have a copy of their shared PMK.

The PMK is used to generate the **pairwise transient key (PTK)**, which in fact consists of three keys to be used for communication between an STA and AP after they have been mutually authenticated. To derive the PTK, the HMAC-SHA-1 function is applied to the PMK, the MAC addresses of the STA and AP, and nonces generated when needed. Using the STA and AP addresses in the generation of the PTK provides protection against session hijacking and impersonation; using nonces provides additional random keying material.

The three parts of the PTK are as follows.

- **EAP Over LAN (EAPOL) Key Confirmation Key (EAPOL-KCK):** Supports the integrity and data origin authenticity of STA-to-AP control frames during operational setup of an RSN. It also performs an access control function: proof-of-possession of the PMK. An entity that possesses the PMK is authorized to use the link.
- **EAPOL Key Encryption Key (EAPOL-KEK):** Protects the confidentiality of keys and other data during some RSN association procedures.
- **Temporal Key (TK):** Provides the actual protection for user traffic.

GROUP KEYS Group keys are used for multicast communication in which one STA sends MPDU's to multiple STAs. At the top level of the group key hierarchy is the **group master key (GMK)**. The GMK is a key-generating key used with other inputs to derive the **group temporal key (GTK)**. Unlike the PTK, which is generated using material from both AP and STA, the GTK is generated by the AP and transmitted to its associated STAs. Exactly how this GTK is generated is undefined. IEEE 802.11i, however, requires that its value is computationally indistinguishable from random. The GTK is distributed securely using the pairwise keys that are already established. The GTK is changed every time a device leaves the network.

PAIRWISE KEY DISTRIBUTION The upper part of Figure 6.9 shows the MPDU exchange for distributing pairwise keys. This exchange is known as the **4-way handshake**. The STA and SP use this handshake to confirm the existence of the PMK, verify the selection of the cipher suite, and derive a fresh PTK for the following data session. The four parts of the exchange are as follows.

- **AP → STA:** Message includes the MAC address of the AP and a nonce (Anonce)
- **STA → AP:** The STA generates its own nonce (Snonce) and uses both nonces and both MAC addresses, plus the PMK, to generate a PTK. The STA then sends a message containing its MAC address and Snonce, enabling the AP to generate the same PTK. This message includes a message integrity code (MIC)[2] using HMAC-MD5 or HMAC-SHA-1-128. The key used with the MIC is KCK.
- **AP → STA:** The AP is now able to generate the PTK. The AP then sends a message to the STA, containing the same information as in the first message, but this time including a MIC.
- **STA → AP:** This is merely an acknowledgment message, again protected by a MIC.

GROUP KEY DISTRIBUTION For group key distribution, the AP generates a GTK and distributes it to each STA in a multicast group. The two-message exchange with each STA consists of the following:

- **AP → STA:** This message includes the GTK, encrypted either with RC4 or with AES. The key used for encryption is KEK. A MIC value is appended.

---

[2]While *MAC* is commonly used in cryptography to refer to a Message Authentication Code, the term *MIC* is used instead in connection with 802.11i because *MAC* has another standard meaning, Media Access Control, in networking.

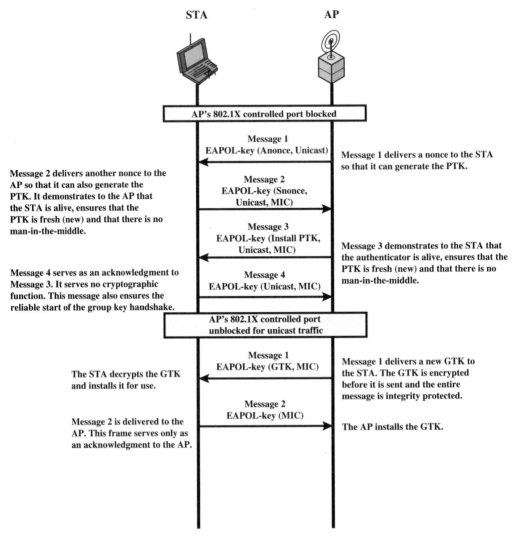

Figure 6.9 IEEE 802.11i Phases of Operation: Four-Way Handshake and Group Key Handshake

- **STA → AP:** The STA acknowledges receipt of the GTK. This message includes a MIC value.

Protected Data Transfer Phase

IEEE 802.11i defines two schemes for protecting data transmitted in 802.11 MPDUs: the Temporal Key Integrity Protocol (TKIP), and the Counter Mode-CBC MAC Protocol (CCMP).

TKIP TKIP is designed to require only software changes to devices that are implemented with the older wireless LAN security approach called Wired Equivalent Privacy (WEP). TKIP provides two services:

- **Message integrity:** TKIP adds a message integrity code (MIC) to the 802.11 MAC frame after the data field. The MIC is generated by an algorithm, called Michael, that computes a 64-bit value using as input the source and destination MAC address values and the Data field, plus key material.
- **Data confidentiality:** Data confidentiality is provided by encrypting the MPDU plus MIC value using RC4.

The 256-bit TK (Figure 6.8) is employed as follows. Two 64-bit keys are used with the Michael message digest algorithm to produce a message integrity code. One key is used to protect STA-to-AP messages, and the other key is used to protect AP-to-STA messages. The remaining 128 bits are truncated to generate the RC4 key used to encrypt the transmitted data.

For additional protection, a monotonically increasing TKIP sequence counter (TSC) is assigned to each frame. The TSC serves two purposes. First, the TSC is included with each MPDU and is protected by the MIC to protect against replay attacks. Second, the TSC is combined with the session TK to produce a dynamic encryption key that changes with each transmitted MPDU, thus making cryptanalysis more difficult.

CCMP CCMP is intended for newer IEEE 802.11 devices that are equipped with the hardware to support this scheme. As with TKIP, CCMP provides two services:

- **Message integrity:** CCMP uses the cipher-block-chaining message authentication code (CBC-MAC), described in Chapter 3.
- **Data confidentiality:** CCMP uses the CTR block cipher mode of operation with AES for encryption. CTR is described in Chapter 2.

The same 128-bit AES key is used for both integrity and confidentiality. The scheme uses a 48-bit packet number to construct a nonce to prevent replay attacks.

The IEEE 802.11i Pseudorandom Function

At a number of places in the IEEE 802.11i scheme, a pseudorandom function (PRF) is used. For example, it is used to generate nonces, to expand pairwise keys, and to generate the GTK. Best security practice dictates that different pseudorandom number streams be used for these different purposes. However, for implementation efficiency, we would like to rely on a single pseudorandom number generator function.

The PRF is built on the use of HMAC-SHA-1 to generate a pseudorandom bit stream. Recall that HMAC-SHA-1 takes a message (block of data) and a key of length at least 160 bits and produces a 160-bit hash value. SHA-1 has the property that the change of a single bit of the input produces a new hash value with no apparent connection to the preceding hash value. This property is the basis for pseudorandom number generation.

The IEEE 802.11i PRF takes four parameters as input and produces the desired number of random bits. The function is of the form PRF(K, A, B, Len), where

K = a secret key

A = a text string specific to the application (e.g., nonce generation or pairwise key expansion)

B = some data specific to each case

Len = desired number of pseudorandom bits

For example, for the pairwise transient key for CCMP:

```
PTK = PRF(PMK, "Pairwise key expansion", min(AP-
      Addr, STA-Addr) || max(AP-Addr, STA-Addr) || min
      (Anonce, Snonce) || max(Anonce, Snonce), 384)
```

So, in this case, the parameters are

K = PMK

A = the text string "Pairwise key expansion"

B = a sequence of bytes formed by concatenating the two MAC addresses and the two nonces

Len = 384 bits

Similarly, a nonce is generated by

```
Nonce = PRF(Random Number, "Init Counter", MAC || Time, 256)
```

where **Time** is a measure of the network time known to the nonce generator. The group temporal key is generated by

```
GTK = PRF(GMK, "Group key expansion", MAC || Gnonce, 256)
```

Figure 6.10 illustrates the function PRF(K, A, B, Len). The parameter K serves as the key input to HMAC. The message input consists of four items concatenated together: the parameter A, a byte with value 0, the parameter B, and a counter i. The counter is initialized to 0. The HMAC algorithm is run once, producing a 160-bit hash value. If more bits are required, HMAC is run again with the same inputs, except that i is incremented each time until the necessary number of bits is generated. We can express the logic as

```
PRF(K, A, B, Len)
    R ← null string
    for i ← 0 to ((Len + 159)/160 - 1) do
    R ← R || HMAC-SHA-1(K, A || 0 || B || i)
    Return Truncate-to-Len(R, Len)
```

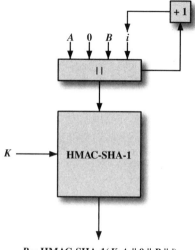

$$R = \text{HMAC-SHA-1}(K, A \parallel 0 \parallel B \parallel i)$$

Figure 6.10   IEEE 802.11i Pseudorandom Function

6.3 WIRELESS APPLICATION PROTOCOL OVERVIEW

The Wireless Application Protocol (WAP) is a universal, open standard developed by the WAP Forum to provide mobile users of wireless phones and other wireless terminals such as pagers and personal digital assistants (PDAs) access to telephony and information services, including the Internet and the Web. WAP is designed to work with all wireless network technologies (e.g., GSM, CDMA, and TDMA). WAP is based on existing Internet standards, such as IP, XML, HTML, and HTTP, as much as possible. It also includes security facilities. At the time of this writing, the current release of the WAP specification is version 2.0.

Strongly affecting the use of mobile phones and terminals for data services are the significant limitations of the devices and the networks that connect them. The devices have limited processors, memory, and battery life. The user interface is also limited, and the displays small. The wireless networks are characterized by relatively low bandwidth, high latency, and unpredictable availability and stability compared to wired connections. Moreover, all of these features vary widely from terminal device to terminal device and from network to network. Finally, mobile, wireless users have different expectations and needs from other information systems users. For instance, mobile terminals must be extremely easy to use — much easier than workstations and personal computers. WAP is designed to deal with these challenges. The WAP specification includes:

- A programming model based on the WWW Programming Model
- A markup language, the Wireless Markup Language, adhering to XML
- A specification of a small browser suitable for a mobile, wireless terminal
- A lightweight communications protocol stack
- A framework for wireless telephony applications (WTAs)

Operational Overview

The WAP Programming Model is based on three elements: the *client*, the *gateway*, and the *original server* (Figure 6.11). HTTP is used between the gateway and the original server to transfer content. The gateway acts as a proxy server for the wireless domain. Its processor(s) provide services that offload the limited capabilities of the hand-held, mobile, wireless terminals. For example, the gateway provides DNS services, converts between WAP protocol stack and the WWW stack (HTTP and TCP/IP), encodes information from the Web into a more compact form that minimizes wireless communication, and in the other direction, decodes the compacted form into standard Web communication conventions. The gateway also caches frequently requested information.

Figure 6.12 illustrates key components in a WAP environment. Using WAP, a mobile user can browse Web content on an ordinary Web server. The Web server provides content in the form of HTML-coded pages that are transmitted using the standard Web protocol stack (HTTP/TCP/IP). The HTML content must go through an HTML filter, which either may be colocated with the WAP proxy or in a separate physical module. The filter translates the HTML content into WML content. If the filter is separate from the proxy, HTTP/TCP/IP is used to deliver the WML to the proxy. The proxy converts the WML to a more compact form known as binary WML and delivers it to the mobile user over a wireless network using the WAP protocol stack.

If the Web server is capable of directly generating WML content, then the WML is delivered using HTTP/TCP/IP to the proxy, which converts the WML to binary WML and then delivers it to the mobile node using WAP protocols.

The WAP architecture is designed to cope with the two principal limitations of wireless Web access: the limitations of the mobile node (small screen size, limited input capability) and the low data rates of wireless digital networks. Even with the introduction of 3G wireless networks, which provide broadband data rates, the small hand-held mobile nodes continue to have limited input and display capabilities. Thus, WAP or a similar capability will be needed for the indefinite future.

Wireless Markup Language

WML was designed to describe content and format for presenting data on devices with limited bandwidth, limited screen size, and limited user input capability. It is designed to work with telephone keypads, styluses, and other input devices common to mobile, wireless communication. WML permits the scaling of displays for use on two-line screens found in some small devices, as well as the larger screens found on smart phones.

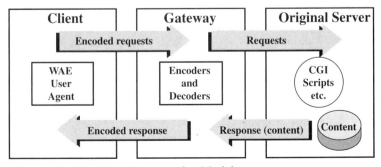

Figure 6.11   The WAP Programming Model

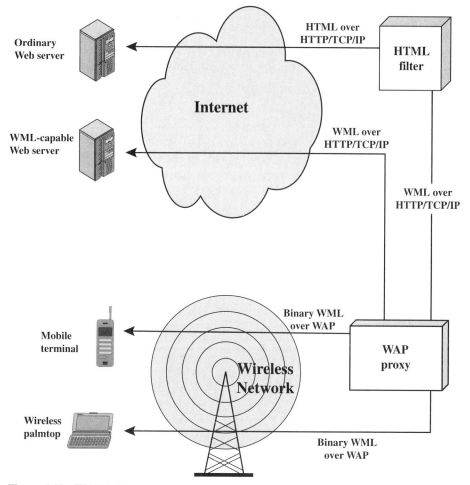

Figure 6.12   WAP Infrastructure

For an ordinary PC, a Web browser provides content in the form of Web pages coded with the Hypertext Markup Language (HTML). To translate an HTML-coded Web page into WML with content and format suitable for wireless devices, much of the information, especially graphics and animation, must be stripped away. WML presents mainly text-based information that attempts to capture the essence of the Web page and that is organized for easy access for users of mobile devices.

Important features of WML include:

- **Text and image support:** Formatting and layout commands are provided for text and limited image capability.

- **Deck/card organizational metaphor:** WML documents are subdivided into small, well-defined units of user interaction called *cards*. Users navigate by moving back and forth between cards. A card specifies one or more units of interaction (a menu, a screen of text, or a text-entry field). A WML deck is similar to an HTML page in that it is identified by a Web address (URL) and is the unit of content transmission.

- **Support for navigation among cards and decks:** WML includes provisions for event handling, which is used for navigation or executing scripts.

In an HTML-based Web browser, a user navigates by clicking on links. At a WML-capable mobile device, a user interacts with cards, moving forward and back through the deck.

WAP Architecture

Figure 6.13, from the WAP architecture document, illustrates the overall stack architecture implemented in a WAP client. In essence, this is a five-layer model. Each layer provides a set of functions and/or services to other services and applications through a set of well-defined interfaces. Each of the layers of the architecture is accessible by the layers above, as well as by other services and applications. Many of the services in the stack may be provided by more than one protocol. For example, either HTTP or WSP may provide the Hypermedia Transfer service.

Common to all five layers are sets of services that are accessible by multiple layers. These common services fall into two categories: security services and service discovery.

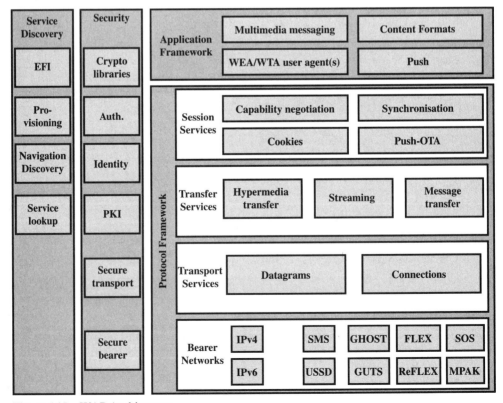

Figure 6.13   WAP Architecture

SECURITY SERVICES The WAP specification includes mechanisms to provide confidentiality, integrity, authentication, and nonrepudiation. The security services include the following.

- **Cryptographic libraries:** This application framework level library provides services for signing of data for integrity and non-repudiation purposes.
- **Authentication:** WAP provides various mechanisms for client and server authentication. At the Session Services layer, HTTP Client Authentication (RFC2617) may be used to authenticate clients to proxies and application servers. At the Transport Services layer, WTLS and TLS handshakes may be used to authenticate clients and servers.
- **Identity:** The WAP Identity Module (WIM) provides the functions that store and process information needed for user identification and authentication.
- **PKI:** The set of security services that enable the use and management of public-key cryptography and certificates.
- **Secure transport:** The Transport Services layer protocols are defined for secure transport over datagrams and connections. WTLS is defined for secure transport over datagrams and TLS is defined for secure transport over connections (i.e., TCP).
- **Secure bearer:** Some bearer networks provide bearer-level security. For example, IP networks (especially in the context of IPv6) provide bearer-level security with IPsec.

SERVICE DISCOVERY There is a collection of service discovery services that enable the WAP client and the Web server to determine capabilities and services. Examples of service discovery services include the following.

- **EFI:** The External Functionality Interface (EFI) allows applications to discover what external functions/services are available on the device.
- **Provisioning:** This service allows a device to be provisioned with the parameters necessary to access network services.
- **Navigation discovery:** This service allows a device to discover new network services (e.g., secure pull proxies) during the course of navigation such as when downloading resources from a hypermedia server. The WAP Transport-Level End-to-End Security specification, described in Section 6.5, defines one navigation discovery protocol.
- **Service lookup:** This service provides for the discovery of a service's parameters through a directory lookup by name. One example of this is the Domain Name System (DNS).

Wireless Application Environment

The WAE specifies an application framework for wireless devices such as mobile telephones, pagers, and PDAs. In essence, the WAE consists of tools and formats that are intended to ease the task of developing applications and devices supported by WAP. The major elements of the WAE model (Figure 6.13) are

- **WAE user agents:** Software that executes in the user's wireless device and that provides specific functionality (e.g., display content) to the end user.
- **Wireless telephony applications (WTA):** A collection of telephony-specific extensions for call and feature control mechanisms that provide authors advanced mobile network services. Using WTA, applications developers can use the microbrowser to originate telephone calls and to respond to events from the telephone network.
- **Standard content encoding:** Defined to allow a WAE user agent (e.g., a browser) to conveniently navigate Web content. On the server side are content generators. These are applications (or services) on origin servers (e.g., CGI scripts) that produce standard content formats in response to requests from user agents in the mobile terminal. WAE does not specify any standard content generators but expects that there will be a variety available running on typical HTTP origin servers commonly used in WWW today.
- **Push:** A service to receive push transmissions from the server, i.e., transmissions that are not in response to a Web client request but are sent on the initiative of the server. This service is supported by the Push-OTA (Push Over The Air) session service.
- **Multimedia messaging:** Provides for the transfer and processing of multimedia messages, such as e-mail and instant messages, to WAP devices.

WAP Protocol Architecture

The WAP architecture illustrated in Figure 6.13 dictates a collection of services at each level and provides interface specifications at the boundary between each pair of layers. Because several of the services in the WAP stack can be provided using different protocols based on the circumstances, there are more than one possible stack configurations. Figure 6.14 depicts a common protocol stack configuration in which a WAP client device connects to a Web server via a WAP gateway. This configuration is common with devices that implement version 1 of the WAP specification but is also used in version 2 devices (WAP2) if the bearer network does not support TCP/IP.

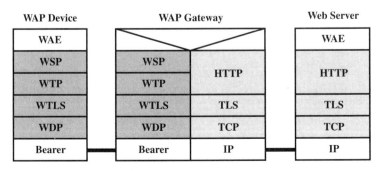

Figure 6.14 WTP 1.x Gateway

In the remainder of this subsection, we provide an overview of the WAP protocols, with the exception of WTLS, which is treated in Section 6.4.

WIRELESS SESSION PROTOCOL WSP provides applications with an interface for two session services. The connection-oriented session service operates above WTP, and the connectionless session service operates above the unreliable transport protocol WDP. In essence, WSP is based on HTTP with some additions and modifications to optimize its use over wireless channels. The principal limitations addressed are low data rate and susceptibility to loss of connection due to poor coverage or cell overloading.

WSP is a transaction-oriented protocol based on the concept of a request and a reply. Each WSP protocol data unit (PDU) consists of a body, which may contain WML, WMLScript, or images; and a header, which contains information about the data in the body and about the transaction. WSP also defines a server push operation, in which the server sends unrequested content to a client device. This may be used for broadcast messages or for services, such as news headlines or stock quotes, that may be tailored to each client device.

WIRELESS TRANSACTION PROTOCOL WTP manages transactions by conveying requests and responses between a user agent (such as a WAP browser) and an application server for such activities as browsing and e-commerce transactions. WTP provides a reliable transport service but dispenses with much of the overhead of TCP, resulting in a lightweight protocol that is suitable for implementation in "thin" clients (e.g., mobile nodes) and suitable for use over low-bandwidth wireless links. WTP includes the following features.

- Three classes of transaction service.
- Optional user-to-user reliability: WTP user triggers the confirmation of each received message.
- Optional out-of-band data on acknowledgments.
- PDU concatenation and delayed acknowledgment to reduce the number of messages sent.
- Asynchronous transactions.

WTP is transaction oriented rather than connection oriented. With WTP, there is no explicit connection setup or teardown but rather a reliable connectionless service.

WTP provides three transaction classes that may be invoked by WSP or another higher layer protocol:

- **Class 0:** Unreliable invoke message with no result message
- **Class 1:** Reliable invoke message with no result message
- **Class 2:** Unreliable invoke message with one reliable result message

Class 0 provides an unreliable datagram service, which can be used for an unreliable push operation. Data from a WTP user are encapsulated by WTP (the initiator, or client) in an invoke PDU and transmitted to the target WTP (the responder, or server) with no acknowledgment. The responder WTP delivers the data to the target WTP user.

Class 1 provides a reliable datagram service, which can be used for a reliable push operation. Data from an initiator are encapsulated in an invoke PDU and transmitted to the responder. The responder delivers the data to the target WTP user and acknowledges receipt of the data by sending back an ACK PDU to the WTP entity on the initiator side, which confirms the transaction to the source WTP user. The responder WTP maintains state information for some time after the ACK has been sent to handle possible retransmission of the ACK if it gets lost and/or the initiator retransmits the invoke PDU.

Class 2 provides a request/response transaction service and supports the execution of multiple transactions during one WSP session. Data from an initiator are encapsulated in an invoke PDU and transmitted to the responder, which delivers the data to the target WTP user. The target WTP user prepares response data, which are handed down to the local WTP entity. The responder WTP entity sends these data back in a result PDU. If there is a delay in generating the response data beyond a timer threshold, the responder may send an ACK PDU before sending the result PDU. This prevents the initiator from unnecessarily retransmitting the invoke message.

WIRELESS DATAGRAM PROTOCOL WDP is used to adapt a higher-layer WAP protocol to the communication mechanism (called the bearer) used between the mobile node and the WAP gateway. Adaptation may include partitioning data into segments of appropriate size for the bearer and interfacing with the bearer network. WDP hides details of the various bearer networks from the other layers of WAP. In some instances, WAP is implemented on top of IP.

6.4 WIRELESS TRANSPORT LAYER SECURITY

WTLS provides security services between the mobile device (client) and the WAP gateway. WTLS is based on the industry-standard Transport Layer Security (TLS) Protocol,[3] which is a refinement of the Secure Sockets Layer (SSL) protocol. TLS is the standard security protocol used between Web browsers and Web servers. WTLS is more efficient that TLS, requiring fewer message exchanges. To provide end-to-end security, WTLS is used between the client and the gateway, and TLS is used between the gateway and the target server (Figure 6.14). WAP systems translate between WTLS and TLS within the WAP gateway. Thus, the gateway is a point of vulnerability and must be given a high level of security from external attacks.

WTLS provides the following features.

- **Data integrity:** Uses message authentication to ensure that data sent between the client and the gateway are not modified.
- **Privacy:** Uses encryption to ensure that the data cannot be read by a third party.
- **Authentication:** Uses digital certificates to authenticate the two parties.
- **Denial-of-service protection:** Detects and rejects messages that are replayed or not successfully verified.

---

[3]See Chapter 5 for a discussion of SSL/TLS. However, the discussion in this section is self-contained; you do not need to read a description of TLS first.

WTLS Sessions and Connections

Two important WTLS concepts are the secure session and the secure connection, which are defined in the specification as:

- **Secure connection:** A connection is a transport (in the OSI layering model definition) that provides a suitable type of service. For SSL, such connections are peer-to-peer relationships. The connections are transient. Every connection is associated with one session.

- **Secure session:** An SSL session is an association between a client and a server. Sessions are created by the Handshake Protocol. Sessions define a set of cryptographic security parameters, which can be shared among multiple connections. Sessions are used to avoid the expensive negotiation of new security parameters for each connection.

Between any pair of parties (applications such as HTTP on client and server), there may be multiple secure connections. In theory, there may also be multiple simultaneous sessions between parties, but this feature is not used in practice.

There are a number of states associated with each session. Once a session is established, there is a current operating state for both read and write (i.e., receive and send). In addition, during the Handshake Protocol, pending read and write states are created. Upon successful conclusion of the Handshake Protocol, the pending states become the current states.

A session state is defined by the following parameters:

- **Session identifier:** An arbitrary byte sequence chosen by the server to identify an active or resumable session state.
- **Protocol version:** WTLS protocol version number.
- **Peer certificate:** Certificate of the peer. This element of the state may be null.
- **Compression method:** The algorithm used to compress data prior to encryption.
- **Cipher spec:** Specifies the bulk data encryption algorithm (such as null, RC5, DES, etc.) and a hash algorithm (such as MD5 or SHA-1) used for MAC calculation. It also defines cryptographic attributes such as the hash_size.
- **Master secret:** A 20-byte secret shared between the client and server.
- **Sequence number:** Which sequence numbering scheme (off, implicit, or explicit) is used in this secure connection.
- **Key refresh:** Defines how often some connection state values (encryption key, MAC secret, and IV) calculations are performed.
- **Is resumable:** A flag indicating whether the session can be used to initiate new connections.

The connection state is the operating environment of the record protocol. It includes all parameters that are needed for the cryptographic operations (encryption/decryption and MAC calculation/verification). Each secure connection has a connection state, which is defined by the following parameters.

- **Connection end:** Whether this entity is considered a client or a server in this secure session.
- **Bulk cipher algorithm:** Includes the key size of this algorithm, how much of that key is secret, whether it is a block or stream cipher, and the block size of the cipher (if appropriate).
- **MAC algorithm:** Includes the size of the key used for MAC calculation and the size of the hash which is returned by the MAC algorithm.
- **Compression algorithm:** Includes all information the algorithm requires to do compression.
- **Master secret:** A 20-byte secret shared between the client and server.
- **Client random:** A 16-byte value provided by the client.
- **Server random:** A 16-byte value provided by the server.
- **Sequence number mode:** Which scheme is used to communicate sequence numbers in this secure connection.
- **Key refresh:** Defines how often some connection state parameters (encryption key, MAC secret, and IV) are updated. New keys are calculated at every $n = 2^{key\_refresh}$ messages, that is, when the sequence number is $0, 2^n, 3^n$, etc.

WTLS Protocol Architecture

WTLS is not a single protocol but rather two layers of protocols, as illustrated in Figure 6.15. The WTLS Record Protocol provides basic security services to various higher-layer protocols. In particular, the Hypertext Transfer Protocol (HTTP), which provides the transfer service for Web client/server interaction, can operate on top of WTLS. Three higher-layer protocols are defined as part of WTLS: the Handshake Protocol, The Change Cipher Spec Protocol, and the Alert Protocol. These WTLS-specific protocols are used in the management of WTLS exchanges and are examined subsequently in this section.

WTLS RECORD PROTOCOL The WTLS Record Protocol takes user data from the next higher layer (WTP, WTLS Handshake Protocol, WTLS Alert Protocol, and WTLS Change Cipher Spec Protocol) and encapsulates these data in a PDU. The following steps occur (Figure 6.16).

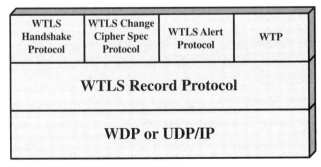

Figure 6.15 WTLS Protocol Stack

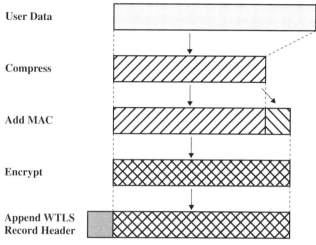

User Data

Compress

Add MAC

Encrypt

Append WTLS
Record Header

Figure 6.16   WTLS Record Protocol Operation

Step 1. The payload is compressed using a lossless compression algorithm.

Step 2. A message authentication code (MAC) is computed over the compressed data, using HMAC. One of several hash algorithms can be used with HMAC, including MD-5 and SHA-1. The length of the hash code is 0, 5, or 10 bytes. The MAC is added after the compressed data.

Step 3. The compressed message plus the MAC code are encrypted using a symmetric encryption algorithm. The allowable encryption algorithms are DES, triple DES, RC5, and IDEA.

Step 4. The Record Protocol prepends a header to the encrypted payload.

The Record Protocol header consists of the following fields (Figure 6.17).

- **Record type** (8 bits): Consisting of the subfields:

  –**Record length field indicator** (1 bit): Indicates whether a record length field is present.

  –**Sequence number field indicator** (1 bit): Indicates whether a sequence number field is present.

  –**Cipher spec indicator** (1 bit): If this bit is zero, it indicates that no compression, MAC protection, or encryption is used.

  –**Content type** (4 bits): The higher-layer protocol above the WTLS Record Protocol.

- **Sequence number** (16 bits): A sequence number associated with this record. This provides reliability over an unreliable transport service.

- **Record length** (16 bits): The length in bytes of the plaintext data (or compressed data if compression is used).

CHANGE CIPHER SPEC PROTOCOL Associated with the current transaction is a cipher spec, which specifies the encryption algorithm, the hash algorithm used as

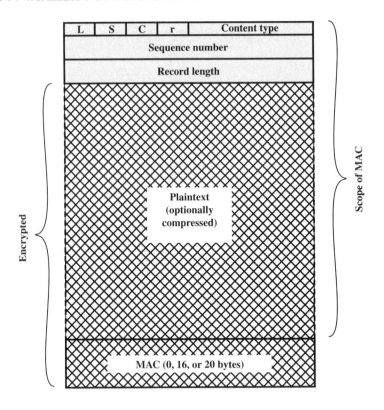

r = reserved
C = cipher spec indicator
S = sequence number field indicator
L = record length field indicator
MAC = message authentication code

Figure 6.17   WTLS Record Format

part of HMAC, and cryptographic attributes, such as MAC code size. There are two states associated with each session. Once a session is established, there is a current operating state for both read and write (i.e., receive and send). In addition, during the Handshake Protocol, pending read and write states are created.

The Change Cipher Spec Protocol is one of the three WTLS-specific protocols that use the WTLS Record Protocol, and it is the simplest. This protocol consists of a single message, which consists of a single byte with the value 1. The sole purpose of this message is to cause the pending state to be copied into the current state, which updates the cipher suite to be used on this connection. Thus, when the Change Cipher Spec message arrives, the sender of the message sets the current write state to the pending state and the receiver sets the current read state to the pending state.

ALERT PROTOCOL The Alert Protocol is used to convey WTLS-related alerts to the peer entity. As with other applications that use WTLS, alert messages are compressed and encrypted, as specified by the current state.

Each message in this protocol consists of 2 bytes. The first byte takes the value warning(1), critical(2), or fatal(3) to convey the severity of the message. The second byte contains a code that indicates the specific alert. If the level is fatal, WTLS immediately terminates the connection. Other connections on the same session may continue, but no new connections on this session may be established. A critical alert message results in termination of the current secure connection. Other connections using the secure session may continue and the secure identifier may also be used for establishing new secure connections.

The connection is closed using the alert messages. Either party may initiate the exchange of the closing messages. If a closing message is received, then any data after this message is ignored. It is also required that the notified party verifies termination of the session by responding to the closing message.

Error handling in the WTLS is based on the alert messages. When an error is detected, the detecting party sends an alert message containing the occurred error. Further procedures depend on the level of the error that occurred.

Examples of fatal alerts:

- **session_close_notify:** notifies the recipient that the sender will not send any more messages using this connection state or the secure session.
- **unexpected_message:** An inappropriate message was received.
- **bad_record_mac:** An incorrect MAC was received.
- **decompression_failure:** The decompression function received improper input (e.g., unable to decompress or decompress to greater than maximum allowable length).
- **handshake_failure:** Sender was unable to negotiate an acceptable set of security parameters given the options available.
- **illegal_parameter:** A field in a handshake message was out of range or inconsistent with other fields.

Examples of nonfatal alerts:

- **connection_close_notify:** Notifies the recipient that the sender will not send any more messages using this connection state.
- **bad_certificate:** A received certificate was corrupt (e.g., contained a signature that did not verify).
- **unsupported_certificate:** The type of the received certificate is not supported.
- **certificate_revoked:** A certificate has been revoked by its signer.
- **certificate_expired:** A certificate has expired.
- **certificate_unknown:** Some other unspecified issue arose in processing the certificate, rendering it unacceptable.

HANDSHAKE PROTOCOL The most complex part of WTLS is the Handshake Protocol. This protocol allows the server and client to authenticate each other and to negotiate an encryption and MAC algorithms and cryptographic keys to be used to protect data sent in a WTLS record. The Handshake Protocol is used before any application data are transmitted. An important function of the Handshake Protocol is the generation of a pre-master secret, which in turn is used to generate a master secret. The master secret is then used to generate various cryptographic keys.

The Handshake Protocol consists of a series of messages exchanged by client and server. Figure 6.18 shows the initial exchange needed to establish a logical

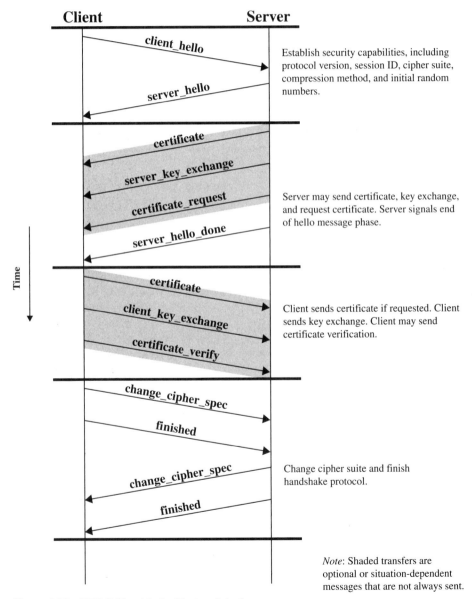

Figure 6.18   WTLS Handshake Protocol Action

connection between client and server. The exchange can be viewed as having four phases.

The **first phase** is used to initiate a logical connection and to establish the security capabilities that will be associated with it. The exchange is initiated by the client. The client sends a `client_hello` message that includes a session ID and a list of cryptographic and compression algorithms supported by the client (in decreasing order of preference for each algorithm type). After sending the `client_hello` message, the client waits for the `server_hello` message. This message indicates which cryptographic and compression algorithms will be used for the exchange.

The **second phase** is used for server authentication and key exchange. The server begins this phase by sending its public-key certificate if it needs to be authenticated. Next, a `server_key_exchange` message may be sent if it is required. This message is needed for certain public-key algorithms used for symmetric key exchange. Next, the server can request a public-key certificate from the client, using the `certificate_request` message. The final message in phase 2 (and one that is always required) is the `server_hello_done` message, which is sent by the server to indicate the end of the server hello and associated messages. After sending this message, the server will wait for a client response. This message has no parameters.

The **third phase** is used for client authentication and key exchange. Upon receipt of the `server_hello_done` message, the client should verify that the server provided a valid certificate if required and check that the `server_hello` parameters are acceptable. If all is satisfactory, the client sends one or more messages back to the server. If the server has requested a certificate, the client sends a certificate message. Next is the `client_key_exchange` message, which must be sent in this phase. The content of the message depends on the type of key exchange. Finally, in this phase, the client may send a `certificate_verify` message to provide explicit verification of a client certificate.

The **fourth phase** completes the setting up of a secure connection. The client sends a `change_cipher_spec` message and copies the pending CipherSpec into the current CipherSpec. Note that this message is not considered part of the Handshake Protocol but is sent using the Change Cipher Spec Protocol. The client then immediately sends the finished message under the new algorithms, keys, and secrets. The finished message verifies that the key exchange and authentication processes were successful. In response to these two messages, the server sends its own `change_cipher_spec` message, transfers the pending to the current CipherSpec, and sends its finished message. At this point, the handshake is complete, and the client and server may begin to exchange application layer data.

Cryptographic Algorithms

AUTHENTICATION Authentication in the WTLS is carried out with certificates. Authentication can occur either between the client and the server or when the client only authenticates the server. The latter procedure can happen only if the server allows it to occur. The server can require the client to authenticate itself to the server.

However, the WTLS specification defines that authentication is an optional procedure. Currently, X.509v3, X9.68, and WTLS certificates are supported. The WTLS certificate is optimized for size, and consists of the following elements (compare with Figure 4.4).

- **Certificate_version:** Version of the certificate.
- **Signature_algorithm:** Algorithm used to sign the certificate.
- **Issuer:** Defines the party who has signed the certificate, usually some CA.
- **Valid_not_before:** The beginning of validity period of the certificate.
- **Valid_not_after:** The point of time after the certificate is no longer valid.
- **Subject:** Owner of the key, associated with the public key being certified.
- **Public_key_type:** Type (algorithm) of the public key.
- **Parameter_specifier:** Specifies parameter relevant for the public key.
- **Public key:** The public key being certified.
- **Signature:** Signed with the CA's private key.

KEY EXCHANGE The purpose of the WTLS protocol is for the client and server to generate a mutually shared pre-master key. This key is then used to generate as master key, as explained subsequently. A number of key exchange protocols are supported by WTLS. They can be grouped into those protocols that include a `server_key_exchange` message as part of the Handshake Protocol (Figure 6.18) and those that don't.

The `server_key_exchange` message is sent by the server only when the server certificate message (if sent) does not contain enough data to allow the client to exchange a pre-master secret. The following three methods require the use of the `server_key_exchange` message.

- **DH_anon:** The conventional Diffie-Hellman computation is performed anonymously (without authentication). The negotiated key (Z) is used as the `pre_master_secret`.
- **ECDH_anon:** The elliptic curve Diffie-Hellman computation is performed. The negotiated key (Z) is used as the `pre_master_secret`.
- **RSA_anon:** This is an RSA key exchange without authentication. The server sends its RSA public key. In this method, a 20-byte secret value is generated by the client, encrypted under the server's public key, and sent to the server. The server uses its private key to decrypt the secret value. The `pre_master_secret` is the secret value appended with the server's public key.

The server key exchange message is not sent for the following key exchange methods.

- **ECDH_ECDSA:** Elliptic curve Diffie-Hellman key exchange with ECDSA-based certificates. The server sends a certificate that contains its ECDH public key. The server certificate is signed with ECDSA by a third party trusted by the client. Depending whether the client is to be authenticated or not, it sends its certificate containing its ECDH public key signed with ECDSA by a third party trusted by the server or just its (temporary) ECDH public key. Each party calculates the pre-master secret based on one's own private key and counterpart's public key received as such or contained in a certificate.

- **RSA:** RSA key exchange with RSA-based certificates. The server sends a certificate that contains its RSA public key. The server certificate is signed with RSA by a third party trusted by the client. The client extracts the server's public key from the received certificate, generates a secret value, encrypts it with the server's public key, and sends it to the server. The pre-master secret is the secret value appended with the server's public key. If the client is to be authenticated, it signs some data (messages sent during the handshake) with its RSA private key and sends its certificate and the signed data.

PSEUDORANDOM FUNCTION(PRF) The PRF is used for a number of purposes in WTLS. The PRF takes as input a secret value, a seed, and an identifying label and produces an output of arbitrary length. In the TLS standard, two hash algorithms were used in order to make the PRF as secure as possible. In order to save resources, WTLS can be implemented using only one hash algorithm. Which hash algorithm is actually used is agreed on during the handshake as a part of the cipher spec.

The PRF is based on the data expansion function

```
P_hash(secret, seed) =   HMAC_hash(secret, A(1) ‖ seed) ‖
                         HMAC_hash(secret, A(2) ‖ seed) ‖
                         HMAC_hash(secret, A(3) ‖ seed) ‖ ...
```

where ‖ indicates concatenation and A() is defined as

```
A(0) = seed
A(i) = HMAC_hash(secret, A(i - 1))
```

Then,

```
PRF(secret, label, seed) = P_hash(secret, label ‖ seed)
```

MASTER KEY GENERATION The shared master secret is a one-time 20-byte value (160 bits) generated for this session by means of secure key exchange. The creation is in two stages. First, a pre_master_secret is exchanged. Second, the master_secret is calculated by both parties, using the function

```
master_secret = PRF(pre_master_secret, "master secret",
                    ClientHello.random ‖ ServerHello.random)
```

where `ClientHello.random` and `ServerHello.random` are the random numbers exchanged during the first phase of the handshake protocol.

The MAC and encryption keys are then derived from the master key. The MAC calculation uses the HMAC algorithm (Chapter 3) and encompasses the fields indicated in the expression

```
HMAC_hash (MAC_secret, seq_number ‖ WTLSCompressed.
    record_type‖ WTLSCompressed.length ‖ WTLS
    Compressed.fragment)
```

where `WTLSCompressed.fragment` refers to the (optionally) compressed plaintext data field.

Either MD5 or SHA-1 may be used for the HMAC hash function.

Encryption is applied to all of the WTLS record, except the header. The following encryption algorithms are permitted.

Algorithm	Key Size (bits)
RC5	40, 56, 64, 128
DES	192
3DES	40
IDEA	40, 56

6.5 WAP END-TO-END SECURITY

The basic WAP transmission model involving a WAP client, a WAP gateway, and a Web server results in a security gap, as illustrated in Figure 6.19. This figure corresponds to the protocol architecture shown in Figure 6.14. The mobile device establishes a secure WTLS session with the WAP gateway. The WAP gateway, in turn,

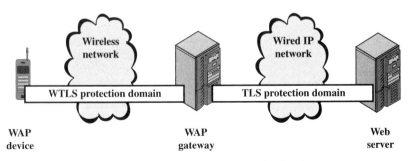

Figure 6.19   Security Zones Using Standard Security Services

establishes a secure SSL or TLS session with the Web server. Within the gateway, data are not encrypted during the translation process. The gateway is thus a point at which the data may be compromised.

There are a number of approaches to providing end-to-end security between the mobile client and the Web server. In the WAP version 2 (known as WAP2) architecture document, the WAP forum defines several protocol arrangements that allow for end-to-end security.

Version 1 of WAP assumed a simplified set of protocols over the wireless network and assumed that the wireless network did not support IP. WAP2 provides the option for the mobile device to implement full TCP/IP-based protocols and operate over an IP-capable wireless network. Figure 6.20 shows two ways in which this IP capability can be exploited to provide end-to-end security. In both approaches, the mobile client implements TCP/IP and HTTP.

The first approach (Figure 6.20a) is to make use of TLS between client and server. A secure TLS session is set up between the endpoints. The WAP gateway acts as a TCP-level gateway and splices together two TCP connections to carry the traffic between the endpoints. However, the TCP user data field (TLS records) remains encrypted as it passes through the gateway, so end-to-end security is maintained.

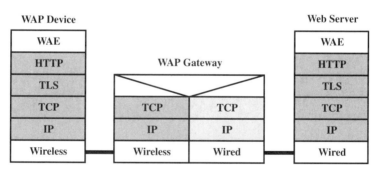

(a) TLS-based security

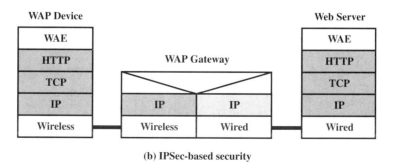

(b) IPSec-based security

Figure 6.20 WAP2 End-to-End Security Approaches

Another possible approach is shown in Figure 6.20b. Here we assume that the WAP gateway acts as a simple Internet router. In this case, end-to-end security can be provided at the IP level using IPsec (discussed in Chapter 8).

Yet another, somewhat more complicated, approach has been defined in more specific terms by the WAP forum in specification entitled "WAP Transport Layer End-to-End Security." This approach is illustrated in Figure 6.21, which is based on a figure in [ASHL01]. In this scenario, the WAP client connects to its usual WAP gateway and attempts to send a request through the gateway to a secure domain. The secure content server determines the need for security that requires that the mobile client connect to its local WAP gateway rather than its default WAP gateway. The Web server responds to the initial client request with an HTTP redirect message that redirects the client to a WAP gateway that is part of the enterprise network. This message passes back through the default gateway, which validates the redirect and sends it to the client. The client caches the redirect information and establishes a secure session with the enterprise WAP gateway using WTLS. After the connection is terminated, the default gateway is reselected and used for subsequent communication to other Web servers. Note that this approach requires that the enterprise maintain a WAP gateway on the wireless network that the client is using.

Figure 6.22, from the WAP specification, illustrates the dialogue.

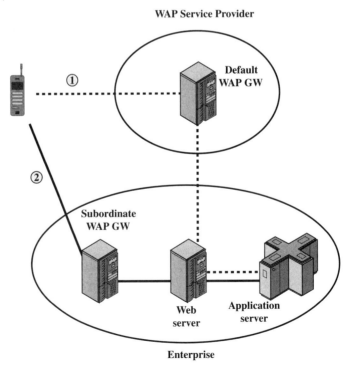

Figure 6.21   WAP2 End-to-End Security Scheme

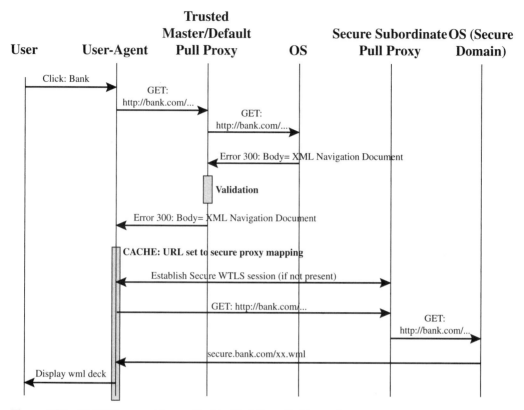

Figure 6.22   WAP Transport Layer End-to-End Security Example

6.6   RECOMMENDED READING AND WEB SITES

The IEEE 802.11 and WiFi specifications are covered in more detail in [STAL07]. A good book-length treatment is [ROSH04]. [FRAN07] is an excellent, detailed treatment of IEEE 802.11i. [CHEN05] provides an overview of IEEE 802.11i.

CHEN05   Chen, J.; Jiang, M.; and Liu, Y. "Wireless LAN Security and IEEE 802.11i." *IEEE Wireless Communications*, February 2005.

FRAN07   Frankel, S.; Eydt, B.; Owens, L.; and Scarfone, K. *Establishing Wireless Robust Security Networks: A Guide to IEEE 802.11i.* NIST Special Publication SP 800-97, February 2007.

ROSH04   Roshan, P., and Leary, J. *802.11 Wireless LAN Fundamentals*. Indianapolis: Cisco Press, 2004.

STAL07   Stallings, W. *Data and Computer Communications, Eighth Edition*. Upper Saddle River, NJ: Prentice Hall, 2007.

Recommended Web Sites:

- **The IEEE 802.11 Wireless LAN Working Group:** Contains working group documents plus discussion archives.
- **Wi-Fi Alliance:** An industry group promoting the interoperability of 802.11 products with each other and with Ethernet.
- **Wireless LAN Association:** Gives an introduction to the technology, including a discussion of implementation considerations and case studies from users. Links to related sites.
- **Extensible Authentication Protocol (EAP) Working Group:** IETF working group responsible for EAP and related issues. Site includes RFCs and Internet drafts.
- **Open Mobile Alliance:** Consolidation of the WAP Forum and the Open Mobile Architecture Initiative. Provides WAP technical specifications and industry links.

6.7   KEY TERMS, REVIEW QUESTIONS, AND PROBLEMS

Key Terms

4-way handshake	media access control (MAC)	Wireless Application Protocol
access point (AP)	MAC protocol data unit	(WAP)
Alert Protocol	(MPDU)	Wireless Datagram Protocol
basic service set (BSS)	MAC service data unit	(WDP)
Change Cipher Spec	(MSDU)	wireless LAN (WLAN)
Protocol	message integrity code (MIC)	Wireless Markup Language
Counter Mode-CBC MAC	Michael	(WML)
Protocol (CCMP)	pairwise keys	Wireless Session Protocol
distribution system (DS)	pseudorandom function	(WSP)
extended service set (ESS)	Robust Security Network	Wireless Transaction Protocol
group keys	(RSN)	(WTP)
Handshake Protocol	Temporal Key Integrity	Wireless Transport Layer
IEEE 802.1X	Protocol (TKIP)	Security (WTLS)
IEEE 802.11	Wired Equivalent Privacy	Wi-Fi
IEEE 802.11i	(WEP)	Wi-Fi Protected Access
independent BSS (IBSS)	Wireless Application	(WPA)
logical link control (LLC)	Environment (WAE)	WTLS Record Protocol

Review Questions

6.1   What is the basic building block of an 802.11 WLAN?

6.2   Define an extended service set.

6.3   List and briefly define IEEE 802.11 services.

6.4   Is a distribution system a wireless network?

6.5   How is the concept of an association related to that of mobility?

6.6　What security areas are addressed by IEEE 802.11i?

6.7　Briefly describe the four IEEE 802.11i phases of operation.

6.8　What is the difference between TKIP and CCMP?

6.9　What is the difference between an HTML filter and a WAP proxy?

6.10　What services are provided by WSP?

6.11　When would each of the three WTP transaction classes be used?

6.12　List and briefly define the security services provided by WTLS.

6.13　Briefly describe the four protocol elements of WTLS.

6.14　List and briefly define all of the keys used in WTLS.

6.15　Describe three alternative approaches to providing WAP end-to-end security.

Problems

6.1　In IEEE 802.11, open system authentication simply consists of two communications. An authentication is requested by the client, which contains the
station ID (typically the MAC address). This is followed by an authentication response from the AP/router containing a success or failure message.
An example of when a failure may occur is if the client's MAC address is
explicitly excluded in the AP/router configuration.
a.　What are the benefits of this authentication scheme?
b.　What are the security vulnerabilities of this authentication scheme?

6.2　Prior to the introduction of IEEE 802.11i, the security scheme for IEEE
802.11 was Wired Equivalent Privacy (WEP). WEP assumed all devices in
the network share a secret key. The purpose of the authentication scenario is
for the STA to prove that it possesses the secret key. Authentication proceeds as shown in Figure 6.23. The STA sends a message to the AP requesting authentication. The AP issues a challenge, which is a sequence of 128
random bytes sent as plaintext. The STA encrypts the challenge with the
shared key and returns it to the AP. The AP decrypts the incoming value and
compares it to the challenge that it sent. If there is a match, the AP confirms
that authentication has succeeded.

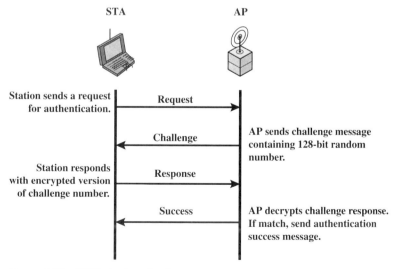

Figure 6.23　WEP Authentication

      a. What are the benefits of this authentication scheme?

      b. This authentication scheme is incomplete. What is missing and why is this important? *Hint:* The addition of one or two messages would fix the problem.

      c. What is a cryptographic weakness of this scheme?

6.3 For WEP, data integrity and data confidentiality are achieved using the RC4 stream encryption algorithm. The transmitter of an MPDU performs the following steps, referred to as encapsulation:

    1. The transmitter selects an initial vector (IV) value.

    2. The IV value is concatenated with the WEP key shared by transmitter and receiver to form the seed, or key input, to RC4.

    3. A 32-bit cyclic redundancy check (CRC) is computed over all the bits of the MAC data field and appended to the data field. The CRC is a common error-detection code used in data link control protocols. In this case, the CRC serves as a integrity check value (ICV).

    4. The result of step 3 is encrypted using RC4 to form the ciphertext block.

    5. The plaintext IV is prepended to the ciphertext block to form the encapsulated MPDU for transmission.

      a. Draw a block diagram that illustrates the encapsulation process.

      b. Describe the steps at the receiver end to recover the plaintext and perform the integrity check.

      c. Draw a block diagram that illustrates part b.

6.4 A potential weakness of the CRC as an integrity check is that it is a linear function. This means that you can predict which bits of the CRC are changed if a single bit of the message is changed. Furthermore, it is possible to determine which combination of bits could be flipped in the message so that the net result is no change in the CRC. Thus, there are a number of combinations of bit flippings of the plaintext message that leave the CRC unchanged, so message integrity is defeated. However, in WEP, if an attacker does not know the encryption key, the attacker does not have access to the plaintext, only to the ciphertext block. Does this mean that the ICV is protected from the bit flipping attack? Explain.

6.5 One potential weakness in WTLS is the use of CBC mode cipher encryption. The standard states that for CBC mode block ciphers, the IV (initialization vector) for each record is calculated in the following way: record_IV = IV $\oplus$ S, where IV is the original IV and S is obtained by concatenating the 2-byte sequence number of the record the needed number of times to obtain as many bytes as in IV. Thus, if the IV is 8 bytes long, the sequence number of the record is concatenated with itself four times. Now, in CBC mode, the first block of plaintext for a record with sequence number i would be encrypted as (Figure 2.10)

$$C_1 = E(K, [IV \oplus S \oplus P_{s,1}])$$

where $P_{s,1}$ is the first block of plaintext of a record with sequence number s and S is the concatenated version of s. Consider a terminal application (such as telnet), where each keypress is sent as an individual record. Alice enters her password into this application, and Eve captures these encrypted records. Note that the sequence number is known to Eve, because this portion of the record is not encrypted (Figure 6.17). Now somehow Eve gets hold of Alice's channel, perhaps through an echo feature in some application. This means that Eve can present unencrypted records to the channel and view the encrypted result. Suggest a brute-force method by which Eve can guess password letters in Alice's password. *Hint*: Exploit these properties of exclusive-OR: $x \oplus x = 1$; $x \oplus 1 = x$.

6.6 An earlier version of WTLS supported a 40-bit XOR MAC and also supported RC4 stream encryption. The XOR MAC works by padding the message with zeros, dividing it into 5-byte blocks and XORing these blocks together. Show that this scheme does not provide message integrity protection.

CHAPTER 7

ELECTRONIC MAIL SECURITY

Despite the refusal of VADM Poindexter and LtCol North to appear, the Board's access to other sources of information filled much of this gap. The FBI provided documents taken from the files of the National Security Advisor and relevant NSC staff members, including messages from the PROF system between VADM Poindexter and LtCol North. The PROF messages were conversations by computer, written at the time events occurred and presumed by the writers to be protected from disclosure. In this sense, they provide a first-hand, contemporaneous account of events.

—The Tower Commission Report to President Reagan on the
Iran-Contra Affair, 1987

KEY POINTS

◆ PGP is an open-source, freely available software package for e-mail security. It provides authentication through the use of digital signature, confidentiality through the use of symmetric block encryption, compression using the ZIP algorithm, and e-mail compatibility using the radix-64 encoding scheme.

◆ PGP incorporates tools for developing a public-key trust model and public-key certificate management.

◆ S/MIME is an Internet standard approach to e-mail security that incorporates the same functionality as PGP.

◆ DKIM is a specification used by e-mail providers for cryptographically signing e-mail messages on behalf of the source domain.

In virtually all distributed environments, electronic mail is the most heavily used network-based application. Users expect to be able to, and do, send e-mail to others who are connected directly or indirectly to the Internet, regardless of host operating system or communications suite. With the explosively growing reliance on e-mail, there grows a demand for authentication and confidentiality services. Two schemes stand out as approaches that enjoy widespread use: Pretty Good Privacy (PGP) and S/MIME. Both are examined in this chapter. The chapter closes with a discussion of DomainKeys Identified Mail.

7.1 PRETTY GOOD PRIVACY

PGP is a remarkable phenomenon. Largely the effort of a single person, Phil Zimmermann, PGP provides a confidentiality and authentication service that can be used for electronic mail and file storage applications. In essence, Zimmermann has done the following:

1. Selected the best available cryptographic algorithms as building blocks.
2. Integrated these algorithms into a general-purpose application that is independent of operating system and processor and that is based on a small set of easy-to-use commands.
3. Made the package and its documentation, including the source code, freely available via the Internet, bulletin boards, and commercial networks such as AOL (America On Line).
4. Entered into an agreement with a company (Viacrypt, now Network Associates) to provide a fully compatible, low-cost commercial version of PGP.

PGP has grown explosively and is now widely used. A number of reasons can be cited for this growth.

1. It is available free worldwide in versions that run on a variety of platforms, including Windows, UNIX, Macintosh, and many more. In addition, the commercial version satisfies users who want a product that comes with vendor support.
2. It is based on algorithms that have survived extensive public review and are considered extremely secure. Specifically, the package includes RSA, DSS, and Diffie-Hellman for public-key encryption; CAST-128, IDEA, and 3DES for symmetric encryption; and SHA-1 for hash coding.
3. It has a wide range of applicability, from corporations that wish to select and enforce a standardized scheme for encrypting files and messages to individuals who wish to communicate securely with others worldwide over the Internet and other networks.
4. It was not developed by, nor is it controlled by, any governmental or standards organization. For those with an instinctive distrust of "the establishment," this makes PGP attractive.
5. PGP is now on an Internet standards track (RFC 3156; *MIME Security with OpenPGP*). Nevertheless, PGP still has an aura of an antiestablishment endeavor.

We begin with an overall look at the operation of PGP. Next, we examine how cryptographic keys are created and stored. Then, we address the vital issue of public-key management.

Notation

Most of the notation used in this chapter has been used before, but a few terms are new. It is perhaps best to summarize those at the beginning. The following symbols are used.

$$K_s \quad = \quad \text{session key used in symmetric encryption scheme}$$
$$PR_a = \quad \text{private key of user A, used in public-key encryption scheme}$$
$$PU_a = \quad \text{public key of user A, used in public-key encryption scheme}$$
$$EP \quad = \quad \text{public-key encryption}$$
$$DP \quad = \quad \text{public-key decryption}$$
$$EC \quad = \quad \text{symmetric encryption}$$
$$DC = \quad \text{symmetric decryption}$$

$$H \quad = \quad \text{hash function}$$
$$|| \quad = \quad \text{concatenation}$$
$$Z \quad = \quad \text{compression using ZIP algorithm}$$
$$R64 = \quad \text{conversion to radix 64 ASCII format}^{[1]}$$

The PGP documentation often uses the term *secret key* to refer to a key paired with a public key in a public-key encryption scheme. As was mentioned earlier, this practice risks confusion with a secret key used for symmetric encryption. Hence, we use the term *private key* instead.

Operational Description

The actual operation of PGP, as opposed to the management of keys, consists of four services: authentication, confidentiality, compression, and e-mail compatibility (Table 7.1). We examine each of these in turn.

AUTHENTICATION   Figure 7.1a illustrates the digital signature service provided by PGP. This is the digital signature scheme discussed in Chapter 3 and illustrated in Figure 4.5. The sequence is as follows.

1. The sender creates a message.
2. SHA-1 is used to generate a 160-bit hash code of the message.
3. The hash code is encrypted with RSA using the sender's private key, and the result is prepended to the message.
4. The receiver uses RSA with the sender's public key to decrypt and recover the hash code.
5. The receiver generates a new hash code for the message and compares it with the decrypted hash code. If the two match, the message is accepted as authentic.

Table 7.1   Summary of PGP Services

Function	Algorithms Used	Description
Digital signature	DSS/SHA or RSA/SHA	A hash code of a message is created using SHA-1. This message digest is encrypted using DSS or RSA with the sender's private key and included with the message.
Message encryption	CAST or IDEA or Three-key Triple DES with Diffie-Hellman or RSA	A message is encrypted using CAST-128 or IDEA or 3DES with a one-time session key generated by the sender. The session key is encrypted using Diffie-Hellman or RSA with the recipient's public key and included with the message.
Compression	ZIP	A message may be compressed for storage or transmission using ZIP.
E-mail compatibility	Radix-64 conversion	To provide transparency for e-mail applications, an encrypted message may be converted to an ASCII string using radix-64 conversion.

---

[1] The American Standard Code for Information Interchange (ASCII) is described in Appendix I.

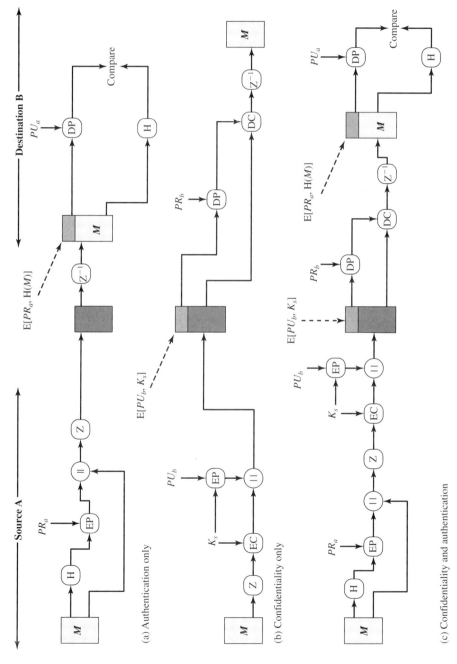

(a) Authentication only

(b) Confidentiality only

(c) Confidentiality and authentication

Figure 7.1 PGP Cryptographic Functions

239

The combination of SHA-1 and RSA provides an effective digital signature scheme. Because of the strength of RSA, the recipient is assured that only the possessor of the matching private key can generate the signature. Because of the strength of SHA-1, the recipient is assured that no one else could generate a new message that matches the hash code and, hence, the signature of the original message.

As an alternative, signatures can be generated using DSS/SHA-1.

Although signatures normally are found attached to the message or file that they sign, this is not always the case: Detached signatures are supported. A detached signature may be stored and transmitted separately from the message it signs. This is useful in several contexts. A user may wish to maintain a separate signature log of all messages sent or received. A detached signature of an executable program can detect subsequent virus infection. Finally, detached signatures can be used when more than one party must sign a document, such as a legal contract. Each person's signature is independent and therefore is applied only to the document. Otherwise, signatures would have to be nested, with the second signer signing both the document and the first signature, and so on.

CONFIDENTIALITY Another basic service provided by PGP is confidentiality, which is provided by encrypting messages to be transmitted or to be stored locally as files. In both cases, the symmetric encryption algorithm CAST-128 may be used. Alternatively, IDEA or 3DES may be used. The 64-bit cipher feedback (CFB) mode is used.

As always, one must address the problem of key distribution. In PGP, each symmetric key is used only once. That is, a new key is generated as a random 128-bit number for each message. Thus, although this is referred to in the documentation as a session key, it is in reality a one-time key. Because it is to be used only once, the session key is bound to the message and transmitted with it. To protect the key, it is encrypted with the receiver's public key. Figure 7.1b illustrates the sequence, which can be described as follows.

1. The sender generates a message and a random 128-bit number to be used as a session key for this message only.

2. The message is encrypted using CAST-128 (or IDEA or 3DES) with the session key.

3. The session key is encrypted with RSA using the recipient's public key and is prepended to the message.

4. The receiver uses RSA with its private key to decrypt and recover the session key.

5. The session key is used to decrypt the message.

As an alternative to the use of RSA for key encryption, PGP provides an option referred to as *Diffie-Hellman*. As was explained in Chapter 3, Diffie-Hellman is a key exchange algorithm. In fact, PGP uses a variant of Diffie-Hellman that does provide encryption/decryption, known as ElGamal.

Several observations may be made. First, to reduce encryption time, the combination of symmetric and public-key encryption is used in preference to simply using

RSA or ElGamal to encrypt the message directly: CAST-128 and the other symmetric algorithms are substantially faster than RSA or ElGamal. Second, the use of the public-key algorithm solves the session-key distribution problem, because only the recipient is able to recover the session key that is bound to the message. Note that we do not need a session-key exchange protocol of the type discussed in Chapter 14, because we are not beginning an ongoing session. Rather, each message is a one-time independent event with its own key. Furthermore, given the store-and-forward nature of electronic mail, the use of handshaking to assure that both sides have the same session key is not practical. Finally, the use of one-time symmetric keys strengthens what is already a strong symmetric encryption approach. Only a small amount of plaintext is encrypted with each key, and there is no relationship among the keys. Thus, to the extent that the public-key algorithm is secure, the entire scheme is secure. To this end, PGP provides the user with a range of key size options from 768 to 3072 bits (the DSS key for signatures is limited to 1024 bits).

CONFIDENTIALITY AND AUTHENTICATION As Figure 7.1c illustrates, both services may be used for the same message. First, a signature is generated for the plaintext message and prepended to the message. Then the plaintext message plus signature is encrypted using CAST-128 (or IDEA or 3DES), and the session key is encrypted using RSA (or ElGamal). This sequence is preferable to the opposite: encrypting the message and then generating a signature for the encrypted message. It is generally more convenient to store a signature with a plaintext version of a message. Furthermore, for purposes of third-party verification, if the signature is performed first, a third party need not be concerned with the symmetric key when verifying the signature.

In summary, when both services are used, the sender first signs the message with its own private key, then encrypts the message with a session key, and finally encrypts the session key with the recipient's public key.

COMPRESSION As a default, PGP compresses the message after applying the signature but before encryption. This has the benefit of saving space both for e-mail transmission and for file storage.

The placement of the compression algorithm, indicated by Z for compression and Z^{-1} for decompression in Figure 7.1, is critical.

1. The signature is generated before compression for two reasons:
   a. It is preferable to sign an uncompressed message so that one can store only the uncompressed message together with the signature for future verification. If one signed a compressed document, then it would be necessary either to store a compressed version of the message for later verification or to recompress the message when verification is required.
   b. Even if one were willing to generate dynamically a recompressed message for verification, PGP's compression algorithm presents a difficulty. The algorithm is not deterministic; various implementations of the algorithm achieve different tradeoffs in running speed versus compression ratio and, as a result, produce different compressed forms. However, these different compression algorithms are interoperable because any version of the algorithm can correctly decompress the output of any other version. Applying the hash

function and signature after compression would constrain all PGP implementations to the same version of the compression algorithm.

2. Message encryption is applied after compression to strengthen cryptographic
   security. Because the compressed message has less redundancy than the
   original plaintext, cryptanalysis is more difficult.

The compression algorithm used is ZIP, which is described in Appendix G.

E-MAIL COMPATIBILITY When PGP is used, at least part of the block to be transmitted
is encrypted. If only the signature service is used, then the message digest is
encrypted (with the sender's private key). If the confidentiality service is used, the
message plus signature (if present) are encrypted (with a one-time symmetric key).
Thus, part or all of the resulting block consists of a stream of arbitrary 8-bit octets.
However, many electronic mail systems only permit the use of blocks consisting of
ASCII text. To accommodate this restriction, PGP provides the service of converting
the raw 8-bit binary stream to a stream of printable ASCII characters.

The scheme used for this purpose is radix-64 conversion. Each group of three
octets of binary data is mapped into four ASCII characters. This format also
appends a CRC to detect transmission errors. See Appendix 7A for a description.

The use of radix 64 expands a message by 33%. Fortunately, the session key
and signature portions of the message are relatively compact, and the plaintext message has been compressed. In fact, the compression should be more than enough to
compensate for the radix-64 expansion. For example, [HELD96] reports an average
compression ratio of about 2.0 using ZIP. If we ignore the relatively small signature
and key components, the typical overall effect of compression and expansion of a
file of length X would be $1.33 \times 0.5 \times X = 0.665 \times X$. Thus, there is still an overall
compression of about one-third.

One noteworthy aspect of the radix-64 algorithm is that it blindly converts the
input stream to radix-64 format regardless of content, even if the input happens to
be ASCII text. Thus, if a message is signed but not encrypted and the conversion is
applied to the entire block, the output will be unreadable to the casual observer,
which provides a certain level of confidentiality. As an option, PGP can be configured to convert to radix-64 format only the signature portion of signed plaintext
messages. This enables the human recipient to read the message without using PGP.
PGP would still have to be used to verify the signature.

Figure 7.2 shows the relationship among the four services so far discussed. On
transmission (if it is required), a signature is generated using a hash code of the
uncompressed plaintext. Then the plaintext (plus signature if present) is compressed. Next, if confidentiality is required, the block (compressed plaintext or compressed signature plus plaintext) is encrypted and prepended with the public-key-
encrypted symmetric encryption key. Finally, the entire block is converted to
radix-64 format.

On reception, the incoming block is first converted back from radix-64 format
to binary. Then, if the message is encrypted, the recipient recovers the session key
and decrypts the message. The resulting block is then decompressed. If the message
is signed, the recipient recovers the transmitted hash code and compares it to its
own calculation of the hash code.

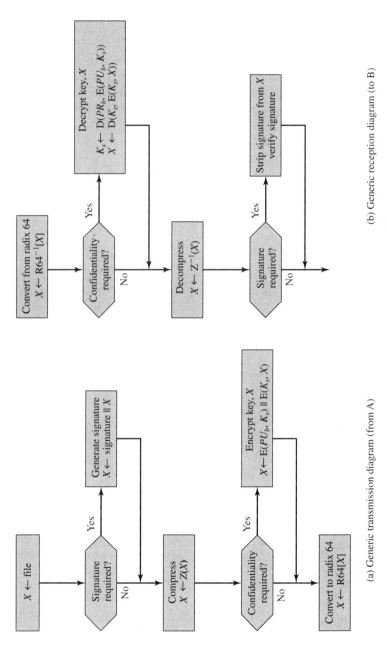

(a) Generic transmission diagram (from A)

(b) Generic reception diagram (to B)

Figure 7.2   Transmission and Reception of PGP Messages

Cryptographic Keys and Key Rings

PGP makes use of four types of keys: one-time session symmetric keys, public keys, private keys, and passphrase-based symmetric keys (explained subsequently). Three separate requirements can be identified with respect to these keys.

1. A means of generating unpredictable session keys is needed.

2. We would like to allow a user to have multiple public-key/private-key pairs. One reason is that the user may wish to change his or her key pair from time to time. When this happens, any messages in the pipeline will be constructed with an obsolete key. Furthermore, recipients will know only the old public key until an update reaches them. In addition to the need to change keys over time, a user may wish to have multiple key pairs at a given time to interact with different groups of correspondents or simply to enhance security by limiting the amount of material encrypted with any one key. The upshot of all this is that there is not a one-to-one correspondence between users and their public keys. Thus, some means is needed for identifying particular keys.

3. Each PGP entity must maintain a file of its own public/private key pairs as well as a file of public keys of correspondents.

We examine each of these requirements in turn.

SESSION KEY GENERATION   Each session key is associated with a single message and is used only for the purpose of encrypting and decrypting that message. Recall that message encryption/decryption is done with a symmetric encryption algorithm. CAST-128 and IDEA use 128-bit keys; 3DES uses a 168-bit key. For the following discussion, we assume CAST-128.

Random 128-bit numbers are generated using CAST-128 itself. The input to the random number generator consists of a 128-bit key and two 64-bit blocks that are treated as plaintext to be encrypted. Using cipher feedback mode, the CAST-128 encrypter produces two 64-bit cipher text blocks, which are concatenated to form the 128-bit session key. The algorithm that is used is based on the one specified in ANSI X12.17.

The "plaintext" input to the random number generator, consisting of two 64-bit blocks, is itself derived from a stream of 128-bit randomized numbers. These numbers are based on keystroke input from the user. Both the keystroke timing and the actual keys struck are used to generate the randomized stream. Thus, if the user hits arbitrary keys at his or her normal pace, a reasonably "random" input will be generated. This random input is also combined with previous session key output from CAST-128 to form the key input to the generator. The result, given the effective scrambling of CAST-128, is to produce a sequence of session keys that is effectively unpredictable.

Appendix H discusses PGP random number generation techniques in more detail.

KEY IDENTIFIERS   As we have discussed, an encrypted message is accompanied by an encrypted form of the session key that was used for message encryption. The session key itself is encrypted with the recipient's public key. Hence, only the recipient will be able to recover the session key and therefore recover the message. If each user employed a single public/private key pair, then the recipient would automatically know which key to use to decrypt the session key: the recipient's unique private key. However, we have stated a requirement that any given user may have multiple public/private key pairs.

How, then, does the recipient know which of its public keys was used to encrypt the session key? One simple solution would be to transmit the public key with the message. The recipient could then verify that this is indeed one of its public keys, and proceed. This scheme would work, but it is unnecessarily wasteful of space. An RSA public key may be hundreds of decimal digits in length. Another solution would be to associate an identifier with each public key that is unique at least within one user. That is, the combination of user ID and key ID would be sufficient to identify a key uniquely. Then only the much shorter key ID would need to be transmitted. This solution, however, raises a management and overhead problem: Key IDs must be assigned and stored so that both sender and recipient could map from key ID to public key. This seems unnecessarily burdensome.

The solution adopted by PGP is to assign a key ID to each public key that is, with very high probability, unique within a user ID. The key ID associated with each public key consists of its least significant 64 bits. That is, the key ID of public key PU_a is $(PU_a \bmod 2^{64})$. This is a sufficient length that the probability of duplicate key IDs is very small.

A key ID is also required for the PGP digital signature. Because a sender may use one of a number of private keys to encrypt the message digest, the recipient must know which public key is intended for use. Accordingly, the digital signature component of a message includes the 64-bit key ID of the required public key. When the message is received, the recipient verifies that the key ID is for a public key that it knows for that sender and then proceeds to verify the signature.

Now that the concept of key ID has been introduced, we can take a more detailed look at the format of a transmitted message, which is shown in Figure 7.3. A message consists of three components: the message component, a signature (optional), and a session key component (optional).

The **message component** includes the actual data to be stored or transmitted, as well as a filename and a timestamp that specifies the time of creation.

The **signature component** includes the following.

- **Timestamp:** The time at which the signature was made.
- **Message digest:** The 160-bit SHA-1 digest encrypted with the sender's private signature key. The digest is calculated over the signature timestamp concatenated with the data portion of the message component. The inclusion of the signature timestamp in the digest insures against replay types of attacks. The exclusion of the filename and timestamp portions of the message component ensures that detached signatures are exactly the same as attached signatures prefixed to the message. Detached signatures are

Content

Operation

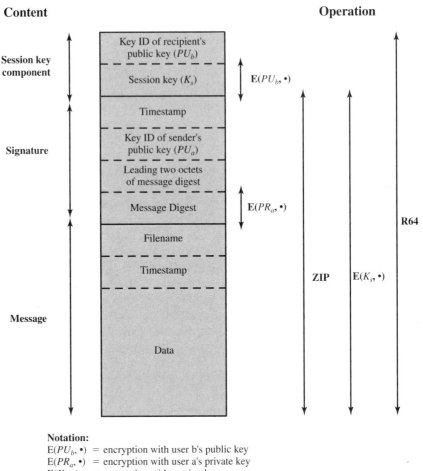

Notation:
$E(PU_b, \bullet)$ = encryption with user b's public key
$E(PR_a, \bullet)$ = encryption with user a's private key
$E(K_s, \bullet)$ = encryption with session key
ZIP = Zip compression function
R64 = Radix-64 conversion function

Figure 7.3   General Format PGP Message (from A to B)

calculated on a separate file that has none of the message component header fields.

- **Leading two octets of message digest:** Enables the recipient to determine if the correct public key was used to decrypt the message digest for authentication by comparing this plaintext copy of the first two octets with the first two octets of the decrypted digest. These octets also serve as a 16-bit frame check sequence for the message.

- **Key ID of sender's public key:** Identifies the public key that should be used to decrypt the message digest and, hence, identifies the private key that was used to encrypt the message digest.

The message component and optional signature component may be compressed using ZIP and may be encrypted using a session key.

The **session key component** includes the session key and the identifier of the recipient's public key that was used by the sender to encrypt the session key.

The entire block is usually encoded with radix-64 encoding.

KEY RINGS We have seen how key IDs are critical to the operation of PGP and that two key IDs are included in any PGP message that provides both confidentiality and authentication. These keys need to be stored and organized in a systematic way for efficient and effective use by all parties. The scheme used in PGP is to provide a pair of data structures at each node, one to store the public/private key pairs owned by that node and one to store the public keys of other users known at this node. These data structures are referred to, respectively, as the private-key ring and the public-key ring.

Figure 7.4 shows the general structure of a **private-key ring.** We can view the ring as a table in which each row represents one of the public/private key pairs owned by this user. Each row contains the entries:

- **Timestamp:** The date/time when this key pair was generated.
- **Key ID:** The least significant 64 bits of the public key for this entry.
- **Public key:** The public-key portion of the pair.
- **Private key:** The private-key portion of the pair; this field is encrypted.

Private-Key Ring

Timestamp	Key ID*	Public Key	Encrypted Private Key	User ID*
• • •	• • •	• • •	• • •	• • •
T_i	$PU_i \bmod 2^{64}$	PU_i	$E(H(P_i), PR_i)$	User i
• • •	• • •	• • •	• • •	• • •

Public-Key Ring

Timestamp	Key ID*	Public Key	Owner Trust	User ID*	Key Legitimacy	Signature(s)	Signature Trust(s)
• • •	• • •	• • •	• • •	• • •	• • •	• • •	• • •
T_i	$PU_i \bmod 2^{64}$	PU_i	trust_flag$_i$	User i	trust_flag$_i$		
• • •	• • •	• • •	• • •	• • •	• • •	• • •	• • •

* = field used to index table

Figure 7.4 General Structure of Private- and Public-Key Rings

- **User ID:** Typically, this will be the user's e-mail address (e.g., stallings@acm.org). However, the user may choose to associate a different name with each pair (e.g., Stallings, WStallings, WilliamStallings, etc.) or to reuse the same User ID more than once.

The private-key ring can be indexed by either User ID or Key ID; later we will see the need for both means of indexing.

Although it is intended that the private-key ring be stored only on the machine of the user that created and owns the key pairs and that it be accessible only to that user, it makes sense to make the value of the private key as secure as possible. Accordingly, the private key itself is not stored in the key ring. Rather, this key is encrypted using CAST-128 (or IDEA or 3DES). The procedure is as follows:

1. The user selects a passphrase to be used for encrypting private keys.

2. When the system generates a new public/private key pair using RSA, it asks the user for the passphrase. Using SHA-1, a 160-bit hash code is generated from the passphrase, and the passphrase is discarded.

3. The system encrypts the private key using CAST-128 with the 128 bits of the hash code as the key. The hash code is then discarded, and the encrypted private key is stored in the private-key ring.

Subsequently, when a user accesses the private-key ring to retrieve a private key, he or she must supply the passphrase. PGP will retrieve the encrypted private key, generate the hash code of the passphrase, and decrypt the encrypted private key using CAST-128 with the hash code.

This is a very compact and effective scheme. As in any system based on passwords, the security of this system depends on the security of the password. To avoid the temptation to write it down, the user should use a passphrase that is not easily guessed but that is easily remembered.

Figure 7.4 also shows the general structure of a **public-key ring.** This data structure is used to store public keys of other users that are known to this user. For the moment, let us ignore some fields shown in the figure and describe the following fields.

- **Timestamp:** The date/time when this entry was generated.
- **Key ID:** The least significant 64 bits of the public key for this entry.
- **Public Key:** The public key for this entry.
- **User ID:** Identifies the owner of this key. Multiple user IDs may be associated with a single public key.

The public-key ring can be indexed by either User ID or Key ID; we will see the need for both means of indexing later.

We are now in a position to show how these key rings are used in message transmission and reception. For simplicity, we ignore compression and radix-64 conversion in the following discussion. First consider message transmission (Figure 7.5) and assume that the message is to be both signed and encrypted. The sending PGP entity performs the following steps.

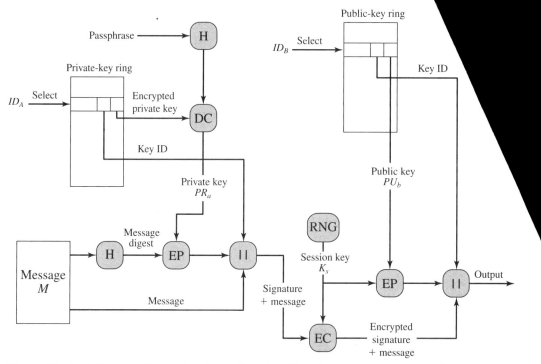

Figure 7.5 PGP Message Generation (from User A to User B: no compression or radix-64 conversion)

1. Signing the message:
   a. PGP retrieves the sender's private key from the private-key ring using `your_userid` as an index. If `your_userid` was not provided in the command, the first private key on the ring is retrieved.
   b. PGP prompts the user for the passphrase to recover the unencrypted private key.
   c. The signature component of the message is constructed.
2. Encrypting the message:
   a. PGP generates a session key and encrypts the message.
   b. PGP retrieves the recipient's public key from the public-key ring using `her_userid` as an index.
   c. The session key component of the message is constructed.

The receiving PGP entity performs the following steps (Figure 7.6).

1. Decrypting the message:
   a. PGP retrieves the receiver's private key from the private-key ring using the Key ID field in the session key component of the message as an index.
   b. PGP prompts the user for the passphrase to recover the unencrypted private key.
   c. PGP then recovers the session key and decrypts the message.

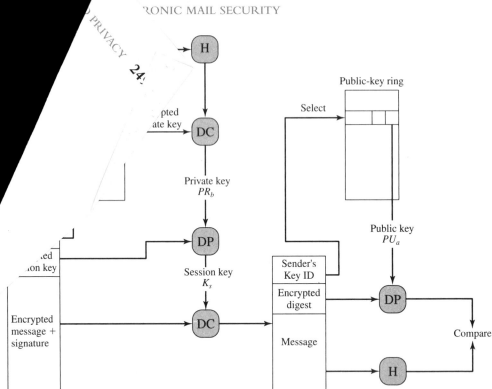

Figure 7.6 PGP Message Reception (from User A to User B; no compression or radix-64 conversion)

2. Authenticating the message:

   a. PGP retrieves the sender's public key from the public-key ring using the Key ID field in the signature key component of the message as an index.

   b. PGP recovers the transmitted message digest.

   c. PGP computes the message digest for the received message and compares it to the transmitted message digest to authenticate.

Public–Key Management

As can be seen from the discussion so far, PGP contains a clever, efficient, interlocking set of functions and formats to provide an effective confidentiality and authentication service. To complete the system, one final area needs to be addressed, that of public-key management. The PGP documentation captures the importance of this area:

> This whole business of protecting public keys from tampering is the single most difficult problem in practical public key applications. It is the "Achilles heel" of public key cryptography, and a lot of software complexity is tied up in solving this one problem.

PGP provides a structure for solving this problem w
options that may be used. Because PGP is intended for use in
and informal environments, no rigid public-key management sch
as we will see in our discussion of S/MIME later in this chapter.

APPROACHES TO PUBLIC-KEY MANAGEMENT The essence of the proble
A must build up a public-key ring containing the public keys of o
interoperate with them using PGP. Suppose that A's key ring contains
attributed to B, but in fact the key is owned by C. This could happen, for
A got the key from a bulletin board system (BBS) that was used by B to
public key but that has been compromised by C. The result is that two thre
exist. First, C can send messages to A and forge B's signature so that A will
the message as coming from B. Second, any encrypted message from A to B ca
read by C.

A number of approaches are possible for minimizing the risk that a use
public-key ring contains false public keys. Suppose that A wishes to obtain a reliable
public key for B. The following are some approaches that could be used.

1. Physically get the key from B. B could store her public key (PU_b) on a floppy
   disk and hand it to A. A could then load the key into his system from the
   floppy disk. This is a very secure method but has obvious practical limitations.

2. Verify a key by telephone. If A can recognize B on the phone, A could call B and
   ask her to dictate the key, in radix-64 format, over the phone. As a more practical
   alternative, B could transmit her key in an e-mail message to A. A could have
   PGP generate a 160-bit SHA-1 digest of the key and display it in hexadecimal
   format; this is referred to as the "fingerprint" of the key. A could then call B and
   ask her to dictate the fingerprint over the phone. If the two fingerprints match,
   the key is verified.

3. Obtain B's public key from a mutual trusted individual D. For this purpose, the
   introducer, D, creates a signed certificate. The certificate includes B's public key,
   the time of creation of the key, and a validity period for the key. D generates an
   SHA-1 digest of this certificate, encrypts it with her private key, and attaches the
   signature to the certificate. Because only D could have created the signature, no
   one else can create a false public key and pretend that it is signed by D. The
   signed certificate could be sent directly to A by B or D, or it could be posted on a
   bulletin board.

4. Obtain B's public key from a trusted certifying authority. Again, a public-key
   certificate is created and signed by the authority. A could then access the
   authority, providing a user name and receiving a signed certificate.

For cases 3 and 4, A already would have to have a copy of the introducer's
public key and trust that this key is valid. Ultimately, it is up to A to assign a level of
trust to anyone who is to act as an introducer.

THE USE OF TRUST Although PGP does not include any specification for establishing
certifying authorities or for establishing trust, it does provide a convenient means of
using trust, associating trust with public keys, and exploiting trust information.

follows. Each entry in the public-key ring is a public-
the preceding subsection. Associated with each such
that indicates the extent to which PGP will trust that
this user; the higher the level of trust, the stronger is the
to this key. This field is computed by PGP. Also associated
or more signatures that the key ring owner has collected that
in turn, each signature has associated with it a **signature trust**
the degree to which this PGP user trusts the signer to certify pub-
legitimacy field is derived from the collection of signature trust
try. Finally, each entry defines a public key associated with a particu-
d an **owner trust field** is included that indicates the degree to which this
is trusted to sign other public-key certificates; this level of trust is
by the user. We can think of the signature trust fields as cached copies of
ner trust field from another entry.

The three fields mentioned in the previous paragraph are each contained in a
ucture referred to as a trust flag byte. The content of this trust flag for each of
these three uses is shown in Table 7.2. Suppose that we are dealing with the public-
key ring of user A. We can describe the operation of the trust processing as follows.

1. When A inserts a new public key on the public-key ring, PGP must assign
   a value to the trust flag that is associated with the owner of this public key. If
   the owner is A, and therefore this public key also appears in the private-key
   ring, then a value of *ultimate trust* is automatically assigned to the trust field.

Table 7.2   Contents of Trust Flag Byte

(a) Trust Assigned to Public-Key Owner (appears after key packet; user defined)	(b) Trust Assigned to Public Key/User ID Pair (appears after User ID packet; computed by PGP)	(c) Trust Assigned to Signature (appears after signature packet; cached copy of OWNERTRUST for this signator)
OWNERTRUST Field —undefined trust —unknown user —usually not trusted to sign other keys —usually trusted to sign other keys —always trusted to sign other keys —this key is present in secret key ring (ultimate trust)	KEYLEGIT Field —unknown or undefined trust —key ownership not trusted —marginal trust in key ownership —complete trust in key ownership	SIGTRUST Field —undefined trust —unknown user —usually not trusted to sign other keys —usually trusted to sign other keys —always trusted to sign other keys —this key is present in secret key ring (ultimate trust)
BUCKSTOP bit —set if this key appears in secret key ring	WARNONLY bit —set if user wants only to be warned when key that is not fully validated is used for encryption	CONTIG bit —set if signature leads up a contiguous trusted certification path back to the ultimately trusted key ring owner

Otherwise, PGP asks A for his assessment o.
owner of this key, and A must enter the desi
that this owner is unknown, untrusted, margin.
trusted.

signed to the
can specify
completely

2. When the new public key is entered, one or more signe
it. More signatures may be added later. When a signat
entry, PGP searches the public-key ring to see if the auth
among the known public-key owners. If so, the OWNERT
owner is assigned to the SIGTRUST field for this signature.
user value is assigned.

ached to
into the
ature is
r this

3. The value of the key legitimacy field is calculated on the basis o
trust fields present in this entry. If at least one signature has a sig
value of *ultimate*, then the key legitimacy value is set to complete.
PGP computes a weighted sum of the trust values. A weight of $1/X$ is
signatures that are always trusted and $1/Y$ to signatures that are
trusted, where X and Y are user-configurable parameters. When the to
weights of the introducers of a Key/UserID combination reaches 1, the bi
ing is considered to be trustworthy, and the key legitimacy value is set to con
plete. Thus, in the absence of ultimate trust, at least X signatures that are
always trusted, Y signatures that are usually trusted, or some combination is
needed.

own
re
t

Periodically, PGP processes the public-key ring to achieve consistency. In
essence, this is a top-down process. For each OWNERTRUST field, PGP scans the
ring for all signatures authored by that owner and updates the SIGTRUST field to
equal the OWNERTRUST field. This process starts with keys for which there is ultimate trust. Then all KEYLEGIT fields are computed on the basis of the attached
signatures.

Figure 7.7 provides an example of the way in which signature trust and key
legitimacy are related.[2] The figure shows the structure of a public-key ring. The user
has acquired a number of public keys—some directly from their owners and some
from a third party such as a key server.

The node labeled "You" refers to the entry in the public-key ring corresponding to this user. This key is legitimate, and the OWNERTRUST value is ultimate
trust. Each other node in the key ring has an OWNERTRUST value of undefined
unless some other value is assigned by the user. In this example, this user has specified that it always trusts the following users to sign other keys: D, E, F, L. This user
partially trusts users A and B to sign other keys.

So the shading, or lack thereof, of the nodes in Figure 7.7 indicates the level of
trust assigned by this user. The tree structure indicates which keys have been signed
by which other users. If a key is signed by a user whose key is also in this key ring,
the arrow joins the signed key to the signatory. If the key is signed by a user whose
key is not present in this key ring, the arrow joins the signed key to a question mark,
indicating that the signatory is unknown to this user.

---

[2]Figure provided to the author by Phil Zimmermann.

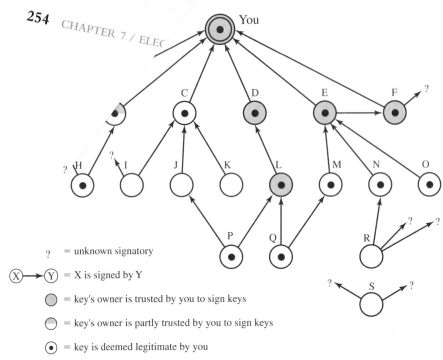

?   = unknown signatory

(X) ———► (Y)   = X is signed by Y

○   = key's owner is trusted by you to sign keys

○   = key's owner is partly trusted by you to sign keys

⊙   = key is deemed legitimate by you

Figure 7.7   PGP Trust Model Example

Several points are illustrated in Figure 7.7.

1. Note that all keys whose owners are fully or partially trusted by this user have been signed by this user, with the exception of node L. Such a user signature is not always necessary, as the presence of node L indicates, but in practice, most users are likely to sign the keys for most owners that they trust. So, for example, even though E's key is already signed by trusted introducer F, the user chose to sign E's key directly.

2. We assume that two partially trusted signatures are sufficient to certify a key. Hence, the key for user H is deemed legitimate by PGP because it is signed by A and B, both of whom are partially trusted.

3. A key may be determined to be legitimate because it is signed by one fully trusted or two partially trusted signatories, but its user may not be trusted to sign other keys. For example, N's key is legitimate because it is signed by E, whom this user trusts, but N is not trusted to sign other keys because this user has not assigned N that trust value. Therefore, although R's key is signed by N, PGP does not consider R's key legitimate. This situation makes perfect sense. If you wish to send a private message to some individual, it is not necessary that you trust that individual in any respect. It is only necessary that you are sure that you have the correct public key for that individual.

4. Figure 7.7 also shows an example of a detached "orphan" node S, with two unknown signatures. Such a key may have been acquired from a key server.

PGP cannot assume that this key is legitimate simply because it came from a reputable server. The user must declare that he or she is willing to trust fully one of the key's signatories by signing it or by telling PGP that it is willing to trust fully one of the key's signatories.

A final point: Earlier it was mentioned that multiple user IDs may be associated with a single public key on the public-key ring. This could be because a person has changed names or has been introduced via signatures under multiple names, indicating different e-mail addresses for the same person, for example. So we can think of a public key as the root of a tree. A public key has a number of user IDs associating with it, with a number of signatures below each user ID. The binding of a particular user ID to a key depends on the signatures associated with that user ID and that key, whereas the level of trust in this key (for use in signing other keys) is a function of all the dependent signatures.

REVOKING PUBLIC KEYS A user may wish to revoke his or her current public key either because compromise is suspected or simply to avoid the use of the same key for an extended period. Note that a compromise would require that an opponent somehow had obtained a copy of your unencrypted private key or that an opponent had obtained both the private key from your private-key ring and your passphrase.

The convention for revoking a public key is for the owner to issue a key revocation certificate, signed by the owner. This certificate has the same form as a normal signature certificate but includes an indicator that the purpose of this certificate is to revoke the use of this public key. Note that the corresponding private key must be used to sign a certificate that revokes a public key. The owner should then attempt to disseminate this certificate as widely and as quickly as possible to enable potential correspondents to update their public-key rings.

Note that an opponent who has compromised the private key of an owner can also issue such a certificate. However, this would deny the opponent as well as the legitimate owner the use of the public key, and therefore, it seems a much less likely threat than the malicious use of a stolen private key.

7.2 S/MIME

Secure/Multipurpose Internet Mail Extension (S/MIME) is a security enhancement to the MIME Internet e-mail format standard based on technology from RSA Data Security. Although both PGP and S/MIME are on an IETF standards track, it appears likely that S/MIME will emerge as the industry standard for commercial and organizational use, while PGP will remain the choice for personal e-mail security for many users. S/MIME is defined in a number of documents—most importantly RFCs 3370, 3850, 3851, and 3852.

To understand S/MIME, we need first to have a general understanding of the underlying e-mail format that it uses, namely MIME. But to understand the significance of MIME, we need to go back to the traditional e-mail format standard, RFC 822, which is still in common use. The most recent version of this format specification is RFC 5322 (*Internet Message Format*). Accordingly, this section first provides an introduction to these two earlier standards and then moves on to a discussion of S/MIME.

RFC 5322

RFC 5322 defines a format for text messages that are sent using electronic mail. It has been the standard for Internet-based text mail messages and remains in common use. In the RFC 5322 context, messages are viewed as having an envelope and contents. The envelope contains whatever information is needed to accomplish transmission and delivery. The contents compose the object to be delivered to the recipient. The RFC 5322 standard applies only to the contents. However, the content standard includes a set of header fields that may be used by the mail system to create the envelope, and the standard is intended to facilitate the acquisition of such information by programs.

The overall structure of a message that conforms to RFC 5322 is very simple. A message consists of some number of header lines (*the header*) followed by unrestricted text (*the body*). The header is separated from the body by a blank line. Put differently, a message is ASCII text, and all lines up to the first blank line are assumed to be header lines used by the user agent part of the mail system.

A header line usually consists of a keyword, followed by a colon, followed by the keyword's arguments; the format allows a long line to be broken up into several lines. The most frequently used keywords are *From*, *To*, *Subject*, and *Date*. Here is an example message:

```
Date: October 8, 2009 2:15:49 PM EDT
From: "William Stallings" <ws@shore.net>
Subject: The Syntax in RFC 5322
To: Smith@Other-host.com
Cc: Jones@Yet-Another-Host.com

Hello. This section begins the actual
message body, which is delimited from the
message heading by a blank line.
```

Another field that is commonly found in RFC 5322 headers is *Message-ID*. This field contains a unique identifier associated with this message.

Multipurpose Internet Mail Extensions

Multipurpose Internet Mail Extension (MIME) is an extension to the RFC 5322 framework that is intended to address some of the problems and limitations of the use of Simple Mail Transfer Protocol (SMTP), defined in RFC 821, or some other mail transfer protocol and RFC 5322 for electronic mail. [PARZ06] lists the following limitations of the SMTP/5322 scheme.

1. SMTP cannot transmit executable files or other binary objects. A number of schemes are in use for converting binary files into a text form that can be used by SMTP mail systems, including the popular UNIX UUencode/UUdecode scheme. However, none of these is a standard or even a *de facto* standard.

2. SMTP cannot transmit text data that includes national language characters, because these are represented by 8-bit codes with values of 128 decimal or higher, and SMTP is limited to 7-bit ASCII.

3. SMTP servers may reject mail message over a certain size.

4. SMTP gateways that translate between ASCII and the character code EBCDIC do not use a consistent set of mappings, resulting in translation problems.

5. SMTP gateways to X.400 electronic mail networks cannot handle nontextual data included in X.400 messages.

6. Some SMTP implementations do not adhere completely to the SMTP standards defined in RFC 821. Common problems include:

   - Deletion, addition, or reordering of carriage return and linefeed
   - Truncating or wrapping lines longer than 76 characters
   - Removal of trailing white space (tab and space characters)
   - Padding of lines in a message to the same length
   - Conversion of tab characters into multiple space characters

MIME is intended to resolve these problems in a manner that is compatible with existing RFC 5322 implementations. The specification is provided in RFCs 2045 through 2049.

OVERVIEW The MIME specification includes the following elements.

1. Five new message header fields are defined, which may be included in an RFC 5322 header. These fields provide information about the body of the message.

2. A number of content formats are defined, thus standardizing representations that support multimedia electronic mail.

3. Transfer encodings are defined that enable the conversion of any content format into a form that is protected from alteration by the mail system.

In this subsection, we introduce the five message header fields. The next two subsections deal with content formats and transfer encodings.

The five header fields defined in MIME are

- **MIME-Version:** Must have the parameter value 1.0. This field indicates that the message conforms to RFCs 2045 and 2046.

- **Content-Type:** Describes the data contained in the body with sufficient detail that the receiving user agent can pick an appropriate agent or mechanism to represent the data to the user or otherwise deal with the data in an appropriate manner.

- **Content-Transfer-Encoding:** Indicates the type of transformation that has been used to represent the body of the message in a way that is acceptable for mail transport.

- **Content-ID:** Used to identify MIME entities uniquely in multiple contexts.

- **Content-Description:** A text description of the object with the body; this is useful when the object is not readable (e.g., audio data).

Any or all of these fields may appear in a normal RFC 5322 header. A compliant implementation must support the MIME-Version, Content-Type, and Content-Transfer-Encoding fields; the Content-ID and Content-Description fields are optional and may be ignored by the recipient implementation.

MIME CONTENT TYPES The bulk of the MIME specification is concerned with the definition of a variety of content types. This reflects the need to provide standardized ways of dealing with a wide variety of information representations in a multimedia environment.

Table 7.3 lists the content types specified in RFC 2046. There are seven different major types of content and a total of 15 subtypes. In general, a content type declares the general type of data, and the subtype specifies a particular format for that type of data.

For the **text type** of body, no special software is required to get the full meaning of the text aside from support of the indicated character set. The primary subtype is *plain text*, which is simply a string of ASCII characters or ISO 8859 characters. The *enriched* subtype allows greater formatting flexibility.

The **multipart type** indicates that the body contains multiple, independent parts. The Content-Type header field includes a parameter (called a boundary) that defines the delimiter between body parts. This boundary should not appear in any parts of the message. Each boundary starts on a new line and consists of two hyphens followed by the boundary value. The final boundary, which indicates the end of the last part, also has a suffix of two hyphens. Within each part, there may be an optional ordinary MIME header.

Table 7.3   MIME Content Types

Type	Subtype	Description
Text	Plain	Unformatted text; may be ASCII or ISO 8859.
	Enriched	Provides greater format flexibility.
Multipart	Mixed	The different parts are independent but are to be transmitted together. They should be presented to the receiver in the order that they appear in the mail message.
	Parallel	Differs from Mixed only in that no order is defined for delivering the parts to the receiver.
	Alternative	The different parts are alternative versions of the same information. They are ordered in increasing faithfulness to the original, and the recipient's mail system should display the "best" version to the user.
	Digest	Similar to Mixed, but the default type/subtype of each part is message/rfc822.
Message	rfc822	The body is itself an encapsulated message that conforms to RFC 822.
	Partial	Used to allow fragmentation of large mail items, in a way that is transparent to the recipient.
	External-body	Contains a pointer to an object that exists elsewhere.
Image	jpeg	The image is in JPEG format, JFIF encoding.
	gif	The image is in GIF format.
Video	mpeg	MPEG format.
Audio	Basic	Single-channel 8-bit ISDN mu-law encoding at a sample rate of 8 kHz.
Application	PostScript	Adobe Postscript format.
	octet-stream	General binary data consisting of 8-bit bytes.

Here is a simple example of a multipart message containing two parts—both consisting of simple text (taken from RFC 2046).

```
From: Nathaniel Borenstein <nsb@bellcore.com>
To: Ned Freed <ned@innosoft.com>
Subject: Sample message
MIME-Version: 1.0
Content-type: multipart/mixed; boundary="simple
boundary"

This is the preamble. It is to be ignored, though it
is a handy place for mail composers to include an
explanatory note to non-MIME conformant readers.
—simple boundary

This is implicitly typed plain ASCII text. It does NOT
end with a linebreak.
—simple boundary
Content-type: text/plain; charset=us-ascii

This is explicitly typed plain ASCII text. It DOES end
with a linebreak.

—simple boundary—
This is the epilogue. It is also to be ignored.
```

There are four subtypes of the multipart type, all of which have the same over-all syntax. The **multipart/mixed subtype** is used when there are multiple independent body parts that need to be bundled in a particular order. For the **multipart/parallel subtype,** the order of the parts is not significant. If the recipient's system is appropriate, the multiple parts can be presented in parallel. For example, a picture or text part could be accompanied by a voice commentary that is played while the picture or text is displayed.

For the **multipart/alternative subtype,** the various parts are different representations of the same information. The following is an example:

```
From: Nathaniel Borenstein <nsb@bellcore.com>
To: Ned Freed <ned@innosoft.com>
Subject: Formatted text mail
MIME-Version: 1.0
Content-Type: multipart/alternative;
boundary=boundary42

    —boundary42

Content-Type: text/plain; charset=us-ascii

    ...plain text version of message goes here....
```

```
—boundary42
Content-Type: text/enriched

     .... RFC 1896 text/enriched version of same message
goes here ...

—boundary42—
```

In this subtype, the body parts are ordered in terms of increasing preference. For this example, if the recipient system is capable of displaying the message in the text/enriched format, this is done; otherwise, the plain text format is used.

The **multipart/digest subtype** is used when each of the body parts is interpreted as an RFC 5322 message with headers. This subtype enables the construction of a message whose parts are individual messages. For example, the moderator of a group might collect e-mail messages from participants, bundle these messages, and send them out in one encapsulating MIME message.

The **message type** provides a number of important capabilities in MIME. The **message/rfc822 subtype** indicates that the body is an entire message, including header and body. Despite the name of this subtype, the encapsulated message may be not only a simple RFC 5322 message but also any MIME message.

The **message/partial subtype** enables fragmentation of a large message into a number of parts, which must be reassembled at the destination. For this subtype, three parameters are specified in the Content-Type: Message/Partial field: an *id* common to all fragments of the same message, a *sequence number* unique to each fragment, and the *total* number of fragments.

The **message/external-body subtype** indicates that the actual data to be conveyed in this message are not contained in the body. Instead, the body contains the information needed to access the data. As with the other message types, the message/external-body subtype has an outer header and an encapsulated message with its own header. The only necessary field in the outer header is the Content-Type field, which identifies this as a message/external-body subtype. The inner header is the message header for the encapsulated message. The Content-Type field in the outer header must include an access-type parameter, which indicates the method of access, such as FTP (file transfer protocol).

The **application type** refers to other kinds of data, typically either uninterpreted binary data or information to be processed by a mail-based application.

MIME TRANSFER ENCODINGS The other major component of the MIME specification, in addition to content type specification, is a definition of transfer encodings for message bodies. The objective is to provide reliable delivery across the largest range of environments.

The MIME standard defines two methods of encoding data. The Content-Transfer-Encoding field can actually take on six values, as listed in Table 7.4. However, three of these values (7bit, 8bit, and binary) indicate that no encoding has been done but provide some information about the nature of the data. For SMTP transfer, it is safe to use the 7bit form. The 8bit and binary forms may be usable in other mail transport contexts. Another Content-Transfer-Encoding value is x-token,

Table 7.4   MIME Transfer Encodings

7bit	The data are all represented by short lines of ASCII characters.
8bit	The lines are short, but there may be non-ASCII characters (octets with the high-order bit set).
binary	Not only may non-ASCII characters be present, but the lines are not necessarily short enough for SMTP transport.
quoted-printable	Encodes the data in such a way that if the data being encoded are mostly ASCII text, the encoded form of the data remains largely recognizable by humans.
base64	Encodes data by mapping 6-bit blocks of input to 8-bit blocks of output, all of which are printable ASCII characters.
x-token	A named nonstandard encoding.

which indicates that some other encoding scheme is used for which a name is to be supplied. This could be a vendor-specific or application-specific scheme. The two actual encoding schemes defined are quoted-printable and base64. Two schemes are defined to provide a choice between a transfer technique that is essentially human readable and one that is safe for all types of data in a way that is reasonably compact.

The **quoted-printable** transfer encoding is useful when the data consists largely of octets that correspond to printable ASCII characters. In essence, it represents nonsafe characters by the hexadecimal representation of their code and introduces reversible (soft) line breaks to limit message lines to 76 characters.

The **base64 transfer encoding,** also known as radix-64 encoding, is a common one for encoding arbitrary binary data in such a way as to be invulnerable to the processing by mail-transport programs. It is also used in PGP and is described in Appendix 7A.

A MULTIPART EXAMPLE Figure 7.8, taken from RFC 2045, is the outline of a complex multipart message. The message has five parts to be displayed serially: two introductory plain text parts, an embedded multipart message, a richtext part, and a closing encapsulated text message in a non-ASCII character set. The embedded multipart message has two parts to be displayed in parallel: a picture and an audio fragment.

CANONICAL FORM An important concept in MIME and S/MIME is that of canonical form. Canonical form is a format, appropriate to the content type, that is standardized for use between systems. This is in contrast to native form, which is a format that may be peculiar to a particular system. Table 7.5, from RFC 2049, should help clarify this matter.

S/MIME Functionality

In terms of general functionality, S/MIME is very similar to PGP. Both offer the ability to sign and/or encrypt messages. In this subsection, we briefly summarize S/MIME capability. We then look in more detail at this capability by examining message formats and message preparation.

```
MIME-Version: 1.0
From: Nathaniel Borenstein <nsb@bellcore.com>
To: Ned Freed <ned@innosoft.com>
Subject: A multipart example
Content-Type: multipart/mixed;
    boundary=unique-boundary-1
```

This is the preamble area of a multipart message. Mail readers that understand multipart format should ignore this preamble. If you are reading this text, you might want to consider changing to a mail reader that understands how to properly display multipart messages.

```
--unique-boundary-1
```

```
    ...Some text appears here...
```
[Note that the preceding blank line means no header fields were given and this is text, with charset US ASCII. It could have been done with explicit typing as in the next part.]

```
--unique-boundary-1
Content-type: text/plain; charset=US-ASCII
```

This could have been part of the previous part, but illustrates explicit versus implicit typing of body parts.

```
--unique-boundary-1
Content-Type: multipart/parallel;   boundary=unique-boundary-2
```

```
--unique-boundary-2
Content-Type: audio/basic
Content-Transfer-Encoding: base64
```

```
    ... base64-encoded 8000 Hz single-channel mu-law-format audio data goes here....
```

```
--unique-boundary-2
Content-Type: image/jpeg
Content-Transfer-Encoding: base64
```

```
    ... base64-encoded image data goes here....
```

```
--unique-boundary-2--
```

```
--unique-boundary-1
Content-type: text/enriched
```

This is <bold><italic>richtext.</italic></bold> <smaller>as defined in RFC 1896</smaller>

Isn't it <bigger><bigger>cool?</bigger></bigger>

```
--unique-boundary-1
Content-Type: message/rfc822
```

```
From: (mailbox in US-ASCII)
To: (address in US-ASCII)
Subject: (subject in US-ASCII)
Content-Type: Text/plain; charset=ISO-8859-1
Content-Transfer-Encoding: Quoted-printable
```

```
    ... Additional text in ISO-8859-1 goes here ...
```

```
--unique-boundary-1--
```

Figure 7.8   Example MIME Message Structure

Table 7.5   Native and Canonical Form

Native Form	The body to be transmitted is created in the system's native format. The native character set is used and, where appropriate, local end-of-line conventions are used as well. The body may be a UNIX-style text file, or a Sun raster image, or a VMS indexed file, or audio data in a system-dependent format stored only in memory, or anything else that corresponds to the local model for the representation of some form of information. Fundamentally, the data is created in the "native" form that corresponds to the type specified by the media type.
Canonical Form	The entire body, including "out-of-band" information such as record lengths and possibly file attribute information, is converted to a universal canonical form. The specific media type of the body as well as its associated attributes dictate the nature of the canonical form that is used. Conversion to the proper canonical form may involve character set conversion, transformation of audio data, compression, or various other operations specific to the various media types. If character set conversion is involved, however, care must be taken to understand the semantics of the media type, which may have strong implications for any character set conversion (e.g., with regard to syntactically meaningful characters in a text subtype other than "plain").

FUNCTIONS S/MIME provides the following functions.

- **Enveloped data:** This consists of encrypted content of any type and encrypted-content encryption keys for one or more recipients.

- **Signed data:** A digital signature is formed by taking the message digest of the content to be signed and then encrypting that with the private key of the signer. The content plus signature are then encoded using base64 encoding. A signed data message can only be viewed by a recipient with S/MIME capability.

- **Clear-signed data:** As with signed data, a digital signature of the content is formed. However, in this case, only the digital signature is encoded using base64. As a result, recipients without S/MIME capability can view the message content, although they cannot verify the signature.

- **Signed and enveloped data:** Signed-only and encrypted-only entities may be nested, so that encrypted data may be signed and signed data or clear-signed data may be encrypted.

CRYPTOGRAPHIC ALGORITHMS Table 7.6 summarizes the cryptographic algorithms used in S/MIME. S/MIME uses the following terminology taken from RFC 2119 (*Key Words for use in RFCs to Indicate Requirement Levels*) to specify the requirement level:

- **MUST:** The definition is an absolute requirement of the specification. An implementation must include this feature or function to be in conformance with the specification.

- **SHOULD:** There may exist valid reasons in particular circumstances to ignore this feature or function, but it is recommended that an implementation include the feature or function.

S/MIME incorporates three public-key algorithms. The Digital Signature Standard (DSS) described in Chapter 3 is the preferred algorithm for digital signature. S/MIME lists Diffie-Hellman as the preferred algorithm for encrypting session keys; in fact, S/MIME uses a variant of Diffie-Hellman that does provide

Table 7.6 Cryptographic Algorithms Used in S/MIME

Function	Requirement
Create a message digest to be used in forming a digital signature.	MUST support SHA-1. Receiver SHOULD support MD5 for backward compatibility.
Encrypt message digest to form a digital signature.	Sending and receiving agents MUST support DSS. Sending agents SHOULD support RSA encryption. Receiving agents SHOULD support verification of RSA signatures with key sizes 512 bits to 1024 bits.
Encrypt session key for transmission with a message.	Sending and receiving agents SHOULD support Diffie-Hellman. Sending and receiving agents MUST support RSA encryption with key sizes 512 bits to 1024 bits.
Encrypt message for transmission with a one-time session key.	Sending and receiving agents MUST support encryption with tripleDES. Sending agents SHOULD support encryption with AES. Sending agents SHOULD support encryption with RC2/40.
Create a message authentication code.	Receiving agents MUST support HMAC with SHA-1. Sending agents SHOULD support HMAC with SHA-1.

encryption/decryption, known as ElGamal. As an alternative, RSA, described in Chapter 3, can be used for both signatures and session key encryption. These are the same algorithms used in PGP and provide a high level of security. For the hash function used to create the digital signature, the specification requires the 160-bit SHA-1 but recommends receiver support for the 128-bit MD5 for backward compatibility with older versions of S/MIME. As we discussed in Chapter 3, there is justifiable concern about the security of MD5, so SHA-1 is clearly the preferred alternative.

For message encryption, three-key triple DES (tripleDES) is recommended, but compliant implementations must support 40-bit RC2. The latter is a weak encryption algorithm but allows compliance with U.S. export controls.

The S/MIME specification includes a discussion of the procedure for deciding which content encryption algorithm to use. In essence, a sending agent has two decisions to make. First, the sending agent must determine if the receiving agent is capable of decrypting using a given encryption algorithm. Second, if the receiving agent is only capable of accepting weakly encrypted content, the sending agent must decide if it is acceptable to send using weak encryption. To support this decision process, a sending agent may announce its decrypting capabilities in order of preference for any message that it sends out. A receiving agent may store that information for future use.

The following rules, in the following order, should be followed by a sending agent.

1. If the sending agent has a list of preferred decrypting capabilities from an intended recipient, it SHOULD choose the first (highest preference) capability on the list that it is capable of using.

2. If the sending agent has no such list of capabilities from an intended recipient but has received one or more messages from the recipient, then the outgoing message SHOULD use the same encryption algorithm as was used on the last signed and encrypted message received from that intended recipient.

3. If the sending agent has no knowledge about the decryption capabilities of the intended recipient and is willing to risk that the recipient may not be able to decrypt the message, then the sending agent SHOULD use triple DES.

4. If the sending agent has no knowledge about the decryption capabilities of the intended recipient and is not willing to risk that the recipient may not be able to decrypt the message, then the sending agent MUST use RC2/40.

If a message is to be sent to multiple recipients and a common encryption algorithm cannot be selected for all, then the sending agent will need to send two messages. However, in that case, it is important to note that the security of the message is made vulnerable by the transmission of one copy with lower security.

S/MIME Messages

S/MIME makes use of a number of new MIME content types, which are shown in Table 7.7. All of the new application types use the designation PKCS. This refers to a set of public-key cryptography specifications issued by RSA Laboratories and made available for the S/MIME effort.

We examine each of these in turn after first looking at the general procedures for S/MIME message preparation.

SECURING A MIME ENTITY S/MIME secures a MIME entity with a signature, encryption, or both. A MIME entity may be an entire message (except for the RFC 5322 headers), or if the MIME content type is multipart, then a MIME entity is one or more of the subparts of the message. The MIME entity is prepared according to the normal rules for MIME message preparation. Then the MIME entity plus some security-related data, such as algorithm identifiers and certificates, are processed by S/MIME to produce what is known as a PKCS object. A PKCS object is then treated as message content and wrapped in MIME (provided with appropriate MIME headers). This process should become clear as we look at specific objects and provide examples.

In all cases, the message to be sent is converted to canonical form. In particular, for a given type and subtype, the appropriate canonical form is used for the message content. For a multipart message, the appropriate canonical form is used for each subpart.

The use of transfer encoding requires special attention. For most cases, the result of applying the security algorithm will be to produce an object that is partially or totally represented in arbitrary binary data. This will then be wrapped in an outer MIME message, and transfer encoding can be applied at that point, typically base64. However, in the case of a multipart signed message (described in more detail later), the message content in one of the subparts is unchanged by the security process. Unless that content is 7bit, it should be transfer encoded using base64 or quoted-printable so that there is no danger of altering the content to which the signature was applied.

We now look at each of the S/MIME content types.

Table 7.7   S/MIME Content Types

Type	Subtype	smime Parameter	Description
Multipart	Signed		A clear-signed message in two parts: one is the message and the other is the signature.
Application	pkcs7-mime	signedData	A signed S/MIME entity.
	pkcs7-mime	envelopedData	An encrypted S/MIME entity.
	pkcs7-mime	degenerate signedData	An entity containing only public-key certificates.
	pkcs7-mime	CompressedData	A compressed S/MIME entity.
	pkcs7-signature	signedData	The content type of the signature subpart of a multipart/signed message.

ENVELOPEDDATA An application/pkcs7-mime subtype is used for one of four categories of S/MIME processing, each with a unique smime-type parameter. In all cases, the resulting entity (referred to as an *object*) is represented in a form known as Basic Encoding Rules (BER), which is defined in ITU-T Recommendation X.209. The BER format consists of arbitrary octet strings and is therefore binary data. Such an object should be transfer encoded with base64 in the outer MIME message. We first look at envelopedData.

The steps for preparing an envelopedData MIME entity are

1. Generate a pseudorandom session key for a particular symmetric encryption algorithm (RC2/40 or triple DES).
2. For each recipient, encrypt the session key with the recipient's public RSA key.
3. For each recipient, prepare a block known as RecipientInfo that contains an identifier of the recipient's public-key certificate,[3] an identifier of the algorithm used to encrypt the session key, and the encrypted session key.
4. Encrypt the message content with the session key.

The RecipientInfo blocks followed by the encrypted content constitute the envelopedData. This information is then encoded into base64. A sample message (excluding the RFC 5322 headers) is

```
Content-Type:  application/pkcs7-mime;   smime-type=enveloped-
         data; name=smime.p7m
Content-Transfer-Encoding: base64
Content-Disposition: attachment; filename=smime.p7m
```

rfvbnj756tbBghyHhHUujhJhjH77n8HHGT9HG4VQpfyF467GhIGfHfYT6
7n8HHGghyHhHUujhJh4VQpfyF467GhIGfHfYGTrfvbnjT6jH7756tbB9H
f8HHGTrfvhJhjH776tbB9HG4VQbnj7567GhIGfHfYT6ghyHhHUujpfyF4
0GhIGfHfQbnj756YT64V

---

[3]This is an X.509 certificate, discussed later in this section.

To recover the encrypted message, the recipient first strips off the base64 encoding. Then the recipient's private key is used to recover the session key. Finally, the message content is decrypted with the session key.

SIGNEDDATA The signedData smime-type can be used with one or more signers. For clarity, we confine our description to the case of a single digital signature. The steps for preparing a signedData MIME entity are

1. Select a message digest algorithm (SHA or MD5).
2. Compute the message digest (hash function) of the content to be signed.
3. Encrypt the message digest with the signer's private key.
4. Prepare a block known as SignerInfo that contains the signer's public-key certificate, an identifier of the message digest algorithm, an identifier of the algorithm used to encrypt the message digest, and the encrypted message digest.

The signedData entity consists of a series of blocks, including a message digest algorithm identifier, the message being signed, and SignerInfo. The signedData entity may also include a set of public-key certificates sufficient to constitute a chain from a recognized root or top-level certification authority to the signer. This information is then encoded into base64. A sample message (excluding the RFC 5322 headers) is

```
Content-Type:  application/pkcs7-mime;  smime-type=signed-
        data; name=smime.p7m
Content-Transfer-Encoding: base64
Content-Disposition: attachment; filename=smime.p7m
```

567GhIGfHfYT6ghyHhHUujpfyF4f8HHGTrfvhJhjH776tbB9HG4VQbnj7
77n8HHGT9HG4VQpfyF467GhIGfHfYT6rfvbnj756tbBghyHhHUujhJhjH
HUujhJh4VQpfyF467GhIGfHfYGTrfvbnjT6jH7756tbB9H7n8HHGghyHh
6YT64V0GhIGfHfQbnj75

To recover the signed message and verify the signature, the recipient first strips off the base64 encoding. Then the signer's public key is used to decrypt the message digest. The recipient independently computes the message digest and compares it to the decrypted message digest to verify the signature.

CLEAR SIGNING Clear signing is achieved using the multipart content type with a signed subtype. As was mentioned, this signing process does not involve transforming the message to be signed, so that the message is sent "in the clear." Thus, recipients with MIME capability but not S/MIME capability are able to read the incoming message.

A multipart/signed message has two parts. The first part can be any MIME type but must be prepared so that it will not be altered during transfer from source to destination. This means that if the first part is not 7bit, then it needs to be encoded using base64 or quoted-printable. Then this part is processed in the same manner as signedData, but in this case an object with signedData format is created that has an empty message content field. This object is a detached signature. It is then transfer encoded using base64 to become the second part of the multipart/signed message. This second part has a MIME content type of application and a subtype of pkcs7-signature. Here is a sample message:

```
Content-Type: multipart/signed;
    protocol="application/pkcs7-signature";
    micalg=sha1; boundary=boundary42

—boundary42
Content-Type: text/plain

This is a clear-signed message.

—boundary42
Content-Type: application/pkcs7-signature; name=smime.p7s
Content-Transfer-Encoding: base64
Content-Disposition: attachment; filename=smime.p7s

ghyHhHUujhJhjH77n8HHGTrfvbnj756tbB9HG4VQpfyF467GhIGfHfYT6
4VQpfyF467GhIGfHfYT6jH77n8HHGghyHhHUujhJh756tbB9HGTrfvbnj
n8HHGTrfvhJhjH776tbB9HG4VQbnj7567GhIGfHfYT6ghyHhHUujpfyF4
7GhIGfHfYT64VQbnj756
—boundary42—
```

The protocol parameter indicates that this is a two-part clear-signed entity. The micalg parameter indicates the type of message digest used. The receiver can verify the signature by taking the message digest of the first part and comparing this to the message digest recovered from the signature in the second part.

REGISTRATION REQUEST   Typically, an application or user will apply to a certification authority for a public-key certificate. The application/pkcs10 S/MIME entity is used to transfer a certification request. The certification request includes certification RequestInfo block, followed by an identifier of the public-key encryption algorithm, followed by the signature of the certificationRequestInfo block made using the sender's private key. The certificationRequestInfo block includes a name of the certificate subject (the entity whose public key is to be certified) and a bit-string representation of the user's public key.

CERTIFICATES-ONLY MESSAGE   A message containing only certificates or a certificate revocation list (CRL) can be sent in response to a registration request. The message is an application/pkcs7-mime type/subtype with an smime-type parameter of degenerate. The steps involved are the same as those for creating a signedData message, except that there is no message content and the signerInfo field is empty.

S/MIME Certificate Processing

S/MIME uses public-key certificates that conform to version 3 of X.509 (see Chapter 4). The key-management scheme used by S/MIME is in some ways a hybrid between a strict X.509 certification hierarchy and PGP's web of trust. As with the PGP model, S/MIME managers and/or users must configure each client with a list of trusted keys and with certificate revocation lists. That is, the responsibility is local for maintaining the certificates needed to verify incoming signatures and to encrypt outgoing messages. On the other hand, the certificates are signed by certification authorities.

USER AGENT ROLE An S/MIME user has several key-management functions to perform.

- **Key generation:** The user of some related administrative utility (e.g., one associated with LAN management) MUST be capable of generating separate Diffie-Hellman and DSS key pairs and SHOULD be capable of generating RSA key pairs. Each key pair MUST be generated from a good source of non-deterministic random input and be protected in a secure fashion. A user agent SHOULD generate RSA key pairs with a length in the range of 768 to 1024 bits and MUST NOT generate a length of less than 512 bits.

- **Registration:** A user's public key must be registered with a certification authority in order to receive an X.509 public-key certificate.

- **Certificate storage and retrieval:** A user requires access to a local list of certificates in order to verify incoming signatures and to encrypt outgoing messages. Such a list could be maintained by the user or by some local administrative entity on behalf of a number of users.

VERISIGN CERTIFICATES There are several companies that provide certification authority (CA) services. For example, Nortel has designed an enterprise CA solution and can provide S/MIME support within an organization. There are a number of Internet-based CAs, including VeriSign, GTE, and the U.S. Postal Service. Of these, the most widely used is the VeriSign CA service, a brief description of which we now provide.

VeriSign provides a CA service that is intended to be compatible with S/MIME and a variety of other applications. VeriSign issues X.509 certificates with the product name VeriSign Digital ID. As of early 1998, over 35,000 commercial Web sites were using VeriSign Server Digital IDs, and over a million consumer Digital IDs had been issued to users of Netscape and Microsoft browsers.

The information contained in a Digital ID depends on the type of Digital ID and its use. At a minimum, each Digital ID contains

- Owner's public key
- Owner's name or alias
- Expiration date of the Digital ID
- Serial number of the Digital ID
- Name of the certification authority that issued the Digital ID
- Digital signature of the certification authority that issued the Digital ID

Digital IDs can also contain other user-supplied information, including

- Address
- E-mail address
- Basic registration information (country, zip code, age, and gender)

VeriSign provides three levels, or classes, of security for public-key certificates, as summarized in Table 7.8. A user requests a certificate online at VeriSign's Web site or other participating Web sites. Class 1 and Class 2 requests are processed on line, and in most cases take only a few seconds to approve. Briefly, the following procedures are used.

- For Class 1 Digital IDs, VeriSign confirms the user's e-mail address by sending a PIN and Digital ID pick-up information to the e-mail address provided in the application.
- For Class 2 Digital IDs, VeriSign verifies the information in the application through an automated comparison with a consumer database in addition to

Table 7.8   Verisign Public-Key Certificate Classes

	Class 1	Class 2	Class 3
Summary of Confirmation of Identity	Automated unambiguous name and e-mail address search.	Same as Class 1, plus automated enrollment information check and automated address check.	Same as Class 1, plus personal presence and ID documents plus Class 2 automated ID check for individuals; business records (or filings) for organizations.
IA Private Key Protection	PCA: trustworthy hardware; CA: trustworthy software or trustworthy hardware.	PCA and CA: trustworthy hardware.	PCA and CA: trustworthy hardware.
Certificate Applicant and Subscriber Private Key Protection	Encryption software (PIN protected) recommended but not required.	Encryption software (PIN protected) required.	Encryption software (PIN protected) required; hardware token recommended but not required.
Applications Implemented or Contemplated by Users	Web-browsing and certain e-mail usage.	Individual and intra- and inter-company e-mail, online subscriptions, password replacement, and software validation.	E-banking, corp. database access, personal banking, membership-based online services, content integrity services, e-commerce server, software validation; authentication of LRAAs; and strong encryption for certain servers.

IA   = Issuing Authority
CA   = Certification Authority
PCA = VeriSign public primary certification authority
PIN = Personal Identification Number
LRAA = Local Registration Authority Administrator

performing all of the checking associated with a Class 1 Digital ID. Finally, confirmation is sent to the specified postal address alerting the user that a Digital ID has been issued in his or her name.

- For Class 3 Digital IDs, VeriSign requires a higher level of identity assurance. An individual must prove his or her identity by providing notarized credentials or applying in person.

Enhanced Security Services

As of this writing, three enhanced security services have been proposed in an Internet draft. The details of these may change, and additional services may be added. The three services are

- **Signed receipts:** A signed receipt may be requested in a `SignedData` object. Returning a signed receipt provides proof of delivery to the originator of a message and allows the originator to demonstrate to a third party that the recipient received the message. In essence, the recipient signs the entire original message plus the original (sender's) signature and appends the new signature to form a new S/MIME message.
- **Security labels:** A security label may be included in the authenticated attributes of a `SignedData` object. A security label is a set of security information regarding the sensitivity of the content that is protected by S/MIME encapsulation. The labels may be used for access control, by indicating which users are permitted access to an object. Other uses include priority (secret, confidential, restricted, and so on) or role based, describing which kind of people can see the information (e.g., patient's health-care team, medical billing agents, etc.).
- **Secure mailing lists:** When a user sends a message to multiple recipients, a certain amount of per-recipient processing is required, including the use of each recipient's public key. The user can be relieved of this work by employing the services of an S/MIME Mail List Agent (MLA). An MLA can take a single incoming message, perform the recipient-specific encryption for each recipient, and forward the message. The originator of a message need only send the message to the MLA with encryption performed using the MLA's public key.

7.3 DOMAINKEYS IDENTIFIED MAIL

DomainKeys Identified Mail (DKIM) is a specification for cryptographically signing e-mail messages, permitting a signing domain to claim responsibility for a message in the mail stream. Message recipients (or agents acting in their behalf) can verify the signature by querying the signer's domain directly to retrieve the appropriate public key and thereby can confirm that the message was attested to by a party in possession of the private key for the signing domain. DKIM is a proposed Internet Standard (RFC 4871: *DomainKeys Identified Mail (DKIM) Signatures*). DKIM has been widely adopted by a range of e-mail providers, including corporations, government agencies, gmail, yahoo, and many Internet Service Providers (ISPs).

This section provides an overview of DKIM. Before beginning our discussion of DKIM, we introduce the standard Internet mail architecture. Then we look at the threat that DKIM is intended to address, and finally provide an overview of DKIM operation.

Internet Mail Architecture

To understand the operation of DKIM, it is useful to have a basic grasp of the Internet mail architecture, which is currently defined in [CROC09]. This subsection provides an overview of the basic concepts.

At its most fundamental level, the Internet mail architecture consists of a user world in the form of Message User Agents (MUA), and the transfer world, in the form of the Message Handling Service (MHS), which is composed of Message Transfer Agents (MTA). The MHS accepts a message from one user and delivers it to one or more other users, creating a virtual MUA-to-MUA exchange environment. This architecture involves three types of interoperability. One is directly between users: messages must be formatted by the MUA on behalf of the message author so that the message can be displayed to the message recipient by the destination MUA. There are also interoperability requirements between the MUA and the MHS—first when a message is posted from an MUA to the MHS and later when it is delivered from the MHS to the destination MUA. Interoperability is required among the MTA components along the transfer path through the MHS.

Figure 7.9 illustrates the key components of the Internet mail architecture, which include the following.

- **Message User Agent (MUA):** Works on behalf of user actors and user applications. It is their representative within the e-mail service. Typically, this function is housed in the user's computer and is referred to as a client e-mail program or a local network e-mail server. The author MUA formats a message and performs initial submission into the MHS via a MSA. The recipient MUA processes received mail for storage and/or display to the recipient user.
- **Mail Submission Agent (MSA):** Accepts the message submitted by an MUA and enforces the policies of the hosting domain and the requirements of Internet standards. This function may be located together with the MUA or as a separate functional model. In the latter case, the Simple Mail Transfer Protocol (SMTP) is used between the MUA and the MSA.
- **Message Transfer Agent (MTA):** Relays mail for one application-level hop. It is like a packet switch or IP router in that its job is to make routing assessments and to move the message closer to the recipients. Relaying is performed by a sequence of MTAs until the message reaches a destination MDA. An MTA also adds trace information to the message header. SMTP is used between MTAs and between an MTA and an MSA or MDA.
- **Mail Delivery Agent (MDA):** Responsible for transferring the message from the MHS to the MS.
- **Message Store (MS):** An MUA can employ a long-term MS. An MS can be located on a remote server or on the same machine as the MUA. Typically, an MUA retrieves messages from a remote server using POP (Post Office Protocol) or IMAP (Internet Message Access Protocol).

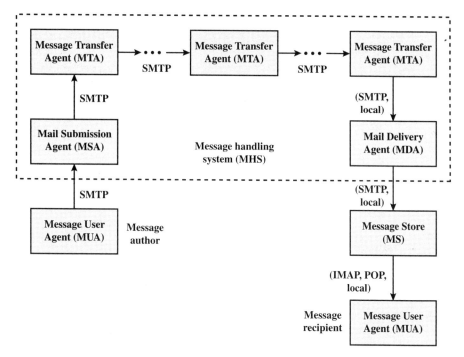

Figure 7.9   Function Modules and Standardized Protocols for the Internet

Two other concepts need to be defined. An **administrative management domain (ADMD)** is an Internet e-mail provider. Examples include a department that operates a local mail relay (MTA), an IT department that operates an enterprise mail relay, and an ISP that operates a public shared e-mail service. Each ADMD can have different operating policies and trust-based decision making. One obvious example is the distinction between mail that is exchanged within an organization and mail that is exchanged between independent organizations. The rules for handling the two types of traffic tend to be quite different.

The **Domain Name System (DNS)** is a directory lookup service that provides a mapping between the name of a host on the Internet and its numerical address.

E-mail Threats

RFC 4684 (*Analysis of Threats Motivating DomainKeys Identified Mail*) describes the threats being addressed by DKIM in terms of the characteristics, capabilities, and location of potential attackers.

CHARACTERISTICS   RFC characterizes the range of attackers on a spectrum of three levels of threat.

1. At the low end are attackers who simply want to send e-mail that a recipient does not want to receive. The attacker can use one of a number of commercially available tools that allow the sender to falsify the origin address of messages. This makes it difficult for the receiver to filter spam on the basis of originating address or domain.

2. At the next level are professional senders of bulk spam mail. These attackers often operate as commercial enterprises and send messages on behalf of third parties. They employ more comprehensive tools for attack, including Mail Transfer Agents (MTAs) and registered domains and networks of compromised computers (zombies) to send messages and (in some cases) to harvest addresses to which to send.

3. The most sophisticated and financially motivated senders of messages are those who stand to receive substantial financial benefit, such as from an e-mail-based fraud scheme. These attackers can be expected to employ all of the above mechanisms and additionally may attack the Internet infrastructure itself, including DNS cache-poisoning attacks and IP routing attacks.

CAPABILITIES RFC 4686 lists the following as capabilities that an attacker might have.

1. Submit messages to MTAs and Message Submission Agents (MSAs) at multiple locations in the Internet.

2. Construct arbitrary Message Header fields, including those claiming to be mailing lists, resenders, and other mail agents.

3. Sign messages on behalf of domains under their control.

4. Generate substantial numbers of either unsigned or apparently signed messages that might be used to attempt a denial-of-service attack.

5. Resend messages that may have been previously signed by the domain.

6. Transmit messages using any envelope information desired.

7. Act as an authorized submitter for messages from a compromised computer.

8. Manipulation of IP routing. This could be used to submit messages from specific IP addresses or difficult-to-trace addresses, or to cause diversion of messages to a specific domain.

9. Limited influence over portions of DNS using mechanisms such as cache poisoning. This might be used to influence message routing or to falsify advertisements of DNS-based keys or signing practices.

10. Access to significant computing resources, for example, through the conscription of worm-infected "zombie" computers. This could allow the "bad actor" to perform various types of brute-force attacks.

11. Ability to eavesdrop on existing traffic, perhaps from a wireless network.

LOCATION DKIM focuses primarily on attackers located outside of the administrative units of the claimed originator and the recipient. These administrative units frequently correspond to the protected portions of the network adjacent to the originator and recipient. It is in this area that the trust relationships required for authenticated message submission do not exist and do not scale adequately to be practical. Conversely, within these administrative units, there are other mechanisms (such as authenticated message submission) that are easier to deploy and more likely to be used than DKIM. External "bad actors" are usually attempting to exploit the "any-to-any" nature of e-mail that motivates most recipient MTAs to accept messages from anywhere for delivery to their local domain. They may generate messages without signatures, with incorrect signatures, or with correct signatures from domains with little traceability. They may also pose as mailing lists, greeting cards, or other agents that legitimately send or resend messages on behalf of others.

DKIM Strategy

DKIM is designed to provide an e-mail authentication technique that is transparent to the end user. In essence, a user's e-mail message is signed by a private key of the administrative domain from which the e-mail originates. The signature covers all of the content of the message and some of the RFC 5322 message headers. At the receiving end, the MDA can access the corresponding public key via a DNS and verify the signature, thus authenticating that the message comes from the claimed administrative domain. Thus, mail that originates from somewhere else but claims to come from a given domain will not pass the authentication test and can be rejected. This approach differs from that of S/MIME and PGP, which use the originator's private key to sign the content of the message. The motivation for DKIM is based on the following reasoning.[4]

1. S/MIME depends on both the sending and receiving users employing S/MIME. For almost all users, the bulk of incoming mail does not use S/MIME, and the bulk of the mail the user wants to send is to recipients not using S/MIME.
2. S/MIME signs only the message content. Thus, RFC 5322 header information concerning origin can be compromised.
3. DKIM is not implemented in client programs (MUAs) and is therefore transparent to the user; the user need take no action.
4. DKIM applies to all mail from cooperating domains.
5. DKIM allows good senders to prove that they did send a particular message and to prevent forgers from masquerading as good senders.

   Figure 7.10 is a simple example of the operation of DKIM. We begin with a message generated by a user and transmitted into the MHS to an MSA that is within the users administrative domain. An e-mail message is generated by an e-mail client program. The content of the message, plus selected RFC 5322 headers, is signed by the e-mail provider using the provider's private key. The signer is associated with a domain, which could be a corporate local network, an ISP, or a public e-mail facility such as gmail. The signed message then passes through the Internet via a sequence of MTAs. At the destination, the MDA retrieves the public key for the incoming signature and verifies the signature before passing the message on to the destination e-mail client. The default signing algorithm is RSA with SHA-256. RSA with SHA-1 also may be used.

DKIM Functional Flow

Figure 7.11 provides a more detailed look at the elements of DKIM operation. Basic message processing is divided between a signing Administrative Management Domain (ADMD) and a verifying ADMD. At its simplest, this is between the

---

[4]The reasoning is expressed in terms of the use of S/MIME. The same argument applies to PGP.

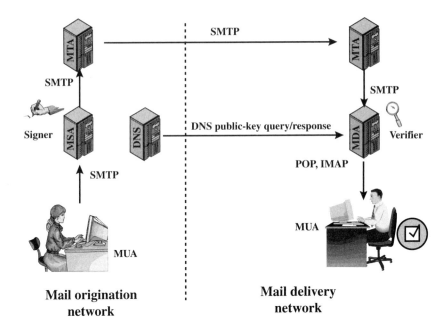

DNS = Domain Name System
MDA = Mail Delivery Agent
MSA = Mail Submission Agent
MTA = Message Transfer Agent
MUA = Message User Agent

Figure 7.10   Simple Example of DKIM Deployment

originating ADMD and the delivering ADMD, but it can involve other ADMDs in the handling path.

Signing is performed by an authorized module within the signing ADMD and uses private information from a Key Store. Within the originating ADMD, this might be performed by the MUA, MSA, or an MTA. Verifying is performed by an authorized module within the verifying ADMD. Within a delivering ADMD, verifying might be performed by an MTA, MDA, or MUA. The module verifies the signature or determines whether a particular signature was required. Verifying the signature uses public information from the Key Store. If the signature passes, reputation information is used to assess the signer and that information is passed to the message filtering system. If the signature fails or there is no signature using the author's domain, information about signing practices related to the author can be retrieved remotely and/or locally, and that information is passed to the message filtering system. For example, if the sender (e.g., gmail) uses DKIM but no DKIM signature is present, then the message may be considered fraudulent.

The signature is inserted into the RFC 5322 message as an additional header entry, starting with the keyword Dkim-Signature. You can view examples from your own incoming mail by using the View Long Headers (or similar wording) option for an incoming message. Here is an example:

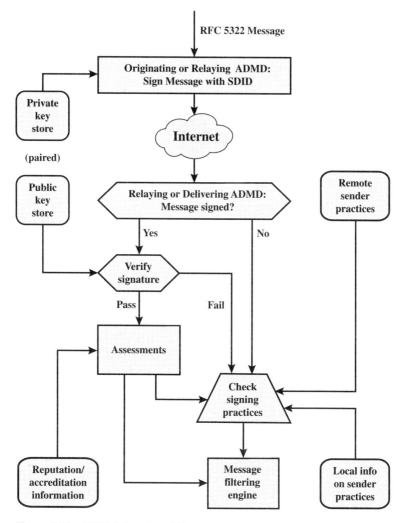

Figure 7.11   DKIM Functional Flow

```
Dkim-Signature:           v=1;  a=rsa-sha256;  c=relaxed/relaxed;
                          d=gmail.com; s=gamma; h=domainkey-signa-
                          ture:mime-version:received:date:message-
                          id:subject   :from:to:content-type:con-
                          tent-transfer-encoding;
                          bh=5mZvQDyCRuyLb1Y28K4zgS2MPOemFToDBgvbJ
                          7GO90s=;
                          b=PcUvPSDygb4ya5Dyj1rbZGp/VyRiScuaz7TTG
                          J5qW5slM+klzv6kcfYdGDHzEVJW+Z
                          FetuPfF1ETOVhELtwH0zjSccOyPkEiblOf6gILO
                          bm3DDRm3Ys1/FVrbhVOlA+/jH9Aei
                          uIIw/5iFnRbSH6qPDVv/beDQqAWQfA/wF7O5k=
```

Before a message is signed, a process known as canonicalization is performed on both the header and body of the RFC 5322 message. Canonicalization is necessary to deal with the possibility of minor changes in the message made en route, including character encoding, treatment of trailing white space in message lines, and the "folding" and "unfolding" of header lines. The intent of canonicalization is to make a minimal transformation of the message (for the purpose of signing; the message itself is not changed, so the canonicalization must be performed again by the verifier) that will give it its best chance of producing the same canonical value at the receiving end. DKIM defines two header canonicalization algorithms ("simple" and "relaxed") and two for the body (with the same names). The simple algorithm tolerates almost no modification, while the relaxed tolerates common modifications.

The signature includes a number of fields. Each field begins with a tag consisting of a tag code followed by an equals sign and ends with a semicolon. The fields include the following:

- **v** = DKIM version.
- **a** = Algorithm used to generate the signature; must be either rsa-sha1 or rsa-sha256.
- **c** = Canonicalization method used on the header and the body.
- **d** = A domain name used as an identifier to refer to the identity of a responsible person or organization. In DKIM, this identifier is called the Signing Domain IDentifier (SDID). In our example, this field indicates that the sender is using a gmail address.
- **s** = In order that different keys may be used in different circumstances for the same signing domain (allowing expiration of old keys, separate departmental signing, or the like), DKIM defines a selector (a name associated with a key), which is used by the verifier to retrieve the proper key during signature verification.
- **h** = Signed Header fields. A colon-separated list of header field names that identify the header fields presented to the signing algorithm. Note that in our example above, the signature covers the domainkey-signature field. This refers to an older algorithm (since replaced by DKIM) that is still in use.
- **bh** = The hash of the canonicalized body part of the message. This provides additional information for diagnosing signature verification failures.
- **b** = The signature data in base64 format; this is the encrypted hash code.

7.4 RECOMMENDED READING AND WEB SITES

[LEIB07] provides an overview of DKIM.

LEIB07 Leiba, B., and Fenton, J. "DomainKeys Identified Mail (DKIM): Using Digital Signatures for Domain Verification." *Proceedings of Fourth Conference on E-mail and Anti-Spam (CEAS 07)*, 2007.

Recommended Web Sites:

- **PGP Home Page:** PGP Web site by PGP Corp., the leading PGP commercial vendor.
- **International PGP Home Page:** Designed to promote worldwide use of PGP. Contains documents and links of interest.
- **PGP Charter:** Latest RFCs and Internet drafts for Open Specification PGP.
- **S/MIME Charter:** Latest RFCs and Internet drafts for S/MIME.
- **DKIM:** Website hosted by Mutual Internet Practices Association, this site contains a wide range of documents and information related to DKIM.
- **DKIM Charter:** Latest RFCs and Internet drafts for DKIM.

7.5 KEY TERMS, REVIEW QUESTIONS, AND PROBLEMS

Key Terms

detached signature DomainKeys Identified Mail (DKIM) electronic mail	Multipurpose Internet Mail Extensions (MIME) Pretty Good Privacy (PGP) radix 64	session key S/MIME trust ZIP

Review Questions

7.1 What are the five principal services provided by PGP?
7.2 What is the utility of a detached signature?
7.3 Why does PGP generate a signature before applying compression?
7.4 What is R64 conversion?
7.5 Why is R64 conversion useful for an e-mail application?
7.6 How does PGP use the concept of trust?
7.7 What is RFC 5322?
7.8 What is MIME?
7.9 What is S/MIME?
7.10 What is DKIM?

Problems

7.1 PGP makes use of the cipher feedback (CFB) mode of CAST-128, whereas most symmetric encryption applications (other than key encryption) use the cipher block chaining (CBC) mode. We have

$$\text{CBC: } C_i = E(K, [C_{i-1} \oplus P_i]); \quad P_i = C_{i-1} \oplus D(K, C_i)$$

$$\text{CFB: } C_i = P_i \oplus E(K, C_{i-1}); \quad P_i = C_i \oplus E(K, C_{i-1})$$

These two appear to provide equal security. Suggest a reason why PGP uses the CFB mode.

7.2 In the PGP scheme, what is the expected number of session keys generated before a previously created key is produced?

7.3 In PGP, what is the probability that a user with N public keys will have at least one duplicate key ID?

7.4 The first 16 bits of the message digest in a PGP signature are translated in the clear.
   a. To what extent does this compromise the security of the hash algorithm?
   b. To what extent does it in fact perform its intended function, namely, to help determine if the correct RSA key was used to decrypt the digest?

7.5 In Figure 7.4, each entry in the public-key ring contains an Owner Trust field that indicates the degree of trust associated with this public-key owner. Why is that not enough? That is, if this owner is trusted and this is supposed to be the owner's public key, why is that trust not enough to permit PGP to use this public key?

7.6 What is the basic difference between X.509 and PGP in terms of key hierarchies and key trust?

7.7 Phil Zimmermann chose IDEA, three-key triple DES, and CAST-128 as symmetric encryption algorithms for PGP. Give reasons why each of the following symmetric encryption algorithms described in this book is suitable or unsuitable for PGP: DES, two-key triple DES, and AES.

7.8 Consider radix-64 conversion as a form of encryption. In this case, there is no key. But suppose that an opponent knew only that some form of substitution algorithm was being used to encrypt English text and did not guess that it was R64. How effective would this algorithm be against cryptanalysis?

7.9 Encode the text "plaintext" using the following techniques. Assume characters are stored in 8-bit ASCII with zero parity.
   a. Radix-64
   b. Quoted-printable

APPENDIX 7A   RADIX-64 CONVERSION

Both PGP and S/MIME make use of an encoding technique referred to as radix-64 conversion. This technique maps arbitrary binary input into printable character output. The form of encoding has the following relevant characteristics:

1. The range of the function is a character set that is universally representable at all sites, not a specific binary encoding of that character set. Thus, the characters themselves can be encoded into whatever form is needed by a specific system. For example, the character "E" is represented in an ASCII-based system as hexadecimal 45 and in an EBCDIC-based system as hexadecimal C5.

2. The character set consists of 65 printable characters, one of which is used for padding. With $2^6 = 64$ available characters, each character can be used to represent 6 bits of input.

3. No control characters are included in the set. Thus, a message encoded in radix 64 can traverse mail-handling systems that scan the data stream for control characters.

4. The hyphen character "-" is not used. This character has significance in the RFC 5322 format and should therefore be avoided.

Table 7.9 Radix-64 Encoding

6-bit Value	Character Encoding	6-bit Value	Character Encoding	6-bit Value	Character Encoding	6-bit Value	Character Encoding
0	A	16	Q	32	g	48	w
1	B	17	R	33	h	49	x
2	C	18	S	34	i	50	y
3	D	19	T	35	j	51	z
4	E	20	U	36	k	52	0
5	F	21	V	37	l	53	1
6	G	22	W	38	m	54	2
7	H	23	X	39	n	55	3
8	I	24	Y	40	o	56	4
9	J	25	Z	41	p	57	5
10	K	26	a	42	q	58	6
11	L	27	b	43	r	59	7
12	M	28	c	44	s	60	8
13	N	29	d	45	t	61	9
14	O	30	e	46	u	62	+
15	P	31	f	47	v	63	/
						(pad)	=

Table 7.9 shows the mapping of 6-bit input values to characters. The character set consists of the alphanumeric characters plus "+" and "/". The "=" character is used as the padding character.

Figure 7.12 illustrates the simple mapping scheme. Binary input is processed in blocks of 3 octets (24 bits). Each set of 6 bits in the 24-bit block is mapped into a character. In the figure, the characters are shown encoded as 8-bit quantities. In this typical case, each 24-bit input is expanded to 32 bits of output.

For example, consider the 24-bit raw text sequence 00100011 01011100 10010001, which can be expressed in hexadecimal as 235C91. We arrange this input in blocks of 6 bits:

$$001000 \quad 110101 \quad 110010 \quad 010001$$

The extracted 6-bit decimal values are 8, 53, 50, and 17. Looking these up in Table 7.9 yields the radix-64 encoding as the following characters: I1yR. If these characters are stored in 8-bit ASCII format with parity bit set to zero, we have

$$01001001 \quad 00110001 \quad 01111001 \quad 01010010$$

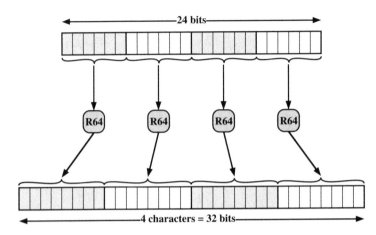

Figure 7.12 Printable Encoding of Binary Data into Radix-64 Format

In hexadecimal, this is 49317952. To summarize:

Input Data	
Binary representation	00100011 01011100 10010001
Hexadecimal representation	235C91
Radix-64 Encoding of Input Data	
Character representation	I1yR
ASCII code (8 bit, zero parity)	01001001 00110001 01111001 01010010
Hexadecimal representation	49317952

CHAPTER 8

IP SECURITY

If a secret piece of news is divulged by a spy before the time is ripe, he must be put to death, together with the man to whom the secret was told.

— The Art of War, Sun Tzu

KEY POINTS

◆ IP security (IPsec) is a capability that can be added to either current version of the Internet Protocol (IPv4 or IPv6) by means of additional headers.

◆ IPsec encompasses three functional areas: authentication, confidentiality, and key management.

◆ Authentication makes use of the HMAC message authentication code. Authentication can be applied to the entire original IP packet (tunnel mode) or to all of the packet except for the IP header (transport mode).

◆ Confidentiality is provided by an encryption format known as encapsulating security payload. Both tunnel and transport modes can be accommodated.

◆ IKE defines a number of techniques for key management.

There are application-specific security mechanisms for a number of application areas, including electronic mail (S/MIME, PGP), client/server (Kerberos), Web access (Secure Sockets Layer), and others. However, users have security concerns that cut across protocol layers. For example, an enterprise can run a secure, private IP network by disallowing links to untrusted sites, encrypting packets that leave the premises, and authenticating packets that enter the premises. By implementing security at the IP level, an organization can ensure secure networking not only for applications that have security mechanisms but also for the many security-ignorant applications.

IP-level security encompasses three functional areas: authentication, confidentiality, and key management. The authentication mechanism assures that a received packet was, in fact, transmitted by the party identified as the source in the packet header. In addition, this mechanism assures that the packet has not been altered in transit. The confidentiality facility enables communicating nodes to encrypt messages to prevent eavesdropping by third parties. The key management facility is concerned with the secure exchange of keys.

We begin this chapter with an overview of IP security (IPsec) and an introduction to the IPsec architecture. We then look at each of the three functional areas in detail. Appendix D reviews Internet protocols.

8.1 IP SECURITY OVERVIEW

In 1994, the Internet Architecture Board (IAB) issued a report titled "Security in the Internet Architecture" (RFC 1636). The report identified key areas for security mechanisms. Among these were the need to secure the network infrastructure from unauthorized monitoring and control of network traffic and the need to secure end-user-to-end-user traffic using authentication and encryption mechanisms.

To provide security, the IAB included authentication and encryption as necessary security features in the next-generation IP, which has been issued as IPv6. Fortunately, these security capabilities were designed to be usable both with the current IPv4 and the future IPv6. This means that vendors can begin offering these features now, and many vendors now do have some IPsec capability in their products. The IPsec specification now exists as a set of Internet standards.

Applications of IPsec

IPsec provides the capability to secure communications across a LAN, across private and public WANs, and across the Internet. Examples of its use include:

- **Secure branch office connectivity over the Internet:** A company can build a secure virtual private network over the Internet or over a public WAN. This enables a business to rely heavily on the Internet and reduce its need for private networks, saving costs and network management overhead.
- **Secure remote access over the Internet:** An end user whose system is equipped with IP security protocols can make a local call to an Internet Service Provider (ISP) and gain secure access to a company network. This reduces the cost of toll charges for traveling employees and telecommuters.
- **Establishing extranet and intranet connectivity with partners:** IPsec can be used to secure communication with other organizations, ensuring authentication and confidentiality and providing a key exchange mechanism.
- **Enhancing electronic commerce security:** Even though some Web and electronic commerce applications have built-in security protocols, the use of IPsec enhances that security. IPsec guarantees that all traffic designated by the network administrator is both encrypted and authenticated, adding an additional layer of security to whatever is provided at the application layer.

The principal feature of IPsec that enables it to support these varied applications is that it can encrypt and/or authenticate *all* traffic at the IP level. Thus, all distributed applications (including remote logon, client/server, e-mail, file transfer, Web access, and so on) can be secured.

Figure 8.1 is a typical scenario of IPsec usage. An organization maintains LANs at dispersed locations. Nonsecure IP traffic is conducted on each LAN. For traffic offsite, through some sort of private or public WAN, IPsec protocols are used. These protocols operate in networking devices, such as a router or firewall, that connect each LAN to the outside world. The IPsec networking device will typically encrypt and compress all traffic going into the WAN and decrypt and decompress traffic coming from the WAN; these operations are transparent to workstations and servers on the LAN. Secure transmission is also possible with individual users who dial into the WAN. Such user workstations must implement the IPsec protocols to provide security.

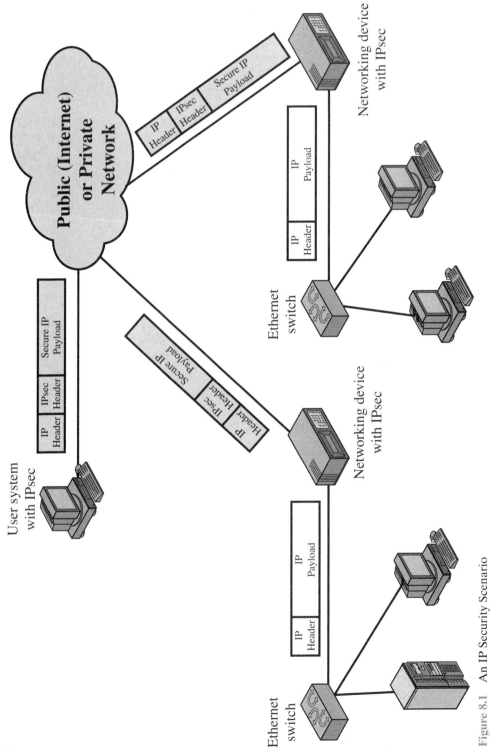

Figure 8.1 An IP Security Scenario

Benefits of IPsec

Some of the benefits of IPsec:

- When IPsec is implemented in a firewall or router, it provides strong security that can be applied to all traffic crossing the perimeter. Traffic within a company or workgroup does not incur the overhead of security-related processing.
- IPsec in a firewall is resistant to bypass if all traffic from the outside must use IP and the firewall is the only means of entrance from the Internet into the organization.
- IPsec is below the transport layer (TCP, UDP) and so is transparent to applications. There is no need to change software on a user or server system when IPsec is implemented in the firewall or router. Even if IPsec is implemented in end systems, upper-layer software, including applications, is not affected.
- IPsec can be transparent to end users. There is no need to train users on security mechanisms, issue keying material on a per-user basis, or revoke keying material when users leave the organization.
- IPsec can provide security for individual users if needed. This is useful for offsite workers and for setting up a secure virtual subnetwork within an organization for sensitive applications.

Routing Applications

In addition to supporting end users and protecting premises systems and networks, IPsec can play a vital role in the routing architecture required for internetworking. [HUIT98] lists the following examples of the use of IPsec. IPsec can assure that

- A router advertisement (a new router advertises its presence) comes from an authorized router.
- A neighbor advertisement (a router seeks to establish or maintain a neighbor relationship with a router in another routing domain) comes from an authorized router.
- A redirect message comes from the router to which the initial IP packet was sent.
- A routing update is not forged.

Without such security measures, an opponent can disrupt communications or divert some traffic. Routing protocols such as Open Shortest Path First (OSPF) should be run on top of security associations between routers that are defined by IPsec.

IPsec Documents

IPsec encompasses three functional areas: authentication, confidentiality, and key management. The totality of the IPsec specification is scattered across dozens of RFCs and draft IETF documents, making this the most complex and difficult to grasp of all IETF specifications. The best way to grasp the scope of IPsec is to consult the latest version of the IPsec document roadmap, which as of this writing is [FRAN09]. The documents can be categorized into the following groups.

- **Architecture:** Covers the general concepts, security requirements, definitions, and mechanisms defining IPsec technology. The current specification is RFC 4301, *Security Architecture for the Internet Protocol.*

- **Authentication Header (AH):** AH is an extension header to provide message authentication. The current specification is RFC 4302, *IP Authentication Header.* Because message authentication is provided by ESP, the use of AH is deprecated. It is included in IPsecv3 for backward compatibility but should not be used in new applications. We do not discuss AH in this chapter.

- **Encapsulating Security Payload (ESP):** ESP consists of an encapsulating header and trailer used to provide encryption or combined encryption/authentication. The current specification is RFC 4303, *IP Encapsulating Security Payload (ESP).*

- **Internet Key Exchange (IKE):** This is a collection of documents describing the key management schemes for use with IPsec. The main specification is RFC 4306, *Internet Key Exchange (IKEv2) Protocol,* but there are a number of related RFCs.

- **Cryptographic algorithms:** This category encompasses a large set of documents that define and describe cryptographic algorithms for encryption, message authentication, pseudorandom functions (PRFs), and cryptographic key exchange.

- **Other:** There are a variety of other IPsec-related RFCs, including those dealing with security policy and management information base (MIB) content.

IPsec Services

IPsec provides security services at the IP layer by enabling a system to select required security protocols, determine the algorithm(s) to use for the service(s), and put in place any cryptographic keys required to provide the requested services. Two protocols are used to provide security: an authentication protocol designated by the header of the protocol, Authentication Header (AH); and a combined encryption/authentication protocol designated by the format of the packet for that protocol, Encapsulating Security Payload (ESP). RFC 4301 lists the following services:

- Access control
- Connectionless integrity
- Data origin authentication
- Rejection of replayed packets (a form of partial sequence integrity)
- Confidentiality (encryption)
- Limited traffic flow confidentiality

Transport and Tunnel Modes

Both AH and ESP support two modes of use: transport and tunnel mode. The operation of these two modes is best understood in the context of a description of ESP, which is covered in Section 8.3. Here we provide a brief overview.

TRANSPORT MODE Transport mode provides protection primarily for upper-layer protocols. That is, transport mode protection extends to the payload of an IP packet.[1] Examples include a TCP or UDP segment or an ICMP packet, all of which operate directly above IP in a host protocol stack. Typically, transport mode is used for end-to-end communication between two hosts (e.g., a client and a server, or two workstations). When a host runs AH or ESP over IPv4, the payload is the data that normally follow the IP header. For IPv6, the payload is the data that normally follow both the IP header and any IPv6 extensions headers that are present, with the possible exception of the destination options header, which may be included in the protection.

ESP in transport mode encrypts and optionally authenticates the IP payload but not the IP header. AH in transport mode authenticates the IP payload and selected portions of the IP header.

TUNNEL MODE Tunnel mode provides protection to the entire IP packet. To achieve this, after the AH or ESP fields are added to the IP packet, the entire packet plus security fields is treated as the payload of new outer IP packet with a new outer IP header. The entire original, inner, packet travels through a tunnel from one point of an IP network to another; no routers along the way are able to examine the inner IP header. Because the original packet is encapsulated, the new, larger packet may have totally different source and destination addresses, adding to the security. Tunnel mode is used when one or both ends of a security association (SA) are a security gateway, such as a firewall or router that implements IPsec. With tunnel mode, a number of hosts on networks behind firewalls may engage in secure communications without implementing IPsec. The unprotected packets generated by such hosts are tunneled through external networks by tunnel mode SAs set up by the IPsec software in the firewall or secure router at the boundary of the local network.

Here is an example of how tunnel mode IPsec operates. Host A on a network generates an IP packet with the destination address of host B on another network. This packet is routed from the originating host to a firewall or secure router at the boundary of A's network. The firewall filters all outgoing packets to determine the need for IPsec processing. If this packet from A to B requires IPsec, the firewall performs IPsec processing and encapsulates the packet with an outer IP header. The source IP address of this outer IP packet is this firewall, and the destination address may be a firewall that forms the boundary to B's local network. This packet is now routed to B's firewall, with intermediate routers examining only the outer IP header. At B's firewall, the outer IP header is stripped off, and the inner packet is delivered to B.

ESP in tunnel mode encrypts and optionally authenticates the entire inner IP packet, including the inner IP header. AH in tunnel mode authenticates the entire inner IP packet and selected portions of the outer IP header.

Table 8.1 summarizes transport and tunnel mode functionality.

---

[1]In this chapter, the term *IP packet* refers to either an IPv4 datagram or an IPv6 packet.

Table 8.1   Tunnel Mode and Transport Mode Functionality

	Transport Mode SA	**Tunnel Mode SA**
AH	Authenticates IP payload and selected portions of IP header and IPv6 extension headers.	Authenticates entire inner IP packet (inner header plus IP payload) plus selected portions of outer IP header and outer IPv6 extension headers.
ESP	Encrypts IP payload and any IPv6 extension headers following the ESP header.	Encrypts entire inner IP packet.
ESP with Authentication	Encrypts IP payload and any IPv6 extension headers following the ESP header. Authenticates IP payload but not IP header.	Encrypts entire inner IP packet. Authenticates inner IP packet.

8.2   IP SECURITY POLICY

Fundamental to the operation of IPsec is the concept of a security policy applied to each IP packet that transits from a source to a destination. IPsec policy is determined primarily by the interaction of two databases, the **security association database (SAD)** and the **security policy database (SPD)**. This section provides an overview of these two databases and then summarizes their use during IPsec operation. Figure 8.2 illustrates the relevant relationships.

Security Associations

A key concept that appears in both the authentication and confidentiality mechanisms for IP is the security association (SA). An association is a one-way logical connection between a sender and a receiver that affords security services to the traffic carried on it. If a peer relationship is needed for two-way secure exchange, then two security associations are required. Security services are afforded to an SA for the use of AH or ESP, but not both.

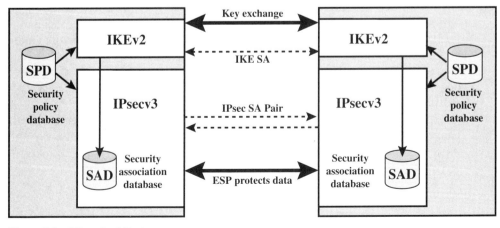

Figure 8.2   IPsec Architecture

A security association is uniquely identified by three parameters.

- **Security Parameters Index (SPI):** A bit string assigned to this SA and having local significance only. The SPI is carried in AH and ESP headers to enable the receiving system to select the SA under which a received packet will be processed.
- **IP Destination Address:** This is the address of the destination endpoint of the SA, which may be an end-user system or a network system such as a firewall or router.
- **Security Protocol Identifier:** This field from the outer IP header indicates whether the association is an AH or ESP security association.

Hence, in any IP packet, the security association is uniquely identified by the Destination Address in the IPv4 or IPv6 header and the SPI in the enclosed extension header (AH or ESP).

Security Association Database

In each IPsec implementation, there is a nominal[2] Security Association Database that defines the parameters associated with each SA. A security association is normally defined by the following parameters in an SAD entry.

- **Security Parameter Index:** A 32-bit value selected by the receiving end of an SA to uniquely identify the SA. In an SAD entry for an outbound SA, the SPI is used to construct the packet's AH or ESP header. In an SAD entry for an inbound SA, the SPI is used to map traffic to the appropriate SA.
- **Sequence Number Counter:** A 32-bit value used to generate the Sequence Number field in AH or ESP headers, described in Section 8.3 (required for all implementations).
- **Sequence Counter Overflow:** A flag indicating whether overflow of the Sequence Number Counter should generate an auditable event and prevent further transmission of packets on this SA (required for all implementations).
- **Anti-Replay Window:** Used to determine whether an inbound AH or ESP packet is a replay, described in Section 8.3 (required for all implementations).
- **AH Information:** Authentication algorithm, keys, key lifetimes, and related parameters being used with AH (required for AH implementations).
- **ESP Information:** Encryption and authentication algorithm, keys, initialization values, key lifetimes, and related parameters being used with ESP (required for ESP implementations).
- **Lifetime of this Security Association:** A time interval or byte count after which an SA must be replaced with a new SA (and new SPI) or terminated, plus an indication of which of these actions should occur (required for all implementations).

---

[2]Nominal in the sense that the functionality provided by a Security Association Database must be present in any IPsec implementation, but the way in which that functionality is provided is up to the implementer.

- **IPsec Protocol Mode:** Tunnel, transport, or wildcard.
- **Path MTU:** Any observed path maximum transmission unit (maximum size of a packet that can be transmitted without fragmentation) and aging variables (required for all implementations).

The key management mechanism that is used to distribute keys is coupled to the authentication and privacy mechanisms only by way of the Security Parameters Index (SPI). Hence, authentication and privacy have been specified independent of any specific key management mechanism.

IPsec provides the user with considerable flexibility in the way in which IPsec services are applied to IP traffic. As we will see later, SAs can be combined in a number of ways to yield the desired user configuration. Furthermore, IPsec provides a high degree of granularity in discriminating between traffic that is afforded IPsec protection and traffic that is allowed to bypass IPsec, as in the former case relating IP traffic to specific SAs.

Security Policy Database

The means by which IP traffic is related to specific SAs (or no SA in the case of traffic allowed to bypass IPsec) is the nominal Security Policy Database (SPD). In its simplest form, an SPD contains entries, each of which defines a subset of IP traffic and points to an SA for that traffic. In more complex environments, there may be multiple entries that potentially relate to a single SA or multiple SAs associated with a single SPD entry. The reader is referred to the relevant IPsec documents for a full discussion.

Each SPD entry is defined by a set of IP and upper-layer protocol field values, called *selectors*. In effect, these selectors are used to filter outgoing traffic in order to map it into a particular SA. Outbound processing obeys the following general sequence for each IP packet.

1. Compare the values of the appropriate fields in the packet (the selector fields) against the SPD to find a matching SPD entry, which will point to zero or more SAs.
2. Determine the SA if any for this packet and its associated SPI.
3. Do the required IPsec processing (i.e., AH or ESP processing).

The following selectors determine an SPD entry:

- **Remote IP Address:** This may be a single IP address, an enumerated list or range of addresses, or a wildcard (mask) address. The latter two are required to support more than one destination system sharing the same SA (e.g., behind a firewall).
- **Local IP Address:** This may be a single IP address, an enumerated list or range of addresses, or a wildcard (mask) address. The latter two are required to support more than one source system sharing the same SA (e.g., behind a firewall).
- **Next Layer Protocol:** The IP protocol header (IPv4, IPv6, or IPv6 Extension) includes a field (Protocol for IPv4, Next Header for IPv6 or IPv6 Extension) that designates the protocol operating over IP. This is an individual protocol number, ANY, or for IPv6 only, OPAQUE. If AH or ESP is used, then this IP protocol header immediately precedes the AH or ESP header in the packet.

Table 8.2   Host SPD Example

Protocol	Local IP	Port	Remote IP	Port	Action	Comment
UDP	1.2.3.101	500	*	500	BYPASS	IKE
ICMP	1.2.3.101	*	*	*	BYPASS	Error messages
*	1.2.3.101	*	1.2.3.0/24	*	PROTECT: ESP intransport-mode	Encrypt intranet traffic
TCP	1.2.3.101	*	1.2.4.10	80	PROTECT: ESP intransport-mode	Encrypt to server
TCP	1.2.3.101	*	1.2.4.10	443	BYPASS	TLS: avoid double encryption
*	1.2.3.101	*	1.2.4.0/24	*	DISCARD	Others in DMZ
*	1.2.3.101	*	*	*	BYPASS	Internet

- **Name:** A user identifier from the operating system. This is not a field in the IP or upper-layer headers but is available if IPsec is running on the same operating system as the user.
- **Local and Remote Ports:** These may be individual TCP or UDP port values, an enumerated list of ports, or a wildcard port.

Table 8.2 provides an example of an SPD on a host system (as opposed to a network system such as a firewall or router). This table reflects the following configuration: A local network configuration consists of two networks. The basic corporate network configuration has the IP network number 1.2.3.0/24. The local configuration also includes a secure LAN, often known as a DMZ, that is identified as 1.2.4.0/24. The DMZ is protected from both the outside world and the rest of the corporate LAN by firewalls. The host in this example has the IP address 1.2.3.10, and it is authorized to connect to the server 1.2.4.10 in the DMZ.

The entries in the SPD should be self-explanatory. For example, UDP port 500 is the designated port for IKE. Any traffic from the local host to a remote host for purposes of an IKE exchange bypasses the IPsec processing.

IP Traffic Processing

IPsec is executed on a packet-by-packet basis. When IPsec is implemented, each outbound IP packet is processed by the IPsec logic before transmission, and each inbound packet is processed by the IPsec logic after reception and before passing the packet contents on to the next higher layer (e.g., TCP or UDP). We look at the logic of these two situations in turn.

OUTBOUND PACKETS Figure 8.3 highlights the main elements of IPsec processing for outbound traffic. A block of data from a higher layer, such as TCP, is passed down to the IP layer and an IP packet is formed, consisting of an IP header and an IP body. Then the following steps occur:

1. IPsec searches the SPD for a match to this packet.
2. If no match is found, then the packet is discarded and an error message is generated.

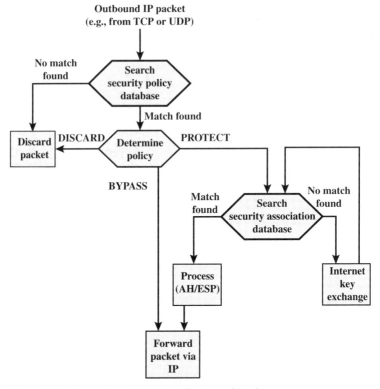

Figure 8.3 Processing Model for Outbound Packets

3. If a match is found, further processing is determined by the first matching entry in the SPD. If the policy for this packet is DISCARD, then the packet is discarded. If the policy is BYPASS, then there is no further IPsec processing; the packet is forwarded to the network for transmission.

4. If the policy is PROTECT, then a search is made of the SAD for a matching entry. If no entry is found, then IKE is invoked to create an SA with the appropriate keys and an entry is made in the SA.

5. The matching entry in the SAD determines the processing for this packet. Either encryption, authentication, or both can be performed, and either transport or tunnel mode can be used. The packet is then forwarded to the network for transmission.

INBOUND PACKETS Figure 8.4 highlights the main elements of IPsec processing for inbound traffic. An incoming IP packet triggers the IPsec processing. The following steps occur:

1. IPsec determines whether this is an unsecured IP packet or one that has ESP or AH headers/trailers, by examining the IP Protocol field (IPv4) or Next Header field (IPv6).

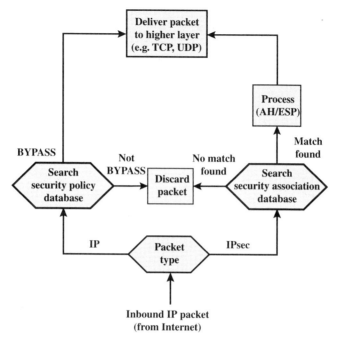

Figure 8.4   Processing Model for Inbound Packets

2. If the packet is unsecured, IPsec searches the SPD for a match to this packet. If the first matching entry has a policy of BYPASS, the IP header is processed and stripped off and the packet body is delivered to the next higher layer, such as TCP. If the first matching entry has a policy of PROTECT or DISCARD, or if there is no matching entry, the packet is discarded.

3. For a secured packet, IPsec searches the SAD. If no match is found, the packet is discarded. Otherwise, IPsec applies the appropriate ESP or AH processing. Then, the IP header is processed and stripped off and the packet body is delivered to the next higher layer, such as TCP.

8.3 ENCAPSULATING SECURITY PAYLOAD

ESP can be used to provide confidentiality, data origin authentication, connectionless integrity, an anti-replay service (a form of partial sequence integrity), and (limited) traffic flow confidentiality. The set of services provided depends on options selected at the time of Security Association (SA) establishment and on the location of the implementation in a network topology.

ESP can work with a variety of encryption and authentication algorithms, including authenticated encryption algorithms such as GCM.

ESP Format

Figure 8.5a shows the top-level format of an ESP packet. It contains the following fields.

- **Security Parameters Index (32 bits):** Identifies a security association.
- **Sequence Number (32 bits):** A monotonically increasing counter value; this provides an anti-replay function, as discussed for AH.
- **Payload Data (variable):** This is a transport-level segment (transport mode) or IP packet (tunnel mode) that is protected by encryption.
- **Padding (0–255 bytes):** The purpose of this field is discussed later.
- **Pad Length (8 bits):** Indicates the number of pad bytes immediately preceding this field.
- **Next Header (8 bits):** Identifies the type of data contained in the payload data field by identifying the first header in that payload (for example, an extension header in IPv6, or an upper-layer protocol such as TCP).

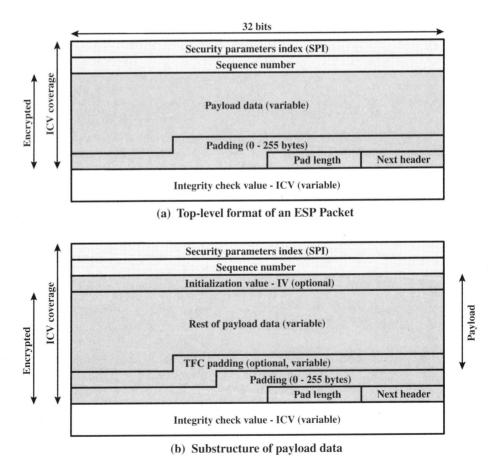

(a) **Top-level format of an ESP Packet**

(b) **Substructure of payload data**

Figure 8.5   ESP Packet Format

- **Integrity Check Value (variable):** A variable-length field (must be an integral number of 32-bit words) that contains the Integrity Check Value computed over the ESP packet minus the Authentication Data field.

When any combined mode algorithm is employed, the algorithm itself is expected to return both decrypted plaintext and a pass/fail indication for the integrity check. For combined mode algorithms, the ICV that would normally appear at the end of the ESP packet (when integrity is selected) may be omitted. When the ICV is omitted and integrity is selected, it is the responsibility of the combined mode algorithm to encode within the Payload Data an ICV-equivalent means of verifying the integrity of the packet.

Two additional fields may be present in the payload (Figure 8.5b). An **initialization value (IV)**, or nonce, is present if this is required by the encryption or authenticated encryption algorithm used for ESP. If tunnel mode is being used, then the IPsec implementation may add **traffic flow confidentiality (TFC)** padding after the Payload Data and before the Padding field, as explained subsequently.

Encryption and Authentication Algorithms

The Payload Data, Padding, Pad Length, and Next Header fields are encrypted by the ESP service. If the algorithm used to encrypt the payload requires cryptographic synchronization data, such as an initialization vector (IV), then these data may be carried explicitly at the beginning of the Payload Data field. If included, an IV is usually not encrypted, although it is often referred to as being part of the ciphertext.

The ICV field is optional. It is present only if the integrity service is selected and is provided by either a separate integrity algorithm or a combined mode algorithm that uses an ICV. The ICV is computed after the encryption is performed. This order of processing facilitates rapid detection and rejection of replayed or bogus packets by the receiver prior to decrypting the packet, hence potentially reducing the impact of denial of service (DoS) attacks. It also allows for the possibility of parallel processing of packets at the receiver, i.e., decryption can take place in parallel with integrity checking. Note that because the ICV is not protected by encryption, a keyed integrity algorithm must be employed to compute the ICV.

Padding

The Padding field serves several purposes:

- If an encryption algorithm requires the plaintext to be a multiple of some number of bytes (e.g., the multiple of a single block for a block cipher), the Padding field is used to expand the plaintext (consisting of the Payload Data, Padding, Pad Length, and Next Header fields) to the required length.
- The ESP format requires that the Pad Length and Next Header fields be right aligned within a 32-bit word. Equivalently, the ciphertext must be an integer multiple of 32 bits. The Padding field is used to assure this alignment.
- Additional padding may be added to provide partial traffic-flow confidentiality by concealing the actual length of the payload.

Anti-Replay Service

A **replay attack** is one in which an attacker obtains a copy of an authenticated packet and later transmits it to the intended destination. The receipt of duplicate, authenticated IP packets may disrupt service in some way or may have some other undesired consequence. The Sequence Number field is designed to thwart such attacks. First, we discuss sequence number generation by the sender, and then we look at how it is processed by the recipient.

When a new SA is established, the **sender** initializes a sequence number counter to 0. Each time that a packet is sent on this SA, the sender increments the counter and places the value in the Sequence Number field. Thus, the first value to be used is 1. If anti-replay is enabled (the default), the sender must not allow the sequence number to cycle past $2^{32} - 1$ back to zero. Otherwise, there would be multiple valid packets with the same sequence number. If the limit of $2^{32} - 1$ is reached, the sender should terminate this SA and negotiate a new SA with a new key.

Because IP is a connectionless, unreliable service, the protocol does not guarantee that packets will be delivered in order and does not guarantee that all packets will be delivered. Therefore, the IPsec authentication document dictates that the **receiver** should implement a window of size W, with a default of $W = 64$. The right edge of the window represents the highest sequence number, N, so far received for a valid packet. For any packet with a sequence number in the range from $N - W + 1$ to N that has been correctly received (i.e., properly authenticated), the corresponding slot in the window is marked (Figure 8.6). Inbound processing proceeds as follows when a packet is received:

1. If the received packet falls within the window and is new, the MAC is checked. If the packet is authenticated, the corresponding slot in the window is marked.

2. If the received packet is to the right of the window and is new, the MAC is checked. If the packet is authenticated, the window is advanced so that this sequence number is the right edge of the window, and the corresponding slot in the window is marked.

3. If the received packet is to the left of the window or if authentication fails, the packet is discarded; this is an auditable event.

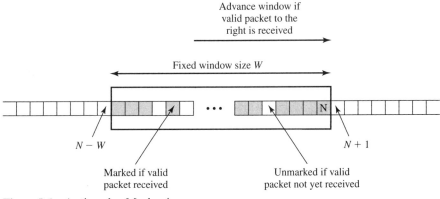

Figure 8.6 Anti-replay Mechanism

Transport and Tunnel Modes

Figure 8.7 shows two ways in which the IPsec ESP service can be used. In the upper part of the figure, encryption (and optionally authentication) is provided directly between two hosts. Figure 8.7b shows how tunnel mode operation can be used to set up a **virtual private network**. In this example, an organization has four private networks interconnected across the Internet. Hosts on the internal networks use the Internet for transport of data but do not interact with other Internet-based hosts. By terminating the tunnels at the security gateway to each internal network, the configuration allows the hosts to avoid implementing the security capability. The former technique is supported by a transport mode SA, while the latter technique uses a tunnel mode SA.

In this section, we look at the scope of ESP for the two modes. The considerations are somewhat different for IPv4 and IPv6. We use the packet formats of Figure 8.8a as a starting point.

TRANSPORT MODE ESP Transport mode ESP is used to encrypt and optionally authenticate the data carried by IP (e.g., a TCP segment), as shown in Figure 8.8b.

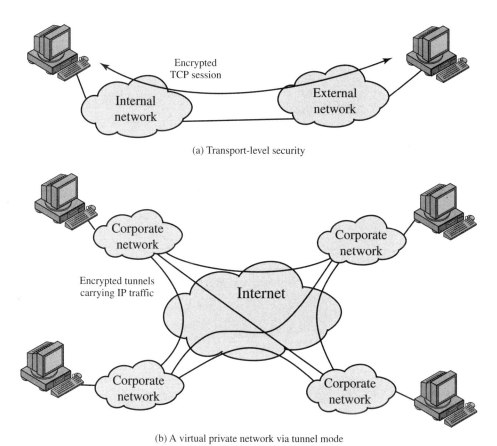

(a) Transport-level security

(b) A virtual private network via tunnel mode

Figure 8.7   Transport-Mode versus Tunnel-Mode Encryption

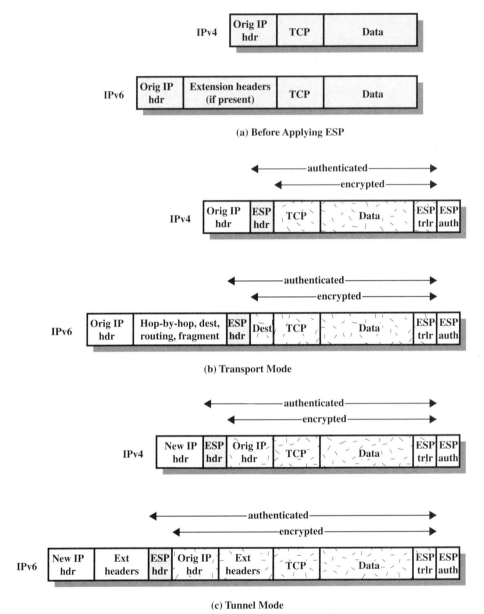

Figure 8.8   Scope of ESP Encryption and Authentication

For this mode using IPv4, the ESP header is inserted into the IP packet immediately prior to the transport-layer header (e.g., TCP, UDP, ICMP), and an ESP trailer (Padding, Pad Length, and Next Header fields) is placed after the IP packet. If authentication is selected, the ESP Authentication Data field is added after the ESP trailer. The entire transport-level segment plus the ESP trailer are encrypted. Authentication covers all of the ciphertext plus the ESP header.

In the context of IPv6, ESP is viewed as an end-to-end payload; that is, it is not examined or processed by intermediate routers. Therefore, the ESP header appears after the IPv6 base header and the hop-by-hop, routing, and fragment extension headers. The destination options extension header could appear before or after the ESP header, depending on the semantics desired. For IPv6, encryption covers the entire transport-level segment plus the ESP trailer plus the destination options extension header if it occurs after the ESP header. Again, authentication covers the ciphertext plus the ESP header.

Transport mode operation may be summarized as follows.

1. At the source, the block of data consisting of the ESP trailer plus the entire transport-layer segment is encrypted and the plaintext of this block is replaced with its ciphertext to form the IP packet for transmission. Authentication is added if this option is selected.

2. The packet is then routed to the destination. Each intermediate router needs to examine and process the IP header plus any plaintext IP extension headers but does not need to examine the ciphertext.

3. The destination node examines and processes the IP header plus any plaintext IP extension headers. Then, on the basis of the SPI in the ESP header, the destination node decrypts the remainder of the packet to recover the plaintext transport-layer segment.

Transport mode operation provides confidentiality for any application that uses it, thus avoiding the need to implement confidentiality in every individual application. One drawback to this mode is that it is possible to do traffic analysis on the transmitted packets.

TUNNEL MODE ESP Tunnel mode ESP is used to encrypt an entire IP packet (Figure 8.8c). For this mode, the ESP header is prefixed to the packet and then the packet plus the ESP trailer is encrypted. This method can be used to counter traffic analysis.

Because the IP header contains the destination address and possibly source routing directives and hop-by-hop option information, it is not possible simply to transmit the encrypted IP packet prefixed by the ESP header. Intermediate routers would be unable to process such a packet. Therefore, it is necessary to encapsulate the entire block (ESP header plus ciphertext plus Authentication Data, if present) with a new IP header that will contain sufficient information for routing but not for traffic analysis.

Whereas the transport mode is suitable for protecting connections between hosts that support the ESP feature, the tunnel mode is useful in a configuration that includes a firewall or other sort of security gateway that protects a trusted network from external networks. In this latter case, encryption occurs only between an external host and the security gateway or between two security gateways. This relieves hosts on the internal network of the processing burden of encryption and simplifies the key distribution task by reducing the number of needed keys. Further, it thwarts traffic analysis based on ultimate destination.

Consider a case in which an external host wishes to communicate with a host on an internal network protected by a firewall, and in which ESP is implemented in the external host and the firewalls. The following steps occur for transfer of a transport-layer segment from the external host to the internal host.

1. The source prepares an inner IP packet with a destination address of the target internal host. This packet is prefixed by an ESP header; then the packet and ESP trailer are encrypted and Authentication Data may be added. The resulting block is encapsulated with a new IP header (base header plus optional extensions such as routing and hop-by-hop options for IPv6) whose destination address is the firewall; this forms the outer IP packet.

2. The outer packet is routed to the destination firewall. Each intermediate router needs to examine and process the outer IP header plus any outer IP extension headers but does not need to examine the ciphertext.

3. The destination firewall examines and processes the outer IP header plus any outer IP extension headers. Then, on the basis of the SPI in the ESP header, the destination node decrypts the remainder of the packet to recover the plaintext inner IP packet. This packet is then transmitted in the internal network.

4. The inner packet is routed through zero or more routers in the internal network to the destination host.

Figure 8.9 shows the protocol architecture for the two modes.

8.4 COMBINING SECURITY ASSOCIATIONS

An individual SA can implement either the AH or ESP protocol but not both. Sometimes a particular traffic flow will call for the services provided by both AH and ESP. Further, a particular traffic flow may require IPsec services between hosts and, for that same flow, separate services between security gateways, such as firewalls. In all of these cases, multiple SAs must be employed for the same traffic flow to achieve the desired IPsec services. The term *security association bundle* refers to a sequence of SAs through which traffic must be processed to provide a desired set of IPsec services. The SAs in a bundle may terminate at different endpoints or at the same endpoints.

Security associations may be combined into bundles in two ways:

- **Transport adjacency:** Refers to applying more than one security protocol to the same IP packet without invoking tunneling. This approach to combining AH and ESP allows for only one level of combination; further nesting yields no added benefit since the processing is performed at one IPsec instance: the (ultimate) destination.

- **Iterated tunneling:** Refers to the application of multiple layers of security protocols effected through IP tunneling. This approach allows for multiple levels of nesting, since each tunnel can originate or terminate at a different IPsec site along the path.

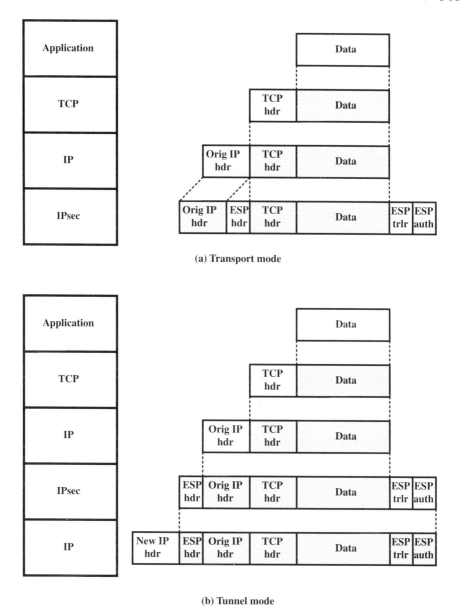

(a) Transport mode

(b) Tunnel mode

Figure 8.9   Protocol Operation for ESP

The two approaches can be combined, for example, by having a transport SA between hosts travel part of the way through a tunnel SA between security gateways.

One interesting issue that arises when considering SA bundles is the order in which authentication and encryption may be applied between a given pair of endpoints and the ways of doing so. We examine that issue next. Then we look at combinations of SAs that involve at least one tunnel.

Authentication Plus Confidentiality

Encryption and authentication can be combined in order to transmit an IP packet that has both confidentiality and authentication between hosts. We look at several approaches.

ESP WITH AUTHENTICATION OPTION This approach is illustrated in Figure 8.8. In this approach, the user first applies ESP to the data to be protected and then appends the authentication data field. There are actually two subcases:

- **Transport mode ESP:** Authentication and encryption apply to the IP payload delivered to the host, but the IP header is not protected.

- **Tunnel mode ESP:** Authentication applies to the entire IP packet delivered to the outer IP destination address (e.g., a firewall), and authentication is performed at that destination. The entire inner IP packet is protected by the privacy mechanism for delivery to the inner IP destination.

For both cases, authentication applies to the ciphertext rather than the plaintext.

TRANSPORT ADJACENCY Another way to apply authentication after encryption is to use two bundled transport SAs, with the inner being an ESP SA and the outer being an AH SA. In this case, ESP is used without its authentication option. Because the inner SA is a transport SA, encryption is applied to the IP payload. The resulting packet consists of an IP header (and possibly IPv6 header extensions) followed by an ESP. AH is then applied in transport mode, so that authentication covers the ESP plus the original IP header (and extensions) except for mutable fields. The advantage of this approach over simply using a single ESP SA with the ESP authentication option is that the authentication covers more fields, including the source and destination IP addresses. The disadvantage is the overhead of two SAs versus one SA.

TRANSPORT-TUNNEL BUNDLE The use of authentication prior to encryption might be preferable for several reasons. First, because the authentication data are protected by encryption, it is impossible for anyone to intercept the message and alter the authentication data without detection. Second, it may be desirable to store the authentication information with the message at the destination for later reference. It is more convenient to do this if the authentication information applies to the unencrypted message; otherwise the message would have to be reencrypted to verify the authentication information.

One approach to applying authentication before encryption between two hosts is to use a bundle consisting of an inner AH transport SA and an outer ESP tunnel SA. In this case, authentication is applied to the IP payload plus the IP header (and extensions) except for mutable fields. The resulting IP packet is then processed in tunnel mode by ESP; the result is that the entire, authenticated inner packet is encrypted and a new outer IP header (and extensions) is added.

Basic Combinations of Security Associations

The IPsec Architecture document lists four examples of combinations of SAs that must be supported by compliant IPsec hosts (e.g., workstation, server) or security gateways (e.g. firewall, router). These are illustrated in Figure 8.10. The lower part of

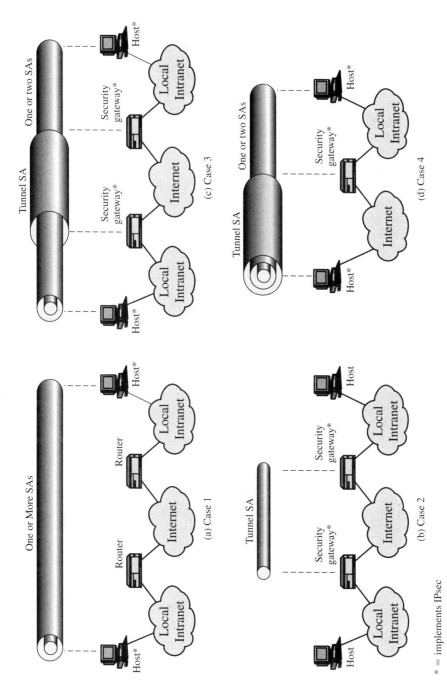

* = implements IPsec

Figure 8.10 Basic Combinations of Security Associations

each case in the figure represents the physical connectivity of the elements; the upper part represents logical connectivity via one or more nested SAs. Each SA can be either AH or ESP. For host-to-host SAs, the mode may be either transport or tunnel; otherwise it must be tunnel mode.

Case 1. All security is provided between end systems that implement IPsec. For any two end systems to communicate via an SA, they must share the appropriate secret keys. Among the possible combinations are

a. AH in transport mode

b. ESP in transport mode

c. ESP followed by AH in transport mode (an ESP SA inside an AH SA)

d. Any one of a, b, or c inside an AH or ESP in tunnel mode

We have already discussed how these various combinations can be used to support authentication, encryption, authentication before encryption, and authentication after encryption.

Case 2. Security is provided only between gateways (routers, firewalls, etc.) and no hosts implement IPsec. This case illustrates simple virtual private network support. The security architecture document specifies that only a single tunnel SA is needed for this case. The tunnel could support AH, ESP, or ESP with the authentication option. Nested tunnels are not required, because the IPsec services apply to the entire inner packet.

Case 3. This builds on case 2 by adding end-to-end security. The same combinations discussed for cases 1 and 2 are allowed here. The gateway-to-gateway tunnel provides either authentication, confidentiality, or both for all traffic between end systems. When the gateway-to-gateway tunnel is ESP, it also provides a limited form of traffic confidentiality. Individual hosts can implement any additional IPsec services required for given applications or given users by means of end-to-end SAs.

Case 4. This provides support for a remote host that uses the Internet to reach an organization's firewall and then to gain access to some server or workstation behind the firewall. Only tunnel mode is required between the remote host and the firewall. As in case 1, one or two SAs may be used between the remote host and the local host.

8.5 INTERNET KEY EXCHANGE

The key management portion of IPsec involves the determination and distribution of secret keys. A typical requirement is four keys for communication between two applications: transmit and receive pairs for both integrity and confidentiality. The IPsec Architecture document mandates support for two types of key management:

- **Manual:** A system administrator manually configures each system with its own keys and with the keys of other communicating systems. This is practical for small, relatively static environments.

- **Automated:** An automated system enables the on-demand creation of keys for SAs and facilitates the use of keys in a large distributed system with an evolving configuration.

The default automated key management protocol for IPsec is referred to as ISAKMP/Oakley and consists of the following elements:

- **Oakley Key Determination Protocol:** Oakley is a key exchange protocol based on the Diffie-Hellman algorithm but providing added security. Oakley is generic in that it does not dictate specific formats.
- **Internet Security Association and Key Management Protocol (ISAKMP):** ISAKMP provides a framework for Internet key management and provides the specific protocol support, including formats, for negotiation of security attributes.

ISAKMP by itself does not dictate a specific key exchange algorithm; rather, ISAKMP consists of a set of message types that enable the use of a variety of key exchange algorithms. Oakley is the specific key exchange algorithm mandated for use with the initial version of ISAKMP.

In IKEv2, the terms Oakley and ISAKMP are no longer used, and there are significant differences from the use of Oakley and ISAKMP in IKEv1. Nevertheless, the basic functionality is the same. In this section, we describe the IKEv2 specification.

Key Determination Protocol

IKE key determination is a refinement of the Diffie-Hellman key exchange algorithm. Recall that Diffie-Hellman involves the following interaction between users A and B. There is prior agreement on two global parameters: q, a large prime number; and α, a primitive root of q. A selects a random integer X_A as its private key and transmits to B its public key $Y_A = \alpha^{X_A} \bmod q$. Similarly, B selects a random integer X_B as its private key and transmits to A its public key $Y_B = \alpha^{X_B} \bmod q$. Each side can now compute the secret session key:

$$K = (Y_B)^{X_A} \bmod q = (Y_A)^{X_B} \bmod q = \alpha^{X_A X_B} \bmod q$$

The Diffie-Hellman algorithm has two attractive features:

- Secret keys are created only when needed. There is no need to store secret keys for a long period of time, exposing them to increased vulnerability.
- The exchange requires no pre-existing infrastructure other than an agreement on the global parameters.

However, there are a number of weaknesses to Diffie-Hellman, as pointed out in [HUIT98].

- It does not provide any information about the identities of the parties.
- It is subject to a man-in-the-middle attack, in which a third party C impersonates B while communicating with A and impersonates A while communicating with B. Both A and B end up negotiating a key with C, which can then listen to and pass on traffic. The man-in-the-middle attack proceeds as
  1. B sends his public key Y_B in a message addressed to A (see Figure 3.13).
  2. The enemy (E) intercepts this message. E saves B's public key and sends a message to A that has B's User ID but E's public key Y_E. This message is

sent in such a way that it appears as though it was sent from B's host system. A receives E's message and stores E's public key with B's User ID. Similarly, E sends a message to B with E's public key, purporting to come from A.

3. B computes a secret key K_1 based on B's private key and Y_E. A computes a secret key K_2 based on A's private key and Y_E. E computes K_1 using E's secret key X_E and Y_B and computers K_2 using X_E and Y_A.

4. From now on, E is able to relay messages from A to B and from B to A, appropriately changing their encipherment en route in such a way that neither A nor B will know that they share their communication with E.

- It is computationally intensive. As a result, it is vulnerable to a clogging attack, in which an opponent requests a high number of keys. The victim spends considerable computing resources doing useless modular exponentiation rather than real work.

IKE key determination is designed to retain the advantages of Diffie-Hellman, while countering its weaknesses.

FEATURES OF IKE KEY DETERMINATION The IKE key determination algorithm is characterized by five important features:

1. It employs a mechanism known as cookies to thwart clogging attacks.
2. It enables the two parties to negotiate a *group*; this, in essence, specifies the global parameters of the Diffie-Hellman key exchange.
3. It uses nonces to ensure against replay attacks.
4. It enables the exchange of Diffie-Hellman public key values.
5. It authenticates the Diffie-Hellman exchange to thwart man-in-the-middle attacks.

We have already discussed Diffie-Hellman. Let us look at the remainder of these elements in turn. First, consider the problem of clogging attacks. In this attack, an opponent forges the source address of a legitimate user and sends a public Diffie-Hellman key to the victim. The victim then performs a modular exponentiation to compute the secret key. Repeated messages of this type can *clog* the victim's system with useless work. The **cookie exchange** requires that each side send a pseudorandom number, the cookie, in the initial message, which the other side acknowledges. This acknowledgment must be repeated in the first message of the Diffie-Hellman key exchange. If the source address was forged, the opponent gets no answer. Thus, an opponent can only force a user to generate acknowledgments and not to perform the Diffie-Hellman calculation.

IKE mandates that cookie generation satisfy three basic requirements:

1. The cookie must depend on the specific parties. This prevents an attacker from obtaining a cookie using a real IP address and UDP port and then using it to swamp the victim with requests from randomly chosen IP addresses or ports.
2. It must not be possible for anyone other than the issuing entity to generate cookies that will be accepted by that entity. This implies that the issuing entity will use local secret information in the generation and subsequent verification of a

cookie. It must not be possible to deduce this secret information from any particular cookie. The point of this requirement is that the issuing entity need not save
copies of its cookies, which are then more vulnerable to discovery, but can verify
an incoming cookie acknowledgment when it needs to.

3. The cookie generation and verification methods must be fast to thwart attacks
   intended to sabotage processor resources.

The recommended method for creating the cookie is to perform a fast hash
(e.g., MD5) over the IP Source and Destination addresses, the UDP Source and
Destination ports, and a locally generated secret value.

IKE key determination supports the use of different **groups** for the Diffie-
Hellman key exchange. Each group includes the definition of the two global parameters and the identity of the algorithm. The current specification includes the following
groups.

- Modular exponentiation with a 768-bit modulus

$$q = 2^{768} - 2^{704} - 1 + 2^{64} \times (\lfloor 2^{638} \times \pi \rfloor + 149686)$$
$$\alpha = 2$$

- Modular exponentiation with a 1024-bit modulus

$$q = 2^{1024} - 2^{960} - 1 + 2^{64} \times (\lfloor 2^{894} \times \pi \rfloor + 129093)$$
$$\alpha = 2$$

- Modular exponentiation with a 1536-bit modulus
  - Parameters to be determined
- Elliptic curve group over 2^{155}
  - Generator (hexadecimal): X = 7B, Y = 1C8
  - Elliptic curve parameters (hexadecimal): A = 0, Y = 7338F
- Elliptic curve group over 2^{185}
  - Generator (hexadecimal): X = 18, Y = D
  - Elliptic curve parameters (hexadecimal): A = 0, Y = 1EE9

The first three groups are the classic Diffie-Hellman algorithm using modular
exponentiation. The last two groups use the elliptic curve analog to Diffie-Hellman,
which was described in Chapter 3.

IKE key determination employs **nonces** to ensure against replay attacks. Each
nonce is a locally generated pseudorandom number. Nonces appear in responses
and are encrypted during certain portions of the exchange to secure their use.

Three different **authentication** methods can be used with IKE key determination:

- **Digital signatures:** The exchange is authenticated by signing a mutually
  obtainable hash; each party encrypts the hash with its private key. The hash is
  generated over important parameters, such as user IDs and nonces.

- **Public-key encryption:** The exchange is authenticated by encrypting parameters such as IDs and nonces with the sender's private key.

- **Symmetric-key encryption:** A key derived by some out-of-band mechanism can be used to authenticate the exchange by symmetric encryption of exchange parameters.

IKEv2 EXCHANGES The IKEv2 protocol involves the exchange of messages in pairs. The first two pairs of exchanges are referred to as the **initial exchanges** (Figure 8.11a). In the first exchange, the two peers exchange information concerning cryptographic algorithms and other security parameters they are willing to use along with nonces and Diffie-Hellman (DH) values. The result of this exchange is to set up a special SA called the IKE SA (see Figure 8.2). This SA defines parameters for a secure channel between the peers over which subsequent message exchanges take place. Thus, all subsequent IKE message exchanges are protected by encryption and message authentication. In the second exchange, the two parties authenticate one another and set up a first IPsec SA to be placed in the SADB and used for protecting ordinary (i.e. non-IKE) communications between the peers. Thus, four messages are needed to establish the first SA for general use.

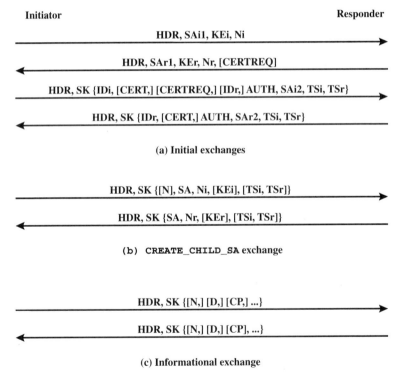

Initiator   Responder

HDR, SAi1, KEi, Ni →

← HDR, SAr1, KEr, Nr, [CERTREQ]

HDR, SK {IDi, [CERT,] [CERTREQ,] [IDr,] AUTH, SAi2, TSi, TSr} →

← HDR, SK {IDr, [CERT,] AUTH, SAr2, TSi, TSr}

(a) Initial exchanges

HDR, SK {[N], SA, Ni, [KEi], [TSi, TSr]} →

← HDR, SK {SA, Nr, [KEr], [TSi, TSr]}

(b) CREATE_CHILD_SA exchange

HDR, SK {[N,] [D,] [CP,] ...} →

← HDR, SK {[N,] [D,] [CP], ...}

(c) Informational exchange

HDR = IKE header	SK {...} = MAC and encrypt
SAx1 = offered and chosen algorithms, DH group	AUTH = Authentication
KEx = Diffie-Hellman public key	SAx2 = algorithms, parameters for IPsec SA
Nx = nonces	TSx = traffic selectors for IPsec SA
CERTREQ = Certificate request	N = Notify
IDx = identity	D = Delete
CERT = certificate	CP = Configuration

Figure 8.11   IKEv2 Exchanges

The **CREATE_CHILD_SA exchange** can be used to establish further SAs for protecting traffic. The **informational exchange** is used to exchange management information, IKEv2 error messages, and other notifications.

Header and Payload Formats

IKE defines procedures and packet formats to establish, negotiate, modify, and delete security associations. As part of SA establishment, IKE defines payloads for exchanging key generation and authentication data. These payload formats provide a consistent framework independent of the specific key exchange protocol, encryption algorithm, and authentication mechanism.

IKE HEADER FORMAT An IKE message consists of an IKE header followed by one or more payloads. All of this is carried in a transport protocol. The specification dictates that implementations must support the use of UDP for the transport protocol.

Figure 8.12a shows the header format for an IKE message. It consists of the following fields.

- **Initiator SPI (64 bits):** A value chosen by the initiator to identify a unique IKE security association (SA).
- **Responder SPI (64 bits):** A value chosen by the responder to identify a unique IKE SA.
- **Next Payload (8 bits):** Indicates the type of the first payload in the message; payloads are discussed in the next subsection.
- **Major Version (4 bits):** Indicates major version of IKE in use.
- **Minor Version (4 bits):** Indicates minor version in use.

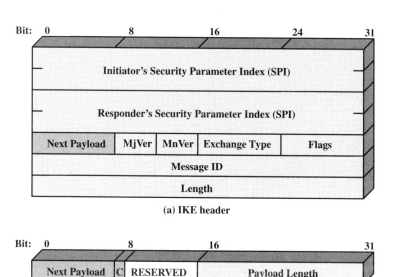

(a) IKE header

(b) Generic Payload header

Figure 8.12 IKE Formats

- **Exchange Type (8 bits):** Indicates the type of exchange; these are discussed later in this section.

- **Flags (8 bits):** Indicates specific options set for this IKE exchange. Three bits are defined so far. The initiator bit indicates whether this packet is sent by the SA initiator. The version bit indicates whether the transmitter is capable of using a higher major version number than the one currently indicated. The response bit indicates whether this is a response to a message containing the same message ID.

- **Message ID (32 bits):** Used to control retransmission of lost packets and matching of requests and responses.

- **Length (32 bits):** Length of total message (header plus all payloads) in octets.

IKE PAYLOAD TYPES   All IKE payloads begin with the same generic payload header shown in Figure 8.12b. The Next Payload field has a value of 0 if this is the last payload in the message; otherwise its value is the type of the next payload. The Payload Length field indicates the length in octets of this payload, including the generic payload header.

The critical bit is 0 if the sender wants the recipient to skip this payload if it does not understand the payload type code in the Next Payload field of the previous payload. It is set to 1 if the sender wants the recipient to reject this entire message if it does not understand the payload type.

Table 8.3 summarizes the payload types defined for IKE and lists the fields, or parameters, that are part of each payload. The **SA payload** is used to begin

Table 8.3   IKE Payload Types

Type	Parameters
Security Association	Proposals
Key Exchange	DH Group #, Key Exchange Data
Identification	ID Type, ID Data
Certificate	Cert Encoding, Certificate Data
Certificate Request	Cert Encoding, Certification Authority
Authentication	Auth Method, Authentication Data
Nonce	Nonce Data
Notify	Protocol-ID, SPI Size, Notify Message Type, SPI, Notification Data
Delete	Protocol-ID, SPI Size, # of SPIs, SPI (one or more)
Vendor ID	Vendor ID
Traffic Selector	Number of TSs, Traffic Selectors
Encrypted	IV, Encrypted IKE payloads, Padding, Pad Length, ICV
Configuration	CFG Type, Configuration Attributes
Extensible Authentication Protocol	EAP Message

the establishment of an SA. The payload has a complex, hierarchical structure. The payload may contain multiple proposals. Each proposal may contain multiple protocols. Each protocol may contain multiple transforms. And each transform may contain multiple attributes. These elements are formatted as substructures within the payload as follows.

- **Proposal:** This substructure includes a proposal number, a protocol ID (AH, ESP, or IKE), an indicator of the number of transforms, and then a transform substructure. If more than one protocol is to be included in a proposal, then there is a subsequent proposal substructure with the same proposal number.
- **Transform:** Different protocols support different transform types. The transforms are used primarily to define cryptographic algorithms to be used with a particular protocol.
- **Attribute:** Each transform may include attributes that modify or complete the specification of the transform. An example is key length.

The **Key Exchange payload** can be used for a variety of key exchange techniques, including Oakley, Diffie-Hellman, and the RSA-based key exchange used by PGP. The Key Exchange data field contains the data required to generate a session key and is dependent on the key exchange algorithm used.

The **Identification payload** is used to determine the identity of communicating peers and may be used for determining authenticity of information. Typically the ID Data field will contain an IPv4 or IPv6 address.

The **Certificate payload** transfers a public-key certificate. The Certificate Encoding field indicates the type of certificate or certificate-related information, which may include the following:

- PKCS #7 wrapped X.509 certificate
- PGP certificate
- DNS signed key
- X.509 certificate—signature
- X.509 certificate—key exchange
- Kerberos tokens
- Certificate Revocation List (CRL)
- Authority Revocation List (ARL)
- SPKI certificate

At any point in an IKE exchange, the sender may include a **Certificate Request** payload to request the certificate of the other communicating entity. The payload may list more than one certificate type that is acceptable and more than one certificate authority that is acceptable.

The **Authentication** payload contains data used for message authentication purposes. The authentication method types so far defined are RSA digital signature, shared-key message integrity code, and DSS digital signature.

The **Nonce** payload contains random data used to guarantee liveness during an exchange and to protect against replay attacks.

The **Notify** payload contains either error or status information associated with this SA or this SA negotiation. The following table lists the IKE notify messages.

Error Messages	Status Messages
Unsupported Critical	Initial Contact
Payload	Set Window Size
Invalid IKE SPI	Additional TS Possible
Invalid Major Version	IPCOMP Supported
Invalid Syntax	NAT Detection Source IP
Invalid Payload Type	NAT Detection Destination IP
Invalid Message ID	Cookie
Invalid SPI	Use Transport Mode
No Proposal Chosen	HTTP Cert Lookup Supported
Invalid KE Payload	Rekey SA
Authentication Failed	ESP TFC Padding Not Supported
Single Pair Required	Non First Fragments Also
No Additional SAS	
Internal Address Failure	
Failed CP Required	
TS Unacceptable	
Invalid Selectors	

The **Delete** payload indicates one or more SAs that the sender has deleted from its database and that therefore are no longer valid.

The **Vendor ID** payload contains a vendor-defined constant. The constant is used by vendors to identify and recognize remote instances of their implementations. This mechanism allows a vendor to experiment with new features while maintaining backward compatibility.

The **Traffic Selector** payload allows peers to identify packet flows for processing by IPsec services.

The **Encrypted** payload contains other payloads in encrypted form. The encrypted payload format is similar to that of ESP. It may include an IV if the encryption algorithm requires it and an ICV if authentication is selected.

The **Configuration** payload is used to exchange configuration information between IKE peers.

The **Extensible Authentication Protocol (EAP)** payload allows IKE SAs to be authenticated using EAP, which was discussed in Chapter 6.

8.6 CRYPTOGRAPHIC SUITES

The IPsecv3 and IKEv3 protocols rely on a variety of types of cryptographic algorithms. As we have seen in this book, there are many cryptographic algorithms of each type, each with a variety of parameters, such as key size. To promote interoperability, two RFCs define recommended suites of cryptographic algorithms and parameters for various applications.

RFC 4308 defines two cryptographic suites for establishing virtual private networks. Suite VPN-A matches the commonly used corporate VPN security used in older IKEv1 implementations at the time of the issuance of IKEv2 in 2005. Suite VPN-B provides stronger security and is recommended for new VPNs that implement IPsecv3 and IKEv2.

Table 8.4a lists the algorithms and parameters for the two suites. There are several points to note about these two suites. Note that for symmetric

Table 8.4 Cryptographic Suites for IPsec

	VPN-A	VPN-B
ESP encryption	3DES-CBC	AES-CBC (128-bit key)
ESP integrity	HMAC-SHA1-96	AES-XCBC-MAC-96
IKE encryption	3DES-CBC	AES-CBC (128-bit key)
IKE PRF	HMAC-SHA1	AES-XCBC-PRF-128
IKE Integrity	HMAC-SHA1-96	AES-XCBC-MAC-96
IKE DH group	1024-bit MODP	2048-bit MODP

(a) Virtual private networks (RFC 4308)

	GCM-128	GCM-256	GMAC-128	GMAC-256
ESP encryption/Integrity	AES-GCM (128-bit key)	AES-GCM (256-bit key)	Null	Null
ESP integrity	Null	Null	AES-GMAC (128-bit key)	AES-GMAC (256-bit key)
IKE encryption	AES-CBC (128-bit key)	AES-CBC (256-bit key)	AES-CBC (128-bit key)	AES-CBC (256-bit key)
IKE PRF	HMAC-SHA-256	HMAC-SHA-384	HMAC-SHA-256	HMAC-SHA-384
IKE Integrity	HMAC-SHA-256-128	HMAC-SHA-384-192	HMAC-SHA-256-128	HMAC-SHA-384-192
IKE DH group	256-bit random ECP	384-bit random ECP	256-bit random ECP	384-bit random ECP
IKE authentication	ECDSA-256	ECDSA-384	ECDSA-256	ECDSA-384

(b) NSA Suite B (RFC 4869)

cryptography, VPN-A relies on 3DES and HMAC, while VPN-B relies exclusively on AES. Three types of secret-key algorithms are used:

- **Encryption:** For encryption, the cipher block chaining (CBC) mode is used.
- **Message authentication:** For message authentication, VPN-A relies on HMAC with SHA-1 with the output truncated to 96 bits. VPN-B relies on a variant of CMAC with the output truncated to 96 bits.
- **Pseudorandom function:** IKEv2 generates pseudorandom bits by repeated use of the MAC used for message authentication.

RFC 4869 defines four optional cryptographic suites that are compatible with the United States National Security Agency's Suite B specifications. In 2005, the NSA issued Suite B, which defined the algorithms and strengths needed to protect both sensitive but unclassified (SBU) and classified information for use in its Cryptographic Modernization program [LATT09]. The four suites defined in RFC 4869 provide choices for ESP and IKE. The four suites are differentiated by the choice of cryptographic algorithm strengths and a choice of whether ESP is to provide both confidentiality and integrity or integrity only. All of the suites offer greater protection than the two VPN suites defined in RFC 4308.

Table 8.4b lists the algorithms and parameters for the two suites. As with RFC 4308, three categories of secret key algorithms are listed:

- **Encryption:** For ESP, authenticated encryption is provided using the GCM mode with either 128-bit or 256-bit AES keys. For IKE encryption, CBC is used, as it was for the VPN suites.
- **Message authentication:** For ESP, if only authentication is required, then GMAC is used. GMAC is a message authentication code algorithm based on the CRT mode of operation discussed in Chapter 2. For IKE, message authentication is provided using HMAC with one of the SHA-3 hash functions.
- **Pseudorandom function:** As with the VPN suites, IKEv2 in these suites generates pseudorandom bits by repeated use of the MAC used for message authentication.

For the Diffie-Hellman algorithm, the use of elliptic curve groups modulo a prime is specified. For authentication, elliptic curve digital signatures are listed. The original IKEv2 documents used RSA-based digital signatures. Equivalent or greater strength can be achieved using ECC with fewer key bits.

8.7 RECOMMENDED READING AND WEB SITES

IPv6 and IPv4 are covered in more detail in [STAL07]. [CHEN98] provides a good discussion of an IPsec design. [FRAN05] is a more comprehensive treatment of IPsec. [PATE06] is a useful overview of IPsecv3 and IKEv2 with an emphasis on cryptographic aspects.

CHEN98 Cheng, P., et al. "A Security Architecture for the Internet Protocol." *IBM Systems Journal,* Number 1, 1998.

FRAN05 Frankel, S., et al. *Guide to IPsec VPNs.* NIST SP 800-77, 2005.

PATE06 Paterson, K. "A Cryptographic Tour of the IPsec Standards." " *Cryptology ePrint Archive: Report 2006/097,* April 2006.

STAL07 Stallings, W. *Data and Computer Communications, Eighth Edition.* Upper Saddle River, NJ: Prentice Hall, 2007.

Recommended Web Sites:

- **NIST IPsec Project:** Contains papers, presentations, and reference implementations.
- **IPsec Maintenance and Extensions Charter:** Latest RFCs and internet drafts for IPsec.

8.8 KEY TERMS, REVIEW QUESTIONS, AND PROBLEMS

Key Terms

anti-replay service	Internet Key Exchange (IKE)	replay attack
Authentication Header (AH)	IP Security (IPsec)	security association (SA)
Encapsulating Security Payload (ESP)	IPv4	transport mode
	IPv6	tunnel mode
Internet Security Association and Key Management Protocol (ISAKMP)	Oakley key determination protocol	

Review Questions

8.1 Give examples of applications of IPsec.

8.2 What services are provided by IPsec?

8.3 What parameters identify an SA and what parameters characterize the nature of a particular SA?

8.4 What is the difference between transport mode and tunnel mode?

8.5 What is a replay attack?

8.6 Why does ESP include a padding field?

8.7 What are the basic approaches to bundling SAs?

8.8 What are the roles of the Oakley key determination protocol and ISAKMP in IPsec?

Problems

8.1   Describe and explain each of the entries in Table 8.2.

8.2   Draw a figure similar to Figure 8.8 for AH.

8.3   List the major security services provided by AH and ESP, respectively.

8.4   In discussing AH processing, it was mentioned that not all of the fields in an IP header are included in MAC calculation.
   a.   For each of the fields in the IPv4 header, indicate whether the field is immutable, mutable but predictable, or mutable (zeroed prior to ICV calculation).
   b.   Do the same for the IPv6 header.
   c.   Do the same for the IPv6 extension headers.
   In each case, justify your decision for each field.

8.5   Suppose that the current replay window spans from 120 to 530.
   a.   If the next incoming authenticated packet has sequence number 105, what will the receiver do with the packet, and what will be the parameters of the window after that?
   b.   If instead the next incoming authenticated packet has sequence number 440, what will the receiver do with the packet, and what will be the parameters of the window after that?
   c.   If instead the next incoming authenticated packet has sequence number 540, what will the receiver do with the packet, and what will be the parameters of the window after that?

8.6   When tunnel mode is used, a new outer IP header is constructed. For both IPv4 and IPv6, indicate the relationship of each outer IP header field and each extension header in the outer packet to the corresponding field or extension header of the inner IP packet. That is, indicate which outer values are derived from inner values and which are constructed independently of the inner values.

8.7   End-to-end authentication and encryption are desired between two hosts. Draw figures similar to Figure 8.8 that show each of the following.
   a.   Transport adjacency with encryption applied before authentication.
   b.   A transport SA bundled inside a tunnel SA with encryption applied before authentication.
   c.   A transport SA bundled inside a tunnel SA with authentication applied before encryption.

8.8   The IPsec architecture document states that when two transport mode SAs are bundled to allow both AH and ESP protocols on the same end-to-end flow, only one ordering of security protocols seems appropriate: performing the ESP protocol before performing the AH protocol. Why is this approach recommended rather than authentication before encryption?

8.9   For the IKE key exchange, indicate which parameters in each message go in which ISAKMP payload types.

8.10   Where does IPsec reside in a protocol stack?

CHAPTER 9

INTRUDERS

*They agreed that Graham should set the test for Charles Mabledene. It was nei-
ther more nor less than that Dragon should get Stern's code. If he had the 'in' at
Utting which he claimed to have this should be possible, only loyalty to Moscow
Centre would prevent it. If he got the key to the code he would prove his loyalty
to London Central beyond a doubt.*

— Talking to Strange Men, Ruth Rendell

KEY POINTS

- ◆ Unauthorized intrusion into a computer system or network is one of the most serious threats to computer security.

- ◆ Intrusion detection systems have been developed to provide early warning of an intrusion so that defensive action can be taken to prevent or minimize damage.

- ◆ Intrusion detection involves detecting unusual patterns of activity or patterns of activity that are known to correlate with intrusions.

- ◆ One important element of intrusion prevention is password management, with the goal of preventing unauthorized users from having access to the passwords of others.

A significant security problem for networked systems is hostile, or at least unwanted, trespass by users or software. User trespass can take the form of unauthorized logon to a machine or, in the case of an authorized user, acquisition of privileges or performance of actions beyond those that have been authorized. Software trespass can take the form of a virus, worm, or Trojan horse.

All these attacks relate to network security because system entry can be achieved by means of a network. However, these attacks are not confined to network-based attacks. A user with access to a local terminal may attempt trespass without using an intermediate network. A virus or Trojan horse may be introduced into a system by means of an optical disc. Only the worm is a uniquely network phenomenon. Thus, system trespass is an area in which the concerns of network security and computer security overlap.

Because the focus of this book is network security, we do not attempt a comprehensive analysis of either the attacks or the security countermeasures related to system trespass. Instead, in this Part we present a broad overview of these concerns.

This chapter covers the subject of intruders. First, we examine the nature of the attack and then look at strategies intended for prevention and, failing that, detection. Next we examine the related topic of password management.

9.1 INTRUDERS

One of the two most publicized threats to security is the intruder (the other is viruses), often referred to as a hacker or cracker. In an important early study of intrusion, Anderson [ANDE80] identified three classes of intruders:

- **Masquerader:** An individual who is not authorized to use the computer and who penetrates a system's access controls to exploit a legitimate user's account
- **Misfeasor:** A legitimate user who accesses data, programs, or resources for which such access is not authorized, or who is authorized for such access but misuses his or her privileges
- **Clandestine user:** An individual who seizes supervisory control of the system and uses this control to evade auditing and access controls or to suppress audit collection

The masquerader is likely to be an outsider; the misfeasor generally is an insider; and the clandestine user can be either an outsider or an insider.

Intruder attacks range from the benign to the serious. At the benign end of the scale, there are many people who simply wish to explore internets and see what is out there. At the serious end are individuals who are attempting to read privileged data, perform unauthorized modifications to data, or disrupt the system.

[GRAN04] lists the following examples of intrusion:

- Performing a remote root compromise of an e-mail server
- Defacing a Web server
- Guessing and cracking passwords
- Copying a database containing credit card numbers
- Viewing sensitive data, including payroll records and medical information, without authorization
- Running a packet sniffer on a workstation to capture usernames and passwords
- Using a permission error on an anonymous FTP server to distribute pirated software and music files
- Dialing into an unsecured modem and gaining internal network access
- Posing as an executive, calling the help desk, resetting the executive's e-mail password, and learning the new password
- Using an unattended, logged-in workstation without permission

Intruder Behavior Patterns

The techniques and behavior patterns of intruders are constantly shifting, to exploit newly discovered weaknesses and to evade detection and countermeasures. Even so, intruders typically follow one of a number of recognizable behavior patterns, and these patterns typically differ from those of ordinary users. In the following, we look at three broad examples of intruder behavior patterns, to give the reader some feel for the challenge facing the security administrator. Table 9.1, based on [RADC04], summarizes the behavior.

HACKERS Traditionally, those who hack into computers do so for the thrill of it or for status. The hacking community is a strong meritocracy in which status is determined by level of competence. Thus, attackers often look for targets of opportunity and then share the information with others. A typical example is a break-in at a large financial institution reported in [RADC04]. The intruder took advantage of the fact that the corporate network was running unprotected services, some of which were not even needed. In this case, the key to the break-in was the pcAnywhere application. The manufacturer, Symantec, advertises this program as a remote control solution that enables secure connection to remote devices. But the attacker had an easy time gaining access to pcAnywhere; the administrator used the same three-letter username and password for the program. In this case, there was no intrusion detection system on the 700-node corporate network. The intruder was only discovered when a vice president walked into her office and saw the cursor moving files around on her Windows workstation.

Table 9.1   Some Examples of Intruder Patterns of Behavior

(a) Hacker

1. Select the target using IP lookup tools such as NSLookup, Dig, and others.
2. Map network for accessible services using tools such as NMAP.
3. Identify potentially vulnerable services (in this case, pcAnywhere).
4. Brute force (guess) pcAnywhere password.
5. Install remote administration tool called DameWare.
6. Wait for administrator to log on and capture his password.
7. Use that password to access remainder of network.

(b) Criminal Enterprise

1. Act quickly and precisely to make their activities harder to detect.
2. Exploit perimeter through vulnerable ports.
3. Use Trojan horses (hidden software) to leave back doors for reentry.
4. Use sniffers to capture passwords.
5. Do not stick around until noticed.
6. Make few or no mistakes.

(c) Internal Threat

1. Create network accounts for themselves and their friends.
2. Access accounts and applications they wouldn't normally use for their daily jobs.
3. E-mail former and prospective employers.
4. Conduct furtive instant-messaging chats.
5. Visit Web sites that cater to disgruntled employees, such as f'dcompany.com.
6. Perform large downloads and file copying.
7. Access the network during off hours.

Benign intruders might be tolerable, although they do consume resources and may slow performance for legitimate users. However, there is no way in advance to know whether an intruder will be benign or malign. Consequently, even for systems with no particularly sensitive resources, there is a motivation to control this problem.

Intrusion detection systems (IDSs) and intrusion prevention systems (IPSs) are designed to counter this type of hacker threat. In addition to using such systems, organizations can consider restricting remote logons to specific IP addresses and/or use virtual private network technology.

One of the results of the growing awareness of the intruder problem has been the establishment of a number of computer emergency response teams (CERTs). These cooperative ventures collect information about system vulnerabilities and disseminate it to systems managers. Hackers also routinely read CERT reports. Thus, it is important for system administrators to quickly insert all software patches to discovered vulnerabilities. Unfortunately, given the complexity of many IT systems, and the rate at which patches are released, this is increasingly difficult to achieve without automated updating. Even then, there are problems caused by incompatibilities resulting from the updated software. Hence the need for multiple layers of defense in managing security threats to IT systems.

CRIMINALS Organized groups of hackers have become a widespread and common threat to Internet-based systems. These groups can be in the employ of a corporation or government but often are loosely affiliated gangs of hackers. Typically, these gangs are young, often Eastern European, Russian, or southeast Asian hackers who do business on the Web [ANTE06]. They meet in underground forums with names like DarkMarket.org and theftservices.com to trade tips and data and coordinate attacks. A common target is a credit card file at an e-commerce server. Attackers attempt to gain root access. The card numbers are used by organized crime gangs to purchase expensive items and are then posted to carder sites, where others can access and use the account numbers; this obscures usage patterns and complicates investigation.

Whereas traditional hackers look for targets of opportunity, criminal hackers usually have specific targets, or at least classes of targets in mind. Once a site is penetrated, the attacker acts quickly, scooping up as much valuable information as possible and exiting.

IDSs and IPSs can also be used for these types of attackers, but may be less effective because of the quick in-and-out nature of the attack. For e-commerce sites, database encryption should be used for sensitive customer information, especially credit cards. For hosted e-commerce sites (provided by an outsider service), the e-commerce organization should make use of a dedicated server (not used to support multiple customers) and closely monitor the provider's security services.

INSIDER ATTACKS Insider attacks are among the most difficult to detect and prevent. Employees already have access and knowledge about the structure and content of corporate databases. Insider attacks can be motivated by revenge or simply a feeling of entitlement. An example of the former is the case of Kenneth Patterson, fired from his position as data communications manager for American Eagle Outfitters. Patterson disabled the company's ability to process credit card purchases during five days of the holiday season of 2002. As for a sense of entitlement, there have always been many employees who felt entitled to take extra office supplies for home use, but this now extends to corporate data. An example is that of a vice president of sales for a stock analysis firm who quit to go to a competitor. Before she left, she copied the customer database to take with her. The offender reported feeling no animus toward her former employee; she simply wanted the data because it would be useful to her.

Although IDS and IPS facilities can be useful in countering insider attacks, other more direct approaches are of higher priority. Examples include the following:

- Enforce least privilege, only allowing access to the resources employees need to do their job.
- Set logs to see what users access and what commands they are entering.
- Protect sensitive resources with strong authentication.
- Upon termination, delete employee's computer and network access.
- Upon termination, make a mirror image of employee's hard drive before reissuing it. That evidence might be needed if your company information turns up at a competitor.

In this section, we look at the techniques used for intrusion. Then we examine ways to detect intrusion.

Intrusion Techniques

The objective of the intruder is to gain access to a system or to increase the range of privileges accessible on a system. Most initial attacks use system or software vulnerabilities that allow a user to execute code that opens a back door into the system. Alternatively, the intruder attempts to acquire information that should have been protected. In some cases, this information is in the form of a user password. With knowledge of some other user's password, an intruder can log in to a system and exercise all the privileges accorded to the legitimate user.

Typically, a system must maintain a file that associates a password with each authorized user. If such a file is stored with no protection, then it is an easy matter to gain access to it and learn passwords. The password file can be protected in one of two ways:

- **One-way function:** The system stores only the value of a function based on the user's password. When the user presents a password, the system transforms that password and compares it with the stored value. In practice, the system usually performs a one-way transformation (not reversible) in which the password is used to generate a key for the one-way function and in which a fixed-length output is produced.
- **Access control:** Access to the password file is limited to one or a very few accounts.

If one or both of these countermeasures are in place, some effort is needed for a potential intruder to learn passwords. On the basis of a survey of the literature and interviews with a number of password crackers, [ALVA90] reports the following techniques for learning passwords:

1. Try default passwords used with standard accounts that are shipped with the system. Many administrators do not bother to change these defaults.
2. Exhaustively try all short passwords (those of one to three characters).
3. Try words in the system's online dictionary or a list of likely passwords. Examples of the latter are readily available on hacker bulletin boards.
4. Collect information about users, such as their full names, the names of their spouse and children, pictures in their office, and books in their office that are related to hobbies.
5. Try users' phone numbers, Social Security numbers, and room numbers.
6. Try all legitimate license plate numbers for this state.
7. Use a Trojan horse (described in Chapter 10) to bypass restrictions on access.
8. Tap the line between a remote user and the host system.

The first six methods are various ways of guessing a password. If an intruder has to verify the guess by attempting to log in, it is a tedious and easily countered means of attack. For example, a system can simply reject any login after three password attempts, thus requiring the intruder to reconnect to the host to try again. Under these circumstances, it is not practical to try more than a handful of passwords. However, the intruder is unlikely to try such crude methods. For example, if an intruder can gain access with a low level of privileges to an encrypted password file, then the strategy would be to capture that file and then use the encryption mechanism of that particular system at leisure until a valid password that provided greater privileges was discovered.

Guessing attacks are feasible, and indeed highly effective, when a large number of guesses can be attempted automatically and each guess verified, without the guessing process being detectable. Later in this chapter, we have much to say about thwarting guessing attacks.

The seventh method of attack listed earlier, the Trojan horse, can be particularly difficult to counter. An example of a program that bypasses access controls was cited in [ALVA90]. A low-privilege user produced a game program and invited the system operator to use it in his or her spare time. The program did indeed play a game, but in the background it also contained code to copy the password file, which was unencrypted but access protected, into the user's file. Because the game was running under the operator's high-privilege mode, it was able to gain access to the password file.

The eighth attack listed, line tapping, is a matter of physical security.

Other intrusion techniques do not require learning a password. Intruders can get access to a system by exploiting attacks such as buffer overflows on a program that runs with certain privileges. Privilege escalation can be done this way as well.

We turn now to a discussion of the two principal countermeasures: detection and prevention. Detection is concerned with learning of an attack, either before or after its success. Prevention is a challenging security goal and an uphill battle at all times. The difficulty stems from the fact that the defender must attempt to thwart all possible attacks, whereas the attacker is free to try to find the weakest link in the defense chain and attack at that point.

9.2 INTRUSION DETECTION

Inevitably, the best intrusion prevention system will fail. A system's second line of defense is intrusion detection, and this has been the focus of much research in recent years. This interest is motivated by a number of considerations, including the following:

1. If an intrusion is detected quickly enough, the intruder can be identified and ejected from the system before any damage is done or any data are compromised. Even if the detection is not sufficiently timely to preempt the intruder, the sooner that the intrusion is detected, the less the amount of damage and the more quickly that recovery can be achieved.

2. An effective intrusion detection system can serve as a deterrent, so acting to prevent intrusions.

3. Intrusion detection enables the collection of information about intrusion techniques that can be used to strengthen the intrusion prevention facility.

Intrusion detection is based on the assumption that the behavior of the intruder differs from that of a legitimate user in ways that can be quantified. Of course, we cannot expect that there will be a crisp, exact distinction between an attack by an intruder and the normal use of resources by an authorized user. Rather, we must expect that there will be some overlap.

Figure 9.1 suggests, in very abstract terms, the nature of the task confronting the designer of an intrusion detection system. Although the typical behavior of an

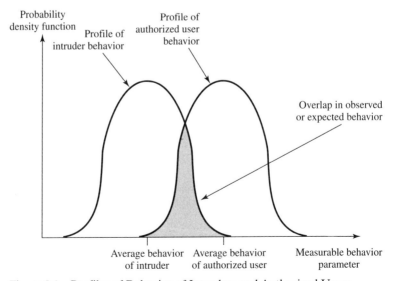

Figure 9.1 Profiles of Behavior of Intruders and Authorized Users

intruder differs from the typical behavior of an authorized user, there is an overlap in these behaviors. Thus, a loose interpretation of intruder behavior, which will catch more intruders, will also lead to a number of "false positives," or authorized users identified as intruders. On the other hand, an attempt to limit false positives by a tight interpretation of intruder behavior will lead to an increase in false negatives, or intruders not identified as intruders. Thus, there is an element of compromise and art in the practice of intrusion detection.

In Anderson's study [ANDE80], it was postulated that one could, with reasonable confidence, distinguish between a masquerader and a legitimate user. Patterns of legitimate user behavior can be established by observing past history, and significant deviation from such patterns can be detected. Anderson suggests that the task of detecting a misfeasor (legitimate user performing in an unauthorized fashion) is more difficult, in that the distinction between abnormal and normal behavior may be small. Anderson concluded that such violations would be undetectable solely through the search for anomalous behavior. However, misfeasor behavior might nevertheless be detectable by intelligent definition of the class of conditions that suggest unauthorized use. Finally, the detection of the clandestine user was felt to be beyond the scope of purely automated techniques. These observations, which were made in 1980, remain true today.

[PORR92] identifies the following approaches to intrusion detection:

1. **Statistical anomaly detection:** Involves the collection of data relating to the behavior of legitimate users over a period of time. Then statistical tests are applied to observed behavior to determine with a high level of confidence whether that behavior is not legitimate user behavior.

   a. Threshold detection: This approach involves defining thresholds, independent of user, for the frequency of occurrence of various events.

   b. Profile based: A profile of the activity of each user is developed and used to detect changes in the behavior of individual accounts.

2. **Rule-based detection:** Involves an attempt to define a set of rules that can be used to decide that a given behavior is that of an intruder.

   a. Anomaly detection: Rules are developed to detect deviation from previous usage patterns.

   b. Penetration identification: An expert system approach that searches for suspicious behavior.

In a nutshell, statistical approaches attempt to define normal, or expected, behavior, whereas rule-based approaches attempt to define proper behavior.

In terms of the types of attackers listed earlier, statistical anomaly detection is effective against masqueraders, who are unlikely to mimic the behavior patterns of the accounts they appropriate. On the other hand, such techniques may be unable to deal with misfeasors. For such attacks, rule-based approaches may be able to recognize events and sequences that, in context, reveal penetration. In practice, a system may exhibit a combination of both approaches to be effective against a broad range of attacks.

Audit Records

A fundamental tool for intrusion detection is the audit record. Some record of ongoing activity by users must be maintained as input to an intrusion detection system. Basically, two plans are used:

- **Native audit records:** Virtually all multiuser operating systems include accounting software that collects information on user activity. The advantage of using this information is that no additional collection software is needed. The disadvantage is that the native audit records may not contain the needed information or may not contain it in a convenient form.

- **Detection-specific audit records:** A collection facility can be implemented that generates audit records containing only that information required by the intrusion detection system. One advantage of such an approach is that it could be made vendor independent and ported to a variety of systems. The disadvantage is the extra overhead involved in having, in effect, two accounting packages running on a machine.

A good example of detection-specific audit records is one developed by Dorothy Denning [DENN87]. Each audit record contains the following fields:

- **Subject:** Initiators of actions. A subject is typically a terminal user but might also be a process acting on behalf of users or groups of users. All activity arises through commands issued by subjects. Subjects may be grouped into different access classes, and these classes may overlap.

- **Action:** Operation performed by the subject on or with an object; for example, login, read, perform I/O, execute.

- **Object:** Receptors of actions. Examples include files, programs, messages, records, terminals, printers, and user- or program-created structures. When a subject is the recipient of an action, such as electronic mail, then that subject is considered an object. Objects may be grouped by type. Object granularity may vary by object type and by environment. For example, database actions may be audited for the database as a whole or at the record level.

- **Exception-Condition:** Denotes which, if any, exception condition is raised on return.

- **Resource-Usage:** A list of quantitative elements in which each element gives the amount used of some resource (e.g., number of lines printed or displayed, number of records read or written, processor time, I/O units used, session elapsed time).

- **Time-Stamp:** Unique time-and-date stamp identifying when the action took place.

Most user operations are made up of a number of elementary actions. For example, a file copy involves the execution of the user command, which includes doing access validation and setting up the copy, plus the read from one file, plus the write to another file. Consider the command

COPY GAME.EXE TO <Libray>GAME.EXE

issued by Smith to copy an executable file GAME from the current directory to the <Library> directory. The following audit records may be generated:

| Smith | execute | `<Library>COPY.EXE` | 0 | CPU = 00002 | 11058721678 |

| Smith | read | `<Smith>GAME.EXE` | 0 | RECORDS = 0 | 11058721679 |

| Smith | execute | `<Library>COPY.EXE` | write-viol | RECORDS = 0 | 11058721680 |

In this case, the copy is aborted because Smith does not have write permission to <Library>.

The decomposition of a user operation into elementary actions has three advantages:

1. Because objects are the protectable entities in a system, the use of elementary actions enables an audit of all behavior affecting an object. Thus, the system can detect attempted subversions of access controls (by noting an abnormality in the number of exception conditions returned) and can detect successful subversions by noting an abnormality in the set of objects accessible to the subject.

2. Single-object, single-action audit records simplify the model and the implementation.

3. Because of the simple, uniform structure of the detection-specific audit records, it may be relatively easy to obtain this information or at least part of it by a straightforward mapping from existing native audit records to the detection-specific audit records.

Statistical Anomaly Detection

As was mentioned, statistical anomaly detection techniques fall into two broad categories: threshold detection and profile-based systems. Threshold detection involves counting the number of occurrences of a specific event type over an interval of time. If the count surpasses what is considered a reasonable number that one might expect to occur, then intrusion is assumed.

Threshold analysis, by itself, is a crude and ineffective detector of even moderately sophisticated attacks. Both the threshold and the time interval must be determined. Because of the variability across users, such thresholds are likely to generate either a lot of false positives or a lot of false negatives. However, simple threshold detectors may be useful in conjunction with more sophisticated techniques.

Profile-based anomaly detection focuses on characterizing the past behavior of individual users or related groups of users and then detecting significant deviations. A profile may consist of a set of parameters, so that deviation on just a single parameter may not be sufficient in itself to signal an alert.

The foundation of this approach is an analysis of audit records. The audit records provide input to the intrusion detection function in two ways. First, the designer must decide on a number of quantitative metrics that can be used to measure user behavior. An analysis of audit records over a period of time can be used to determine the activity profile of the average user. Thus, the audit records serve to define typical behavior. Second, current audit records are the input used to detect intrusion. That is, the intrusion detection model analyzes incoming audit records to determine deviation from average behavior.

Examples of metrics that are useful for profile-based intrusion detection are the following:

- **Counter:** A nonnegative integer that may be incremented but not decremented until it is reset by management action. Typically, a count of certain event types is kept over a particular period of time. Examples include the number of logins by a single user during an hour, the number of times a given command is executed during a single user session, and the number of password failures during a minute.
- **Gauge:** A nonnegative integer that may be incremented or decremented. Typically, a gauge is used to measure the current value of some entity. Examples include the number of logical connections assigned to a user application and the number of outgoing messages queued for a user process.
- **Interval timer:** The length of time between two related events. An example is the length of time between successive logins to an account.
- **Resource utilization:** Quantity of resources consumed during a specified period. Examples include the number of pages printed during a user session and total time consumed by a program execution.

Given these general metrics, various tests can be performed to determine whether current activity fits within acceptable limits. [DENN87] lists the following approaches that may be taken:

- Mean and standard deviation
- Multivariate
- Markov process
- Time series
- Operational

The simplest statistical test is to measure the **mean and standard deviation** of a parameter over some historical period. This gives a reflection of the average behavior and its variability. The use of mean and standard deviation is applicable to a wide variety of counters, timers, and resource measures. But these measures, by themselves, are typically too crude for intrusion detection purposes.

A **multivariate** model is based on correlations between two or more variables. Intruder behavior may be characterized with greater confidence by considering such correlations (for example, processor time and resource usage, or login frequency and session elapsed time).

A **Markov process** model is used to establish transition probabilities among various states. As an example, this model might be used to look at transitions between certain commands.

A **time series** model focuses on time intervals, looking for sequences of events that happen too rapidly or too slowly. A variety of statistical tests can be applied to characterize abnormal timing.

Finally, an **operational model** is based on a judgment of what is considered abnormal, rather than an automated analysis of past audit records. Typically, fixed limits are defined and intrusion is suspected for an observation that is outside the limits. This type of approach works best where intruder behavior can be deduced from certain types of activities. For example, a large number of login attempts over a short period suggests an attempted intrusion.

As an example of the use of these various metrics and models, Table 9.2 shows various measures considered or tested for the Stanford Research Institute (SRI) intrusion detection system (IDES) [DENN87, JAVI91, LUNT88].

The main advantage of the use of statistical profiles is that a prior knowledge of security flaws is not required. The detector program learns what is "normal" behavior and then looks for deviations. The approach is not based on system-dependent characteristics and vulnerabilities. Thus, it should be readily portable among a variety of systems.

Rule-Based Intrusion Detection

Rule-based techniques detect intrusion by observing events in the system and applying a set of rules that lead to a decision regarding whether a given pattern of activity is or is not suspicious. In very general terms, we can characterize all approaches as focusing on either anomaly detection or penetration identification, although there is some overlap in these approaches.

Rule-based anomaly detection is similar in terms of its approach and strengths to statistical anomaly detection. With the rule-based approach, historical audit records are analyzed to identify usage patterns and to generate automatically rules that describe those patterns. Rules may represent past behavior patterns of users, programs, privileges, time slots, terminals, and so on. Current behavior is then observed, and each transaction is matched against the set of rules to determine if it conforms to any historically observed pattern of behavior.

As with statistical anomaly detection, rule-based anomaly detection does not require knowledge of security vulnerabilities within the system. Rather, the scheme is based on observing past behavior and, in effect, assuming that the future will be like the past. In order for this approach to be effective, a rather large database of rules will be needed. For example, a scheme described in [VACC89] contains anywhere from 10^4 to 10^6 rules.

Rule-based penetration identification takes a very different approach to intrusion detection. The key feature of such systems is the use of rules for identifying known penetrations or penetrations that would exploit known weaknesses. Rules can also be defined that identify suspicious behavior, even when the behavior is within the bounds of established patterns of usage. Typically, the rules used in these systems are specific to the machine and operating system. The most fruitful approach to developing such rules is to analyze attack tools and scripts collected on the Internet. These rules can be supplemented with rules generated by knowledgeable security personnel. In this latter case, the normal procedure is to interview

Table 9.2   Measures That May Be Used for Intrusion Detection

Measure	Model	Type of Intrusion Detected
Login and Session Activity		
Login frequency by day and time	Mean and standard deviation	Intruders may be likely to log in during off-hours.
Frequency of login at different locations	Mean and standard deviation	Intruders may log in from a location that a particular user rarely or never uses.
Time since last login	Operational	Break-in on a "dead" account.
Elapsed time per session	Mean and standard deviation	Significant deviations might indicate masquerader.
Quantity of output to location	Mean and standard deviation	Excessive amounts of data transmitted to remote locations could signify leakage of sensitive data.
Session resource utilization	Mean and standard deviation	Unusual processor or I/O levels could signal an intruder.
Password failures at login	Operational	Attempted break-in by password guessing.
Failures to login from specified terminals	Operational	Attempted break-in.
Command or Program Execution Activity		
Execution frequency	Mean and standard deviation	May detect intruders, who are likely to use different commands, or a successful penetration by a legitimate user, who has gained access to privileged commands.
Program resource utilization	Mean and standard deviation	An abnormal value might suggest injection of a virus or Trojan horse, which performs side-effects that increase I/O or processor utilization.
Execution denials	Operational model	May detect penetration attempt by individual user who seeks higher privileges.
File Access Activity		
Read, write, create, delete frequency	Mean and standard deviation	Abnormalities for read and write access for individual users may signify masquerading or browsing.
Records read, written	Mean and standard deviation	Abnormality could signify an attempt to obtain sensitive data by inference and aggregation.
Failure count for read, write, create, delete	Operational	May detect users who persistently attempt to access unauthorized files.

system administrators and security analysts to collect a suite of known penetration scenarios and key events that threaten the security of the target system.

A simple example of the type of rules that can be used is found in NIDX, an early system that used heuristic rules that can be used to assign degrees of suspicion to activities [BAUE88]. Example heuristics are the following:

1. Users should not read files in other users' personal directories.
2. Users must not write other users' files.

3. Users who log in after hours often access the same files they used earlier.
4. Users do not generally open disk devices directly but rely on higher-level operating system utilities.
5. Users should not be logged in more than once to the same system.
6. Users do not make copies of system programs.

The penetration identification scheme used in IDES is representative of the strategy followed. Audit records are examined as they are generated, and they are matched against the rule base. If a match is found, then the user's *suspicion rating* is increased. If enough rules are matched, then the rating will pass a threshold that results in the reporting of an anomaly.

The IDES approach is based on an examination of audit records. A weakness of this plan is its lack of flexibility. For a given penetration scenario, there may be a number of alternative audit record sequences that could be produced, each varying from the others slightly or in subtle ways. It may be difficult to pin down all these variations in explicit rules. Another method is to develop a higher-level model independent of specific audit records. An example of this is a state transition model known as USTAT [ILGU93]. USTAT deals in general actions rather than the detailed specific actions recorded by the UNIX auditing mechanism. USTAT is implemented on a SunOS system that provides audit records on 239 events. Of these, only 28 are used by a preprocessor, which maps these onto 10 general actions (Table 9.3). Using just these actions and the parameters that are invoked with each action, a state transition diagram is developed that characterizes suspicious activity. Because a number of different auditable events map into a smaller number of actions, the rule-creation process is simpler. Furthermore, the state transition diagram model is easily modified to accommodate newly learned intrusion behaviors.

Table 9.3   USTAT Actions versus SunOS Event Types

USTAT Action	SunOS Event Type
Read	open_r, open_rc, open_rtc, open_rwc, open_rwtc, open_rt, open_rw, open_rwt
Write	truncate, ftruncate, creat, open_rtc, open_rwc, open_rwtc, open_rt, open_rw, open_rwt, open_w, open_wt, open_wc, open_wct
Create	mkdir, creat, open_rc, open_rtc, open_rwc, open_rwtc, open_wc, open_wtc, mknod
Delete	rmdir, unlink
Execute	exec, execve
Exit	exit
Modify_Owner	chown, fchown
Modify_Perm	chmod, fchmod
Rename	rename
Hardlink	link

The Base-Rate Fallacy

To be of practical use, an intrusion detection system should detect a substantial percentage of intrusions while keeping the false alarm rate at an acceptable level. If only a modest percentage of actual intrusions are detected, the system provides a false sense of security. On the other hand, if the system frequently triggers an alert when there is no intrusion (a false alarm), then either system managers will begin to ignore the alarms, or much time will be wasted analyzing the false alarms.

Unfortunately, because of the nature of the probabilities involved, it is very difficult to meet the standard of high rate of detections with a low rate of false alarms. In general, if the actual numbers of intrusions is low compared to the number of legitimate uses of a system, then the false alarm rate will be high unless the test is extremely discriminating. A study of existing intrusion detection systems, reported in [AXEL00], indicated that current systems have not overcome the problem of the base-rate fallacy. See Appendix 9A for a brief background on the mathematics of this problem.

Distributed Intrusion Detection

Until recently, work on intrusion detection systems focused on single-system stand-alone facilities. The typical organization, however, needs to defend a distributed collection of hosts supported by a LAN or internetwork. Although it is possible to mount a defense by using stand-alone intrusion detection systems on each host, a more effective defense can be achieved by coordination and cooperation among intrusion detection systems across the network.

Porras points out the following major issues in the design of a distributed intrusion detection system [PORR92]:

- A distributed intrusion detection system may need to deal with different audit record formats. In a heterogeneous environment, different systems will employ different native audit collection systems and, if using intrusion detection, may employ different formats for security-related audit records.

- One or more nodes in the network will serve as collection and analysis points for the data from the systems on the network. Thus, either raw audit data or summary data must be transmitted across the network. Therefore, there is a requirement to assure the integrity and confidentiality of these data. Integrity is required to prevent an intruder from masking his or her activities by altering the transmitted audit information. Confidentiality is required because the transmitted audit information could be valuable.

- Either a centralized or decentralized architecture can be used. With a centralized architecture, there is a single central point of collection and analysis of all audit data. This eases the task of correlating incoming reports but creates a potential bottleneck and single point of failure. With a decentralized architecture, there are more than one analysis centers, but these must coordinate their activities and exchange information.

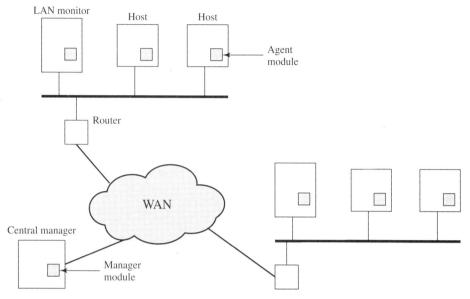

Figure 9.2   Architecture for Distributed Intrusion Detection

A good example of a distributed intrusion detection system is one developed at the University of California at Davis [HEBE92, SNAP91]. Figure 9.2 shows the overall architecture, which consists of three main components:

- **Host agent module:** An audit collection module operating as a background process on a monitored system. Its purpose is to collect data on security-related events on the host and transmit these to the central manager.

- **LAN monitor agent module:** Operates in the same fashion as a host agent module except that it analyzes LAN traffic and reports the results to the central manager.

- **Central manager module:** Receives reports from LAN monitor and host agents and processes and correlates these reports to detect intrusion.

The scheme is designed to be independent of any operating system or system auditing implementation. Figure 9.3 [SNAP91] shows the general approach that is taken. The agent captures each audit record produced by the native audit collection system. A filter is applied that retains only those records that are of security interest. These records are then reformatted into a standardized format referred to as the host audit record (HAR). Next, a template-driven logic module analyzes the records for suspicious activity. At the lowest level, the agent scans for notable events that are of interest independent of any past events. Examples include failed file accesses, accessing system files, and changing a file's access control. At the next higher level, the agent looks for sequences of events, such as known attack patterns (signatures). Finally, the agent looks for anomalous behavior of an individual user based on a historical profile of that user, such as number of programs executed, number of files accessed, and the like.

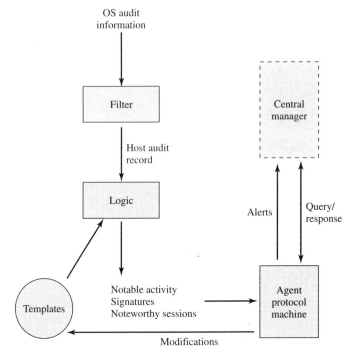

Figure 9.3 Agent Architecture

When suspicious activity is detected, an alert is sent to the central manager. The central manager includes an expert system that can draw inferences from received data. The manager may also query individual systems for copies of HARs to correlate with those from other agents.

The LAN monitor agent also supplies information to the central manager. The LAN monitor agent audits host-host connections, services used, and volume of traffic. It searches for significant events, such as sudden changes in network load, the use of security-related services, and network activities such as *rlogin*.

The architecture depicted in Figures 9.2 and 9.3 is quite general and flexible. It offers a foundation for a machine-independent approach that can expand from stand-alone intrusion detection to a system that is able to correlate activity from a number of sites and networks to detect suspicious activity that would otherwise remain undetected.

Honeypots

A relatively recent innovation in intrusion detection technology is the honeypot. Honeypots are decoy systems that are designed to lure a potential attacker away from critical systems. Honeypots are designed to

- divert an attacker from accessing critical systems
- collect information about the attacker's activity
- encourage the attacker to stay on the system long enough for administrators to respond

These systems are filled with fabricated information designed to appear valuable but that a legitimate user of the system wouldn't access. Thus, any access to the honeypot is suspect. The system is instrumented with sensitive monitors and event loggers that detect these accesses and collect information about the attacker's activities. Because any attack against the honeypot is made to seem successful, administrators have time to mobilize and log and track the attacker without ever exposing productive systems.

Initial efforts involved a single honeypot computer with IP addresses designed to attract hackers. More recent research has focused on building entire honeypot networks that emulate an enterprise, possibly with actual or simulated traffic and data. Once hackers are within the network, administrators can observe their behavior in detail and figure out defenses.

Intrusion Detection Exchange Format

To facilitate the development of distributed intrusion detection systems that can function across a wide range of platforms and environments, standards are needed to support interoperability. Such standards are the focus of the IETF Intrusion Detection Working Group. The purpose of the working group is to define data formats and exchange procedures for sharing information of interest to intrusion detection and response systems and to management systems that may need to interact with them. The outputs of this working group include:

1. A requirements document, which describes the high-level functional requirements for communication between intrusion detection systems and requirements for communication between intrusion detection systems and with management systems, including the rationale for those requirements. Scenarios will be used to illustrate the requirements.

2. A common intrusion language specification, which describes data formats that satisfy the requirements.

3. A framework document, which identifies existing protocols best used for communication between intrusion detection systems, and describes how the devised data formats relate to them.

As of this writing, all of these documents are in an Internet-draft document stage.

9.3 PASSWORD MANAGEMENT

Password Protection

The front line of defense against intruders is the password system. Virtually all multiuser systems require that a user provide not only a name or identifier (ID) but also a password. The password serves to authenticate the ID of the individual logging on to the system. In turn, the ID provides security in the following ways:

- The ID determines whether the user is authorized to gain access to a system. In some systems, only those who already have an ID filed on the system are allowed to gain access.

- The ID determines the privileges accorded to the user. A few users may have supervisory or "superuser" status that enables them to read files and perform functions that are especially protected by the operating system. Some systems have guest or anonymous accounts, and users of these accounts have more limited privileges than others.

- The ID is used in what is referred to as discretionary access control. For example, by listing the IDs of the other users, a user may grant permission to them to read files owned by that user.

THE VULNERABILITY OF PASSWORDS To understand the nature of the threat to password-based systems, let us consider a scheme that is widely used on UNIX, in which passwords are never stored in the clear. Rather, the following procedure is employed (Figure 9.4a). Each user selects a password of up to eight printable characters in length. This is converted into a 56-bit value (using 7-bit ASCII) that serves as the key input to an encryption routine. The encryption routine, known as crypt(3), is based on DES. The DES algorithm is modified using a 12-bit "salt" value. Typically, this value is related to the time at which the password is assigned to the user. The modified DES algorithm is exercised with a data input consisting of a 64-bit block of zeros. The output of the algorithm then serves as input for a second encryption. This process is repeated for a total of 25 encryptions. The resulting 64-bit output is then translated into an 11-character sequence. The hashed password is then stored, together with a plaintext copy of the salt, in the password file for the corresponding user ID. This method has been shown to be secure against a variety of cryptanalytic attacks [WAGN00].

The salt serves three purposes:

- It prevents duplicate passwords from being visible in the password file. Even if two users choose the same password, those passwords will be assigned at different times. Hence, the "extended" passwords of the two users will differ.

- It effectively increases the length of the password without requiring the user to remember two additional characters. Hence, the number of possible passwords is increased by a factor of 4096, increasing the difficulty of guessing a password.

- It prevents the use of a hardware implementation of DES, which would ease the difficulty of a brute-force guessing attack.

When a user attempts to log on to a UNIX system, the user provides an ID and a password. The operating system uses the ID to index into the password file and retrieve the plaintext salt and the encrypted password. The salt and user-supplied password are used as input to the encryption routine. If the result matches the stored value, the password is accepted.

The encryption routine is designed to discourage guessing attacks. Software implementations of DES are slow compared to hardware versions, and the use of 25 iterations multiplies the time required by 25. However, since the original design of this algorithm, two changes have occurred. First, newer implementations of the algorithm itself have resulted in speedups. For example, the Morris worm described in Chapter 10 was able to do online password guessing of a few hundred passwords

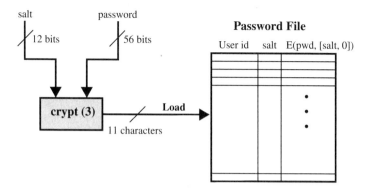

(a) Loading a new password

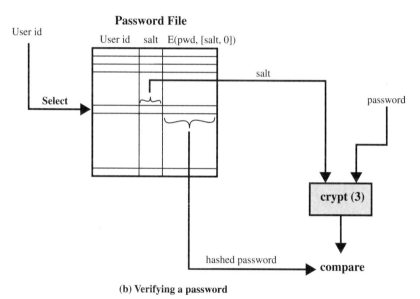

(b) Verifying a password

Figure 9.4   UNIX Password Scheme

in a reasonably short time by using a more efficient encryption algorithm than the standard one stored on the UNIX systems that it attacked. Second, hardware performance continues to increase, so that any software algorithm executes more quickly.

Thus, there are two threats to the UNIX password scheme. First, a user can gain access on a machine using a guest account or by some other means and then run a password guessing program, called a password cracker, on that machine. The attacker should be able to check hundreds and perhaps thousands of possible passwords with little resource consumption. In addition, if an opponent is able to obtain a copy of the password file, then a cracker program can be run on another machine at leisure. This enables the opponent to run through many thousands of possible passwords in a reasonable period.

As an example, a password cracker was reported on the Internet in August 1993 [MADS93]. Using a Thinking Machines Corporation parallel computer, a performance of 1560 encryptions per second per vector unit was achieved. With four vector units per processing node (a standard configuration), this works out to 800,000 encryptions per second on a 128-node machine (which is a modest size) and 6.4 million encryptions per second on a 1024-node machine.

Even these stupendous guessing rates do not yet make it feasible for an attacker to use a dumb brute-force technique of trying all possible combinations of characters to discover a password. Instead, password crackers rely on the fact that some people choose easily guessable passwords.

Some users, when permitted to choose their own password, pick one that is absurdly short. The results of one study at Purdue University are shown in Table 9.4. The study observed password change choices on 54 machines, representing approximately 7000 user accounts. Almost 3% of the passwords were three characters or fewer in length. An attacker could begin the attack by exhaustively testing all possible passwords of length 3 or fewer. A simple remedy is for the system to reject any password choice of fewer than, say, six characters or even to require that all passwords be exactly eight characters in length. Most users would not complain about such a restriction.

Password length is only part of the problem. Many people, when permitted to choose their own password, pick a password that is guessable, such as their own name, their street name, a common dictionary word, and so forth. This makes the job of password cracking straightforward. The cracker simply has to test the password file against lists of likely passwords. Because many people use guessable passwords, such a strategy should succeed on virtually all systems.

One demonstration of the effectiveness of guessing is reported in [KLEI90]. From a variety of sources, the author collected UNIX password files, containing nearly 14,000 encrypted passwords. The result, which the author rightly characterizes

Table 9.4 Observed Password Lengths [SPAF92a]

Length	Number	Fraction of Total
1	55	.004
2	87	.006
3	212	.02
4	449	.03
5	1260	.09
6	3035	.22
7	2917	.21
8	5772	.42
Total	13787	1.0

as frightening, is shown in Table 9.5. In all, nearly one-fourth of the passwords were guessed. The following strategy was used:

1. Try the user's name, initials, account name, and other relevant personal information. In all, 130 different permutations for each user were tried.
2. Try words from various dictionaries. The author compiled a dictionary of over 60,000 words, including the online dictionary on the system itself, and various other lists as shown.

Table 9.5 Passwords Cracked from a Sample Set of 13,797 Accounts [KLEI90]

Type of Password	Search Size	Number of Matches	Percentage of Passwords Matched	Cost/Benefit Ratio[a]
User/account name	130	368	2.7%	2.830
Character sequences	866	22	0.2%	0.025
Numbers	427	9	0.1%	0.021
Chinese	392	56	0.4%	0.143
Place names	628	82	0.6%	0.131
Common names	2239	548	4.0%	0.245
Female names	4280	161	1.2%	0.038
Male names	2866	140	1.0%	0.049
Uncommon names	4955	130	0.9%	0.026
Myths & legends	1246	66	0.5%	0.053
Shakespearean	473	11	0.1%	0.023
Sports terms	238	32	0.2%	0.134
Science fiction	691	59	0.4%	0.085
Movies and actors	99	12	0.1%	0.121
Cartoons	92	9	0.1%	0.098
Famous people	290	55	0.4%	0.190
Phrases and patterns	933	253	1.8%	0.271
Surnames	33	9	0.1%	0.273
Biology	58	1	0.0%	0.017
System dictionary	19683	1027	7.4%	0.052
Machine names	9018	132	1.0%	0.015
Mnemonics	14	2	0.0%	0.143
King James bible	7525	83	0.6%	0.011
Miscellaneous words	3212	54	0.4%	0.017
Yiddish words	56	0	0.0%	0.000
Asteroids	2407	19	0.1%	0.007
TOTAL	62727	3340	24.2%	0.053

[a]Computed as the number of matches divided by the search size. The more words that needed to be tested for a match, the lower the cost/benefit ratio.

3. Try various permutations on the words from step 2. This included making the first letter uppercase or a control character, making the entire word uppercase, reversing the word, changing the letter "o" to the digit "zero," and so on. These permutations added another 1 million words to the list.

4. Try various capitalization permutations on the words from step 2 that were not considered in step 3. This added almost 2 million additional words to the list.

Thus, the test involved in the neighborhood of 3 million words. Using the fastest Thinking Machines implementation listed earlier, the time to encrypt all these words for all possible salt values is under an hour. Keep in mind that such a thorough search could produce a success rate of about 25%, whereas even a single hit may be enough to gain a wide range of privileges on a system.

ACCESS CONTROL One way to thwart a password attack is to deny the opponent access to the password file. If the encrypted password portion of the file is accessible only by a privileged user, then the opponent cannot read it without already knowing the password of a privileged user. [SPAF92a] points out several flaws in this strategy:

- Many systems, including most UNIX systems, are susceptible to unanticipated break-ins. Once an attacker has gained access by some means, he or she may wish to obtain a collection of passwords in order to use different accounts for different logon sessions to decrease the risk of detection. Or a user with an account may desire another user's account to access privileged data or to sabotage the system.
- An accident of protection might render the password file readable, thus compromising all the accounts.
- Some of the users have accounts on other machines in other protection domains, and they use the same password. Thus, if the passwords could be read by anyone on one machine, a machine in another location might be compromised.

Thus, a more effective strategy would be to force users to select passwords that are difficult to guess.

Password Selection Strategies

The lesson from the two experiments just described (Tables 9.4 and 9.5) is that, left to their own devices, many users choose a password that is too short or too easy to guess. At the other extreme, if users are assigned passwords consisting of eight randomly selected printable characters, password cracking is effectively impossible. But it would be almost as impossible for most users to remember their passwords. Fortunately, even if we limit the password universe to strings of characters that are reasonably memorable, the size of the universe is still too large to permit practical cracking. Our goal, then, is to eliminate guessable passwords while allowing the user to select a password that is memorable. Four basic techniques are in use:

- User education
- Computer-generated passwords

- Reactive password checking
- Proactive password checking

Users can be told the importance of using hard-to-guess passwords and can be provided with guidelines for selecting strong passwords. This **user education** strategy is unlikely to succeed at most installations, particularly where there is a large user population or a lot of turnover. Many users will simply ignore the guidelines. Others may not be good judges of what is a strong password. For example, many users (mistakenly) believe that reversing a word or capitalizing the last letter makes a password unguessable.

Computer-generated passwords also have problems. If the passwords are quite random in nature, users will not be able to remember them. Even if the password is pronounceable, the user may have difficulty remembering it and so be tempted to write it down. In general, computer-generated password schemes have a history of poor acceptance by users. FIPS PUB 181 defines one of the best-designed automated password generators. The standard includes not only a description of the approach but also a complete listing of the C source code of the algorithm. The algorithm generates words by forming pronounceable syllables and concatenating them to form a word. A random number generator produces a random stream of characters used to construct the syllables and words.

A **reactive password checking** strategy is one in which the system periodically runs its own password cracker to find guessable passwords. The system cancels any passwords that are guessed and notifies the user. This tactic has a number of drawbacks. First, it is resource intensive if the job is done right. Because a determined opponent who is able to steal a password file can devote full CPU time to the task for hours or even days, an effective reactive password checker is at a distinct disadvantage. Furthermore, any existing passwords remain vulnerable until the reactive password checker finds them.

The most promising approach to improved password security is a **proactive password checker**. In this scheme, a user is allowed to select his or her own password. However, at the time of selection, the system checks to see if the password is allowable and, if not, rejects it. Such checkers are based on the philosophy that, with sufficient guidance from the system, users can select memorable passwords from a fairly large password space that are not likely to be guessed in a dictionary attack.

The trick with a proactive password checker is to strike a balance between user acceptability and strength. If the system rejects too many passwords, users will complain that it is too hard to select a password. If the system uses some simple algorithm to define what is acceptable, this provides guidance to password crackers to refine their guessing technique. In the remainder of this subsection, we look at possible approaches to proactive password checking.

The first approach is a simple system for rule enforcement. For example, the following rules could be enforced:

- All passwords must be at least eight characters long.
- In the first eight characters, the passwords must include at least one each of uppercase, lowercase, numeric digits, and punctuation marks.

These rules could be coupled with advice to the user. Although this approach is superior to simply educating users, it may not be sufficient to thwart password crackers. This scheme alerts crackers as to which passwords *not* to try but may still make it possible to do password cracking.

Another possible procedure is simply to compile a large dictionary of possible "bad" passwords. When a user selects a password, the system checks to make sure that it is not on the disapproved list. There are two problems with this approach:

- **Space:** The dictionary must be very large to be effective. For example, the dictionary used in the Purdue study [SPAF92a] occupies more than 30 megabytes of storage.
- **Time:** The time required to search a large dictionary may itself be large. In addition, to check for likely permutations of dictionary words, either those words most be included in the dictionary, making it truly huge, or each search must also involve considerable processing.

Two techniques for developing an effective and efficient proactive password checker that is based on rejecting words on a list show promise. One of these develops a Markov model for the generation of guessable passwords [DAVI93]. Figure 9.5 shows a simplified version of such a model. This model shows a language consisting of an alphabet of three characters. The state of the system at any time is the identity of the most recent letter. The value on the transition from one state to another represents the probability that one letter follows another. Thus, the probability that the next letter is b, given that the current letter is a, is 0.5.

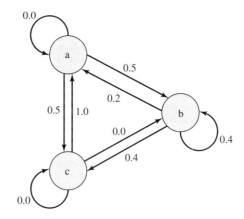

$$M = \{3, \{a, b, c\}, T, 1\} \quad \text{where}$$

$$T = \begin{bmatrix} 0.0 & 0.5 & 0.5 \\ 0.2 & 0.4 & 0.4 \\ 1.0 & 0.0 & 0.0 \end{bmatrix}$$

e.g., string probably from this language: abbcacaba

e.g., string probably not from this language: aacccbaaa

Figure 9.5   An Example Markov Model

In general, a Markov model is a quadruple $[m, A, \mathbf{T}, k]$, where m is the number of states in the model, A is the state space, $\mathbf{T}$ is the matrix of transition probabilities, and k is the order of the model. For a kth-order model, the probability of making a transition to a particular letter depends on the previous k letters that have been generated. Figure 9.5 shows a simple first-order model.

The authors report on the development and use of a second-order model. To begin, a dictionary of guessable passwords is constructed. Then the transition matrix is calculated as follows:

1. Determine the frequency matrix $\mathbf{f}$, where $\mathbf{f}(i, j, k)$ is the number of occurrences of the trigram consisting of the ith, jth, and kth character. For example, the password *parsnips* yields the trigrams par, ars, rsn, sni, nip, and ips.

2. For each bigram ij, calculate $\mathbf{f}(i, j, \infty)$ as the total number of trigrams beginning with ij. For example, $\mathbf{f}(a, b, \infty)$ would be the total number of trigrams of the form aba, abb, abc, and so on.

3. Compute the entries of $\mathbf{T}$ as follows:

$$\mathbf{T}(i, j, k) = \frac{\mathbf{f}(i, j, k)}{\mathbf{f}(i, j, \infty)}$$

The result is a model that reflects the structure of the words in the dictionary. With this model, the question "Is this a bad password?" is transformed into the question "Was this string (password) generated by this Markov model?" For a given password, the transition probabilities of all its trigrams can be looked up. Some standard statistical tests can then be used to determine if the password is likely or unlikely for that model. Passwords that are likely to be generated by the model are rejected. The authors report good results for a second-order model. Their system catches virtually all the passwords in their dictionary and does not exclude so many potentially good passwords as to be user unfriendly.

A quite different approach has been reported by Spafford [SPAF92a, SPAF92b]. It is based on the use of a Bloom filter [BLOO70]. To begin, we explain the operation of the Bloom filter. A Bloom filter of order k consists of a set of k independent hash functions $H_1(x), H_2(x), \ldots, H_k(x)$, where each function maps a password into a hash value in the range 0 to $N - 1$. That is,

$$H_i(X_j) = y \qquad 1 \le i \le k; \qquad 1 \le j \le D; \qquad 0 \le y \le N - 1$$

where

$X_j = $ jth word in password dictionary

$D = $ number of words in password dictionary

The following procedure is then applied to the dictionary:

1. A hash table of N bits is defined, with all bits initially set to 0.

2. For each password, its k hash values are calculated, and the corresponding bits in the hash table are set to 1. Thus, if $H_i(X_j) = 67$ for some (i, j), then the sixty-seventh bit of the hash table is set to 1; if the bit already has the value 1, it remains at 1.

When a new password is presented to the checker, its k hash values are calcu-lated. If all the corresponding bits of the hash table are equal to 1, then the password is rejected. All passwords in the dictionary will be rejected. But there will also be some "false positives" (that is, passwords that are not in the dictionary but that pro-duce a match in the hash table). To see this, consider a scheme with two hash func-tions. Suppose that the passwords *undertaker* and *hulkhogan* are in the dictionary, but *xG%#jj98* is not. Further suppose that

$$H_1(\text{undertaker}) = 25 \qquad H_1(\text{hulkhogan}) = 83 \qquad H_1(\text{xG%\#jj98}) = 665$$

$$H_2(\text{undertaker}) = 998 \qquad H_2(\text{hulkhogan}) = 665 \qquad H_2(\text{xG%\#jj98}) = 998$$

If the password xG%#jj98 is presented to the system, it will be rejected even though it is not in the dictionary. If there are too many such false positives, it will be difficult for users to select passwords. Therefore, we would like to design the hash scheme to minimize false positives. It can be shown that the probability of a false positive can be approximated by:

$$P \approx \left(1 - e^{kD/N}\right)^k = \left(1 - e^{k/R}\right)^k$$

or, equivalently,

$$R \approx \frac{-k}{\ln(1 - P^{1/k})}$$

where

$$k = \text{number of hash functions}$$
$$N = \text{number of bits in hash table}$$
$$D = \text{number of words in dictionary}$$
$$R = N/D, \text{ratio of hash table size (bits) to dictionary size (words)}$$

Figure 9.6 plots P as a function of R for various values of k. Suppose we have a dictionary of 1 million words and we wish to have a 0.01 probability of rejecting a password not in the dictionary. If we choose six hash functions, the required ratio is $R = 9.6$. Therefore, we need a hash table of 9.6×10^6 bits or about 1.2 MBytes of storage. In contrast, storage of the entire dictionary would require on the order of 8 MBytes. Thus, we achieve a compression of almost a factor of 7. Furthermore, password checking involves the straightforward calculation of six hash functions and is independent of the size of the dictionary, whereas with the use of the full dictionary, there is substantial searching.[1]

---

[1]Both the Markov model and the Bloom filter involve the use of probabilistic techniques. In the case of the Markov model, there is a small probability that some passwords in the dictionary will not be caught and a small probability that some passwords not in the dictionary will be rejected. In the case of the Bloom filter, there is a small probability that some passwords not in the dictionary will be rejected.

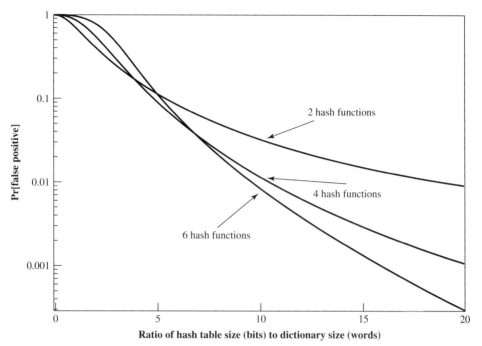

Figure 9.6 Performance of Bloom Filter

9.4 RECOMMENDED READING AND WEB SITES

Two thorough treatments of intrusion detection are [BACE00] and [PROC01]. A more concise but very worthwhile treatment is [SCAR07]. Two short but useful survey articles on the subject are [KENT00] and [MCHU00]. [NING04] surveys recent advances in intrusion detection techniques. [HONE01] is the definitive account on honeypots and provides a detailed analysis of the tools and methods of hackers.

BACE00   Bace, R. *Intrusion Detection.* Indianapolis, IN: Macmillan Technical Publishing, 2000.

HONE01   The Honeynet Project. *Know Your Enemy: Revealing the Security Tools, Tactics, and Motives of the Blackhat Community.* Reading, MA: Addison-Wesley, 2001.

KENT00   Kent, S. "On the Trail of Intrusions into Information Systems." *IEEE Spectrum*, December 2000.

MCHU00   McHugh, J.; Christie, A.; and Allen, J. "The Role of Intrusion Detection Systems." *IEEE Software*, September/October 2000.

NING04   Ning, P., et al. "Techniques and Tools for Analyzing Intrusion Alerts." *ACM Transactions on Information and System Security*, May 2004.

PROC01   Proctor, P., *The Practical Intrusion Detection Handbook.* Upper Saddle River, NJ: Prentice Hall, 2001.

SCAR07   Scarfone, K., and Mell, P. *Guide to Intrusion Detection and Prevention Systems.* NIST Special Publication SP 800-94, February 2007.

Recommended Web Sites:

- **CERT Coordination Center:** The organization that grew from the computer emergency response team formed by the Defense Advanced Research Projects Agency. Site provides good information on Internet security threats, vulnerabilities, and attack statistics.
- **Packet Storm:** Resource of up-to-date and historical security tools, exploits, and advisories.
- **Honeynet Project:** A research project studying the techniques of predatory hackers and developing honeypot products.
- **Honeypots:** A good collection of research papers and technical articles.
- **Intrusion Detection Working Group:** IETF group developing standards for exchange formats and exchange procedures for intrusion detection systems. Includes RFCs and Internet drafts.
- **STAT Project:** A research and open-source project at the University of California, Santa Barbara that focuses on signature-based intrusion detection tools for hosts, applications, and networks.
- **Password Usage and Generation:** NIST documents on this topic.

9.5 KEY TERMS, REVIEW QUESTIONS, AND PROBLEMS

Key Terms

audit record	intruder	password
Bayes' Theorem	intrusion detection	rule-based intrusion detection
base-rate fallacy	intrusion detection exchange	salt
honeypot	format	statistical anomaly detection

Review Questions

9.1 List and briefly define three classes of intruders.

9.2 What are two common techniques used to protect a password file?

9.3 What are three benefits that can be provided by an intrusion detection system?

9.4 What is the difference between statistical anomaly detection and rule-based intrusion detection?

9.5 What metrics are useful for profile-based intrusion detection?

9.6 What is the difference between rule-based anomaly detection and rule-based penetration identification?

9.7 What is a honeypot?

9.8 What is a salt in the context of UNIX password management?

9.9 List and briefly define four techniques used to avoid guessable passwords.

Problems

9.1 In the context of an IDS, we define a false positive to be an alarm generated by an IDS in which the IDS alerts to a condition that is actually benign. A false negative occurs when an IDS fails to generate an alarm when an alert-worthy condition is in effect. Using the following diagram, depict two curves that roughly indicate false positives and false negatives, respectively.

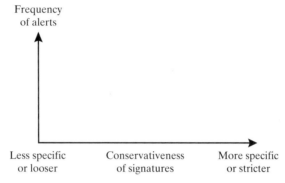

9.2 The overlapping area of the two probability density functions of Figure 9.1 represents the region in which there is the potential for false positives and false negatives. Further, Figure 9.1 is an idealized and not necessarily representative depiction of the relative shapes of the two density functions. Suppose there is 1 actual intrusion for every 1000 authorized users, and the overlapping area covers 1% of the authorized users and 50% of the intruders.

  a. Sketch such a set of density functions and argue that this is not an unreasonable depiction.
  b. What is the probability that an event that occurs in this region is that of an authorized user? Keep in mind that 50% of all intrusions fall in this region.

9.3 An example of a host-based intrusion detection tool is the tripwire program. This is a file integrity checking tool that scans files and directories on the system on a regular basis and notifies the administrator of any changes. It uses a protected database of cryptographic checksums for each file checked and compares this value with that recomputed on each file as it is scanned. It must be configured with a list of files and directories to check, and what changes, if any, are permissible to each. It can allow, for example, log files to have new entries appended, but not for existing entries to be changed. What are the advantages and disadvantages of using such a tool? Consider the problem of determining which files should only change rarely, which files may change more often and how, and which change frequently and hence cannot be checked. Hence consider the amount of work in both the configuration of the program and on the system administrator monitoring the responses generated.

9.4 A taxicab was involved in a fatal hit-and-run accident at night. Two cab companies, the Green and the Blue, operate in the city. You are told that:

  • 85% of the cabs in the city are Green and 15% are Blue.
  • A witness identified the cab as Blue.

The court tested the reliability of the witness under the same circumstances that existed on the night of the accident and concluded that the witness was correct in identifying the color of the cab 80% of the time. What is the probability that the cab involved in the incident was Blue rather than Green?

9.5 Explain the suitability or unsuitability of the following passwords:

  a. YK 334   **b.** mfmitm (for "my favorite   **c.** Natalie1   **d.** Washington
                          movie is tender mercies)
  e. Aristotle **f.** tv9stove   **g.** 12345678   **h.** dribgib

9.6   An early attempt to force users to use less predictable passwords involved computer-supplied passwords. The passwords were eight characters long and were taken from the character set consisting of lowercase letters and digits. They were generated by a pseudorandom number generator with 2^{15} possible starting values. Using the technology of the time, the time required to search through all character strings of length 8 from a 36-character alphabet was 112 years. Unfortunately, this is not a true reflection of the actual security of the system. Explain the problem.

9.7   Assume that passwords are selected from four-character combinations of 26 alphabetic characters. Assume that an adversary is able to attempt passwords at a rate of one per second.
   a.   Assuming no feedback to the adversary until each attempt has been completed, what is the expected time to discover the correct password?
   b.   Assuming feedback to the adversary flagging an error as each incorrect character is entered, what is the expected time to discover the correct password?

9.8   Assume that source elements of length k are mapped in some uniform fashion into a target elements of length p. If each digit can take on one of r values, then the number of source elements is r^k and the number of target elements is the smaller number r^p. A particular source element x_i is mapped to a particular target element y_j.
   a.   What is the probability that the correct source element can be selected by an adversary on one try?
   b.   What is the probability that a different source element $x_k (x_i \neq x_k)$ that results in the same target element, y_j, could be produced by an adversary?
   c.   What is the probability that the correct target element can be produced by an adversary on one try?

9.9   A phonetic password generator picks two segments randomly for each six-letter password. The form of each segment is CVC (consonant, vowel, consonant), where $V = <a, e, i, o, u>$ and $C = \overline{V}$.
   a.   What is the total password population?
   b.   What is the probability of an adversary guessing a password correctly?

9.10 Assume that passwords are limited to the use of the 95 printable ASCII characters and that all passwords are 10 characters in length. Assume a password cracker with an encryption rate of 6.4 million encryptions per second. How long will it take to test exhaustively all possible passwords on a UNIX system?

9.11 Because of the known risks of the UNIX password system, the SunOS-4.0 documentation recommends that the password file be removed and replaced with a publicly readable file called /etc/publickey. An entry in the file for user A consists of a user's identifier ID_A, the user's public key, PU_a, and the corresponding private key PR_a. This private key is encrypted using DES with a key derived from the user's login password P_a. When A logs in, the system decrypts $E(P_a, PR_a)$ to obtain PR_a.
   a.   The system then verifies that P_a was correctly supplied. How?
   b.   How can an opponent attack this system?

9.12 The encryption scheme used for UNIX passwords is one way; it is not possible to reverse it. Therefore, would it be accurate to say that this is, in fact, a hash code rather than an encryption of the password?

9.13 It was stated that the inclusion of the salt in the UNIX password scheme increases the difficulty of guessing by a factor of 4096. But the salt is stored in plaintext in the same entry as the corresponding ciphertext password. Therefore, those two characters are known to the attacker and need not be guessed. Why is it asserted that the salt increases security?

9.14 Assuming that you have successfully answered the preceding problem and understand the significance of the salt, here is another question. Wouldn't it be possible to thwart completely all password crackers by dramatically increasing the salt size to, say, 24 or 48 bits?

9.15 Consider the Bloom filter discussed in Section 9.3. Define k = number of hash functions; N = number of bits in hash table; and D = number of words in dictionary.

a. Show that the expected number of bits in the hash table that are equal to zero is expressed as

$$\phi = \left(1 - \frac{k}{N}\right)^D$$

b. Show that the probability that an input word, not in the dictionary, will be falsely accepted as being in the dictionary is

$$P = (1 - \phi)^k$$

c. Show that the preceding expression can be approximated as

$$P \approx \left(1 - e^{-kD/N}\right)^k$$

9.16 Design a file access system to allow certain users read and write access to a file, depending on authorization set up by the system. The instructions should be of the format:

READ (F, User A): attempt by User A to read file F
READ (F, User A): attempt by User A to store a possibly modified copy of F

Each file has a *header record*, which contains authorization privileges; that is, a list of users who can read and write. The file is to be encrypted by a key that is not shared by the users but known only to the system.

APPENDIX 9A   THE BASE-RATE FALLACY

We begin with a review of important results from probability theory, then demonstrate the base-rate fallacy.

Conditional Probability and Independence

We often want to know a probability that is conditional on some event. The effect of the condition is to remove some of the outcomes from the sample space. For example, what is the probability of getting a sum of 8 on the roll of two dice, if we know that the face of at least one die is an even number? We can reason as follows. Because one die is even and the sum is even, the second die must show an even number. Thus, there are three equally likely successful outcomes: (2, 6), (4, 4) and (6, 2), out of a total set of possibilities of [36−(number of events with both faces odd)] = 36−(3 × 3) = 27. The resulting probability is 3/27 = 1/9.

Formally, the **conditional probability** of an event A assuming the event B has occurred, denoted by $\Pr[A|B]$, is defined as the ratio

$$\Pr[A \mid B] = \frac{\Pr[AB]}{\Pr[B]}$$

where we assume $\Pr[B]$ is not zero.

In our example, A = {sum of 8} and B = {at least one die even}. The quantity $\Pr[AB]$ encompasses all of those outcomes in which the sum is 8 and at least one die is even. As we have seen, there are three such outcomes. Thus, $\Pr[AB]$ = 3/36 = 1/12. A moment's thought should convince you that $\Pr[B]$ = 3/4. We can now calculate

$$Pr[A \mid B] = \frac{1/12}{3/4} = \frac{1}{9}$$

This agrees with our previous reasoning.

Two events A and B are called **independent** if $Pr[AB] = Pr[A]Pr[B]$. It can easily be seen that if A and B are independent, $Pr[A|B] = Pr[A]$ and $Pr[B|A] = Pr[B]$.

Bayes' Theorem

One of the most important results from probability theory is known as Bayes' theorem. First we need to state the total probability formula. Given a set of mutually exclusive events $E_1, E_2, \ldots, E_n$, such that the union of these events covers all possible outcomes, and given an arbitrary event A, then it can be shown that

$$Pr[A] = \sum_{i=1}^{n} Pr[A|E_i]Pr[E_i] \tag{9.1}$$

Bayes' theorem may be stated as follows:

$$Pr[E_i|A] = \frac{Pr[A|E_i]P[E_i]}{Pr[A]} = \frac{Pr[A|E_i]P[E_i]}{\sum_{j=1}^{n} Pr[A|E_j]Pr[E_j]} \tag{9.2}$$

Figure 9.7a illustrates the concepts of total probability and Bayes' theorem.

Bayes' theorem is used to calculate "posterior odds," that is, the probability that something really is the case, given evidence in favor of it. For example, suppose we are transmitting a sequence of zeroes and ones over a noisy transmission line. Let S0 and S1 be the events a zero is sent at a given time and a one is sent, respectively, and R0 and R1 be the events that a zero is received and a one is received. Suppose we know the probabilities of the source, namely $Pr[S1] = p$ and $Pr[S0] = 1 - p$. Now the line is observed to determine how frequently an error occurs when a one is sent and when a zero is sent, and the following probabilities are calculated: $Pr[R0|S0] = p_a$ and $Pr[R1|S0] = p_b$. If a zero is received, we can then

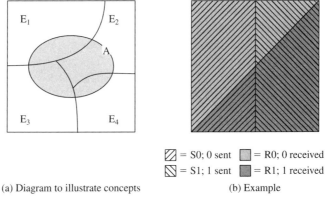

= S0; 0 sent   = R0; 0 received
= S1; 1 sent   = R1; 1 received

(a) Diagram to illustrate concepts   (b) Example

Figure 9.7 Illustration of Total Probability and Bayes' Theorem

calculate the conditional probability of an error, namely the conditional probability that a one was sent given that a zero was received, using Bayes' theorem:

$$\Pr[S1 \mid R0] = \frac{\Pr[R0 \mid S1]\Pr[S1]}{\Pr[R0 \mid S1]\Pr[S1] + \Pr[R0 \mid S0]\Pr[S0]} = \frac{p_a p}{p_a p + (1 - p_b)(1 - p)}$$

Figure 9.7b illustrates the preceding equation. In the figure, the sample space is represented by a unit square. Half of the square corresponds to S0 and half to S1, so $\Pr[S0] = \Pr[S1] = 0.5$. Similarly, half of the square corresponds to R0 and half to R1, so $\Pr[R0] = \Pr[R1] = 0.5$. Within the area representing S0, 1/4 of that area corresponds to R1, so $\Pr[R1/S0] = 0.25$. Other conditional probabilities are similarly evident.

The Base–Rate Fallacy Demonstrated

Consider the following situation. A patient has a test for some disease that comes back positive (indicating he has the disease). You are told that

- The accuracy of the test is 87% (i.e., if a patient has the disease, 87% of the time, the test yields the correct result, and if the patient does not have the disease, 87% of the time, the test yields the correct result).

- The incidence of the disease in the population is 1%.

Given that the test is positive, how probable is it that the patient does not have the disease? That is, what is the probability that this is a false alarm? We need Bayes' theorem to get the correct answer:

$$\Pr[\text{well/positive}] = \frac{\Pr[\text{positive/well}]\Pr[\text{well}]}{\Pr[\text{positive/disease}]\Pr[\text{disease}] + \Pr[\text{positive/well}]\Pr[\text{well}]}$$

$$= \frac{(0.13)(0.99)}{(0.87)(0.01) + (0.13)(0.99)} = 0.937$$

Thus, in the vast majority of cases, when a disease condition is detected, it is a false alarm.

This problem, used in a study [PIAT91], was presented to a number of people. Most subjects gave the answer 13%. The vast majority, including many physicians, gave a number below 50%. Many physicians who guessed wrong lamented, "If you are right, there is no point in making clinical tests!" The reason most people get it wrong is that they do not take into account the basic rate of incidence (the base rate) when intuitively solving the problem. This error is known as the *base-rate fallacy*.

How could this problem be fixed? Suppose we could drive both of the correct result rates to 99.9%. That is, suppose we have $\Pr[\text{positive/disease}] = 0.999$ and $\Pr[\text{negative/well}] = 0.999$. Plugging these numbers into the Equation (9.2), we get $\Pr[\text{well/positive}] = 0.09$. Thus, if we can accurately detect disease and accurately detect lack of disease at a level of 99.9%, then the rate of false alarms will be 9%. This is much better, but still not ideal. Moreover, again assume 99.9% accuracy, but now suppose that the incidence of the disease in the population is only $1/10000 = 0.0001$. We then end up with a rate of false alarms of 91%. In actual situations, [AXEL00] found that the probabilities associated with intrusion detection systems were such that the false alarm rate was unsatisfactory.

MALICIOUS SOFTWARE

What is the concept of defense: The parrying of a blow. What is its characteristic feature: Awaiting the blow.

— *On War*, Carl Von Clausewitz

KEY POINTS

◆ Malicious software is software that is intentionally included or inserted in a system for a harmful purpose.

◆ A virus is a piece of software that can "infect" other programs by modifying them; the modification includes a copy of the virus program, which can then go on to infect other programs.

◆ A worm is a program that can replicate itself and send copies from computer to computer across network connections. Upon arrival, the worm may be activated to replicate and propagate again. In addition to propagation, the worm usually performs some unwanted function.

◆ A denial of service (DoS) attack is an attempt to prevent legitimate users of a service from using that service.

◆ A distributed denial of service attack is launched from multiple coordinated sources.

Perhaps the most sophisticated types of threats to computer systems are presented by programs that exploit vulnerabilities in computing systems. Such threats are referred to as **malicious software**, or **malware**. In this context, we are concerned with threats to application programs as well as utility programs, such as editors and compilers, and kernel-level programs.

This chapter examines malicious software, with a special emphasis on viruses and worms. The chapter begins with a survey of various types of malware, with a more detailed look at the nature of viruses and worms. We then turn to distributed denial-of-service attacks. Throughout, the discussion presents both threats and countermeasures.

10.1 TYPES OF MALICIOUS SOFTWARE

The terminology in this area presents problems because of a lack of universal agreement on all of the terms and because some of the categories overlap. Table 10.1 is a useful guide.

Malicious software can be divided into two categories: those that need a host program, and those that are independent. The former, referred to as **parasitic**, are essentially fragments of programs that cannot exist independently of some actual application program, utility, or system program. Viruses, logic bombs,

Table 10.1 Terminology of Malicious Programs

Name	Description
Virus	Malware that, when executed, tries to replicate itself into other executable code; when it succeeds the code is said to be infected. When the infected code is executed, the virus also executes.
Worm	A computer program that can run independently and can propagate a complete working version of itself onto other hosts on a network.
Logic bomb	A program inserted into software by an intruder. A logic bomb lies dormant until a predefined condition is met; the program then triggers an unauthorized act.
Trojan horse	A computer program that appears to have a useful function, but also has a hidden and potentially malicious function that evades security mechanisms, sometimes by exploiting legitimate authorizations of a system entity that invokes the Trojan horse program.
Backdoor (trapdoor)	Any mechanism that bypasses a normal security check; it may allow unauthorized access to functionality.
Mobile code	Software (e.g., script, macro, or other portable instruction) that can be shipped unchanged to a heterogeneous collection of platforms and execute with identical semantics.
Exploits	Code specific to a single vulnerability or set of vulnerabilities.
Downloaders	Program that installs other items on a machine that is under attack. Usually, a downloader is sent in an e-mail.
Auto-rooter	Malicious hacker tools used to break into new machines remotely.
Kit (virus generator)	Set of tools for generating new viruses automatically.
Spammer programs	Used to send large volumes of unwanted e-mail.
Flooders	Used to attack networked computer systems with a large volume of traffic to carry out a denial-of-service (DoS) attack.
Keyloggers	Captures keystrokes on a compromised system.
Rootkit	Set of hacker tools used after attacker has broken into a computer system and gained root-level access.
Zombie, bot	Program activated on an infected machine that is activated to launch attacks on other machines.
Spyware	Software that collects information from a computer and transmits it to another system.
Adware	Advertising that is integrated into software. It can result in pop-up ads or redirection of a browser to a commercial site.

and backdoors are examples. Independent malware is a self-contained program that can be scheduled and run by the operating system. Worms and bot programs are examples.

We can also differentiate between those software threats that do not replicate and those that do. The former are programs or fragments of programs that are activated by a trigger. Examples are logic bombs, backdoors, and bot programs. The latter consist of either a program fragment or an independent program that, when executed, may produce one or more copies of itself to be activated later on the same system or some other system. Viruses and worms are examples.

In the remainder of this section, we briefly survey some of the key categories of malicious software, deferring discussion on the key topics of viruses and worms until the following sections.

Backdoor

A **backdoor**, also known as a **trapdoor**, is a secret entry point into a program that allows someone who is aware of the backdoor to gain access without going through the usual security access procedures. Programmers have used backdoors legitimately for many years to debug and test programs; such a backdoor is called a **maintenance hook**. This usually is done when the programmer is developing an application that has an authentication procedure, or a long setup, requiring the user to enter many different values to run the application. To debug the program, the developer may wish to gain special privileges or to avoid all the necessary setup and authentication. The programmer may also want to ensure that there is a method of activating the program should something be wrong with the authentication procedure that is being built into the application. The backdoor is code that recognizes some special sequence of input or is triggered by being run from a certain user ID or by an unlikely sequence of events.

Backdoors become threats when unscrupulous programmers use them to gain unauthorized access. The backdoor was the basic idea for the vulnerability portrayed in the movie *War Games*. Another example is that during the development of Multics, penetration tests were conducted by an Air Force "tiger team" (simulating adversaries). One tactic employed was to send a bogus operating system update to a site running Multics. The update contained a Trojan horse (described later) that could be activated by a backdoor and that allowed the tiger team to gain access. The threat was so well implemented that the Multics developers could not find it, even after they were informed of its presence [ENGE80].

It is difficult to implement operating system controls for backdoors. Security measures must focus on the program development and software update activities.

Logic Bomb

One of the oldest types of program threat, predating viruses and worms, is the logic bomb. The logic bomb is code embedded in some legitimate program that is set to "explode" when certain conditions are met. Examples of conditions that can be used as triggers for a logic bomb are the presence or absence of certain files, a particular day of the week or date, or a particular user running the application. Once triggered, a bomb may alter or delete data or entire files, cause a machine halt, or do some other damage. A striking example of how logic bombs can be employed was the case of Tim Lloyd, who was convicted of setting a logic bomb that cost his employer, Omega Engineering, more than $10 million, derailed its corporate growth strategy, and eventually led to the layoff of 80 workers [GAUD00]. Ultimately, Lloyd was sentenced to 41 months in prison and ordered to pay $2 million in restitution.

Trojan Horses

A Trojan horse[1] is a useful, or apparently useful, program or command procedure containing hidden code that, when invoked, performs some unwanted or harmful function.

Trojan horse programs can be used to accomplish functions indirectly that an unauthorized user could not accomplish directly. For example, to gain access to the files of another user on a shared system, a user could create a Trojan horse program that, when executed, changes the invoking user's file permissions so that the files are readable by any user. The author could then induce users to run the program by placing it in a common directory and naming it such that it appears to be a useful utility program or application. An example is a program that ostensibly produces a listing of the user's files in a desirable format. After another user has run the program, the author of the program can then access the information in the user's files. An example of a Trojan horse program that would be difficult to detect is a compiler that has been modified to insert additional code into certain programs as they are compiled, such as a system login program [THOM84]. The code creates a backdoor in the login program that permits the author to log on to the system using a special password. This Trojan horse can never be discovered by reading the source code of the login program.

Another common motivation for the Trojan horse is data destruction. The program appears to be performing a useful function (e.g., a calculator program), but it may also be quietly deleting the user's files. For example, a CBS executive was victimized by a Trojan horse that destroyed all information contained in his computer's memory [TIME90]. The Trojan horse was implanted in a graphics routine offered on an electronic bulletin board system.

Trojan horses fit into one of three models:

- Continuing to perform the function of the original program and additionally performing a separate malicious activity
- Continuing to perform the function of the original program but modifying the function to perform malicious activity (e.g., a Trojan horse version of a login program that collects passwords) or to disguise other malicious activity (e.g., a Trojan horse version of a process listing program that does not display certain processes that are malicious)
- Performing a malicious function that completely replaces the function of the original program

---

[1] In Greek mythology, the Trojan horse was used by the Greeks during their siege of Troy. Epeios constructed a giant hollow wooden horse in which thirty of the most valiant Greek heroes concealed themselves. The rest of the Greeks burned their encampment and pretended to sail away but actually hid nearby. The Trojans, convinced the horse was a gift and the siege over, dragged the horse into the city. That night, the Greeks emerged from the horse and opened the city gates to the Greek army. A blood-bath ensued, resulting in the destruction of Troy and the death or enslavement of all its citizens.

Mobile Code

Mobile code refers to programs (e.g., script, macro, or other portable instruction) that can be shipped unchanged to a heterogeneous collection of platforms and execute with identical semantics [JANS01]. The term also applies to situations involving a large homogeneous collection of platforms (e.g., Microsoft Windows).

Mobile code is transmitted from a remote system to a local system and then executed on the local system without the user's explicit instruction. Mobile code often acts as a mechanism for a virus, worm, or Trojan horse to be transmitted to the user's workstation. In other cases, mobile code takes advantage of vulnerabilities to perform its own exploits, such as unauthorized data access or root compromise. Popular vehicles for mobile code include Java applets, ActiveX, JavaScript, and VBScript. The most common ways of using mobile code for malicious operations on local system are cross-site scripting, interactive and dynamic Web sites, e-mail attachments, and downloads from untrusted sites or of untrusted software.

Multiple-Threat Malware

Viruses and other malware may operate in multiple ways. The terminology is far from uniform; this subsection gives a brief introduction to several related concepts that could be considered multiple-threat malware.

A **multipartite** virus infects in multiple ways. Typically, the multipartite virus is capable of infecting multiple types of files, so that virus eradication must deal with all of the possible sites of infection.

A **blended attack** uses multiple methods of infection or transmission, to maximize the speed of contagion and the severity of the attack. Some writers characterize a blended attack as a package that includes multiple types of malware. An example of a blended attack is the Nimda attack, erroneously referred to as simply a worm. Nimda uses four distribution methods:

- **E-mail:** A user on a vulnerable host opens an infected e-mail attachment; Nimda looks for e-mail addresses on the host and then sends copies of itself to those addresses.

- **Windows shares:** Nimda scans hosts for unsecured Windows file shares; it can then use NetBIOS86 as a transport mechanism to infect files on that host in the hopes that a user will run an infected file, which will activate Nimda on that host.

- **Web servers:** Nimda scans Web servers, looking for known vulnerabilities in Microsoft IIS. If it finds a vulnerable server, it attempts to transfer a copy of itself to the server and infect it and its files.

- **Web clients:** If a vulnerable Web client visits a Web server that has been infected by Nimda, the client's workstation will become infected.

Thus, Nimda has worm, virus, and mobile code characteristics. Blended attacks may also spread through other services, such as instant messaging and peer-to-peer file sharing.

10.2 VIRUSES

The Nature of Viruses

A computer virus is a piece of software that can "infect" other programs by modifying them; the modification includes injecting the original program with a routine to make copies of the virus program, which can then go on to infect other programs. Computer viruses first appeared in the early 1980s, and the term itself is attributed to Fred Cohen in 1983. Cohen is the author of a groundbreaking book on the subject [COHE94].

Biological viruses are tiny scraps of genetic code—DNA or RNA—that can take over the machinery of a living cell and trick it into making thousands of flawless replicas of the original virus. Like its biological counterpart, a computer virus carries in its instructional code the recipe for making perfect copies of itself. The typical virus becomes embedded in a program on a computer. Then, whenever the infected computer comes into contact with an uninfected piece of software, a fresh copy of the virus passes into the new program. Thus, the infection can be spread from computer to computer by unsuspecting users who either swap disks or send programs to one another over a network. In a network environment, the ability to access applications and system services on other computers provides a perfect culture for the spread of a virus.

A virus can do anything that other programs do. The difference is that a virus attaches itself to another program and executes secretly when the host program is run. Once a virus is executing, it can perform any function, such as erasing files and programs that is allowed by the privileges of the current user.

A computer virus has three parts [AYCO06]:

- **Infection mechanism:** The means by which a virus spreads, enabling it to replicate. The mechanism is also referred to as the **infection vector**.
- **Trigger:** The event or condition that determines when the payload is activated or delivered.
- **Payload:** What the virus does, besides spreading. The payload may involve damage or may involve benign but noticeable activity.

During its lifetime, a typical virus goes through the following four phases:

- **Dormant phase:** The virus is idle. The virus will eventually be activated by some event, such as a date, the presence of another program or file, or the capacity of the disk exceeding some limit. Not all viruses have this stage.
- **Propagation phase:** The virus places a copy of itself into other programs or into certain system areas on the disk. The copy may not be identical to the propagating version; viruses often morph to evade detection. Each infected program will now contain a clone of the virus, which will itself enter a propagation phase.
- **Triggering phase:** The virus is activated to perform the function for which it was intended. As with the dormant phase, the triggering phase can be caused by a variety of system events, including a count of the number of times that this copy of the virus has made copies of itself.

- **Execution phase:** The function is performed. The function may be harmless, such as a message on the screen, or damaging, such as the destruction of programs and data files.

Most viruses carry out their work in a manner that is specific to a particular operating system and, in some cases, specific to a particular hardware platform. Thus, they are designed to take advantage of the details and weaknesses of particular systems.

VIRUS STRUCTURE A virus can be prepended or postpended to an executable program, or it can be embedded in some other fashion. The key to its operation is that the infected program, when invoked, will first execute the virus code and then execute the original code of the program.

A very general depiction of virus structure is shown in Figure 10.1 (based on [COHE94]). In this case, the virus code, V, is prepended to infected programs, and it is assumed that the entry point to the program, when invoked, is the first line of the program.

The infected program begins with the virus code and works as follows. The first line of code is a jump to the main virus program. The second line is a special marker that is used by the virus to determine whether or not a potential victim program has already been infected with this virus. When the program is invoked, control is immediately transferred to the main virus program. The virus program may first seek out uninfected executable files and infect them. Next, the virus may perform some action, usually detrimental to the system. This action could be performed every time the program is invoked, or it could be a logic bomb that triggers only under certain conditions. Finally, the virus transfers control to the original program. If the infection

```
        program V :=

{goto main;
       1234567;

       subroutine infect-executable :=
              {loop:
              file := get-random-executable-file;
              if (first-line-of-file = 1234567)
                     then goto loop
                     else prepend V to file; }

       subroutine do-damage :=
              {whatever damage is to be done}

       subroutine trigger-pulled :=
              {return true if some condition holds}

   main:   main-program :=
              {infect-executable;
              if trigger-pulled then do-damage;
              goto next;}
   next:

   }
```

Figure 10.1   A Simple Virus

```
        program CV :=

     {goto main;
         01234567;

         subroutine infect-executable :=
              {loop:
                       file := get-random-executable-file;
                   if (first-line-of-file = 01234567) then goto loop;
              (1)   compress file;
              (2)   prepend CV to file;
              }

     main:   main-program :=
                   {if ask-permission then infect-executable;
              (3)   uncompress rest-of-file;
              (4)   run uncompressed file;}
              }
```

Figure 10.2   Logic for a Compression Virus

phase of the program is reasonably rapid, a user is unlikely to notice any difference between the execution of an infected and an uninfected program.

A virus such as the one just described is easily detected because an infected version of a program is longer than the corresponding uninfected one. A way to thwart such a simple means of detecting a virus is to compress the executable file so that both the infected and uninfected versions are of identical length. Figure 10.2 [COHE94] shows in general terms the logic required. The key lines in this virus are numbered, and Figure 10.3 [COHE94] illustrates the operation. We assume that program P1 is infected with the virus CV. When this program is invoked, control passes to its virus, which performs the following steps:

1. For each uninfected file P_2 that is found, the virus first compresses that file to produce P_2', which is shorter than the original program by the size of the virus.

2. A copy of the virus is prepended to the compressed program.

3. The compressed version of the original infected program, P_1', is uncompressed.

4. The uncompressed original program is executed.

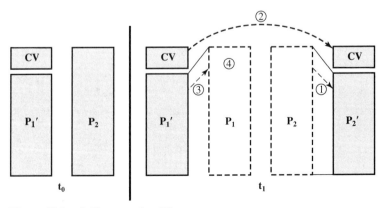

Figure 10.3   A Compression Virus

In this example, the virus does nothing other than propagate. As previously mentioned, the virus may include a logic bomb.

INITIAL INFECTION Once a virus has gained entry to a system by infecting a single program, it is in a position to potentially infect some or all other executable files on that system when the infected program executes. Thus, viral infection can be completely prevented by preventing the virus from gaining entry in the first place. Unfortunately, prevention is extraordinarily difficult because a virus can be part of any program outside a system. Thus, unless one is content to take an absolutely bare piece of iron and write all one's own system and application programs, one is vulnerable. Many forms of infection can also be blocked by denying normal users the right to modify programs on the system.

The lack of access controls on early PCs is a key reason why traditional machine code based viruses spread rapidly on these systems. In contrast, while it is easy enough to write a machine code virus for UNIX systems, they were almost never seen in practice because the existence of access controls on these systems prevented effective propagation of the virus. Traditional machine code based viruses are now less prevalent, because modern PC OSs do have more effective access controls. However, virus creators have found other avenues, such as macro and e-mail viruses, as discussed subsequently.

Viruses Classification

There has been a continuous arms race between virus writers and writers of antivirus software since viruses first appeared. As effective countermeasures are developed for existing types of viruses, newer types are developed. There is no simple or universally agreed upon classification scheme for viruses, In this section, we follow [AYCO06] and classify viruses along two orthogonal axes: the type of target the virus tries to infect and the method the virus uses to conceal itself from detection by users and antivirus software.

A virus **classification by target** includes the following categories:

- **Boot sector infector:** Infects a master boot record or boot record and spreads when a system is booted from the disk containing the virus.
- **File infector:** Infects files that the operating system or shell consider to be executable.
- **Macro virus:** Infects files with macro code that is interpreted by an application.

A virus classification by concealment strategy includes the following categories:

- **Encrypted virus:** A typical approach is as follows. A portion of the virus creates a random encryption key and encrypts the remainder of the virus. The key is stored with the virus. When an infected program is invoked, the virus uses the stored random key to decrypt the virus. When the virus replicates, a different random key is selected. Because the bulk of the virus is encrypted with a different key for each instance, there is no constant bit pattern to observe.

- **Stealth virus:** A form of virus explicitly designed to hide itself from detection by antivirus software. Thus, the entire virus, not just a payload is hidden.
- **Polymorphic virus:** A virus that mutates with every infection, making detection by the "signature" of the virus impossible.
- **Metamorphic virus:** As with a polymorphic virus, a metamorphic virus mutates with every infection. The difference is that a metamorphic virus rewrites itself completely at each iteration, increasing the difficulty of detection. Metamorphic viruses may change their behavior as well as their appearance.

One example of a **stealth virus** was discussed earlier: a virus that uses compression so that the infected program is exactly the same length as an uninfected version. Far more sophisticated techniques are possible. For example, a virus can place intercept logic in disk I/O routines, so that when there is an attempt to read suspected portions of the disk using these routines, the virus will present back the original, uninfected program. Thus, *stealth* is not a term that applies to a virus as such but, rather, refers to a technique used by a virus to evade detection.

A **polymorphic virus** creates copies during replication that are functionally equivalent but have distinctly different bit patterns. As with a stealth virus, the purpose is to defeat programs that scan for viruses. In this case, the "signature" of the virus will vary with each copy. To achieve this variation, the virus may randomly insert superfluous instructions or interchange the order of independent instructions. A more effective approach is to use encryption. The strategy of the encryption virus is followed. The portion of the virus that is responsible for generating keys and performing encryption/decryption is referred to as the *mutation engine*. The mutation engine itself is altered with each use.

Virus Kits

Another weapon in the virus writers' armory is the virus-creation toolkit. Such a toolkit enables a relative novice to quickly create a number of different viruses. Although viruses created with toolkits tend to be less sophisticated than viruses designed from scratch, the sheer number of new viruses that can be generated using a toolkit creates a problem for antivirus schemes.

Macro Viruses

In the mid-1990s, macro viruses became by far the most prevalent type of virus. Macro viruses are particularly threatening for a number of reasons:

1. A macro virus is platform independent. Many macro viruses infect Microsoft Word documents or other Microsoft Office documents. Any hardware platform and operating system that supports these applications can be infected.
2. Macro viruses infect documents, not executable portions of code. Most of the information introduced onto a computer system is in the form of a document rather than a program.
3. Macro viruses are easily spread. A very common method is by electronic mail.
4. Because macro viruses infect user documents rather than system programs, traditional file system access controls are of limited use in preventing their spread.

Macro viruses take advantage of a feature found in Word and other office applications such as Microsoft Excel, namely the macro. In essence, a macro is an executable program embedded in a word processing document or other type of file. Typically, users employ macros to automate repetitive tasks and thereby save keystrokes. The macro language is usually some form of the Basic programming language. A user might define a sequence of keystrokes in a macro and set it up so that the macro is invoked when a function key or special short combination of keys is input.

Successive releases of MS Office products provide increased protection against macro viruses. For example, Microsoft offers an optional Macro Virus Protection tool that detects suspicious Word files and alerts the customer to the potential risk of opening a file with macros. Various antivirus product vendors have also developed tools to detect and correct macro viruses. As in other types of viruses, the arms race continues in the field of macro viruses, but they no longer are the predominant virus threat.

E-Mail Viruses

A more recent development in malicious software is the e-mail virus. The first rapidly spreading e-mail viruses, such as Melissa, made use of a Microsoft Word macro embedded in an attachment. If the recipient opens the e-mail attachment, the Word macro is activated. Then

1. The e-mail virus sends itself to everyone on the mailing list in the user's e-mail package.
2. The virus does local damage on the user's system.

In 1999, a more powerful version of the e-mail virus appeared. This newer version can be activated merely by opening an e-mail that contains the virus rather than opening an attachment. The virus uses the Visual Basic scripting language supported by the e-mail package.

Thus we see a new generation of malware that arrives via e-mail and uses e-mail software features to replicate itself across the Internet. The virus propagates itself as soon as it is activated (either by opening an e-mail attachment or by opening the e-mail) to all of the e-mail addresses known to the infected host. As a result, whereas viruses used to take months or years to propagate, they now do so in hours. This makes it very difficult for antivirus software to respond before much damage is done. Ultimately, a greater degree of security must be built into Internet utility and application software on PCs to counter the growing threat.

10.3 VIRUS COUNTERMEASURES

Antivirus Approaches

The ideal solution to the threat of viruses is prevention: Do not allow a virus to get into the system in the first place, or block the ability of a virus to modify any files containing executable code or macros. This goal is, in general, impossible to achieve, although prevention can reduce the number of successful viral attacks. The next best approach is to be able to do the following:

- **Detection:** Once the infection has occurred, determine that it has occurred and locate the virus.
- **Identification:** Once detection has been achieved, identify the specific virus that has infected a program.
- **Removal:** Once the specific virus has been identified, remove all traces of the virus from the infected program and restore it to its original state. Remove the virus from all infected systems so that the virus cannot spread further.

If detection succeeds but either identification or removal is not possible, then the alternative is to discard the infected file and reload a clean backup version.

Advances in virus and antivirus technology go hand in hand. Early viruses were relatively simple code fragments and could be identified and purged with relatively simple antivirus software packages. As the virus arms race has evolved, both viruses and, necessarily, antivirus software have grown more complex and sophisticated.

[STEP93] identifies four generations of antivirus software:

- First generation: simple scanners
- Second generation: heuristic scanners
- Third generation: activity traps
- Fourth generation: full-featured protection

A **first-generation** scanner requires a virus signature to identify a virus. The virus may contain "wildcards" but has essentially the same structure and bit pattern in all copies. Such signature-specific scanners are limited to the detection of known viruses. Another type of first-generation scanner maintains a record of the length of programs and looks for changes in length.

A **second-generation** scanner does not rely on a specific signature. Rather, the scanner uses heuristic rules to search for probable virus infection. One class of such scanners looks for fragments of code that are often associated with viruses. For example, a scanner may look for the beginning of an encryption loop used in a polymorphic virus and discover the encryption key. Once the key is discovered, the scanner can decrypt the virus to identify it, then remove the infection and return the program to service.

Another second-generation approach is integrity checking. A checksum can be appended to each program. If a virus infects the program without changing the checksum, then an integrity check will catch the change. To counter a virus that is sophisticated enough to change the checksum when it infects a program, an encrypted hash function can be used. The encryption key is stored separately from the program so that the virus cannot generate a new hash code and encrypt that. By using a hash function rather than a simpler checksum, the virus is prevented from adjusting the program to produce the same hash code as before.

Third-generation programs are memory-resident programs that identify a virus by its actions rather than its structure in an infected program. Such programs have the advantage that it is not necessary to develop signatures and heuristics for a wide array of viruses. Rather, it is necessary only to identify the small set of actions that indicate an infection is being attempted and then to intervene.

Fourth-generation products are packages consisting of a variety of antivirus techniques used in conjunction. These include scanning and activity trap components. In addition, such a package includes access control capability, which limits the ability of viruses to penetrate a system and then limits the ability of a virus to update files in order to pass on the infection.

The arms race continues. With fourth-generation packages, a more comprehensive defense strategy is employed, broadening the scope of defense to more general-purpose computer security measures.

Advanced Antivirus Techniques

More sophisticated antivirus approaches and products continue to appear. In this subsection, we highlight some of the most important.

GENERIC DECRYPTION Generic decryption (GD) technology enables the antivirus program to easily detect even the most complex polymorphic viruses while maintaining fast scanning speeds [NACH97]. Recall that when a file containing a polymorphic virus is executed, the virus must decrypt itself to activate. In order to detect such a structure, executable files are run through a GD scanner, which contains the following elements:

- **CPU emulator:** A software-based virtual computer. Instructions in an executable file are interpreted by the emulator rather than executed on the underlying processor. The emulator includes software versions of all registers and other processor hardware, so that the underlying processor is unaffected by programs interpreted on the emulator.
- **Virus signature scanner:** A module that scans the target code looking for known virus signatures.
- **Emulation control module:** Controls the execution of the target code.

At the start of each simulation, the emulator begins interpreting instructions in the target code, one at a time. Thus, if the code includes a decryption routine that decrypts and hence exposes the virus, that code is interpreted. In effect, the virus does the work for the antivirus program by exposing the virus. Periodically, the control module interrupts interpretation to scan the target code for virus signatures.

During interpretation, the target code can cause no damage to the actual personal computer environment, because it is being interpreted in a completely controlled environment.

The most difficult design issue with a GD scanner is to determine how long to run each interpretation. Typically, virus elements are activated soon after a program begins executing, but this need not be the case. The longer the scanner emulates a particular program, the more likely it is to catch any hidden viruses. However, the antivirus program can take up only a limited amount of time and resources before users complain of degraded system performance.

DIGITAL IMMUNE SYSTEM The digital immune system is a comprehensive approach to virus protection developed by IBM [KEPH97a, KEPH97b, WHIT99] and subsequently refined by Symantec [SYMA01]. The motivation for this development has been the rising threat of Internet-based virus propagation. We first say a few words about this threat and then summarize IBM's approach.

Traditionally, the virus threat was characterized by the relatively slow spread of new viruses and new mutations. Antivirus software was typically updated on a monthly basis, and this was sufficient to control the problem. Also traditionally, the Internet played a comparatively small role in the spread of viruses. But as [CHES97] points out, two major trends in Internet technology have had an increasing impact on the rate of virus propagation in recent years:

- **Integrated mail systems:** Systems such as Lotus Notes and Microsoft Outlook make it very simple to send anything to anyone and to work with objects that are received.
- **Mobile-program systems:** Capabilities such as Java and ActiveX allow programs to move on their own from one system to another.

In response to the threat posed by these Internet-based capabilities, IBM has developed a prototype digital immune system. This system expands on the use of program emulation discussed in the preceding subsection and provides a general-purpose emulation and virus-detection system. The objective of this system is to provide rapid response time so that viruses can be stamped out almost as soon as they are introduced. When a new virus enters an organization, the immune system automatically captures it, analyzes it, adds detection and shielding for it, removes it, and passes information about that virus to systems running IBM AntiVirus so that it can be detected before it is allowed to run elsewhere.

Figure 10.4 illustrates the typical steps in digital immune system operation:

1. A monitoring program on each PC uses a variety of heuristics based on system behavior, suspicious changes to programs, or family signature to infer that a virus may be present. The monitoring program forwards a copy of any program thought to be infected to an administrative machine within the organization.
2. The administrative machine encrypts the sample and sends it to a central virus analysis machine.
3. This machine creates an environment in which the infected program can be safely run for analysis. Techniques used for this purpose include emulation, or the creation of a protected environment within which the suspect program can be executed and monitored. The virus analysis machine then produces a prescription for identifying and removing the virus.
4. The resulting prescription is sent back to the administrative machine.
5. The administrative machine forwards the prescription to the infected client.
6. The prescription is also forwarded to other clients in the organization.
7. Subscribers around the world receive regular antivirus updates that protect them from the new virus.

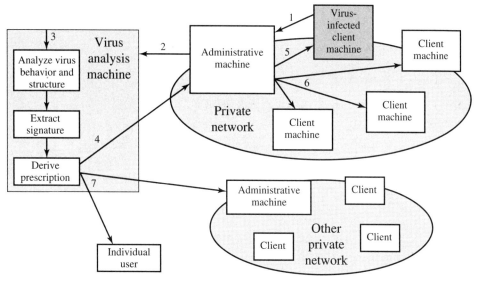

Figure 10.4   Digital Immune System

The success of the digital immune system depends on the ability of the virus analysis machine to detect new and innovative virus strains. By constantly analyzing and monitoring the viruses found in the wild, it should be possible to continually update the digital immune software to keep up with the threat.

BEHAVIOR-BLOCKING SOFTWARE   Unlike heuristics or fingerprint-based scanners, behavior-blocking software integrates with the operating system of a host computer and monitors program behavior in real-time for malicious actions [CONR02, NACH02]. The behavior blocking software then blocks potentially malicious actions before they have a chance to affect the system. Monitored behaviors can include

- Attempts to open, view, delete, and/or modify files;
- Attempts to format disk drives and other unrecoverable disk operations;
- Modifications to the logic of executable files or macros;
- Modification of critical system settings, such as start-up settings;
- Scripting of e-mail and instant messaging clients to send executable content; and
- Initiation of network communications.

Figure 10.5 illustrates the operation of a behavior blocker. Behavior-blocking software runs on server and desktop computers and is instructed through policies set by the network administrator to let benign actions take place but to intercede when unauthorized or suspicious actions occur. The module blocks any suspicious software from executing. A blocker isolates the code in a sandbox, which restricts the code's access to various OS resources and applications. The blocker then sends an alert.

Because a behavior blocker can block suspicious software in real-time, it has an advantage over such established antivirus detection techniques as fingerprinting or

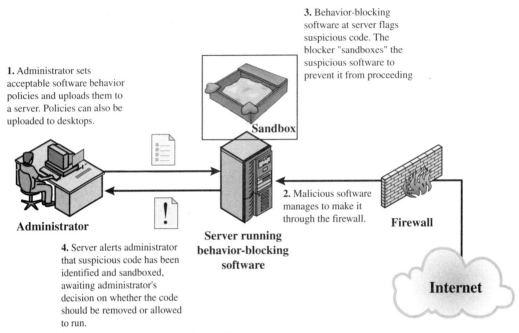

3. Behavior-blocking software at server flags suspicious code. The blocker "sandboxes" the suspicious software to prevent it from proceeding

1. Administrator sets acceptable software behavior policies and uploads them to a server. Policies can also be uploaded to desktops.

Sandbox

Administrator

2. Malicious software manages to make it through the firewall.

Firewall

4. Server alerts administrator that suspicious code has been identified and sandboxed, awaiting administrator's decision on whether the code should be removed or allowed to run.

Server running behavior-blocking software

Internet

Figure 10.5   Behavior-Blocking Software Operation

heuristics. While there are literally trillions of different ways to obfuscate and rearrange the instructions of a virus or worm, many of which will evade detection by a fingerprint scanner or heuristic, eventually malicious code must make a well-defined request to the operating system. Given that the behavior blocker can intercept all such requests, it can identify and block malicious actions regardless of how obfuscated the program logic appears to be.

Behavior blocking alone has limitations. Because the malicious code must run on the target machine before all its behaviors can be identified, it can cause harm before it has been detected and blocked. For example, a new virus might shuffle a number of seemingly unimportant files around the hard drive before infecting a single file and being blocked. Even though the actual infection was blocked, the user may be unable to locate his or her files, causing a loss to productivity or possibly worse.

10.4 WORMS

A worm is a program that can replicate itself and send copies from computer to computer across network connections. Upon arrival, the worm may be activated to replicate and propagate again. In addition to propagation, the worm usually performs some unwanted function. An e-mail virus has some of the characteristics of a worm because it propagates itself from system to system. However, we can still classify it as a virus because it uses a document modified to contain viral macro content and requires human action. A worm actively seeks out more machines to infect and each machine that is infected serves as an automated launching pad for attacks on other machines.

The concept of a computer worm was introduced in John Brunner's 1975 SF novel *The Shockwave Rider*. The first known worm implementation was done in Xerox Palo Alto Labs in the early 1980s. It was nonmalicious, searching for idle systems to use to run a computationally intensive task.

Network worm programs use network connections to spread from system to system. Once active within a system, a network worm can behave as a computer virus or bacteria, or it could implant Trojan horse programs or perform any number of disruptive or destructive actions.

To replicate itself, a network worm uses some sort of network vehicle. Examples include the following:

- **Electronic mail facility:** A worm mails a copy of itself to other systems, so that its code is run when the e-mail or an attachment is received or viewed.
- **Remote execution capability:** A worm executes a copy of itself on another system, either using an explicit remote execution facility or by exploiting a program flaw in a network service to subvert its operations.
- **Remote login capability:** A worm logs onto a remote system as a user and then uses commands to copy itself from one system to the other, where it then executes.

The new copy of the worm program is then run on the remote system where, in addition to any functions that it performs at that system, it continues to spread in the same fashion.

A network worm exhibits the same characteristics as a computer virus: a dormant phase, a propagation phase, a triggering phase, and an execution phase. The propagation phase generally performs the following functions:

1. Search for other systems to infect by examining host tables or similar reposi-tories of remote system addresses.
2. Establish a connection with a remote system.
3. Copy itself to the remote system and cause the copy to be run.

The network worm may also attempt to determine whether a system has previously been infected before copying itself to the system. In a multiprogramming system, it may also disguise its presence by naming itself as a system process or using some other name that may not be noticed by a system operator.

As with viruses, network worms are difficult to counter.

The Morris Worm

Until the current generation of worms, the best known was the worm released onto the Internet by Robert Morris in 1988 [ORMA03]. The Morris worm was designed to spread on UNIX systems and used a number of different techniques for propagation.

When a copy began execution, its first task was to discover other hosts known to this host that would allow entry from this host. The worm performed this task by examining a variety of lists and tables, including system tables that declared which other machines were trusted by this host, users' mail forwarding files, tables by which users gave themselves permission for access to remote accounts, and from a program that reported the status of network connections. For each discovered host, the worm tried a number of methods for gaining access:

1. It attempted to log on to a remote host as a legitimate user. In this method, the worm first attempted to crack the local password file and then used the discovered passwords and corresponding user IDs. The assumption was that many users would use the same password on different systems. To obtain the passwords, the worm ran a password-cracking program that tried

   a. Each user's account name and simple permutations of it
   b. A list of 432 built-in passwords that Morris thought to be likely candidates[2]
   c. All the words in the local system dictionary

2. It exploited a bug in the UNIX finger protocol, which reports the whereabouts of a remote user.

3. It exploited a trapdoor in the debug option of the remote process that receives and sends mail.

If any of these attacks succeeded, the worm achieved communication with the operating system command interpreter. It then sent this interpreter a short bootstrap program, issued a command to execute that program, and then logged off. The bootstrap program then called back the parent program and downloaded the remainder of the worm. The new worm was then executed.

Worm Propagation Model

[ZOU05] describes a model for worm propagation based on an analysis of recent worm attacks. The speed of propagation and the total number of hosts infected depend on a number of factors, including the mode of propagation, the vulnerability or vulnerabilities exploited, and the degree of similarity to preceding attacks. For the latter factor, an attack that is a variation of a recent previous attack may be countered more effectively than a more novel attack. Figure 10.6 shows the dynamics for one typical set of parameters. Propagation proceeds through three phases. In the initial phase, the number of hosts increases exponentially. To see that this is so, consider a simplified case in which a worm is launched from a single host and infects two nearby hosts. Each of these hosts infects two more hosts, and so on. This results in exponential growth. After a time, infecting hosts waste some time attacking already infected hosts, which reduces the rate of infection. During this middle phase, growth is approximately linear, but the rate of infection is rapid. When most vulnerable computers have been infected, the attack enters a slow finish phase as the worm seeks out those remaining hosts that are difficult to identify.

---

[2]The complete list is provided at this book's Web site.

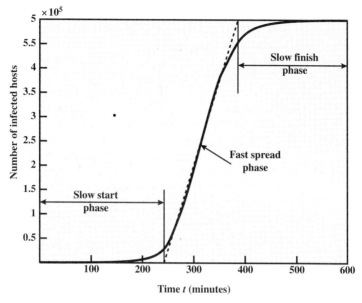

Figure 10.6   Worm Propagation Model

Clearly, the objective in countering a worm is to catch the worm in its slow start phase, at a time when few hosts have been infected.

Recent Worm Attacks

The contemporary era of worm threats began with the release of the Code Red worm in July of 2001. Code Red exploits a security hole in the Microsoft Internet Information Server (IIS) to penetrate and spread. It also disables the system file checker in Windows. The worm probes random IP addresses to spread to other hosts. During a certain period of time, it only spreads. It then initiates a denial-of-service attack against a government Web site by flooding the site with packets from numerous hosts. The worm then suspends activities and reactivates periodically. In the second wave of attack, Code Red infected nearly 360,000 servers in 14 hours. In addition to the havoc it caused at the targeted server, Code Red consumed enormous amounts of Internet capacity, disrupting service.

Code Red II is a variant that targets Microsoft IISs. In addition, this newer worm installs a backdoor, allowing a hacker to remotely execute commands on victim computers.

In early 2003, the SQL Slammer worm appeared. This worm exploited a buffer overflow vulnerability in Microsoft SQL server. The Slammer was extremely compact and spread rapidly, infecting 90% of vulnerable hosts within 10 minutes. Late 2003 saw the arrival of the Sobig.f worm, which exploited open proxy servers to turn infected machines into spam engines. At its peak, Sobig.f reportedly accounted for one in every 17 messages and produced more than one million copies of itself within the first 24 hours.

Mydoom is a mass-mailing e-mail worm that appeared in 2004. It followed a growing trend of installing a backdoor in infected computers, thereby enabling hackers to gain remote access to data such as passwords and credit card numbers. Mydoom replicated up to 1000 times per minute and reportedly flooded the Internet with 100 million infected messages in 36 hours.

A recent worm that rapidly became prevalent in a variety of versions is the Warezov family of worms [KIRK06]. When the worm is launched, it creates several executable in system directories and sets itself to run every time Windows starts, by creating a registry entry. Warezov scans several types of files for e-mail addresses and sends itself as an e-mail attachment. Some variants are capable of downloading other malware, such as Trojan horses and adware. Many variants disable security-related products and/or disable their updating capability.

State of Worm Technology

The state of the art in worm technology includes the following:

- **Multiplatform:** Newer worms are not limited to Windows machines but can attack a variety of platforms, especially the popular varieties of UNIX.
- **Multi-exploit:** New worms penetrate systems in a variety of ways, using exploits against Web servers, browsers, e-mail, file sharing, and other network-based applications.
- **Ultrafast spreading:** One technique to accelerate the spread of a worm is to conduct a prior Internet scan to accumulate Internet addresses of vulnerable machines.
- **Polymorphic:** To evade detection, skip past filters, and foil real-time analysis, worms adopt the virus polymorphic technique. Each copy of the worm has new code generated on the fly using functionally equivalent instructions and encryption techniques.
- **Metamorphic:** In addition to changing their appearance, metamorphic worms have a repertoire of behavior patterns that are unleashed at different stages of propagation.
- **Transport vehicles:** Because worms can rapidly compromise a large number of systems, they are ideal for spreading other distributed attack tools, such as distributed denial of service bots.
- **Zero-day exploit:** To achieve maximum surprise and distribution, a worm should exploit an unknown vulnerability that is only discovered by the general network community when the worm is launched.

Mobile Phone Worms

Worms first appeared on mobile phones in 2004. These worms communicate through Bluetooth wireless connections or via the multimedia messaging service (MMS). The target is the smartphone, which is a mobile phone that permits users to install software applications from sources other than the cellular network operator. Mobile phone malware can completely disable the phone, delete data on the phone, or force the device to send costly messages to premium-priced numbers.

An example of a mobile phone worm is CommWarrior, which was launched in 2005. This worm replicates by means of Bluetooth to other phones in the receiving area. It also sends itself as an MMS file to numbers in the phone's address book and in automatic replies to incoming text messages and MMS messages. In addition, it copies itself to the removable memory card and inserts itself into the program installation files on the phone.

Worm Countermeasures

There is considerable overlap in techniques for dealing with viruses and worms. Once a worm is resident on a machine, antivirus software can be used to detect it. In addition, because worm propagation generates considerable network activity, network activity and usage monitoring can form the basis of a worm defense.

To begin, let us consider the requirements for an effective worm countermeasure scheme:

- **Generality:** The approach taken should be able to handle a wide variety of worm attacks, including polymorphic worms.
- **Timeliness:** The approach should respond quickly so as to limit the number of infected systems and the number of generated transmissions from infected systems.
- **Resiliency:** The approach should be resistant to evasion techniques employed by attackers to evade worm countermeasures.
- **Minimal denial-of-service costs:** The approach should result in minimal reduction in capacity or service due to the actions of the countermeasure software. That is, in an attempt to contain worm propagation, the countermeasure should not significantly disrupt normal operation.
- **Transparency:** The countermeasure software and devices should not require modification to existing (legacy) OSs, application software, and hardware.
- **Global and local coverage:** The approach should be able to deal with attack sources both from outside and inside the enterprise network.

No existing worm countermeasure scheme appears to satisfy all these requirements. Thus, administrators typically need to use multiple approaches in defending against worm attacks.

COUNTERMEASURE APPROACHES Following [JHI07], we list six classes of worm defense:

- A. **Signature-based worm scan filtering:** This type of approach generates a worm signature, which is then used to prevent worm scans from entering/leaving a network/host. Typically, this approach involves identifying suspicious flows and generating a worm signature. This approach is vulnerable to the use of polymorphic worms: Either the detection software misses the worm or, if it is sufficiently sophisticated to deal with polymorphic worms, the scheme may take a long time to react. [NEWS05] is an example of this approach.
- B. **Filter-based worm containment:** This approach is similar to class A but focuses on worm content rather than a scan signature. The filter checks a message to

determine if it contains worm code. An example is Vigilante [COST05], which relies on collaborative worm detection at end hosts. This approach can be quite effective but requires efficient detection algorithms and rapid alert dissemination.

C. **Payload-classification-based worm containment:** These network-based techniques examine packets to see if they contain a worm. Various anomaly detection techniques can be used, but care is needed to avoid high levels of false positives or negatives. An example of this approach is reported in [CHIN05], which looks for exploit code in network flows. This approach does not generate signatures based on byte patterns but rather looks for control and data flow structures that suggest an exploit.

D. **Threshold random walk (TRW) scan detection:** TRW exploits randomness in picking destinations to connect to as a way of detecting if a scanner is in operation [JUNG04]. TRW is suitable for deployment in high-speed, low-cost network devices. It is effective against the common behavior seen in worm scans.

E. **Rate limiting:** This class limits the rate of scanlike traffic from an infected host. Various strategies can be used, including limiting the number of new machines a host can connect to in a window of time, detecting a high connection failure rate, and limiting the number of unique IP addresses a host can scan in a window of time. [CHEN04] is an example. This class of countermeasures may introduce longer delays for normal traffic. This class is also not suited for slow, stealthy worms that spread slowly to avoid detection based on activity level.

F. **Rate halting:** This approach immediately blocks outgoing traffic when a threshold is exceeded either in outgoing connection rate or diversity of connection attempts [JHI07]. The approach must include measures to quickly unblock mistakenly blocked hosts in a transparent way. Rate halting can integrate with a signature- or filter-based approach so that once a signature or filter is generated, every blocked host can be unblocked. Rate halting appears to offer a very effective countermeasure. As with rate limiting, rate halting techniques are not suitable for slow, stealthy worms.

We look now at two approaches in more detail.

PROACTIVE WORM CONTAINMENT The PWC scheme [JHI07] is host based rather than being based on network devices such as honeypots, firewalls, and network IDSs. PWC is designed to address the threat of worms that spread rapidly. The software on a host looks for surges in the rate of frequency of outgoing connection attempts and the diversity of connections to remote hosts. When such a surge is detected, the software immediately blocks its host from further connection attempts. The developers estimate that only a few dozen infected packets may be sent out to other systems before PWC quarantines that attack. In contrast, the Slammer worm on average sent out 4000 infected packets per second.

A deployed PWC system consists of a PWC manager and PWC agents in hosts. Figure 10.7 is an example of an architecture that includes PWC. In this example, the security manager, signature extractor, and PWC manager are implemented in a single network device. In practice, these three modules could be implemented as two or three separate devices.

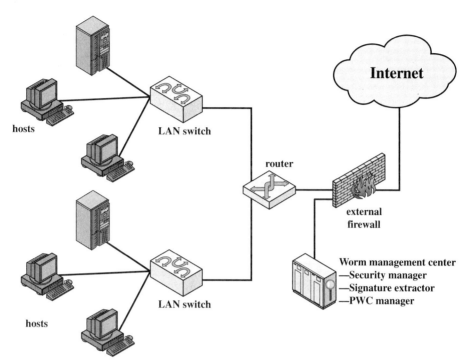

Figure 10.7 Example PWC Deployment

The operation of the PWC architecture can be described as follows:

A. A PWC agent monitors outgoing traffic for scan activity, determined by a surge in UDP or TCP connection attempts to remote hosts. If a surge is detected, the agent performs the following actions: (1) issues an alert to local system; (2) blocks all outgoing connection attempts; (3) transmits the alert to the PWC manager; and (4) starts a relaxation analysis, described in D.

B. A PWC manager receives an alert. The PWC propagates the alert to all other agents (beside the originating agent).

C. The host receives an alert. The agent must decide whether to ignore the alert, in the following way. If the time since the last incoming packet has been sufficiently long so that the agent would have detected a worm if infected, then the alert is ignored. Otherwise, the agent assumes that it might be infected and performs the following actions: (1) blocks all outgoing connection attempts from the specific alerting port; and (2) starts a relaxation analysis, described in D.

D. Relaxation analysis is performed as follows. An agent monitors outgoing activity for a fixed window of time to see if outgoing connections exceed a threshold. If so, blockage is continued and relaxation analysis is performed for another window of time. This process continues until the outgoing connection rate drops below the threshold, at which time the agent removes the block. If the threshold continues to be exceeded over a sufficient number of relaxation windows, the agent isolates the host and reports to the PWC manager.

Meanwhile, a separate aspect of the worm defense system is in operation. The signature extractor functions as a passive sensor that monitors all traffic and attempts to detect worms by signature analysis. When a new worm is detected, its signature is sent by the security manager to the firewall to filter out any more copies of the worm. In addition, the PWC manager sends the signature to PWC agents, enabling them to immediately recognize infection and disable the worm.

NETWORK-BASED WORM DEFENSE The key element of a network-based worm defense is worm monitoring software. Consider an enterprise network at a site, consisting of one or an interconnected set of LANs. Two types of monitoring software are needed:

- **Ingress monitors:** These are located at the border between the enterprise network and the Internet. They can be part of the ingress filtering software of a border router or external firewall or a separate passive monitor. A honeypot can also capture incoming worm traffic. An example of a detection technique for an ingress monitor is to look for incoming traffic to unused local IP addresses.

- **Egress monitors:** These can be located at the egress point of individual LANs on the enterprise network as well as at the border between the enterprise network and the Internet. In the former case, the egress monitor can be part of the egress filtering software of a LAN router or switch. As with ingress monitors, the external firewall or a honeypot can house the monitoring software. Indeed, the two types of monitors can be collocated. The egress monitor is designed to catch the source of a worm attack by monitoring outgoing traffic for signs of scanning or other suspicious behavior.

Worm monitors can act in the manner of intrusion detection systems and generate alerts to a central administrative system. It is also possible to implement a system that attempts to react in real time to a worm attack, so as to counter zero-day exploits effectively. This is similar to the approach taken with the digital immune system (Figure 10.4).

Figure 10.8 shows an example of a worm countermeasure architecture [SIDI05]. The system works as follows (numbers in figure refer to numbers in the following list):

1. Sensors deployed at various network locations detect a potential worm. The sensor logic can also be incorporated in IDS sensors.

2. The sensors send alerts to a central server that correlates and analyzes the incoming alerts. The correlation server determines the likelihood that a worm attack is being observed and the key characteristics of the attack.

3. The server forwards its information to a protected environment, where the potential worm may be sandboxed for analysis and testing.

4. The protected system tests the suspicious software against an appropriately instrumented version of the targeted application to identify the vulnerability.

5. The protected system generates one or more software patches and tests these.

6. If the patch is not susceptible to the infection and does not compromise the application's functionality, the system sends the patch to the application host to update the targeted application.

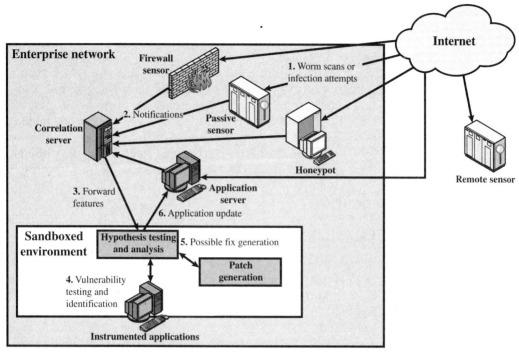

Figure 10.8 Placement of Worm Monitors

The success of such an automated patching system depends on maintaining a current list of potential attacks and developing general tools for patching software to counter such attacks. Examples of approaches are as follows:

- Increasing the size of buffers
- Using minor code-randomization techniques [BHAT03] so that the infection no longer works because the code to be attacked is no longer in the same form and location
- Adding filters to the application that enable it to recognize and ignore an attack

10.5 DISTRIBUTED DENIAL OF SERVICE ATTACKS

Distributed denial of service (DDoS) attacks present a significant security threat to corporations, and the threat appears to be growing [VIJA02]. In one study, covering a three-week period in 2001, investigators observed more than 12,000 attacks against more than 5000 distinct targets, ranging from well-known ecommerce companies such as Amazon and Hotmail to small foreign ISPs and dial-up connections [MOOR01]. DDoS attacks make computer systems inaccessible by flooding servers, networks, or even end user systems with useless traffic so that legitimate users can no longer gain access to those resources. In a typical DDoS attack, a large number of compromised hosts are amassed to send useless packets. In recent years, the attack methods and tools have become more sophisticated, effective, and more difficult to trace to the real attackers, while defense technologies have been unable to withstand large-scale attacks [CHAN02].

A denial of service (DoS) attack is an attempt to prevent legitimate users of a service from using that service. When this attack comes from a single host or network node, then it is simply referred to as a DoS attack. A more serious threat is posed by a DDoS attack. In a DDoS attack, an attacker is able to recruit a number of hosts throughout the Internet to simultaneously or in a coordinated fashion launch an attack upon the target. This section is concerned with DDoS attacks. First, we look at the nature and types of attacks. Next, we examine means by which an attacker is able to recruit a network of hosts for attack launch. Finally, this section looks at countermeasures.

DDoS Attack Description

A DDoS attack attempts to consume the target's resources so that it cannot provide service. One way to classify DDoS attacks is in terms of the type of resource that is consumed. Broadly speaking, the resource consumed is either an internal host resource on the target system or data transmission capacity in the local network to which the target is attacked.

A simple example of an **internal resource attack** is the SYN flood attack. Figure 10.9a shows the steps involved:

1. The attacker takes control of multiple hosts over the Internet, instructing them to contact the target Web server.

2. The slave hosts begin sending TCP/IP SYN (synchronize/initialization) packets, with erroneous return IP address information, to the target.

3. Each SYN packet is a request to open a TCP connection. For each such packet, the Web server responds with a SYN/ACK (synchronize/acknowledge) packet, trying to establish a TCP connection with a TCP entity at a spurious IP address. The Web server maintains a data structure for each SYN request waiting for a response back and becomes bogged down as more traffic floods in. The result is that legitimate connections are denied while the victim machine is waiting to complete bogus "half-open" connections.

The TCP state data structure is a popular internal resource target but by no means the only one. [CERT01] gives the following examples:

1. In many systems, a limited number of data structures are available to hold process information (process identifiers, process table entries, process slots, etc.). An intruder may be able to consume these data structures by writing a simple program or script that does nothing but repeatedly create copies of itself.

2. An intruder may also attempt to consume disk space in other ways, including
   - generating excessive numbers of mail messages
   - intentionally generating errors that must be logged
   - placing files in anonymous ftp areas or network-shared areas

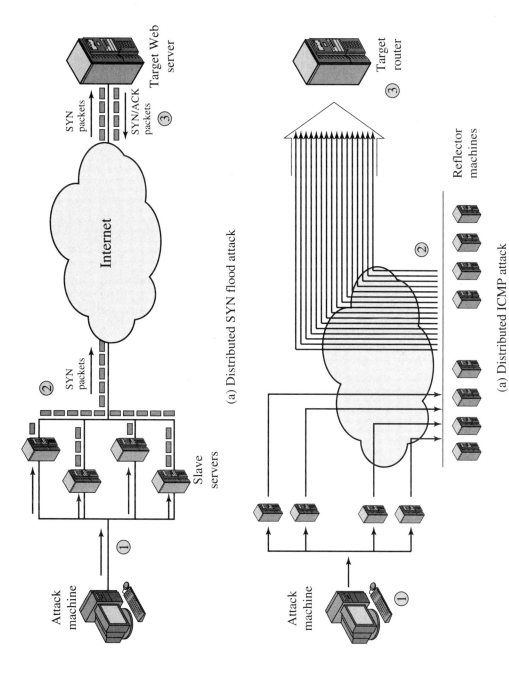

(a) Distributed SYN flood attack

(a) Distributed ICMP attack

Figure 10.9 Examples of Simple DDoS Attacks

381

Figure 10.9b illustrates an example of an **attack that consumes data transmission resources**. The following steps are involved:

1. The attacker takes control of multiple hosts over the Internet, instructing them to send ICMP ECHO packets[3] with the target's spoofed IP address to a group of hosts that act as reflectors, as described subsequently.

2. Nodes at the bounce site receive multiple spoofed requests and respond by sending echo reply packets to the target site.

3. The target's router is flooded with packets from the bounce site, leaving no data transmission capacity for legitimate traffic.

Another way to classify DDoS attacks is as either direct or reflector DDoS attacks. In a **direct DDoS** attack (Figure 10.10a), the attacker is able to implant zombie software on a number of sites distributed throughout the Internet. Often, the DDoS attack involves two levels of zombie machines: master zombies and slave zombies. The hosts of both machines have been infected with malicious code. The attacker coordinates and triggers the master zombies, which in turn coordinate and trigger the slave zombies. The use of two levels of zombies makes it more difficult to trace the attack back to its source and provides for a more resilient network of attackers.

A **reflector DDoS** attack adds another layer of machines (Figure 10.10b). In this type of attack, the slave zombies construct packets requiring a response that contains the target's IP address as the source IP address in the packet's IP header. These packets are sent to uninfected machines known as reflectors. The uninfected machines respond with packets directed at the target machine. A reflector DDoS attack can easily involve more machines and more traffic than a direct DDoS attack and hence be more damaging. Further, tracing back the attack or filtering out the attack packets is more difficult because the attack comes from widely dispersed uninfected machines.

Constructing the Attack Network

The first step in a DDoS attack is for the attacker to infect a number of machines with zombie software that will ultimately be used to carry out the attack. The essential ingredients in this phase of the attack are the following:

1. Software that can carry out the DDoS attack. The software must be able to run on a large number of machines, must be able to conceal its existence, must be able to communicate with the attacker or have some sort of time-triggered mechanism, and must be able to launch the intended attack toward the target.

2. A vulnerability in a large number of systems. The attacker must become aware of a vulnerability that many system administrators and individual users have failed to patch and that enables the attacker to install the zombie software.

3. A strategy for locating vulnerable machines, a process known as scanning.

---

[3]The Internet Control Message Protocol (ICMP) is an IP-level protocol for the exchange of control packets between a router and a host or between hosts. The ECHO packet requires the recipient to respond with an echo reply to check that communication is possible between entities.

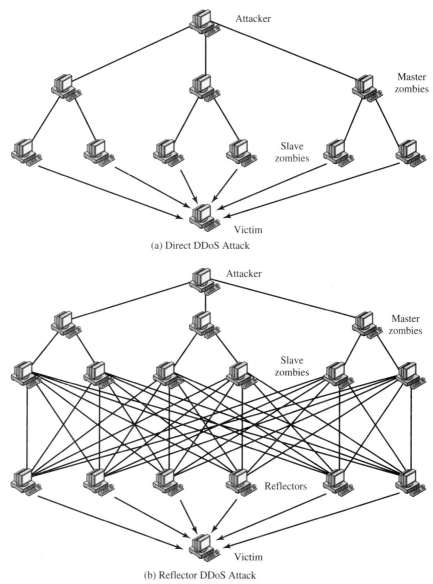

(a) Direct DDoS Attack

(b) Reflector DDoS Attack

Figure 10.10   Types of Flooding-Based DDoS Attacks

In the scanning process, the attacker first seeks out a number of vulnerable machines and infects them. Then, typically, the zombie software that is installed in the infected machines repeats the same scanning process, until a large distributed network of infected machines is created. [MIRK04] lists the following types of scanning strategies:

- **Random:** Each compromised host probes random addresses in the IP address space, using a different seed. This technique produces a high volume of

Internet traffic, which may cause generalized disruption even before the actual attack is launched.

- **Hit-List:** The attacker first compiles a long list of potential vulnerable machines. This can be a slow process done over a long period to avoid detection that an attack is underway. Once the list is compiled, the attacker begins infecting machines on the list. Each infected machine is provided with a portion of the list to scan. This strategy results in a very short scanning period, which may make it difficult to detect that infection is taking place.

- **Topological:** This method uses information contained on an infected victim machine to find more hosts to scan.

- **Local subnet:** If a host can be infected behind a firewall, that host then looks for targets in its own local network. The host uses the subnet address structure to find other hosts that would otherwise be protected by the firewall.

DDoS Countermeasures

In general, there are three lines of defense against DDoS attacks [CHAN02]:

- **Attack prevention and preemption (before the attack):** These mechanisms enable the victim to endure attack attempts without denying service to legitimate clients. Techniques include enforcing policies for resource consumption and providing backup resources available on demand. In addition, prevention mechanisms modify systems and protocols on the Internet to reduce the possibility of DDoS attacks.

- **Attack detection and filtering (during the attack):** These mechanisms attempt to detect the attack as it begins and respond immediately. This minimizes the impact of the attack on the target. Detection involves looking for suspicious patterns of behavior. Response involves filtering out packets likely to be part of the attack.

- **Attack source traceback and identification (during and after the attack):** This is an attempt to identify the source of the attack as a first step in preventing future attacks. However, this method typically does not yield results fast enough, if at all, to mitigate an ongoing attack.

The challenge in coping with DDoS attacks is the sheer number of ways in which they can operate. Thus DDoS countermeasures must evolve with the threat.

10.6 RECOMMENDED READING AND WEB SITES

For a thorough understanding of viruses, the book to read is [SZOR05]. Another excellent treatment is [AYCO06]. Good overview articles on viruses and worms are [CASS01], [FORR97], [KEPH97a], and [NACH97]. [MEIN01] provides a good treatment of the Code Red worm. [WEAV03] is a comprehensive survey of worm characteristics. [HYPP06] discusses worm attacks on mobile phones.

[PATR04] is a worthwhile survey of DDoS attacks. [MIRK04] is a thorough description of the variety of DDoS attacks and countermeasures. [CHAN02] is a good examination of DDoS defense strategies.

AYCO06 Aycock, J. *Computer Viruses and Malware.* New York: Springer, 2006.

CASS01 Cass, S. "Anatomy of Malice." *IEEE Spectrum*, November 2001.

CHAN02 Chang, R. "Defending Against Flooding-Based Distributed Denial-of-Service Attacks: A Tutorial." *IEEE Communications Magazine*, October 2002.

FORR97 Forrest, S.; Hofmeyr, S.; and Somayaji, A. "Computer Immunology." *Communications of the ACM*, October 1997.

HYPP06 Hypponen, M. "Malware Goes Mobile." *Scientific American*, November 2006.

KEPH97a Kephart, J.; Sorkin, G.; Chess, D.; and White, S. "Fighting Computer Viruses." *Scientific American*, November 1997.

MEIN01 Meinel, C. "Code Red for the Web." *Scientific American*, October 2001.

MIRK04 Mirkovic, J., and Relher, P. "A Taxonomy of DDoS Attack and DDoS Defense Mechanisms." *ACM SIGCOMM Computer Communications Review*, April 2004.

NACH97 Nachenberg, C. "Computer Virus-Antivirus Coevolution." *Communications of the ACM*, January 1997.

PATR04 Patrikakis, C.; Masikos, M.; and Zouraraki, O. "Distributed Denial of Service Attacks." *The Internet Protocol Journal*, December 2004.

SZOR05 Szor, P., *The Art of Computer Virus Research and Defense.* Reading, MA: Addison-Wesley, 2005.

WEAV03 Weaver, N., et al. "A Taxonomy of Computer Worms." *The First ACM Workshop on Rapid Malcode (WORM)*, 2003.

Recommended Web Sites:

- **AntiVirus Online:** IBM's site on virus information.
- **Vmyths:** Dedicated to exposing virus hoaxes and dispelling misconceptions about real viruses.
- **VirusList:** Site maintained by commercial antivirus software provider. Good collection of useful information.
- **DDoS Attacks/Tools:** Extensive list of links and documents.

10.7 KEY TERMS, REVIEW QUESTIONS, AND PROBLEMS

Key Terms

backdoor	distributed denial of service (DDoS)	macro virus
behavior-blocking software	downloaders	malicious software
blended attack	downloaders	malware
boot-sector virus	e-mail virus	metamorphic virus
digital immune system	flooder	mobile code
direct DDoS attack	logic bomb	parasitic virus

polymorphic virus	stealth virus	virus
reflector DDoS attack	trapdoor	worm
scanning	Trojan horse	zero-day exploit

Review Questions

10.1 What is the role of compression in the operation of a virus?

10.2 What is the role of encryption in the operation of a virus?

10.3 What are typical phases of operation of a virus or worm?

10.4 What is a digital immune system?

10.5 How does behavior-blocking software work?

10.6 In general terms, how does a worm propagate?

10.7 Describe some worm countermeasures.

10.8 What is a DDoS?

Problems

10.1 There is a flaw in the virus program of Figure 10.1. What is it?

10.2 The question arises as to whether it is possible to develop a program that can analyze a piece of software to determine if it is a virus. Consider that we have a program D that is supposed to be able to do that. That is, for any program P, if we run D(P), the result returned is TRUE (P is a virus) or FALSE (P is not a virus). Now consider the following program:

```
Program CV :=
  { ...
  main-program :=
            {if D(CV) then goto next:
                  else infect-executable;
            }
  next:
       }
```

In the preceding program, infect-executable is a module that scans memory for executable programs and replicates itself in those programs. Determine if D can correctly decide whether CV is a virus.

10.3 The point of this problem is to demonstrate the type of puzzles that must be solved in the design of malicious code and therefore, the type of mindset that one wishing to counter such attacks must adopt.

a. Consider the following C program:

```
begin
     print (*begin print (); end.*);
end
```

What do you think the program was intended to do? Does it work?

b. Answer the same questions for the following program:

```
char [] = {'0', ' ', '}', ';', 'm', 'a', 'i', 'n',
'(', ')', '{', and so on... 't', ')', '0'};

main ()
{
   int I;
   printf(*char t[] = (*);
```

```
        for (i=0; t[i]!=0; i=i+1)
            printf("%d, ", t[i]);
        printf("%s", t);
    }
```

c. What is the specific relevance of this problem to this chapter?

10.4 Consider the following fragment:

```
        legitimate code
        if data is Friday the 13th;
            crash_computer();
        legitimate code
```

What type of malicious software is this?

10.5 Consider the following fragment in an authentication program:

```
        username = read_username();
        password = read_password();
        if username is "133t h4ck0r"
            return ALLOW_LOGIN;
        if username and password are valid
            return ALLOW_LOGIN
        else return DENY_LOGIN
```

What type of malicious software is this?

10.6 The following code fragments show a sequence of virus instructions and a metamorphic version of the virus. Describe the effect produced by the metamorphic code.

Original Code	Metamorphic Code
mov eax, 5	mov eax, 5
add eax, ebx	push ecx
call [eax]	pop ecx
	add eax, ebx
	swap eax, ebx
	swap ebx, eax
	call [eax]
	nop

10.7 The list of passwords used by the Morris worm is provided at this book's Web site.
   a. The assumption has been expressed by many people that this list represents words commonly used as passwords. Does this seem likely? Justify your answer.
   b. If the list does not reflect commonly used passwords, suggest some approaches that Morris may have used to construct the list.

10.8 Suggest some methods of attacking the PWC worm defense that could be used by worm creators and suggest countermeasures to these methods.

CHAPTER 11

FIREWALLS

The function of a strong position is to make the forces holding it practically unassailable.

— *On War*, Carl Von Clausewitz

On the day that you take up your command, block the frontier passes, destroy the official tallies, and stop the passage of all emissaries.

— *The Art of War*, Sun Tzu

KEY POINTS

◆ A firewall forms a barrier through which the traffic going in each direction must pass. A firewall security policy dictates which traffic is authorized to pass in each direction.

◆ A firewall may be designed to operate as a filter at the level of IP packets, or may operate at a higher protocol layer.

Firewalls can be an effective means of protecting a local system or network of systems from network-based security threats while at the same time affording access to the outside world via wide area networks and the Internet.

11.1 THE NEED FOR FIREWALLS

Information systems in corporations, government agencies, and other organizations have undergone a steady evolution. The following are notable developments:

- Centralized data processing system, with a central mainframe supporting a number of directly connected terminals
- Local area networks (LANs) interconnecting PCs and terminals to each other and the mainframe
- Premises network, consisting of a number of LANs, interconnecting PCs, servers, and perhaps a mainframe or two
- Enterprise-wide network, consisting of multiple, geographically distributed premises networks interconnected by a private wide area network (WAN)
- Internet connectivity, in which the various premises networks all hook into the Internet and may or may not also be connected by a private WAN

Internet connectivity is no longer optional for organizations. The information and services available are essential to the organization. Moreover, individual users within the organization want and need Internet access, and if this is not provided via their LAN, they will use dial-up capability from their PC to an Internet service provider (ISP). However, while Internet access provides benefits to the organization, it enables the outside world to reach and interact with local network assets. This creates a threat to the organization. While it is possible to equip each workstation and server on the premises network with strong security features, such as intrusion protection, this may not be sufficient and in some cases is not cost-effective. Consider a network with hundreds or even thousands of systems, running various operating systems, such as different versions of UNIX and Windows. When a security flaw is discovered, each potentially affected system must be upgraded to fix that flaw. This requires scaleable configuration management and aggressive patching to function effectively. While difficult, this is possible and is necessary if only host-based security is used. A widely accepted alternative or at least complement to host-based security services is the firewall. The firewall is inserted between the premises network and the Internet to establish a controlled link and to erect an outer security wall or perimeter. The aim of this perimeter is to protect the premises network from Internet-based attacks and to provide a single choke point where security and auditing can be imposed. The firewall may be a single computer system or a set of two or more systems that cooperate to perform the firewall function.

The firewall, then, provides an additional layer of defense, insulating the internal systems from external networks. This follows the classic military doctrine of "defense in depth," which is just as applicable to IT security.

11.2 FIREWALL CHARACTERISTICS

[BELL94b] lists the following design goals for a firewall:

1. All traffic from inside to outside, and vice versa, must pass through the firewall. This is achieved by physically blocking all access to the local network except via the firewall. Various configurations are possible, as explained later in this chapter.

2. Only authorized traffic, as defined by the local security policy, will be allowed to pass. Various types of firewalls are used, which implement various types of security policies, as explained later in this chapter.

3. The firewall itself is immune to penetration. This implies the use of a hardened system with a secured operating system. Trusted computer systems are suitable for hosting a firewall and often required in government applications.

[SMIT97] lists four general techniques that firewalls use to control access and enforce the site's security policy. Originally, firewalls focused primarily on service control, but they have since evolved to provide all four:

- **Service control:** Determines the types of Internet services that can be accessed, inbound or outbound. The firewall may filter traffic on the basis of IP address, protocol, or port number; may provide proxy software that receives and interprets each service request before passing it on; or may host the server software itself, such as a Web or mail service.

- **Direction control:** Determines the direction in which particular service requests may be initiated and allowed to flow through the firewall.

- **User control:** Controls access to a service according to which user is attempting to access it. This feature is typically applied to users inside the firewall perimeter (local users). It may also be applied to incoming traffic from external users; the latter requires some form of secure authentication technology, such as is provided in IPsec (Chapter 8).

- **Behavior control:** Controls how particular services are used. For example, the firewall may filter e-mail to eliminate spam, or it may enable external access to only a portion of the information on a local Web server.

Before proceeding to the details of firewall types and configurations, it is best to summarize what one can expect from a firewall. The following capabilities are within the scope of a firewall:

1. A firewall defines a single choke point that keeps unauthorized users out of the protected network, prohibits potentially vulnerable services from entering or leaving the network, and provides protection from various kinds of IP spoofing and routing attacks. The use of a single choke point simplifies security management because security capabilities are consolidated on a single system or set of systems.

2. A firewall provides a location for monitoring security-related events. Audits and alarms can be implemented on the firewall system.

3. A firewall is a convenient platform for several Internet functions that are not security related. These include a network address translator, which maps local addresses to Internet addresses, and a network management function that audits or logs Internet usage.

4. A firewall can serve as the platform for IPsec. Using the tunnel mode capability described in Chapter 8, the firewall can be used to implement virtual private networks.

Firewalls have their limitations, including the following:

1. The firewall cannot protect against attacks that bypass the firewall. Internal systems may have dial-out capability to connect to an ISP. An internal LAN may support a modem pool that provides dial-in capability for traveling employees and telecommuters.

2. The firewall may not protect fully against internal threats, such as a disgruntled employee or an employee who unwittingly cooperates with an external attacker.

3. An improperly secured wireless LAN may be accessed from outside the organization. An internal firewall that separates portions of an enterprise network cannot guard against wireless communications between local systems on different sides of the internal firewall.

4. A laptop, PDA, or portable storage device may be used and infected outside the corporate network, and then attached and used internally.

11.3 TYPES OF FIREWALLS

A firewall may act as a packet filter. It can operate as a positive filter, allowing to pass only packets that meet specific criteria, or as a negative filter, rejecting any packet that meets certain criteria. Depending on the type of firewall, it may examine one or more protocol headers in each packet, the payload of each packet, or the pattern generated by a sequence of packets. In this section, we look at the principal types of firewalls.

Packet Filtering Firewall

A packet filtering firewall applies a set of rules to each incoming and outgoing IP packet and then forwards or discards the packet (Figure 11.1b). The firewall is typically configured to filter packets going in both directions (from and to the internal network). Filtering rules are based on information contained in a network packet:

- **Source IP address:** The IP address of the system that originated the IP packet (e.g., 192.178.1.1)
- **Destination IP address:** The IP address of the system the IP packet is trying to reach (e.g., 192.168.1.2)
- **Source and destination transport-level address:** The transport-level (e.g., TCP or UDP) port number, which defines applications such as SNMP or TELNET
- **IP protocol field:** Defines the transport protocol
- **Interface:** For a firewall with three or more ports, which interface of the firewall the packet came from or which interface of the firewall the packet is destined for

The packet filter is typically set up as a list of rules based on matches to fields in the IP or TCP header. If there is a match to one of the rules, that rule is invoked to determine whether to forward or discard the packet. If there is no match to any rule, then a default action is taken. Two default policies are possible:

- **Default = discard:** That which is not expressly permitted is prohibited.
- **Default = forward:** That which is not expressly prohibited is permitted.

The default discard policy is more conservative. Initially, everything is blocked, and services must be added on a case-by-case basis. This policy is more visible to users, who are more likely to see the firewall as a hindrance. However, this is the policy likely to be preferred by businesses and government organizations. Further, visibility to users diminishes as rules are created. The default forward policy increases ease of use for end users but provides reduced security; the security administrator must, in essence, react to each new security threat as it becomes known. This policy may be used by generally more open organizations, such as universities.

Table 11.1, from [BELL94b], gives some examples of packet filtering rulesets. In each set, the rules are applied top to bottom. The "*" in a field is a wildcard

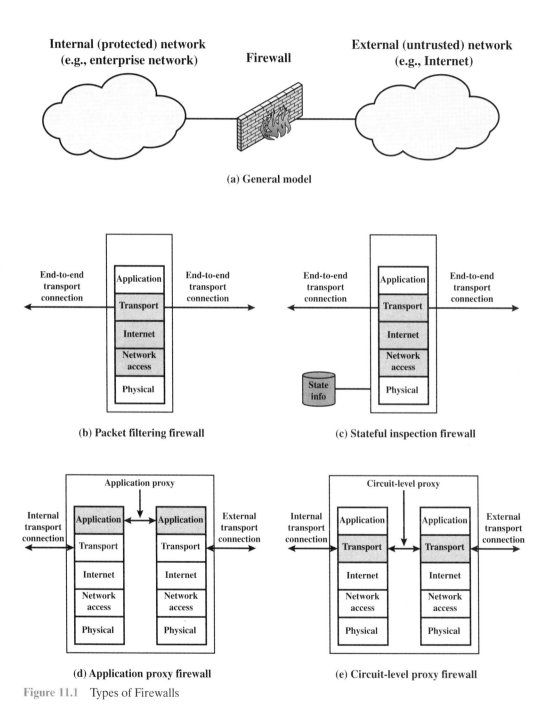

Figure 11.1   Types of Firewalls

Table 11.1 Packet-Filtering Examples

Rule Set A

action	ourhost	port	theirhost	port	comment
block	*	*	SPIGOT	*	we don't trust these people
allow	OUR-GW	25	*	*	connection to our SMTP port

Rule Set B

action	ourhost	port	theirhost	port	comment
block	*	*	*	*	default

Rule Set C

action	ourhost	port	theirhost	port	comment
allow	*	*	*	25	connection to their SMTP port

Rule Set D

action	src	port	dest	port	flags	comment
allow	{our hosts}	*	*	25		our packets to their SMTP port
allow	*	25	*	*	ACK	their replies

Rule Set E

action	src	port	dest	port	flags	comment
allow	{our hosts}	*	*	*		our outgoing calls
allow	*	*	*	*	ACK	replies to our calls
allow	*	*	*	>1024		traffic to nonservers

designator that matches everything. We assume that the default = discard policy is in force.

A. Inbound mail is allowed (port 25 is for SMTP incoming), but only to a gateway host. However, packets from a particular external host, SPIGOT, are blocked because that host has a history of sending massive files in e-mail messages.

B. This is an explicit statement of the default policy. All rulesets include this rule implicitly as the last rule.

C. This ruleset is intended to specify that any inside host can send mail to the outside. A TCP packet with a destination port of 25 is routed to the SMTP server on the destination machine. The problem with this rule is that the use of port 25 for SMTP receipt is only a default; an outside machine could be configured to have some other application linked to port 25. As this rule is written, an attacker could gain access to internal machines by sending packets with a TCP source port number of 25.

D. This ruleset achieves the intended result that was not achieved in C. The rules take advantage of a feature of TCP connections. Once a connection is set up, the ACK flag of a TCP segment is set to acknowledge segments sent from the other side. Thus, this ruleset states that it allows IP packets where the source IP address is one of a list of designated internal hosts and the destination TCP port number is 25. It also allows incoming packets with a source port number of 25 that include the ACK flag in the TCP segment. Note that we explicitly designate source and destination systems to define these rules explicitly.

E. This ruleset is one approach to handling FTP connections. With FTP, two TCP connections are used: a control connection to set up the file transfer and a data connection for the actual file transfer. The data connection uses a different port number that is dynamically assigned for the transfer. Most servers, and hence most attack targets, use low-numbered ports; most outgoing calls tend to use a higher-numbered port, typically above 1023. Thus, this ruleset allows

— Packets that originate internally

— Reply packets to a connection initiated by an internal machine

— Packets destined for a high-numbered port on an internal machine

This scheme requires that the systems be configured so that only the appropriate port numbers are in use.

Rule set E points out the difficulty in dealing with applications at the packet-filtering level. Another way to deal with FTP and similar applications is either stateful packet filters or an application-level gateway, both described subsequently in this section.

One advantage of a packet filtering firewall is its simplicity. Also, packet filters typically are transparent to users and are very fast. [WACK02] lists the following weaknesses of packet filter firewalls:

- Because packet filter firewalls do not examine upper-layer data, they cannot prevent attacks that employ application-specific vulnerabilities or functions. For example, a packet filter firewall cannot block specific application commands; if a packet filter firewall allows a given application, all functions available within that application will be permitted.

- Because of the limited information available to the firewall, the logging functionality present in packet filter firewalls is limited. Packet filter logs normally contain the same information used to make access control decisions (source address, destination address, and traffic type).

- Most packet filter firewalls do not support advanced user authentication schemes. Once again, this limitation is mostly due to the lack of upper-layer functionality by the firewall.

- Packet filter firewalls are generally vulnerable to attacks and exploits that take advantage of problems within the TCP/IP specification and protocol stack, such as *network layer address spoofing*. Many packet filter firewalls cannot detect a network packet in which the OSI Layer 3 addressing information has been altered. Spoofing attacks are generally employed by intruders to bypass the security controls implemented in a firewall platform.

- Finally, due to the small number of variables used in access control decisions, packet filter firewalls are susceptible to security breaches caused by improper configurations. In other words, it is easy to accidentally configure a packet filter firewall to allow traffic types, sources, and destinations that should be denied based on an organization's information security policy.

Some of the attacks that can be made on packet filtering firewalls and the appropriate countermeasures are the following:

- **IP address spoofing:** The intruder transmits packets from the outside with a source IP address field containing an address of an internal host. The attacker hopes that the use of a spoofed address will allow penetration of systems that employ simple source address security, in which packets from specific trusted internal hosts are accepted. The countermeasure is to discard packets with an inside source address if the packet arrives on an external interface. In fact, this countermeasure is often implemented at the router external to the firewall.
- **Source routing attacks:** The source station specifies the route that a packet should take as it crosses the Internet, in the hopes that this will bypass security measures that do not analyze the source routing information. The counter-measure is to discard all packets that use this option.
- **Tiny fragment attacks:** The intruder uses the IP fragmentation option to create extremely small fragments and force the TCP header information into a sepa-rate packet fragment. This attack is designed to circumvent filtering rules that depend on TCP header information. Typically, a packet filter will make a fil-tering decision on the first fragment of a packet. All subsequent fragments of that packet are filtered out solely on the basis that they are part of the packet whose first fragment was rejected. The attacker hopes that the filtering firewall examines only the first fragment and that the remaining fragments are passed through. A tiny fragment attack can be defeated by enforcing a rule that the first fragment of a packet must contain a predefined minimum amount of the transport header. If the first fragment is rejected, the filter can remember the packet and discard all subsequent fragments.

Stateful Inspection Firewalls

A traditional packet filter makes filtering decisions on an individual packet basis and does not take into consideration any higher layer context. To understand what is meant by *context* and why a traditional packet filter is limited with regard to con-text, a little background is needed. Most standardized applications that run on top of TCP follow a client/server model. For example, for the Simple Mail Transfer Protocol (SMTP), e-mail is transmitted from a client system to a server system. The client system generates new e-mail messages, typically from user input. The server system accepts incoming e-mail messages and places them in the appropriate user mailboxes. SMTP operates by setting up a TCP connection between client and server, in which the TCP server port number, which identifies the SMTP server application, is 25. The TCP port number for the SMTP client is a number between 1024 and 65535 that is generated by the SMTP client.

In general, when an application that uses TCP creates a session with a remote host, it creates a TCP connection in which the TCP port number for the remote (server) application is a number less than 1024 and the TCP port number for the local (client) application is a number between 1024 and 65535. The numbers less than 1024 are the "well-known" port numbers and are assigned permanently to particular applications (e.g., 25 for server SMTP). The numbers between 1024 and 65535 are generated dynamically and have temporary significance only for the lifetime of a TCP connection.

A simple packet filtering firewall must permit inbound network traffic on all these high-numbered ports for TCP-based traffic to occur. This creates a vulnerability that can be exploited by unauthorized users.

A stateful inspection packet firewall tightens up the rules for TCP traffic by creating a directory of outbound TCP connections, as shown in Table 11.2. There is an entry for each currently established connection. The packet filter will now allow incoming traffic to high-numbered ports only for those packets that fit the profile of one of the entries in this directory.

A stateful packet inspection firewall reviews the same packet information as a packet filtering firewall, but also records information about TCP connections (Figure 11.1c). Some stateful firewalls also keep track of TCP sequence numbers to prevent attacks that depend on the sequence number, such as session hijacking. Some even inspect limited amounts of application data for some well-known protocols like FTP, IM and SIPS commands, in order to identify and track related connections.

Application-Level Gateway

An application-level gateway, also called an **application proxy**, acts as a relay of application-level traffic (Figure 11.1d). The user contacts the gateway using a TCP/IP application, such as Telnet or FTP, and the gateway asks the user for the name of the remote host to be accessed. When the user responds and provides a valid user ID and authentication information, the gateway contacts the application on the remote host and relays TCP segments containing the application data between the two endpoints. If the gateway does not implement the proxy code for a specific application, the service is not supported and cannot be forwarded across the firewall. Further, the gateway can be configured to support only specific features of

Table 11.2   Example Stateful Firewall Connection State Table [WACK02]

Source Address	Source Port	Destination Address	Destination Port	Connection State
192.168.1.100	1030	210.22.88.29	80	Established
192.168.1.102	1031	216.32.42.123	80	Established
192.168.1.101	1033	173.66.32.122	25	Established
192.168.1.106	1035	177.231.32.12	79	Established
223.43.21.231	1990	192.168.1.6	80	Established
2122.22.123.32	2112	192.168.1.6	80	Established
210.922.212.18	3321	192.168.1.6	80	Established
24.102.32.23	1025	192.168.1.6	80	Established
223.21.22.12	1046	192.168.1.6	80	Established

an application that the network administrator considers acceptable while denying all other features.

Application-level gateways tend to be more secure than packet filters. Rather than trying to deal with the numerous possible combinations that are to be allowed and forbidden at the TCP and IP level, the application-level gateway need only scrutinize a few allowable applications. In addition, it is easy to log and audit all incoming traffic at the application level.

A prime disadvantage of this type of gateway is the additional processing overhead on each connection. In effect, there are two spliced connections between the end users, with the gateway at the splice point, and the gateway must examine and forward all traffic in both directions.

Circuit–Level Gateway

A fourth type of firewall is the circuit-level gateway or **circuit-level proxy** (Figure 11.1e). This can be a stand-alone system or it can be a specialized function performed by an application-level gateway for certain applications. As with an application gateway, a circuit-level gateway does not permit an end-to-end TCP connection; rather, the gateway sets up two TCP connections, one between itself and a TCP user on an inner host and one between itself and a TCP user on an outside host. Once the two connections are established, the gateway typically relays TCP segments from one connection to the other without examining the contents. The security function consists of determining which connections will be allowed.

A typical use of circuit-level gateways is a situation in which the system administrator trusts the internal users. The gateway can be configured to support application-level or proxy service on inbound connections and circuit-level functions for outbound connections. In this configuration, the gateway can incur the processing overhead of examining incoming application data for forbidden functions but does not incur that overhead on outgoing data.

An example of a circuit-level gateway implementation is the SOCKS package [KOBL92]; version 5 of SOCKS is specified in RFC 1928. The RFC defines SOCKS in the following fashion:

> The protocol described here is designed to provide a framework for client-server applications in both the TCP and UDP domains to conveniently and securely use the services of a network firewall. The protocol is conceptually a "shim-layer" between the application layer and the transport layer, and as such does not provide network-layer gateway services, such as forwarding of ICMP messages.

SOCKS consists of the following components:

- The SOCKS server, which often runs on a UNIX-based firewall. SOCKS is also implemented on Windows systems.
- The SOCKS client library, which runs on internal hosts protected by the firewall.

- SOCKS-ified versions of several standard client programs such as FTP and TELNET. The implementation of the SOCKS protocol typically involves either the recompilation or relinking of TCP-based client applications, or the use of alternate dynamically loaded libraries, to use the appropriate encapsulation routines in the SOCKS library.

When a TCP-based client wishes to establish a connection to an object that is reachable only via a firewall (such determination is left up to the implementation), it must open a TCP connection to the appropriate SOCKS port on the SOCKS server system. The SOCKS service is located on TCP port 1080. If the connection request succeeds, the client enters a negotiation for the authentication method to be used, authenticates with the chosen method, and then sends a relay request. The SOCKS server evaluates the request and either establishes the appropriate connection or denies it. UDP exchanges are handled in a similar fashion. In essence, a TCP connection is opened to authenticate a user to send and receive UDP segments, and the UDP segments are forwarded as long as the TCP connection is open.

11.4 FIREWALL BASING

It is common to base a firewall on a stand-alone machine running a common operating system, such as UNIX or Linux. Firewall functionality can also be implemented as a software module in a router or LAN switch. In this section, we look at some additional firewall basing considerations.

Bastion Host

A bastion host is a system identified by the firewall administrator as a critical strong point in the network's security. Typically, the bastion host serves as a platform for an application-level or circuit-level gateway. Common characteristics of a bastion host are as follows:

- The bastion host hardware platform executes a secure version of its operating system, making it a hardened system.
- Only the services that the network administrator considers essential are installed on the bastion host. These could include proxy applications for DNS, FTP, HTTP, and SMTP.
- The bastion host may require additional authentication before a user is allowed access to the proxy services. In addition, each proxy service may require its own authentication before granting user access.
- Each proxy is configured to support only a subset of the standard application's command set.
- Each proxy is configured to allow access only to specific host systems. This means that the limited command/feature set may be applied only to a subset of systems on the protected network.

- Each proxy maintains detailed audit information by logging all traffic, each connection, and the duration of each connection. The audit log is an essential tool for discovering and terminating intruder attacks.

- Each proxy module is a very small software package specifically designed for network security. Because of its relative simplicity, it is easier to check such modules for security flaws. For example, a typical UNIX mail application may contain over 20,000 lines of code, while a mail proxy may contain fewer than 1000.

- Each proxy is independent of other proxies on the bastion host. If there is a problem with the operation of any proxy, or if a future vulnerability is discovered, it can be uninstalled without affecting the operation of the other proxy applications. Also, if the user population requires support for a new service, the network administrator can easily install the required proxy on the bastion host.

- A proxy generally performs no disk access other than to read its initial configuration file. Hence, the portions of the file system containing executable code can be made read only. This makes it difficult for an intruder to install Trojan horse sniffers or other dangerous files on the bastion host.

- Each proxy runs as a nonprivileged user in a private and secured directory on the bastion host.

Host-Based Firewalls

A host-based firewall is a software module used to secure an individual host. Such modules are available in many operating systems or can be provided as an add-on package. Like conventional stand-alone firewalls, host-resident firewalls filter and restrict the flow of packets. A common location for such firewalls is a server. There are several advantages to the use of a server-based or workstation-based firewall:

- Filtering rules can be tailored to the host environment. Specific corporate security policies for servers can be implemented, with different filters for servers used for different application.

- Protection is provided independent of topology. Thus both internal and external attacks must pass through the firewall.

- Used in conjunction with stand-alone firewalls, the host-based firewall provides an additional layer of protection. A new type of server can be added to the network, with its own firewall, without the necessity of altering the network firewall configuration.

Personal Firewall

A personal firewall controls the traffic between a personal computer or workstation on one side and the Internet or enterprise network on the other side. Personal firewall functionality can be used in the home environment and on corporate intranets. Typically, the personal firewall is a software module on the personal computer. In a home environment with multiple computers connected to the Internet, firewall functionality can also be housed in a router that connects all of the home computers to a DSL, cable modem, or other Internet interface.

Personal firewalls are typically much less complex than either server-based firewalls or stand-alone firewalls. The primary role of the personal firewall is to deny unauthorized remote access to the computer. The firewall can also monitor outgoing activity in an attempt to detect and block worms and other malware.

An example of a personal firewall is the capability built in to the Mac OS X operating system. When the user enables the personal firewall in Mac OS X, all inbound connections are denied except for those the user explicitly permits. Figure 11.2 shows this simple interface. The list of inbound services that can be selectively reenabled, with their port numbers, includes the following:

- Personal file sharing (548, 427)
- Windows sharing (139)
- Personal Web sharing (80, 427)
- Remote login - SSH (22)
- FTP access (20-21, 1024-64535 from 20-21)
- Remote Apple events (3031)
- Printer sharing (631, 515)
- IChat Rendezvous (5297, 5298)
- ITunes Music Sharing (3869)
- CVS (2401)

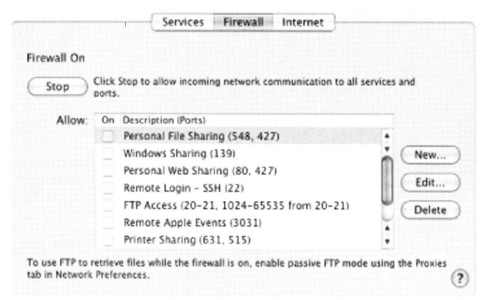

Figure 11.2   Example Personal Firewall Interface

- Gnutella/Limewire (6346)
- ICQ (4000)
- IRC (194)
- MSN Messenger (6891-6900)
- Network Time (123)
- Retrospect (497)
- SMB (without netbios-445)
- Timbuktu (407)
- VNC (5900-5902)
- WebSTAR Admin (1080, 1443)

When FTP access is enabled, ports 20 and 21 on the local machine are opened for FTP; if others connect to this computer from ports 20 or 21, the ports 1024 through 64535 are open.

For increased protection, advanced firewall features are available through easy-to-configure checkboxes. Stealth mode hides the Mac on the Internet by dropping unsolicited communication packets, making it appear as though no Mac is present. UDP packets can be blocked, restricting network traffic to TCP packets only for open ports. The firewall also supports logging, an important tool for checking on unwanted activity.

11.5 FIREWALL LOCATION AND CONFIGURATIONS

As Figure 11.1a indicates, a firewall is positioned to provide a protective barrier between an external, potentially untrusted source of traffic and an internal network. With that general principle in mind, a security administrator must decide on the location and on the number of firewalls needed. In this section, we look at some common options.

DMZ Networks

Figure 11.3 suggests the most common distinction, that between an internal and an external firewall. An external firewall is placed at the edge of a local or enterprise network, just inside the boundary router that connects to the Internet or some wide area network (WAN). One or more internal firewalls protect the bulk of the enterprise network. Between these two types of firewalls are one or more networked devices in a region referred to as a DMZ (demilitarized zone) network. Systems that are externally accessible but need some protections are usually located on DMZ networks. Typically, the systems in the DMZ require or foster external connectivity, such as a corporate Web site, an e-mail server, or a DNS (domain name system) server.

The external firewall provides a measure of access control and protection for the DMZ systems consistent with their need for external connectivity. The external

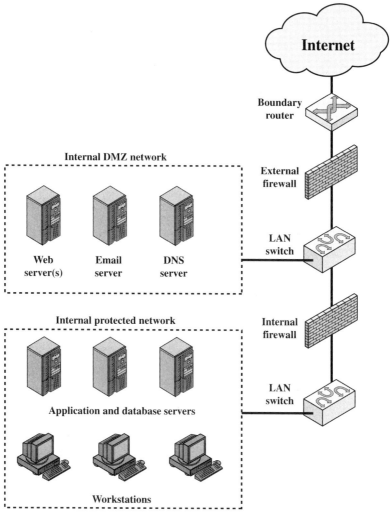

Figure 11.3   Example Firewall Configuration

firewall also provides a basic level of protection for the remainder of the enterprise network. In this type of configuration, internal firewalls serve three purposes:

1. The internal firewall adds more stringent filtering capability, compared to the external firewall, in order to protect enterprise servers and workstations from external attack.

2. The internal firewall provides two-way protection with respect to the DMZ. First, the internal firewall protects the remainder of the network from attacks launched from DMZ systems. Such attacks might originate from worms, rootkits, bots, or other malware lodged in a DMZ system. Second, an internal firewall can protect the DMZ systems from attack from the internal protected network.

3. Multiple internal firewalls can be used to protect portions of the internal network from each other. For example, firewalls can be configured so that internal servers are protected from internal workstations and vice versa. A common practice is to place the DMZ on a different network interface on the external firewall from that used to access the internal networks.

Virtual Private Networks

In today's distributed computing environment, the **virtual private network (VPN)** offers an attractive solution to network managers. In essence, a VPN consists of a set of computers that interconnect by means of a relatively unsecure network and that make use of encryption and special protocols to provide security. At each corporate site, workstations, servers, and databases are linked by one or more local area networks (LANs). The Internet or some other public network can be used to interconnect sites, providing a cost savings over the use of a private network and offloading the wide area network management task to the public network provider. That same public network provides an access path for telecommuters and other mobile employees to log on to corporate systems from remote sites.

But the manager faces a fundamental requirement: security. Use of a public network exposes corporate traffic to eavesdropping and provides an entry point for unauthorized users. To counter this problem, a VPN is needed. In essence, a VPN uses encryption and authentication in the lower protocol layers to provide a secure connection through an otherwise insecure network, typically the Internet. VPNs are generally cheaper than real private networks using private lines but rely on having the same encryption and authentication system at both ends. The encryption may be performed by firewall software or possibly by routers. The most common protocol mechanism used for this purpose is at the IP level and is known as IPsec.

An organization maintains LANs at dispersed locations. A logical means of implementing an IPsec is in a firewall, as shown in Figure 11.4, which essentially repeats Figure 8.1. If IPsec is implemented in a separate box behind (internal to) the firewall, then VPN traffic passing through the firewall in both directions is encrypted. In this case, the firewall is unable to perform its filtering function or other security functions, such as access control, logging, or scanning for viruses. IPsec could be implemented in the boundary router, outside the firewall. However, this device is likely to be less secure than the firewall and thus less desirable as an IPsec platform.

Distributed Firewalls

A distributed firewall configuration involves stand-alone firewall devices plus host-based firewalls working together under a central administrative control. Figure 11.5 suggests a distributed firewall configuration. Administrators can configure host-resident firewalls on hundreds of servers and workstations as well as configure personal firewalls on local and remote user systems. Tools let the network administrator set policies and monitor security across the entire network. These firewalls protect against internal attacks and provide protection tailored to specific machines and applications. Stand-alone firewalls provide global protection, including internal firewalls and an external firewall, as discussed previously.

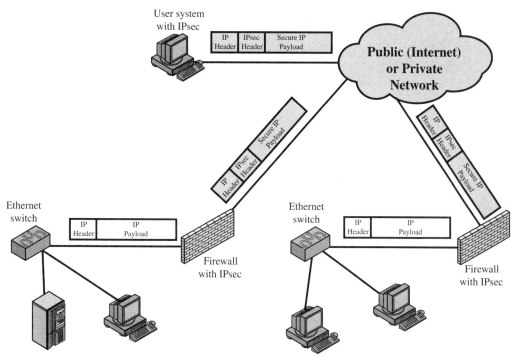

Figure 11.4   A VPN Security Scenario

With distributed firewalls, it may make sense to establish both an internal and an external DMZ. Web servers that need less protection because they have less critical information on them could be placed in an external DMZ, outside the external firewall. What protection is needed is provided by host-based firewalls on these servers.

An important aspect of a distributed firewall configuration is security monitoring. Such monitoring typically includes log aggregation and analysis, firewall statistics, and fine-grained remote monitoring of individual hosts if needed.

Summary of Firewall Locations and Topologies

We can now summarize the discussion from Sections 11.4 and 11.5 to define a spectrum of firewall locations and topologies. The following alternatives can be identified:

- **Host-resident firewall:** This category includes personal firewall software and firewall software on servers. Such firewalls can be used alone or as part of an in-depth firewall deployment.
- **Screening router:** A single router between internal and external networks with stateless or full packet filtering. This arrangement is typical for small office/home office (SOHO) applications.

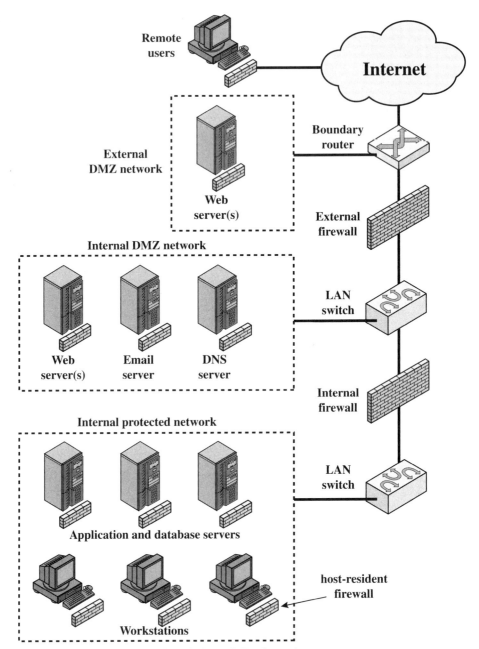

Figure 11.5   Example Distributed Firewall Configuration

- **Single bastion inline:** A single firewall device between an internal and external router (e.g., Figure 11.1a). The firewall may implement stateful filters and/or application proxies. This is the typical firewall appliance configuration for small to medium-sized organizations.

- **Single bastion T:** Similar to single bastion inline but has a third network interface on bastion to a DMZ where externally visible servers are placed. Again, this is a common appliance configuration for medium to large organizations.

- **Double bastion inline:** Figure 11.3 illustrates this configuration, where the DMZ is sandwiched between bastion firewalls. This configuration is common for large businesses and government organizations.

- **Double bastion T:** The DMZ is on a separate network interface on the bastion firewall. This configuration is also common for large businesses and government organizations and may be required. For example, this configuration is required for Australian government use (Australian Government Information Technology Security Manual - ACSI33).

- **Distributed firewall configuration:** Illustrated in Figure 11.5. This configuration is used by some large businesses and government organizations.

11.6 RECOMMENDED READING AND WEB SITE

A classic treatment of firewalls is [CHES03]. [LODI98], [OPPL97], and [BELL94b] are good overview articles on the subject. [WACK02] is an excellent overview of firewall technology and firewall policies. [AUDI04] and [WILS05] provide useful discussions of firewalls.

AUDI04   Audin, G. "Next-Gen Firewalls: What to Expect." *Business Communications Review*, June 2004.

BELL94b   Bellovin, S., and Cheswick, W. "Network Firewalls." *IEEE Communications Magazine*, September 1994.

CHAP00   Chapman, D., and Zwicky, E. *Building Internet Firewalls.* Sebastopol, CA: O'Reilly, 2000.

CHES03   Cheswick, W., and Bellovin, S. *Firewalls and Internet Security: Repelling the Wily Hacker.* Reading, MA: Addison-Wesley, 2003.

LODI98   Lodin, S., and Schuba, C. "Firewalls Fend Off Invasions from the Net." *IEEE Spectrum*, February 1998.

OPPL97   Oppliger, R. "Internet Security: Firewalls and Beyond." *Communications of the ACM*, May 1997.

WACK02   Wack, J.; Cutler, K.; and Pole, J. *Guidelines on Firewalls and Firewall Policy.* NIST Special Publication SP 800-41, January 2002.

WILS05   Wilson, J. "The Future of the Firewall." *Business Communications Review*, May 2005.

Recommended Web Site:

- **Firewall.com:** Numerous links to firewall references and software resources.

11.7 KEY TERMS, REVIEW QUESTIONS, AND PROBLEMS

Key Terms

application-level gateway	firewall	personal firewall
bastion host	host-based firewall	proxy
circuit-level gateway	IP address spoofing	stateful inspection firewall
distributed firewalls	IP security (IPsec)	tiny fragment attack
DMZ	packet filtering firewall	virtual private network (VPN)

Review Questions

11.1 List three design goals for a firewall.

11.2 List four techniques used by firewalls to control access and enforce a security policy.

11.3 What information is used by a typical packet filtering firewall?

11.4 What are some weaknesses of a packet filtering firewall?

11.5 What is the difference between a packet filtering firewall and a stateful inspection firewall?

11.6 What is an application-level gateway?

11.7 What is a circuit-level gateway?

11.8 What are the differences among the firewalls of Figure 11.1?

11.9 What are the common characteristics of a bastion host?

11.10 Why is it useful to have host-based firewalls?

11.11 What is a DMZ network and what types of systems would you expect to find on such networks?

11.12 What is the difference between an internal and an external firewall?

Problems

11.1 As was mentioned in Section 11.3, one approach to defeating the tiny fragment attack is to enforce a minimum length of the transport header that must be contained in the first fragment of an IP packet. If the first fragment is rejected, all subsequent fragments can be rejected. However, the nature of IP is such that fragments may arrive out of order. Thus, an intermediate fragment may pass through the filter before the initial fragment is rejected. How can this situation be handled?

11.2 In an IPv4 packet, the size of the payload in the first fragment, in octets, is equal to Total Length $- (4 \times \text{IHL})$. If this value is less than the required minimum (8 octets for TCP), then this fragment and the entire packet are rejected. Suggest an alternative method of achieving the same result using only the Fragment Offset field.

11.3 RFC 791, the IPv4 protocol specification, describes a reassembly algorithm that results in new fragments overwriting any overlapped portions of previously received fragments. Given such a reassembly implementation, an attacker could construct a series of packets in which the lowest (zero-offset) fragment would contain innocuous data (and thereby be passed by administrative packet filters), and in which some subsequent packet having a non-zero offset would overlap TCP header information (destination port, for instance) and cause it to be modified. The second packet would be passed through most filter implementations because it does not have a zero fragment offset. Suggest a method that could be used by a packet filter to counter this attack.

Table 11.3   Sample Packet Filter Firewall Ruleset

	Source Address	Source Port	Dest Address	Dest Port	Action
1	Any	Any	192.168.1.0	> 1023	Allow
2	192.168.1.1	Any	Any	Any	Deny
3	Any	Any	192.168.1.1	Any	Deny
4	192.168.1.0	Any	Any	Any	Allow
5	Any	Any	192.168.1.2	SMTP	Allow
6	Any	Any	192.168.1.3	HTTP	Allow
7	Any	Any	Any	Any	Deny

11.4   Table 11.3 shows a sample of a packet filter firewall ruleset for an imaginary network of IP address that range from 192.168.1.0 to 192.168.1.254. Describe the effect of each rule.

11.5   SMTP (Simple Mail Transfer Protocol) is the standard protocol for transferring mail between hosts over TCP. A TCP connection is set up between a user agent and a server program. The server listens on TCP port 25 for incoming connection requests. The user end of the connection is on a TCP port number above 1023. Suppose you wish to build a packet filter rule set allowing inbound and outbound SMTP traffic. You generate the following ruleset:

Rule	Direction	Src Addr	Dest Addr	Protocol	Dest Port	Action
A	In	External	Internal	TCP	25	Permit
B	Out	Internal	External	TCP	>1023	Permit
C	Out	Internal	External	TCP	25	Permit
D	In	External	Internal	TCP	>1023	Permit
E	Either	Any	Any	Any	Any	Deny

a.   Describe the effect of each rule.
b.   Your host in this example has IP address 172.16.1.1. Someone tries to send e-mail from a remote host with IP address 192.168.3.4. If successful, this generates an SMTP dialogue between the remote user and the SMTP server on your host consisting of SMTP commands and mail. Additionally, assume that a user on your host tries to send e-mail to the SMTP server on the remote system. Four typical packets for this scenario are as shown:

Packet	Direction	Src Addr	Dest Addr	Protocol	Dest Port	Action
1	In	192.168.3.4	172.16.1.1	TCP	25	?
2	Out	172.16.1.1	192.168.3.4	TCP	1234	?
3	Out	172.16.1.1	192.168.3.4	TCP	25	?
4	In	192.168.3.4	172.16.1.1	TCP	1357	?

Indicate which packets are permitted or denied and which rule is used in each case.

c. Someone from the outside world (10.1.2.3) attempts to open a connection from port 5150 on a remote host to the Web proxy server on port 8080 on one of your local hosts (172.16.3.4), in order to carry out an attack. Typical packets are as follows:

Packet	Direction	Src Addr	Dest Addr	Protocol	Dest Port	Action
5	In	10.1.2.3	172.16.3.4	TCP	8080	?
6	Out	172.16.3.4	10.1.2.3	TCP	5150	?

Will the attack succeed? Give details.

11.6 To provide more protection, the ruleset from the preceding problem is modified as follows:

Rule	Direction	Src Addr	Dest Addr	Protocol	Src Port	Dest Port	Action
A	In	External	Internal	TCP	>1023	25	Permit
B	Out	Internal	External	TCP	25	>1023	Permit
C	Out	Internal	External	TCP	>1023	25	Permit
D	In	External	Internal	TCP	25	>1023	Permit
E	Either	Any	Any	Any	Any	Any	Deny

a. Describe the change.
b. Apply this new ruleset to the same six packets of the preceding problem. Indicate which packets are permitted or denied and which rule is used in each case.

11.7 A hacker uses port 25 as the client port on his or her end to attempt to open a connection to your Web proxy server.
a. The following packets might be generated:

Packet	Direction	Src Addr	Dest Addr	Protocol	Src Port	Dest Port	Action
7	In	10.1.2.3	172.16.3.4	TCP	25	8080	?
8	Out	172.16.3.4	10.1.2.3	TCP	8080	25	?

Explain why this attack will succeed, using the ruleset of the preceding problem.
b. When a TCP connection is initiated, the ACK bit in the TCP header is not set. Subsequently, all TCP headers sent over the TCP connection have the ACK bit set. Use this information to modify the ruleset of the preceding problem to prevent the attack just described.

11.8 A common management requirement is that "all external Web traffic must flow via the organization's Web proxy." However, that requirement is easier stated than implemented. Discuss the various problems and issues, possible solutions, and limitations with supporting this requirement. In particular consider issues such as identifying exactly what constitutes "Web traffic" and how it may be monitored, given the large range of ports and various protocols used by Web browsers and servers.

11.9 Consider the threat of "theft/breach of proprietary or confidential information held in key data files on the system." One method by which such a breach might occur is the accidental/deliberate e-mailing of information to a user outside to the organization. A possible countermeasure to this is to require all external e-mail to be given a sensitivity tag (classification if you like) in its subject and for external e-mail to have the lowest sensitivity tag. Discuss how this measure could be implemented in a firewall and what components and architecture would be needed to do this.

11.10 You are given the following "informal firewall policy" details to be implemented using a firewall like that in Figure 11.3:

1. E-mail may be sent using SMTP in both directions through the firewall, but it must be relayed via the DMZ mail gateway that provides header sanitization and content filtering. External e-mail must be destined for the DMZ mail server.
2. Users inside may retrieve their e-mail from the DMZ mail gateway, using either POP3 or POP3S, and authenticate themselves.
3. Users outside may retrieve their e-mail from the DMZ mail gateway, but only if they use the secure POP3 protocol, and authenticate themselves
4. Web requests (both insecure and secure) are allowed from any internal user out through the firewall but must be relayed via the DMZ Web proxy, which provides content filtering (noting this is not possible for secure requests), and users must authenticate with the proxy for logging.
5. Web requests (both insecure and secure) are allowed from anywhere on the Internet to the DMZ Web server
6. DNS lookup requests by internal users allowed via the DMZ DNS server, which queries to the Internet.
7. External DNS requests are provided by the DMZ DNS server.
8. Management and update of information on the DMZ servers is allowed using secure shell connections from relevant authorized internal users (may have different sets of users on each system as appropriate).
9. SNMP management requests are permitted from the internal management hosts to the firewalls, with the firewalls also allowed to send management traps (i.e., notification of some event occurring) to the management hosts

Design suitable packet filter rulesets (similar to those shown in Table 11.1) to be implemented on the "External Firewall" and the "Internal Firewall" to satisfy the aforementioned policy requirements.

APPENDIX A

SOME ASPECTS OF NUMBER THEORY

A.1 **Prime and Relatively Prime Numbers**

> Divisors
> Prime Numbers
> Relatively Prime Numbers

A.2 **Modular Arithmetic**

The Devil said to Daniel Webster: "Set me a task I can't carry out, and I'll give you anything in the world you ask for."

Daniel Webster: "Fair enough. Prove that for n greater than 2, the equation $a^n + b^n = c^n$ has no non-trivial solution in the integers."

They agreed on a three-day period for the labor, and the Devil disappeared.

At the end of three days, the Devil presented himself, haggard, jumpy, biting his lip. Daniel Webster said to him, "Well, how did you do at my task? Did you prove the theorem?"

"Eh? No . . . no, I haven't proved it."

"Then I can have whatever I ask for? Money? The Presidency?"

"What? Oh, that—of course. But listen! If we could just prove the following two lemmas—"

—*The Mathematical Magpie,* **Clifton Fadiman**

In this appendix, we provide some background on two concepts referenced in this book: prime numbers and modular arithmetic.

A.1 PRIME AND RELATIVELY PRIME NUMBERS

In this section, unless otherwise noted, we deal only with nonnegative integers. The use of negative integers would introduce no essential differences.

Divisors

We say that $b \neq 0$ divides a if $a = mb$ for some m, where a, b, and m are integers. That is, b divides a if there is no remainder on division. The notation $b|a$ is commonly used to mean b divides a. Also, if $b|a$, we say that b is a *divisor* of a. For example, the positive divisors of 24 are $1, 2, 3, 4, 6, 8, 12$, and 24.

The following relations hold:

- If $a|1$, then $a = \pm1$.
- If $a|b$ and $b|a$, then $a = \pm b$.
- Any $b \neq 0$ divides 0.
- If $b|g$ and $b|h$, then $b|(mg + nh)$ for arbitrary integers m and n.

To see this last point, note that

If $b|g$, then g is of the form $g = b \times g_1$ for some integer g_1.

If $b|h$, then h is of the form $h = b \times h_1$ for some integer h_1.

So

$$mg + nh = mbg_1 + nbh_1 = b \times (mg_1 + nh_1)$$

and therefore b divides $mg + nh$.

Prime Numbers

An integer $p > 1$ is a prime number if its only divisors are ±1 and $\pm p$. Prime numbers play a critical role in number theory and in the techniques discussed in Chapter 3.

Any integer $a > 1$ can be factored in a unique way as

$$a = p_1^{a_1} \times p_2^{a_2} \times \ldots \times p_t^{a_t}$$

where $p_1 < p_2 < \ldots < p_t$ are prime numbers and where each a_i is a positive integer. For example, $91 = 7 \times 13$ and $11011 = 7 \times 11^2 \times 13$.

It is useful to cast this another way. If P is the set of all prime numbers, then any positive integer can be written uniquely in the following form:

$$a = \prod_{p \in P} p^{a_p} \quad \text{where each } a_p \geq 0$$

The right-hand side is the product over all possible prime numbers p; for any particular value of a, most of the exponents a_p will be 0.

The value of any given positive integer can be specified by simply listing all the nonzero exponents in the foregoing formulation. Thus, the integer 12 is represented by $\{a_2 = 2, a_3 = 1\}$, and the integer 18 is represented by $\{a_2 = 1, a_3 = 2\}$. Multiplication of two numbers is equivalent to adding the corresponding exponents:

$$k = mn \quad \longrightarrow \quad k_p = m_p + n_p \quad \text{for all } p$$

What does it mean, in terms of these prime factors, to say that $a|b$? Any integer of the form p^k can be divided only by an integer that is of a lesser or equal power of the same prime number, p^j with $j \leq k$. Thus, we can say

$$a|b \quad \longrightarrow \quad a_p \leq b_p \quad \text{for all } p$$

Relatively Prime Numbers

We will use the notation gcd (a, b) to mean the **greatest common divisor** of a and b. The positive integer c is said to be the greatest common divisor of a and b if

1. c is a divisor of a and of b.
2. Any divisor of a and b is a divisor of c.

An equivalent definition is the following:

$$\gcd(a, b) = \max[k, \text{such that } k|a \text{ and } k|b]$$

Because we require that the greatest common divisor be positive, $\gcd(a, b) = \gcd(a, -b) = \gcd(-a, b) = \gcd(-a, -b)$. In general, $\gcd(a, b) = \gcd(|a|, |b|)$. For example, $\gcd(60, 24) = \gcd(60, -24) = 12$. Also, because all nonzero integers divide 0, we have $\gcd(a, 0) = |a|$.

It is easy to determine the greatest common divisor of two positive integers if we express each integer as the product of primes. For example,

$$300 = 2^2 \times 3^1 \times 5^2$$
$$18 = 2^1 \times 3^2$$
$$\gcd(18, 300) = 2^1 \times 3^1 \times 5^0 = 6$$

In general,

$$k = \gcd(a, b) \quad \longrightarrow \quad k_p = \min(a_p, b_p) \quad \text{for all } p$$

Determining the prime factors of a large number is no easy task, so the preceding relationship does not directly lead to a way of calculating the greatest common divisor.

The integers a and b are relatively prime if they have no prime factors in common, that is, if their only common factor is 1. This is equivalent to saying that a and b are relatively prime if $\gcd(a, b) = 1$. For example, 8 and 15 are relatively prime because the divisors of 8 are 1, 2, 4, and 8, and the divisors of 15 are 1, 3, 5, and 15, so 1 is the only number on both lists.

A.2 MODULAR ARITHMETIC

Given any positive integer n and any nonnegative integer a, if we divide a by n, we get an integer quotient q and an integer remainder r that obey the following relationship:

$$a = qn + r \qquad 0 \leq r < n; q = \lfloor a/n \rfloor$$

where $\lfloor x \rfloor$ is the largest integer less than or equal to x.

Figure A.1a demonstrates that, given a and positive n, it is always possible to find q and r that satisfy the preceding relationship. Represent the integers on the number line; a will fall somewhere on that line (positive a is shown, a similar demonstration can be made for negative a). Starting at 0, proceed to $n, 2n$, up to qn such that $qn \leq a$ and $(q + 1)n > a$. The distance from qn to a is r, and we have found the unique values of q and r. The remainder r is often referred to as a **residue**.

If a is an integer and n is a positive integer, we define $a \bmod n$ to be the remainder when a is divided by n. Thus, for any integer a, we can always write:

$$a = \lfloor a/n \rfloor \times n + (a \bmod n)$$

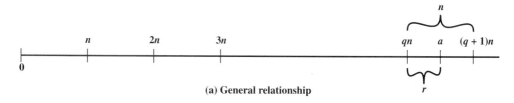

(a) General relationship

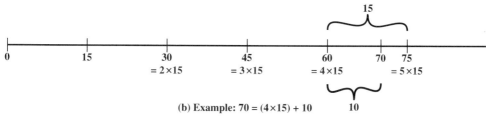

(b) Example: 70 = (4×15) + 10

Figure A.1 The Relationship $a = qn + r; 0 \leq r < n$

Two integers a and b are said to be **congruent modulo** n, if $(a \bmod n) = (b \bmod n)$. This is written $a \equiv b \bmod n$. For example, $73 \equiv 4 \bmod 23$ and $21 \equiv -9 \bmod 10$. Note that if $a \equiv 0 \bmod n$, then $n|a$.

The modulo operator has the following properties:

1. $a \equiv b \bmod n$ if $n|(a - b)$.
2. $(a \bmod n) = (b \bmod n)$ implies $a \equiv b \bmod n$.
3. $a \equiv b \bmod n$ implies $b \equiv a \bmod n$.
4. $a \equiv b \bmod n$ and $b \equiv c \bmod n$ imply $a \equiv c \bmod n$.

To demonstrate the first point, if $n|(a - b)$, then $(a - b) = kn$ for some k. So we can write $a = b + kn$. Therefore, $(a \bmod n) =$ (remainder when $b + kn$ is divided by n) = (remainder when b is divided by n) = $(b \bmod n)$. The remaining points are as easily proved.

The $(\bmod\ n)$ operator maps all integers into the set of integers $\{0, 1, \dots, (n - 1)\}$. This suggests the question: Can we perform arithmetic operations within the confines of this set? It turns out that we can; the technique is known as **modular arithmetic**.

Modular arithmetic exhibits the following properties:

1. $[(a \bmod n) + (b \bmod n)] \bmod n = (a + b) \bmod n$
2. $[(a \bmod n) - (b \bmod n)] \bmod n = (a - b) \bmod n$
3. $[(a \bmod n) \times (b \bmod n)] \bmod n = (a \times b) \bmod n$

We demonstrate the first property. Define $(a \bmod n) = r_a$ and $(b \bmod n) = r_b$. Then we can write $a = r_a + jn$ for some integer j and $b = r_b + kn$ for some integer k. Then

$$(a + b) \bmod n = (r_a + jn + r_b + kn) \bmod n$$
$$= (r_a + r_b + (k + j)n) \bmod n$$
$$= (r_a + r_b) \bmod n$$
$$= [(a \bmod n) + (b \bmod n)] \bmod n$$

The remaining properties are as easily proved.

Appendix B

Projects for Teaching Network Security

Analysis and observation, theory and experience must never disdain or exclude each other; on the contrary, they support each other.

—*On War,* Carl Von Clausewitz

Many instructors believe ,that research or implementation projects are crucial to the clear understanding of network security. Without projects, it may be difficult for students to grasp some of the basic concepts and interactions among components. Projects reinforce the concepts introduced in the book, give the student a greater appreciation of how a cryptographic algorithm or protocol works, and can motivate students and give them confidence that they are capable of not only understanding but implementing the details of a security capability.

In this text, I have tried to present the concepts of network security as clearly as possible and have provided numerous homework problems to reinforce those concepts. However, many instructors will wish to supplement this material with projects. This appendix provides some guidance in that regard and describes support material available in the **Instructor's Resource Center (IRC)** for this book, accessible to instructors from Prentice Hall. The support material covers seven types of projects:

1. Research projects
2. Hacking project
3. Programming projects
4. Laboratory exercises
5. Practical security assessments
6. Writing assignments
7. Reading/report assignments

B.1 RESEARCH PROJECTS

An effective way of reinforcing basic concepts from the course and for teaching students research skills is to assign a research project. Such a project could involve a literature search as well as an Internet search of vendor products, research lab activities, and standardization efforts. Projects could be assigned to teams or, for smaller projects, to individuals. In any case, it is best to require some sort of project proposal early in the term, giving the instructor time to evaluate the proposal for appropriate topic and appropriate level of effort. Student handouts for research projects should include

- A format for the proposal
- A format for the final report
- A schedule with intermediate and final deadlines
- A list of possible project topics

The students can select one of the topics listed in the instructor's manual or devise their own comparable project. The IRC includes a suggested format for the proposal and final report as well as a list of fifteen possible research topics.

B.2 HACKING PROJECT

The aim of this project is to hack into a corporation's network through a series of steps. The Corporation is named Extreme In Security Corporation. As the name indicates, the corporation has some security holes in it, and a clever hacker is able to access critical information by hacking into its network. The IRC includes what is needed to set up the Web site. The student's goal is to capture the secret information about the price on the quote the corporation is placing next week to obtain a contract for a governmental project.

The student should start at the Web site and find his or her way into the network. At each step, if the student succeeds, there are indications as to how to proceed on to the next step as well as the grade until that point.

The project can be attempted in three ways:

1. Without seeking any sort of help.
2. Using some provided hints.
3. Using exact directions.

The IRC includes the files needed for this project:

1. Web Security project.
2. Web Hacking exercises (XSS and Script-attacks) covering client-side and server-side vulnerability exploitations, respectively.
3. Documentation for installation and use for the above.
4. A PowerPoint file describing Web hacking. This file is crucial to understanding how to use the exercises since it clearly explains the operation using screen shots.

This project was designed and implemented by Professor Sreekanth Malladi of Dakota State University.

B.3 PROGRAMMING PROJECTS

The programming project is a useful pedagogical tool. There are several attractive features of stand-alone programming projects that are not part of an existing security facility.

1. The instructor can choose from a wide variety of cryptography and network security concepts to assign projects.
2. The projects can be programmed by the students on any available computer and in any appropriate language; they are platform and language independent.
3. The instructor need not download, install, and configure any particular infra-structure for stand-alone projects.

There is also flexibility in the size of projects. Larger projects give students more a sense of achievement, but students with less ability or fewer organizational skills can be left behind. Larger projects usually elicit more overall effort from the best students. Smaller projects can have a higher concepts-to-code ratio, and because more of them can be assigned, the opportunity exists to address a variety of different areas.

Again, as with research projects, the students should first submit a proposal. The student handout should include the same elements listed in Section A.1. The IRC includes a set of twelve possible programming projects.

The following individuals have supplied the research and programming projects suggested in the instructor's manual: Henning Schulzrinne of Columbia University; Cetin Kaya Koc of Oregon State University; and David M. Balenson of Trusted Information Systems and George Washington University.

B.4 LABORATORY EXERCISES

Professor Sanjay Rao and Ruben Torres of Purdue University have prepared a set of laboratory exercises that are part of the IRC. These are implementation projects designed to be programmed on Linux but could be adapted for any Unix environment. These laboratory exercises provide realistic experience in implementing security functions and applications.

B.5 PRACTICAL SECURITY ASSESSMENTS

Examining the current infrastructure and practices of an existing organization is one of the best ways of developing skills in assessing its security posture. The IRC contains a list of such activities. Students, working either individually or in small groups, select a suitable small-to-medium-sized organization. They then interview some key personnel in that organization in order to conduct a suitable selection of security risk assessment and review tasks as it relates to the organization's IT infrastructure and practices. As a result, they can then recommend suitable changes, which can improve the organization's IT security. These activities help students develop an appreciation of current security practices and the skills needed to review these and recommend changes.

Lawrie Brown of the Australian Defence Force Academy developed these projects.

B.6 WRITING ASSIGNMENTS

Writing assignments can have a powerful multiplier effect in the learning process in a technical discipline such as cryptography and network security. Adherents of the Writing Across the Curriculum (WAC) movement (http://wac.colostate.edu/) report substantial benefits of writing assignments in facilitating learning. Writing assignments lead to more detailed and complete thinking about a particular topic. In addition, writing assignments help to overcome the tendency of students to pursue a subject with a minimum of personal engagement—just learning facts and problem-solving techniques without obtaining a deep understanding of the subject matter.

The IRC contains a number of suggested writing assignments, organized by chapter. Instructors may ultimately find that this is an important part of their approach to teaching the material. I would greatly appreciate any feedback on this area and any suggestions for additional writing assignments.

B.7 READING/REPORT ASSIGNMENTS

Another excellent way to reinforce concepts from the course and to give students research experience is to assign papers from the literature to be read and analyzed. The IRC includes a suggested list of papers, one or two per chapter, to be assigned. The IRC provides a PDF copy of each of the papers. The IRC also includes a suggested assignment wording.

Index

THE WILLIAM STALLINGS BOOKS ON COMPUTER

DATA AND COMPUTER COMMUNICATIONS, EIGHTH EDITION

A comprehensive survey that has become the standard in the field, covering (1) data communications, including transmission, media, signal encoding, link control, and multiplexing; (2) communication networks, including circuit- and packet-switched, frame relay, ATM, and LANs; (3) the TCP/IP protocol suite, including IPv6, TCP, MIME, and HTTP, as well as a detailed treatment of network security. **Received the 2007 Text and Academic Authors Association (TAA) award for the best Computer Science and Engineering Textbook of the year.** ISBN 0-13-243310-9

COMPUTER ORGANIZATION AND ARCHITECTURE, EIGHTH EDITION

A unified view of this broad field. Covers fundamentals such as CPU, control unit, microprogramming, instruction set, I/O, and memory. Also covers advanced topics such as RISC, superscalar, and parallel organization. **Fourth and fifth editions received the TAA award for the best Computer Science and Engineering Textbook of the year.** ISBN 978-0-13-607373-4

OPERATING SYSTEMS, SIXTH EDITION

A state-of-the art survey of operating system principles. Covers fundamental technology as well as contemporary design issues, such as threads, microkernels, SMPs, real-time systems, multiprocessor scheduling, embedded OSs, distributed systems, clusters, security, and object-oriented design. **Received the 2009 Text and Academic Authors Association (TAA) award for the best Computer Science and Engineering Textbook of the year.** ISBN 978-0-13-600632-9

BUSINESS DATA COMMUNICATIONS, SIXTH EDITION

A comprehensive presentation of data communications and telecommunications from a business perspective. Covers voice, data, image, and video communications and applications technology and includes a number of case studies. ISBN 978-0-13-606741-2

COMPUTER NETWORKS WITH INTERNET PROTOCOLS AND TECHNOLOGY

An up-to-date survey of developments in the area of Internet-based protocols and algorithms. Using a top-down approach, this book covers applications, transport layer, Internet QoS, Internet routing, data link layer and computer networks, security, and network management. ISBN 0-13141098-9